Part One

Final

THE NATIONAL TEMPER

Readings in American Culture and Society to 1877

SECOND EDITION

Questions Due April 12

Freddie Douglas

Due April 5

#1 Individualism
Conformity
Idealism
materialism
Equality

#2 Agent of
Progress
or
Disrupter of
Democracy

Bio Friday 19 10   5/15

Well she's walking down the
pathways through the forests
of your mind, if you meet her
Be sure to greet her She'll reply
with, the whispering pines.

As she whispers, she'll enchant you,

time

under the general editorship of John Morton Blum

YALE UNIVERSITY

If you meet her, Be sure to greet h

Part One

know yourself
know others

THE
NATIONAL
TEMPER

Readings in American Culture
and Society to 1877

SECOND EDITION

edited by
Lawrence W. Levine
and
Robert Middlekauff
UNIVERSITY OF CALIFORNIA, BERKELEY

HARCOURT BRACE JOVANOVICH, INC.
NEW YORK   CHICAGO   SAN FRANCISCO   ATLANTA

A Note on the Two-Volume Edition

This volume is part of a variant printing, not a new or revised edition, of *The National Temper: Readings in American Culture and Society,* Second Edition. Many instructors have requested a two-volume version that would enable them to fit the anthology into the particular patterns of their teaching and scheduling. To meet that request, the publishers have prepared this printing, consisting of two separate volumes that exactly reproduce the text of the one-volume version of *The National Temper: Readings in American Culture and Society,* Second Edition. The first of these volumes continues through Reconstruction. The second volume repeats the essay "A Democratic Society Emerges from Total War" by Eric McKitrick, and carries the account forward to the present day. The variant printing, then, is intended as a convenience to those instructors and students who have occasion to use either one part or the other of *The National Temper: Readings in American Culture and Society,* Second Edition. Consequently, the pagination of the one-volume version is retained in the new printing. The difference between the one-volume and two-volume versions of the book is a difference only in form.

ISBN: 0-15-565709-7

Library of Congress Catalog Card Number: 72-177295

Printed in the United States of America

PREFACE

The National Temper: Readings in American Culture and Society, Second Edition, follows the pattern of the first edition in its selection of original and unconventional articles that can be recommended for their significance to the larger terms of American history. About half the articles that appeared in the first edition have been replaced. Most of them have appeared in other places since the first edition of this book was published, so a second edition with fresh selections seemed all the more desirable. For example, we are especially pleased by the essays, now included, on the Civil War, Reconstruction, women, crowds, and Indians. We have retained other essays that seemed particularly impressive in conception and method.

As in the first edition, all the selections bear on concerns important to American historians. They are serious—though occasionally offbeat—attempts to extract meaning from the American past. Such topics as sexual practices, popular novels, and gangster films rarely draw historians' interest as fields of study. But as the articles in this collection demonstrate, they can be dealt with in ways that illuminate cultural development. We have also included the kind of article that takes its distinction largely from its method, though it may deal with an unconventional subject as well. Several of the literary analyses and the sociological studies in our collection fall into this category.

Considered alone or in this collection, the articles do not exhaust the possibilities for investigation into American history. But used seriously, say as supplements to a textbook, a general history, or more ambitious specialized studies, they can inform as well as stimulate. All repay closer reading; and though we believe that they may be most profitable to students in a general American history course, we also hope that any student of the American past will find them rewarding.

We are grateful to the authors and publishers of these essays for permission to reprint them.

LAWRENCE W. LEVINE
ROBERT MIDDLEKAUFF

CONTENTS

Preface

I The Origins
of American
Culture

The Quest for the National Character

David M. Potter

INTRODUCTION

This essay by David M. Potter considers explicitly what every piece in this volume touches implicitly—the question of the American national character. Potter maintains that almost all theories of the American character fall into two primary types. One, first offered by Jefferson, describes the American as an individualist with profound, idealistic impulses; the other, formulated by Alexis de Tocqueville, sees him as a conformist with immense materialistic drives. Although Potter does not contend that the dedication to equality implied in both conceptions effectively reconciles these contrasting images, he does find in its various manifestations a new focus for understanding much that has been persistent in the American character.

Every student of American character can profit from Tocqueville's great *Democracy in America,** edited by Phillips Bradley (1945). More recent studies should be consulted as well; a good starting point is Frederick Jackson Turner, *The Frontier in American History** (1920). Two studies of symbols are also especially revealing: Henry Nash Smith, *Virgin Land: The American West as Symbol and Myth** (1950), and John William Ward, *Andrew Jackson: Symbol for an Age** (1955). David M. Potter, *People of Plenty** (1954), and Elting E. Morison, *The American Style* (1958), suggest some new developments in the national character of Americans. For perceptive discussions by anthropologists, students might consult Clyde Kluckhohn and Henry A. Murray, *Personality in Nature, Society, and Culture* (1949), and Margaret Mead, *And Keep Your Powder Dry** (1942).

* *All books marked with an asterisk are available in paperback.*

UNLIKE most nationality groups in the world today, the people of the United States are not ethnically rooted in the land where they live. The French have remote Gallic antecedents; the Germans, Teutonic; the English, Anglo-Saxon; the Italians, Roman; the Irish, Celtic; but the only people in America who can claim ancient American origins are a remnant of Red Indians. In any deep dimension of time, all other Americans are immigrants. They began as Europeans (or in the case of 10 per cent of the population, as Africans), and if they became Americans it was only, somehow, after a relatively recent passage westbound across the Atlantic.

It is, perhaps, this recency of arrival which has given to Americans a somewhat compulsive preoccupation with the question of their Americanism. No people can really qualify as a nation in the true sense unless they are united by important qualities or values in common. If they share the same ethnic, or linguistic, or religious, or political heritage, the foundations of nationality can hardly be questioned. But when their ethnic, religious, linguistic, and political heritage is mixed, as in the case of the American people, nationality can hardly exist at all unless it takes the form of a common adjustment to conditions of a new land, a common commitment to shared values, a common esteem for certain qualities of character, or a common set of adaptive traits and attitudes. It is partly for this reason that Americans, although committed to the principle of freedom of thought, have nevertheless placed such heavy emphasis upon the obligation to accept certain undefined tenets of "Americanism." It is for this same reason, also, that Americans have insisted upon their distinctiveness from the Old World from which they are derived. More than two centuries ago Hector St. John de Crèvecoeur asked a famous question, "What then is the American, this new man?" He simply assumed, without arguing the point, that the American is a new man, and he only inquired wherein the American is different. A countless array of writers, including not only careful historians and social scientists but also professional patriots, hit-and-run travellers, itinerant lecturers, intuitive-minded amateurs of all sorts, have been repeating Crèvecoeur's question and seeking to answer it ever since.

A thick volume would hardly suffice even to summarize the diverse interpretations which these various writers have advanced in describing or explaining the American character. Almost every trait, good or bad, has been attributed to the American people by someone,[1] and almost every explanation, from Darwinian selection to toilet-training, has been advanced to account for

FROM David M. Potter, "The Quest for the National Character," in John Higham, ed., *The Reconstruction of American History*, New York: Harper & Row Torchbooks, 1962, pp. 197–220. © Hutchinson & Co. (Publishers), Ltd., 1962. Reprinted by permission of Harper & Row, Publishers, Inc.

[1] Lee Coleman, "What Is American: A Study of Alleged American Traits," in *Social Forces,* XIX (1941), surveyed a large body of the literature on the American character and concluded that "almost every conceivable value or trait has at one time or another been imputed to American culture by authoritative observers."

the attributed qualities. But it is probably safe to say that at bottom there have been only two primary ways of explaining the American, and that almost all of the innumerable interpretations which have been formulated can be grouped around or at least oriented to these two basic explanations, which serve as polar points for all the literature.

The most disconcerting fact about these two composite images of the American is that they are strikingly dissimilar and seemingly about as inconsistent with one another as two interpretations of the same phenomenon could possibly be. One depicts the American primarily as an individualist and an idealist, while the other makes him out as a conformist and a materialist. Both images have been developed with great detail and elaborate explanation in extensive bodies of literature, and both are worth a close scrutiny.

For those who have seen the American primarily as an individualist, the story of his evolution as a distinctive type dates back possibly to the actual moment of his decision to migrate from Europe to the New World, for this was a process in which the daring and venturesome were more prone to risk life in a new country while the timid and the conventional were more disposed to remain at home. If the selective factors in the migration had the effect of screening out men of low initiative, the conditions of life in the North American wilderness, it is argued, must have further heightened the exercise of individual resourcefulness, for they constantly confronted the settler with circumstances in which he could rely upon no one but himself, and where the capacity to improvise a solution for a problem was not infrequently necessary to survival.

In many ways the colonial American exemplified attitudes that were individualistic. Although he made his first settlements by the removal of whole communities which were transplanted bodily—complete with all their ecclesiastical and legal institutions—he turned increasingly, in the later process of settlement, to a more and more individualistic mode of pioneering, in which one separate family would take up title to a separate, perhaps an isolated, tract of land, and would move to this land long in advance of any general settlement, leaving churches and courts and schools far behind. His religion, whether Calvinistic Puritanism or emotional revivalism, made him individually responsible for his own salvation, without the intervention of ecclesiastical intermediaries between himself and his God. His economy, which was based very heavily upon subsistence farming, with very little division of labor, also impelled him to cope with a diversity of problems and to depend upon no one but himself.

With all of these conditions at work, the tendency to place a premium upon individual self-reliance was no doubt well developed long before the cult of the American as an individualist crystallized in a conceptual form. But it did crystallize, and it took on almost its classic formulation in the thought of Thomas Jefferson.

It may seem paradoxical to regard Jefferson as a delineator of American national character, for in direct terms he did not attempt to describe the American character at all. But he did conceive that one particular kind of society was necessary to the fulfillment of American ideals, and further that one particular kind of person, namely the independent farmer, was a necessary component in the optimum society. He believed that the principles of liberty and equality, which he cherished so deeply, could not exist in a hierarchical society, such as that of Europe, nor, indeed, in any society where economic and social circumstances enabled one set of men to dominate and exploit the rest. An urban society or a commercial society, with its concentration of financial power into a few hands and its imposition of dependence through a wage system, scarcely lent itself better than an aristocracy to his basic values. In fact, only a society of small husbandmen who tilled their own soil and found sustenance in their own produce could achieve the combination of independence and equalitarianism which he envisioned for the ideal society. Thus, although Jefferson did not write a description of the national character, he erected a model for it, and the model ultimately had more influence than a description could ever have exercised. The model American was a plain, straightforward agrarian democrat, an individualist in his desire for freedom for himself, and an idealist in his desire for equality for all men.

Jefferson's image of the American as a man of independence, both in his values and in his mode of life, has had immense appeal to Americans ever since. They found this image best exemplified in the man of the frontier, for he, as a pioneer, seemed to illustrate the qualities of independence and self-reliance in their most pronounced and most dramatic form. Thus, in a tradition of something like folklore, half-legendary figures like Davy Crockett have symbolized America as well as symbolizing the frontier. In literature, ever since J. Fenimore Cooper's Leatherstocking tales, the frontier scout, at home under the open sky, free from the trammels of an organized and stratified society, has been cherished as an incarnation of American qualities.[2] In American politics the voters showed such a marked preference for men who had been born in log cabins that many an ambitious candidate pretended to pioneer origins which were in fact fictitious.

The pioneer is, of course, not necessarily an agrarian (he may be a hunter, a trapper, a cowboy, a prospector for gold), and the agrarian is not necessarily a pioneer (he may be a European peasant tilling his ancestral acres), but the American frontier was basically an agricultural frontier, and the pioneer was usually a farmer. Thus it was possible to make an equation between the pioneer and the agrarian, and since the pioneer evinced the agrarian traits in their most picturesque and most appealing form there was a strong psychological impulse to concentrate the diffused agrarian ideal into a sharp frontier focus. This is, in part, what Frederick Jackson Turner did in 1893 when he wrote *The Significance of the Frontier in American History*. In this famous essay Turner offered an explanation of what has been distinctive in American history, but it is not as widely realized as it might be that he also penned a major contribution to the literature of national character. Thus Turner affirmed categorically that

> The American intellect owes its striking characteristics to the frontier. That coarseness and strength, combined with acuteness and acquisitiveness; that practical inventive turn of mind, quick to find expedients; that masterful grasp of material things, lacking in the artistic but powerful to effect great ends; that restless, nervous energy; that dominant individualism, working for good and for evil; and withal, that buoyancy and exuberance which comes

[2] Henry Nash Smith, *Virgin Land: The American West as Symbol and Myth* (1950), brilliantly analyzes the power which the image of the Western pioneer has had upon the American imagination.

with freedom—these are traits of the frontier, or traits called out elsewhere because of the existence of the frontier.[3]

A significant but somewhat unnoticed aspect of Turner's treatment is the fact that, in his quest to discover the traits of the American character, he relied for proof not upon descriptive evidence that given traits actually prevailed, but upon the argument that given conditions in the environment would necessarily cause the development of certain traits. Thus the cheapness of land on the frontier would make for universal land-holding which in turn would make for equalitarianism in the society. The absence of division of labor on the frontier would force each man to do most things for himself, and this would breed self-reliance. The pitting of the individual man against the elemental forces of the wilderness and of nature would further reinforce this self-reliance. Similarly, the fact that a man had moved out in advance of society's institutions and its stratified structure would mean that he could find independence, without being overshadowed by the institutions, and could enjoy an equality unknown to stratified society. All of this argument was made without any sustained effort to measure exactly how much recognizable equalitarianism and individualism and self-reliance actually were in evidence either on the American frontier or in American society. There is little reason to doubt that most of his arguments were valid or that most of the traits which he emphasized did actually prevail, but it is nevertheless ironical that Turner's interpretation, which exercised such vast influence upon historians, was not based upon the historian's kind of proof, which is from evidence, but upon an argument from logic which so often fails to work out in historical experience.

But no matter how he arrived at it, Turner's picture reaffirmed some by-now-familiar beliefs about the American character. The American was equalitarian, stoutly maintaining the practices of both social and political democracy; he had a spirit of freedom reflected in his buoyance and exuberance; he was individual-istic—hence "practical and inventive," "quick to find expedients," "restless, nervous, acquisitive." Turner was too much a scholar to let his evident fondness for the frontiersman run away with him entirely, and he took pains to point out that this development was not without its sordid aspects. There was a marked primitivism about the frontier, and with it, to some extent, a regression from civilized standards. The buoyant and exuberant frontiersman sometimes emulated his Indian neighbors in taking the scalps of his adversaries. Coarse qualities sometimes proved to have more survival value than gentle ones. But on the whole this regression was brief, and certainly a rough-and-ready society had its compensating advantages. Turner admired his frontiersman, and thus Turner's American, like Jefferson's American, was partly a realistic portrait from life and partly an idealized model from social philosophy. Also, though one of these figures was an agrarian and the other was a frontiersman, both were very much the same man—democratic, freedom-loving, self-reliant, and individualistic.

An essay like this is hardly the place to prove either the validity or the invalidity of the Jeffersonian and Turnerian conception of the American character. The attempt to do so would involve a review of the entire range of

[3] Frederick J. Turner, *The Frontier in American History* (Henry Holt and Co., 1920), p. 37.

American historical experience, and in the course of such a review the proponents of this conception could point to a vast body of evidence in support of their interpretation. They could argue, with much force, that Americans have consistently been zealous to defend individualism by defending the rights and the welfare of the individual, and that our whole history is a protracted record of our government's recognizing its responsibility to an ever broader range of people—to men without property, to men held in slavery, to women, to small enterprises threatened by monopoly, to children laboring in factories, to industrial workers, to the ill, to the elderly, and to the unemployed. This record, it can further be argued, is also a record of the practical idealism of the American people, unceasingly at work.

But without attempting a verdict on the historical validity of this image of the American as individualist and idealist, it is important to bear in mind that this image has been partly a portrait, but also partly a model. In so far as it is a portrait—a likeness by an observer reporting on Americans whom he knew—it can be regarded as authentic testimony on the American character. But in so far as it is a model—an idealization of what is best in Americanism, and of what Americans should strive to be, it will only be misleading if used as evidence of what ordinary Americans are like in their everyday lives. It is also important to recognize that the Jefferson-Turner image posited several traits as distinctively American, and that they are not all necessarily of equal validity. Particularly, Jefferson and Turner both believed that love of equality and love of liberty go together. For Jefferson the very fact, stated in the Declaration of Independence, that "all men are created equal," carried with it the corollary that they are all therefore "entitled to [and would be eager for] life, liberty, and the pursuit of happiness." From this premise it is easy to slide imperceptibly into the position of holding that equalitarianism and individualism are inseparably linked, or even that they are somehow the same thing. This is, indeed, almost an officially sanctioned ambiguity in the American creed. But it requires only a little thoughtful reflection to recognize that equalitarianism and individualism do not necessarily go together. Alexis de Tocqueville understood this fact more than a century ago, and out of his recognition he framed an analysis which is not only the most brilliant single account of the American character, but is also the only major alternative to the Jefferson-Turner image.

After travelling the length and breadth of the United States for ten months at the height of Andrew Jackson's ascendancy, Tocqueville felt no doubt of the depth of the commitment of Americans to democracy. Throughout two volumes which ranged over every aspect of American life, he consistently emphasized democracy as a pervasive factor. But the democracy which he wrote about was far removed from Thomas Jefferson's dream.

"Liberty," he observed of the Americans, "is not the chief object of their desires; equality is their idol. They make rapid and sudden efforts to obtain liberty, and if they miss their aim resign themselves to their disappointment; but nothing can satisfy them without equality, and they would rather perish than lose it."[4]

This emphasis upon equality was not, in itself, inconsistent with the most

[4] Alexis de Tocqueville, *Democracy in America*, edited by Phillips Bradley (Alfred A. Knopf, 1946), I, pp. 53–4.

orthodox Jeffersonian ideas, and indeed Tocqueville took care to recognize that under certain circumstances equality and freedom might "meet and blend." But such circumstances would be rare, and the usual effects of equality would be to encourage conformity and discourage individualism, to regiment opinion and to inhibit dissent. Tocqueville justified this seemingly paradoxical conclusion by arguing that:

> When the inhabitant of a democratic country compares himself individually with all those about him, he feels with pride that he is the equal of any one of them; but when he comes to survey the totality of his fellows, and to place himself in contrast with so huge a body, he is instantly overwhelmed by the sense of his own insignificance and weakness. The same equality that renders him independent of each of his fellow citizens, taken severally, exposes him alone and unprotected to the influence of the greater number. The public, therefore, among a democratic people, has a singular power, which aristocratic nations cannot conceive; for it does not persuade others to its beliefs, but it imposes them and makes them permeate the thinking of everyone by a sort of enormous pressure of the mind of all upon the individual intelligence.[5]

At the time when Tocqueville wrote, he expressed admiration for the American people in many ways, and when he criticized adversely his tone was abstract, bland, and free of the petulance and the personalities that characterized some critics, like Mrs. Trollope and Charles Dickens. Consequently, Tocqueville was relatively well received in the United States, and we have largely forgotten what a severe verdict his observations implied. But, in fact, he pictured the American character as the very embodiment of conformity, of conformity so extreme that not only individualism but even freedom was endangered. Because of the enormous weight with which the opinion of the majority pressed upon the individual, Tocqueville said, the person in the minority "not only mistrusts his strength, but even doubts of his right; and he is very near acknowledging that he is in the wrong when the greater number of his countrymen assert that he is so. The majority do not need to force him; they convince him." "The principle of equality," as a consequence, had the effect of "prohibiting him from thinking at all," and "freedom of opinion does not exist in America." Instead of reinforcing liberty, therefore, equality constituted a danger to liberty. It caused the majority "to despise and undervalue the rights of private persons," and led on to the pessimistic conclusion that "Despotism appears . . . peculiarly to be dreaded in democratic times."[6]

Tocqueville was perhaps the originator of the criticism of the American as conformist, but he also voiced another criticism which has had many echoes, but which did not originate with him. This was the condemnation of the American as a materialist. As early as 1805 Richard Parkinson had observed that "all men there [in America] make it [money] their pursuit," and in 1823 William Faux had asserted that "two selfish gods, pleasure and gain, enslave the Americans." In the interval between the publication of the first and second parts of Tocqueville's study, Washington Irving coined his classic phrase concerning "the almighty dollar, that great object of universal devotion throughout

[5] *Ibid.*, II, p. 94; II, p. 10.
[6] *Ibid.*, II, p. 261; II, p. 11; I, p. 265; II, p. 326; II, p. 322.

the land."[7] But it remained for Tocqueville, himself, to link materialism with equality, as he had already linked conformity.

> "Of all passions," he said, "which originate in or are fostered by equality, there is one which it renders peculiarly intense, and which it also infuses into the heart of every man: I mean the love of well-being. The taste for well-being is the prominent and indelible feature of democratic times. . . . The effort to satisfy even the least wants of the body and to provide the little conveniences of life is uppermost in every mind."

He described this craving for physical comforts as a "passion," and affirmed that "I know of no country, indeed, where the love of money has taken stronger hold on the affections of men."[8]

For more than a century we have lived with the contrasting images of the American character which Thomas Jefferson and Alexis de Tocqueville visualized. Both of these images presented the American as an equalitarian and therefore as a democrat, but one was an agrarian democrat while the other was a majoritarian democrat; one an independent individualist, the other a mass-dominated conformist; one an idealist, the other a materialist. Through many decades of self-scrutiny Americans have been seeing one or the other of these images whenever they looked into the mirror of self-analysis.

The discrepancy between the two images is so great that it must bring the searcher for the American character up with a jerk, and must force him to grapple with the question whether these seemingly antithetical versions of the American can be reconciled in any way. Can the old familiar formula for embracing opposite reports—that the situation presents a paradox—be stretched to encompass both Tocqueville and Jefferson? Or is there so grave a flaw somewhere that one must question the whole idea of national character and call to mind all the warnings that thoughtful men have uttered against the very concept that national groups can be distinguished from one another in terms of collective group traits.

Certainly there is a sound enough basis for doubting the validity of generalizations about national character. To begin with, many of these generalizations have been derived not from any dispassionate observation or any quest for truth, but from superheated patriotism which sought only to glorify one national group by invidious comparison with other national groups, or from a pseudo-scientific racism which claimed innately superior qualities for favored ethnic groups. Further, the explanations which were offered to account for the ascribed traits were as suspect as the ascriptions themselves. No one today will accept the notions which once prevailed that such qualities as the capacity for self-government are inherited in the genes, nor will anyone credit the notion that national character is a unique quality which manifests itself mystically in all the inhabitants of a given country. Between the chauvinistic purposes for which the concept of national character was used, and the irrationality with which it was supported, it fell during the 1930's into a disrepute from which it has by no means fully recovered.

---

[7] Richard Parkinson, *A Tour in America in 1798–1800* (2 vols., 1805), vol. II, p. 652; William Faux, *Memorable Days in America* (1823), p. 417; Washington Irving, "The Creole Village," in *The Knickerbocker Magazine,* November 1836.

[8] Tocqueville, *Democracy in America,* II, p. 26; II, p. 128; II, p. 129; I, p. 51.

Some thinkers of a skeptical turn of mind had rejected the idea of national character even at a time when most historians accepted it without question. Thus, for instance, John Stuart Mill as early as 1849 observed that "of all vulgar modes of escaping from the consideration of the effect of social and moral influences on the human mind, the most vulgar is that of attributing diversities of character to inherent natural differences." Sir John Seely said, "no explanation is so vague, so cheap, and so difficult to verify."[9]

But it was particularly at the time of the rise of Fascism and Naziism, when the vicious aspects of extreme nationalism and of racism became glaringly conspicuous, that historians in general began to repudiate the idea of national character and to disavow it as an intellectual concept, even though they sometimes continued to employ it as a working device in their treatment of the peoples with whose history they were concerned. To historians whose skepticism had been aroused, the conflicting nature of the images of the American as an individualistic democrat or as a conformist democrat would have seemed simply to illustrate further the already demonstrated flimsiness and fallacious quality of all generalizations about national character.

But to deny that the inhabitants of one country may, as a group, evince a given trait in higher degree than the inhabitants of some other country amounts almost to a denial that the culture of one people can be different from the culture of another people. To escape the pitfalls of racism in this way is to fly from one error into the embrace of another, and students of culture—primarily anthropologists, rather than historians—perceived that rejection of the idea that a group could be distinctive, along with the idea that the distinction was eternal and immutable in the genes, involved the ancient logical fallacy of throwing out the baby along with the bath. Accordingly, the study of national character came under the special sponsorship of cultural anthropology, and in the forties a number of outstanding workers in this field tackled the problem of national character, including the American character, with a methodological precision and objectivity that had never been applied to the subject before. After their investigations, they felt no doubt that national character was a reality—an observable and demonstrable reality. One of them, Margaret Mead, declared that

> In every culture, in Samoa, in Germany, in Iceland, in Bali, and in the United States of America, we will find consistencies and regularities in the way in which newborn babies grow up and assume the attitudes and behavior patterns of their elders—and this we may call "character formation." We will find that Samoans may be said to have a Samoan character structure and Americans an American character structure.[10]

Another, the late Clyde Kluckhohn, wrote: "The statistical prediction can safely be made that a hundred Americans, for example, will display certain defined characteristics more frequently than will a hundred Englishmen comparably distributed as to age, sex, social class, and vocation."[11]

[9] Mill, *The Principles of Political Economy* (1849), I, p. 390; Seely, quoted by Boyd C. Shafer, "Men Are More Alike," in *American Historical Review*, LVII (1952), p. 606.
[10] Margaret Mead, *And Keep Your Powder Dry* (William Morrow and Co., 1942), p. 21. Miss Mead also says, "The way in which people behave is all of a piece, their virtues and their sins, the way they slap the baby, handle their court cases, and bury their dead."
[11] Clyde Kluckhohn and Henry A. Murray, *Personality in Nature, Society, and Culture* (Alfred A. Knopf, 1949), p. 36.

If these new students were correct, it meant that there was some kind of identifiable American character. It might conform to the Jeffersonian image; it might conform to the Tocquevillian image; it might conform in part to both; or it might conform to neither. But in any event discouraged investigators were enjoined against giving up the quest with the conclusion that there is no American character. It has been said that a philosopher is a blind man in a dark room looking for a black cat that isn't there; the student of national character might also, at times, resemble a blind man in a dark room, looking for a black cat, but the cultural anthropologists exhorted him to persevere in spite of the problems of visibility, for the cat was indubitably there.

Still confronted with the conflicting images of the agrarian democrat and the majoritarian democrat, the investigator might avoid an outright rejection of either by taking the position that the American character has changed, and that each of these images was at one time valid and realistic, but that in the twentieth century the qualities of conformity and materialism have grown increasingly prominent, while the qualities of individualism and idealism have diminished. This interpretation of a changing American character has had a number of adherents in the last two decades, for it accords well with the observation that the conditions of the American culture have changed. As they do so, of course the qualities of a character that is derived from the culture might be expected to change correspondingly. Thus, Henry S. Commager, in his *The American Mind* (1950), portrayed in two contrasting chapters "the nineteenth-century American" and "the twentieth-century American." Similarly, David Riesman, in *The Lonely Crowd* (1950), significantly sub-titled *A Study of the Changing American Character,* pictured two types of Americans, first an "inner-directed man," whose values were deeply internalized and who adhered to these values tenaciously, regardless of the opinions of his peers (clearly an individualist), and second an "other-directed man," who subordinated his own internal values to the changing expectations directed toward him by changing peer groups (in short, a conformist).

Although he viewed his inner-directed man as having been superseded historically by his other-directed man, Riesman did not attempt to explain in historical terms the reason for the change. He made a rather limited effort to relate his stages of character formation to stages of population growth, but he has since then not used population phase as a key. Meanwhile, it is fairly clear, from Riesman's own context, as well as from history in general, that there were changes in the culture which would have accounted for the transition in character. Most nineteenth-century Americans were self-employed; most were engaged in agriculture; most produced a part of their own food and clothing. These facts meant that their well-being did not depend on the goodwill or the services of their associates, but upon their resourcefulness in wrestling with the elemental forces of Nature. Even their physical isolation from their fellows added something to the independence of their natures. But most twentieth-century Americans work for wages or salaries, many of them in very large employee groups; most are engaged in office or factory work; most are highly specialized, and are reliant upon many others to supply their needs in an economy with an advanced division of labor. Men now do depend upon the goodwill and the services of their fellows. This means that what they achieve depends less upon stamina and hardihood than upon their capacity to get along with other people and to fit smoothly into a cooperative relationship. In short the culture now places a premium upon the qualities which will enable the individual to function effectively as a member of a large organizational group. The strategic importance of this institutional factor has been well recognized by William H. Whyte, Jr., in his significantly titled book *The Organization Man* (1956)—for the conformity of Whyte's bureaucratized individual results from the fact that he lives under an imperative to succeed in a situation where promotion and even survival depend upon effective inter-action with others in an hierarchical structure.

Thus, by an argument from logic (always a treacherous substitute for direct observation in historical study), one can make a strong case that the nineteenth-century American should have been (and therefore must have been) an individualist, while the twentieth-century American should be (and therefore is) a conformist. But this formula crashes headlong into the obdurate fact that no Americans have ever been more classically conformist than Tocqueville's Jacksonian democrats—hardy specimens of the frontier breed, far back in the nineteenth century, long before the age of corporate images, peer groups, marginal differentiation, and status frustration. In short, Tocqueville's nineteenth-century American, whether frontiersman or no, was to some extent an other-directed man. Carl N. Degler has pointed out this identity in a very cogent paper not yet published, in which he demonstrates very forcibly that most of our easy assumptions about the immense contrast between the nineteenth-century American and the twentieth-century American are vulnerable indeed.[12]

This conclusion should, perhaps, have been evident from the outset, in view of the fact that it was Tocqueville who, in the nineteenth century, gave us the image which we now frequently identify as the twentieth-century American. But in any case, the fact that he did so means that we can hardly resolve the dilemma of our individualist democrat and our majoritarian democrat by assuming that both are historically valid but that one replaced the other. The problem of determining what use we can make of either of these images, in view of the fact that each casts doubt upon the other, still remains. Is it possible to uncover common factors in these apparently contradictory images, and thus to make use of them both in our quest for a definition of the national character? For no matter whether either of these versions of the American is realistic as a type or image, there is no doubt that both of them reflect fundamental aspects of the American experience.

There is no purpose, at this point in this essay, to execute a neat, prearranged sleight-of-hand by which the individualist democrat and the conformist democrat will cast off their disguises and will reveal themselves as identical twin Yankee Doodle Dandies, both born on the fourth of July. On the contrary, intractable, irresolvable discrepancies exist between the two figures, and it will probably never be possible to go very far in the direction of accepting the one without treating the other as a fictitious image, to be rejected as reflecting an anti-democratic bias and as at odds with the evidence from actual observation of the behavior of *Homo Americanus* in his native haunts. At the same time, however, it is both necessary to probe for the common factors, and legitimate to observe that there is one common factor conspicuous in the extreme—namely

[12] Delivered on 30 December 1960, at the annual meeting of the American Historical Association in New York.

the emphasis on equality, so dear both to Jefferson's American and to Tocqueville's. One of these figures, it will be recalled, has held no truth to be more self-evident than that all men are created equal, while the other has made equality his "idol," far more jealously guarded than his liberty.

If the commitment to equality is so dominant a feature in both of these representations of the American, it will perhaps serve as a key to various facets of the national character, even to contradictory aspects of this character. In a society as complex as that of the United States, in fact, it may be that the common factors underlying the various manifestations are all that our quest should seek. For it is evident that American life and American energy have expressed themselves in a great diversity of ways, and any effort to define the American as if nearly two hundred million persons all corresponded to a single type would certainly reduce complex data to a blunt, crude, and oversimplified form. To detect what qualities Americans share in their diversity may be far more revealing than to superimpose the stereotype of a fictitious uniformity. If this is true, it means that our quest must be to discover the varied and dissimilar ways in which the commitment to equality expresses itself—the different forms which it takes in different individuals—rather than to regard it as an undifferentiated component which shows in all individuals in the same way. Figuratively, one might say that in seeking for what is common, one should think of the metal from which Americans are forged, no matter into how many shapes this metal may be cast, rather than thinking of a die with which they all are stamped into an identical shape. If the problem is viewed in this way, it will be readily apparent that Tocqueville made a pregnant statement when he observed that the idea of equality was "the fundamental fact from which all others seem to be derived."

The term "equality" is a loose-fitting garment and it has meant very different things at very different times. It is very frequently used to imply parity or uniformity. The grenadiers in the King of Prussia's guard were equal in that they were all, uniformly, over six feet six inches tall. Particularly, it can mean, and often does mean in some social philosophies, uniformity of material welfare —of income, of medical care, etc. But people are clearly not uniform in strength or intelligence or beauty, and one must ask, therefore, what kind of uniformity Americans believed in. Did they believe in an equal sharing of goods? Tocqueville himself answered this question when he said, "I know of no country . . . where a profounder contempt is expressed for the theory of the permanent equality of property."[13]

At this point in the discussion of equality, someone, and very likely a business man, is always likely to break in with the proposition that Americans believe in equality of opportunity—in giving everyone what is called an equal start, and in removing all handicaps such as illiteracy and all privileges such as monopoly or special priority, which will tend to give one person an advantage over another. But if a person gains the advantage without having society give it to him, by being more clever or more enterprising or even just by being stronger than someone else, he is entitled to enjoy the benefits that accrue from these qualities, particularly in terms of possessing more property or wealth than others.

Historically, equality of opportunity was a particularly apt form of equali-

[13] Tocqueville, *Democracy in America*, I, pp. 57–8.

tarianism for a new, undeveloped frontier country. In the early stages of American history, the developed resources of the country were so few that an equality in the division of these assets would only have meant an insufficiency for everyone. The best economic benefit which the government could give was to offer a person free access in developing undeveloped resources for his own profit, and this is what America did offer. It was an ideal formula for everyone: for the individual it meant a very real chance to gain more wealth than he would have secured by receiving an equal share of the existing wealth. For the community, it meant that no one could prosper appreciably without activities which would develop undeveloped resources, at a time when society desperately needed rapid economic development. For these reasons, equality of opportunity did become the most highly sanctioned form of equalitarianism in the United States.

Because of this sanction, Americans have indeed been tolerant of great discrepancies in wealth. They have approved of wealth much more readily when they believed that it had been earned—as in the case, for instance, of Henry Ford—than when they thought it had been acquired by some special privilege or monopoly. In general, however, they have not merely condoned great wealth; they have admired it. But to say that the ideal of equality means only equality of opportunity is hardly to tell the whole story. The American faith has also held, with intense conviction, the belief that all men are equal in the sense that they share a common humanity—that all are alike in the eyes of God—and that every person has a certain dignity, no matter how low his circumstances, which no one else, no matter how high *his* circumstances, is entitled to disregard. When this concept of the nature of man was translated into a system of social arrangements, the crucial point on which it came to focus was the question of rank. For the concept of rank essentially denies that all men are equally worthy and argues that some are better than others—that some are born to serve and others born to command. The American creed not only denied this view, but even condemned it and placed a taboo upon it. Some people, according to the American creed, might be more fortunate than others, but they must never regard themselves as better than others. Pulling one's rank has therefore been the unforgivable sin against American democracy, and the American people have, accordingly, reserved their heartiest dislike for the officer class in the military, for people with upstage or condescending manners, and for anyone who tries to convert power or wealth (which are not resented) into overt rank or privilege (which are). Thus it is permissible for an American to have servants (which is a matter of function), but he must not put them in livery (which is a matter of rank); permissible to attend expensive schools, but not to speak with a cultivated accent; permissible to rise in the world, but never to repudiate the origins from which he rose. The most palpable and overt possible claim of rank is, of course, the effort of one individual to assert authority, in a personal sense, over others, and accordingly the rejection of authority is the most pronounced of all the concrete expressions of American beliefs in equality.

In almost any enterprise which involves numbers of people working in conjunction, it is necessary for some people to tell other people what to do. This function cannot be wholly abdicated without causing a breakdown, and in America it cannot be exercised overtly without violating the taboos against authority. The result is that the American people have developed an arrangement which skillfully combines truth and fiction, and maintains that the top man does not rule, but leads; and does not give orders, but calls signals; while the men in the lower echelons are not underlings, but members of the team. This view of the relationship is truthful in the sense that the man in charge does depend upon his capacity to elicit the voluntary or spontaneous co-operation of the members of his organization, and he regards the naked use of authority to secure compliance as an evidence of failure; also, in many organizations, the members lend their support willingly, and contribute much more on a voluntary basis than authority could ever exact from them. But the element of fiction sometimes enters, in terms of the fact that both sides understand that in many situations authority would have to be invoked if voluntary compliance were not forthcoming. This would be humiliating to all parties—to the top man because it would expose his failure as a leader and to the others because it would force them to recognize the carefully concealed fact that in an ultimate sense they are subject to coercion. To avoid this mutually undesirable exploration of the ultimate implications, both sides recognize that even when an order has to be given, it is better for it to be expressed in the form of a request or a proposal, and when compliance is mandatory, it should be rendered with an appearance of consent.

It is in this way that the anti-authoritarian aspect of the creed of equality leads to the extraordinarily strong emphasis upon permissiveness, either as a reality or as a mere convention in American life. So strong is the taboo against authority that the father, once a paternal authority, is now expected to be a pal to his children, and to persuade rather than to command. The husband, once a lord and master, to be obeyed under the vows of matrimony, is now a partner. And if, perchance, an adult male in command of the family income uses his control to bully his wife and children, he does not avow his desire to make them obey, but insists that he only wants them to be co-operative. The unlimited American faith in the efficacy of discussion as a means of finding solutions for controversies reflects less a faith in the powers of rational persuasion than a supreme reluctance to let anything reach a point where authority will have to be invoked. If hypocrisy is the tribute that vice pays to virtue, permissiveness is, to some extent, the tribute that authority pays to the principle of equality.

When one recognizes some of these varied strands in the fabric of equalitarianism it becomes easier to see how the concept has contributed to the making both of the Jeffersonian American and the Tocquevillian American. For as one picks at the strands they ravel out in quite dissimilar directions. The strand of equality of opportunity, for instance, if followed out, leads to the theme of individualism. It challenged each individual to pit his skill and talents in a competition against the skill and talents of others and to earn the individual rewards which talent and effort might bring. Even more, the imperatives of the competitive race were so compelling that the belief grew up that everyone had a kind of obligation to enter his talents in this competition and to "succeed." It was but a step from the belief that ability and virtue would produce success to the belief that success was produced by—and was therefore an evidence of —ability and virtue. In short, money not only represented power, it also was a sign of the presence of admirable qualities in the man who attained it. Here, certainly, an equalitarian doctrine fostered materialism, and if aggressiveness and competitiveness are individualistic qualities, then it fostered individualism also.

Of course, neither American individualism nor American materialism can be explained entirely in these terms. Individualism must have derived great strength, for instance, from the reflection that if all men are equal, a man might as well form his own convictions as accept the convictions of someone else no better than himself. It must also have been reinforced by the frontier experience, which certainly compelled every man to rely upon himself. But this kind of individualism is not the quality of independent-mindedness, and it is not the quality which Tocqueville was denying when he said that Americans were conformists. A great deal of confusion has resulted, in the discussion of the American character, from the fact that the term individualism is sometimes used (as by Tocqueville) to mean willingness to think and act separately from the majority, and sometimes (as by Turner) to mean capacity to get along without help. It might be supposed that the two would converge, on the theory that a man who can get along by himself without help will soon recognize that he may as well also think for himself without help. But in actuality, this did not necessarily happen. Self-reliance on the frontier was more a matter of courage and of staying power than of intellectual resourcefulness, for the struggle with the wilderness challenged the body rather than the mind, and a man might be supremely effective in fending for himself, and at the same time supremely conventional in his ideas. In this sense, Turner's individualist is not really an antithesis of Tocqueville's conformist at all.

Still, it remains true that Jefferson's idealist and Tocqueville's conformist both require explanation, and that neither can be accounted for in the terms which make Jefferson's individualist and Tocqueville's materialist understandable. As an explanation of these facets of the American character, it would seem that the strand of equalitarianism which stresses the universal dignity of all men, and which hates rank as a violation of dignity, might be found quite pertinent. For it is the concept of the worth of every man which has stimulated a century and a half of reform, designed at every step to realize in practice the ideal that every human possesses potentialities which he should have a chance to fulfill. Whatever has impeded this fulfillment, whether it be lack of education, chattel slavery, the exploitation of the labor of unorganized workers, the hazards of unemployment, or the handicaps of age and infirmity, has been the object, at one time or another, of a major reforming crusade. The whole American commitment to progress would be impossible without a prior belief in the perfectibility of man and in the practicability of steps to bring perfection nearer. In this sense, the American character has been idealistic. And yet its idealism is not entirely irreconcilable with its materialism, for American idealism has often framed its most altruistic goals in materialistic terms—for instance, of raising the standard of living as a means to a better life. Moreover, Americans are committed to the view that materialistic means are necessary to idealistic ends. Franklin defined what is necessary to a virtuous life by saying "an empty sack cannot stand upright," and Americans have believed that spiritual and humanitarian goals are best achieved by instrumentalities such as universities and hospitals which carry expensive price tags.

If the belief that all men are of equal worth has contributed to a feature of American life so much cherished as our tradition of humanitarian reform, how could it at the same time have contributed to a feature so much deplored as American conformity? Yet it has done both, for the same respect of the American for his fellow men, which has made many a reformer think that his fellow citizens are worth helping, has also made many another American think that he has no business to question the opinions that his neighbors have sanctioned. True, he says, if all men are equal, each ought to think for himself, but on the other hand, no man should consider himself better than his neighbors, and if the majority have adopted an opinion on a matter, how can one man question their opinion, without setting himself up as being better than they. Moreover, it is understood that the majority are pledged not to force him to adopt their opinion. But it is also understood that in return for this immunity he will voluntarily accept the will of the majority in most things. The absence of a formal compulsion to conform seemingly increases the obligation to conform voluntarily. Thus, the other-directed man is seen to be derived as much from the American tradition of equalitarianism as the rugged individualist, and the compulsive seeker of an unequally large share of wealth as much as the humanitarian reformer striving for the fulfillment of democratic ideals.

To say that they are all derived from the same tradition is by no means to say that they are, in some larger, mystic sense, all the same. They are not, even though the idealism of the reformer may seek materialistic goals, and though men who are individualists in their physical lives may be conformists in their ideas. But all of them, it may be argued, do reflect circumstances which are distinctively American, and all present manifestations of a character which is more convincingly American because of its diversity than any wholly uniform character could possibly be. If Americans have never reached the end of their quest for an image that would represent the American character, it may be not because they failed to find one image but because they failed to recognize the futility of attempting to settle upon one, and the necessity of accepting several.

Errand into the Wilderness

Perry Miller

INTRODUCTION

Perry Miller raises a question that perplexes Americans today as it perplexed Puritans three centuries ago: what is the meaning of America? Just as the Puritans first formulated the question, so also they first offered an answer, one that retains much of its original relevance in the present age. Puritans conceived of an American mission as the fulfillment of divine intentions through the actions of human beings; and though, as Miller explains, they felt oppressed by their inability to carry out God's will as well as they might, they never doubted the worth of their conviction. Since the seventeenth century other Americans have redefined their country's purposes and have pointed out its failure of mind and performance. Whatever these departures from the Puritans' sense of destiny, the American character, even a part of its critical cast of mind, owes something to the original formulation of mission as it was defined by the Puritans. Miller's evocative essay deserves our attention for what it tells us both about the Puritans and about ourselves.

For a fuller explication of the ideas expressed in this essay, students should see Perry Miller, *The New England Mind: From Colony to Province** (1953), and *Orthodoxy in Massachusetts** (1933). Edmund S. Morgan, *The Puritan Dilemma: The Story of John Winthrop** (1958), provides a brilliant discussion of the motives of a leading founder. For a different view of Puritan mission see Darrett B. Rutman, *Winthrop's Boston: A Portrait of a Puritan Town, 1630–1649** (1965). And see, too, Robert Middlekauff, *The Mathers: Three Generations of Puritan Intellectuals* (1971), for a recent and revisionist interpretation of Puritan mission. The social origins of the English Puritan emigrants to America is ably reconstructed in Carl Bridenbaugh, *Vexed and Troubled Englishmen, 1590–1642* (1968). Another group of Puritans filled with zeal for a holy experiment, the Quakers, may be studied in William C. Braithwaite, *The Second Period of Quakerism* (second edition prepared by Henry J. Cadbury, 1961); Charles M. Andrews, *The Colonial Period of American History: The Settlements** (1937), Vol. 3; and Frederick B. Tolles, *Meeting House and Counting House** (1948).

I T was a happy inspiration that led the staff of the John Carter Brown Library to choose as the title of its New England exhibition of 1952 a phrase from Samuel Danforth's election sermon, delivered on May 11, 1670: *A Brief Recognition of New England's Errand into the Wilderness*. It was of course an inspiration, if not of genius at least of talent, for Danforth to invent his title in the first place. But all the election sermons of this period—that is to say, the major expressions of the second generation, which, delivered on these forensic occasions, were in the fullest sense community expression—have interesting titles; a mere listing tells the story of what was happening to the minds and emotions of the New England people: John Higginson's *The Cause of God and His People In New England* in 1663, William Stoughton's *New England's True Interest, Not to Lie* in 1668, Thomas Shepard's *Eye-Salve* in 1672, Urian Oakes's *New England Pleaded With* in 1673, and, climactically and most explicitly, Increase Mather's *A Discourse Concerning the Danger of Apostasy* in 1677.

All of these show by their title pages alone—and, as those who have looked into them know, infinitely more by their contents—a deep disquietude. They are troubled utterances, worried, fearful. Something has gone wrong. As in 1662 Wigglesworth already was saying in verse, God has a controversy with New England; He has cause to be angry and to punish it because of its innumerable defections. They say, unanimously, that New England was sent on an errand, and that it has failed.

To our ears these lamentations of the second generation sound strange indeed. We think of the founders as heroic men—of the towering stature of Bradford, Winthrop, and Thomas Hooker—who braved the ocean and the wilderness, who conquered both, and left to their children a goodly heritage. Why then this whimpering?

Some historians suggest that the second and third generations suffered a failure of nerve; they weren't the men their fathers had been, and they knew it. Where the founders could range over the vast body of theology and ecclesiastical polity and produce profound works like the treatises of John Cotton or the subtle psychological analyses of Hooker, or even such a gusty though wrongheaded book as Nathaniel Ward's *Simple Cobler*, let alone such lofty and righteaded pleas as Roger Williams' *Bloudy Tenent*, all these children could do was tell each other that they were on probation and that their chances of making good did not seem very promising.

Since Puritan intellectuals were thoroughly grounded in grammar and rhetoric, we may be certain that Danforth was fully aware of the ambiguity concealed in his word "errand." It already had taken on the double meaning which it still carries with us. Originally, as the word first took form in English,

FROM Perry Miller, *Errand into the Wilderness*, Cambridge: Belknap Press of Harvard University Press, 1956. Copyright, 1956, by the President and Fellows of Harvard College. Reprinted by permission of the publishers and Mrs. Elizabeth Miller.

it meant exclusively a short journey on which an inferior is sent to convey a message or to perform a service for his superior. In that sense we today speak of an "errand boy"; or the husband says that while in town on his lunch hour, he must run an errand for his wife. But by the end of the Middle Ages, errand developed another connotation: it came to mean the actual business on which the actor goes, the purpose itself, the conscious intention in his mind. In this signification, the runner of the errand is working for himself, is his own boss; the wife, while the husband is away at the office, runs her own errands. Now in the 1660's the problem was this: which had New England originally been —an errand boy or a doer of errands? In which sense had it failed? Had it been despatched for a further purpose, or was it an end in itself? Or had it fallen short not only in one or the other, but in both of the meanings? If so, it was indeed a tragedy, in the primitive sense of a fall from a mighty designation.

If the children were in grave doubt about which had been the original errand—if, in fact, those of the founders who lived into the later period and who might have set their progeny to rights found themselves wondering and confused—there is little chance of our answering clearly. Of course, there is no problem about Plymouth Colony. That is the charm about Plymouth: its clarity. The Pilgrims, as we have learned to call them, were reluctant voyagers; they had never wanted to leave England, but had been obliged to depart because the authorities made life impossible for Separatists. They could, naturally, have stayed at home had they given up being Separatists, but that idea simply did not occur to them. Yet they did not go to Holland as though on an errand; neither can we extract the notion of a mission out of the reasons which, as Bradford tells us, persuaded them to leave Leyden for "Virginia." The war with Spain was about to be resumed, and the economic threat was ominous; their migration was not so much an errand as a shrewd forecast, a plan to get out while the getting was good, lest, should they stay, they would be "intrapped or surrounded by their enemies, so as they should neither be able to fight nor flie." True, once the decision was taken, they congratulated themselves that they might become a means for propagating the gospel in remote parts of the world, and thus of serving as steppingstones to others in the performance of this great work; nevertheless, the substance of their decision was that they "thought it better to dislodge betimes to some place of better advantage and less danger, if any such could be found." The great hymn that Bradford, looking back in his old age, chanted about the landfall is one of the greatest passages, if not the very greatest, in all New England's literature; yet it does not resound with the sense of a mission accomplished—instead, it vibrates with the sorrow and exultation of suffering, the sheer endurance, the pain and the anguish, with the somberness of death faced unflinchingly:

> May not and ought not the children of these fathers rightly say: Our fathers were Englishmen which came over this great ocean, and were ready to perish in this wilderness; but they cried unto the Lord, and he heard their voyce, and looked on their adversitie. . . .

We are bound, I think, to see in Bradford's account the prototype of the vast majority of subsequent immigrants—of those Oscar Handlin calls "The Uprooted": they came for better advantage and for less danger, and to give their posterity the opportunity of success.

The Great Migration of 1630 is an entirely other story. True, among the reasons John Winthrop drew up in 1629 to persuade himself and his colleagues that they should commit themselves to the enterprise, the economic motive frankly figures. Wise men thought that England was overpopulated and that the poor would have a better chance in the new land. But Massachusetts Bay was not just an organization of immigrants seeking advantage and opportunity. It had a positive sense of mission—either it was sent on an errand or it had its own intention, but in either case the deed was deliberate. It was an act of will, perhaps of willfulness. These Puritans were not driven out of England (thousands of their fellows stayed and fought the Cavaliers)—they went of their own accord.

So, concerning them, we ask the question, why? If we are not altogether clear about precisely how we should phrase the answer, this is not because they themselves were reticent. They spoke as fully as they knew how, and none more magnificently or cogently than John Winthrop in the midst of the passage itself, when he delivered a lay sermon aboard the flagship *Arbella* and called it "A Modell of Christian Charity." It distinguishes the motives of this great enterprise from those of Bradford's forlorn retreat, and especially from those of the masses who later have come in quest of advancement. Hence, for the student of New England and of America, it is a fact demanding incessant brooding that John Winthrop selected as the "doctrine" of his discourse, and so as the basic proposition to which, it then seemed to him, the errand was committed, the thesis that God had disposed mankind in a hierarchy of social classes, so that "in all times some must be rich, some poor, some highe and eminent in power and dignitie; others mean and in subjeccion." It is as though, preternaturally sensing what the promise of America might come to signify for the rank and file, Winthrop took the precaution to drive out of their heads any notion that in the wilderness the poor and the mean were ever so to improve themselves as to mount above the rich or the eminent in dignity. Were there any who had signed up under the mistaken impression that such was the purpose of their errand, Winthrop told them that, although other peoples, lesser breeds, might come for wealth or pelf, this migration was specifically dedicated to an avowed end that had nothing to do with incomes. We have entered into an explicit covenant with God, "we haue professed to enterprise these accions vpon these and these ends"; we have drawn up indentures with the Almighty, wherefore if we succeed and do not let ourselves get diverted into making money, He will reward us. Whereas if we fail, if we "fall to embrace this present world and prosecute our carnall intencions, seekeing great things for our selves and our posterity, the Lord will surely breake out in wrathe against us be revenged of such a periured people and make us knowe the price of the breache of such a Covenant."

Well, what terms were agreed upon in this covenant? Winthrop could say precisely—"It is by a mutuall consent through a specially overruleing providence, and a more than ordinary approbation of the Churches of Christ to seeke out a place of Cohabitation and Consorteshipp under a due forme of Government both civill and ecclesiasticall." If it could be said thus concretely, why should there be any ambiguity? There was no doubt whatsoever about what Winthrop meant by a due form of ecclesiastical government: he meant the pure Biblical polity set forth in full detail by the New Testament, that method which later generations, in the days of increasing confusion, would settle down to calling Congregational, but which for Winthrop was no denominational peculiarity but the very essence of organized Christianity. What a due form of civil government meant, therefore, became crystal clear: a political regime, possessing power, which would consider its main function to be the erecting, protecting, and preserving of this form of polity. This due form would have, at the very beginning of its list of responsibilities, the duty of suppressing heresy, of subduing or somehow getting rid of dissenters—of being, in short, deliberately, vigorously, and consistently intolerant.

Regarded in this light, the Massachusetts Bay Company came on an errand in the second and later sense of the word: it was, so to speak, on its own business. What it set out to do was the sufficient reason for its setting out. About this Winthrop seems to be perfectly certain, as he declares specifically what the due forms will be attempting: the end is to improve our lives to do more service to the Lord, to increase the body of Christ, and to preserve our posterity from the corruptions of this evil world, so that they in turn shall work out their salvation under the purity and power of Biblical ordinances. Because the errand was so definable in advance, certain conclusions about the method of conducting it were equally evident: one, obviously, was that those sworn to the covenant should not be allowed to turn aside in a lust for mere physical rewards; but another was, in Winthrop's simple but splendid words, "we must be knit together in this worke as one man, wee must entertaine each other in brotherly affection." we must actually delight in each other, "always having before our eyes our Commission and community in the worke, our community as members of the same body." This was to say, were the great purpose kept steadily in mind, if all gazed only at it and strove only for it, then social solidarity (within a scheme of fixed and unalterable class distinctions) would be an automatic consequence. A society despatched upon an errand that is its own reward would want no other rewards: it could go forth to possess a land without ever becoming possessed by it; social gradations would remain eternally what God had originally appointed; there would be no internal contention among groups or interests, and though there would be hard work for everybody, prosperity would be bestowed not as a consequence of labor but as a sign of approval upon the mission itself. For once in the history of humanity (with all its sins), there would be a society so dedicated to a holy cause that success would prove innocent and triumph not raise up sinful pride or arrogant dissension.

Or, at least, this would come about if the people did not deal falsely with God, if they would live up to the articles of their bond. If we do not perform these terms, Winthrop warned, we may expect immediate manifestations of divine wrath; we shall perish out of the land we are crossing the sea to possess. And here in the 1660's and 1670's, all the jeremiads (of which Danforth's is one of the most poignant) are castigations of the people for having defaulted on precisely these articles. They recite the long list of afflictions an angry God had rained upon them, surely enough to prove how abysmally they had deserted the covenant: crop failures, epidemics, grasshoppers, caterpillars, torrid summers, arctic winters, Indian wars, hurricanes, shipwrecks, accidents, and (most grievous of all) unsatisfactory children. The solemn work of the election day, said Stoughton in 1668, is "Foundationwork"—not, that is, to lay a new one, "but to continue, and strengthen, and beautifie, and build upon that which has been laid." It had been laid in the covenant before even a foot was set ashore, and thereon New England should rest. Hence the terms of survival, let alone of prosperity, remained what had first been propounded:

> If we should so frustrate and deceive the Lords Expectations, that his Covenant-interest in us, and the Workings of his Salvation be made to cease, then All were lost indeed; Ruine upon Ruine, Destruction upon Destruction would come, until one stone were not left upon another.

Since so much of the literature after 1660—in fact, just about all of it—dwells on this theme of declension and apostasy, would not the story of New England seem to be simply that of the failure of a mission? Winthrop's dread was realized: posterity had not found their salvation amid pure ordinances but had, despite the ordinances, yielded to the seductions of the good land. Hence distresses were being piled upon them, the slaughter of King Philip's War and now the attack of a profligate king upon the sacred charter. By about 1680, it did in truth seem that shortly no stone would be left upon another, that history would record of New England that the founders had been great men, but that their children and grandchildren progressively deteriorated.

This would certainly seem to be the impression conveyed by the assembled clergy and lay elders who, in 1679, met at Boston in a formal synod, under the leadership of Increase Mather, and there prepared a report on why the land suffered. The result of their deliberation, published under the title *The Necessity of Reformation,* was the first in what has proved to be a distressingly long succession of investigations into the civic health of Americans, and it is probably the most pessimistic. The land was afflicted, it said, because corruption had proceeded apace; assuredly, if the people did not quickly reform, the last blow would fall and nothing but desolation be left. Into what a moral quagmire this dedicated community had sunk, the synod did not leave to imagination; it published a long and detailed inventory of sins, crimes, misdemeanors, and nasty habits, which makes, to say the least, interesting reading.

We hear much talk nowadays about corruption, most of it couched in generalized terms. If we ask our current Jeremiahs to descend to particulars, they tell us that the republic is going on the rocks, or to the dogs, because the wives of politicians aspire to wear mink coats and their husbands take a moderate five per cent cut on certain deals to pay for the garments. The Puritans were devotees of logic, and the verb "methodize" ruled their thinking. When the synod went to work, it had before it a succession of sermons, such as that of Danforth and the other election-day or fast-day orators, as well as such works as Increase Mather's *A Brief History of the Warr With the Indians,* wherein the decimating conflict with Philip was presented as a revenge upon the people for their transgressions. When the synod felt obliged to enumerate the enormities of the land so that the people could recognize just how far short of their errand they had fallen, it did not, in the modern manner, assume that regeneration would be accomplished at the next election by turning the rascals out, but it digested this body of literature; it reduced the contents to method. The result is a staggering compendium of iniquity, organized into twelve headings.

First, there was a great and visible decay of godliness. Second, there were several manifestations of pride—contention in the churches, insubordination of inferiors toward superiors, particularly of those inferiors who had, unaccountably, acquired more wealth than their betters, and, astonishingly, a shocking extravagance in attire, especially on the part of these of the meaner sort, who persisted in dressing beyond their means. Third, there were heretics, especially Quakers and Anabaptists. Fourth, a notable increase in swearing and a spreading disposition to sleep at sermons (these two phenomena seemed basically connected). Fifth, the Sabbath was wantonly violated. Sixth, family government had decayed, and fathers no longer kept their sons and daughters from prowling at night. Seventh, instead of people being knit together as one man in mutual love, they were full of contention, so that lawsuits were on the increase and lawyers were thriving. Under the eighth head, the synod described the sins of sex and alcohol, thus producing some of the juciest prose of the period: militia days had become orgies, taverns were crowded; women threw temptation in the way of befuddled men by wearing false locks and displaying naked necks and arms "or, which is more abominable, naked Breasts"; there were "mixed Dancings," along with light behavior and "Company-keeping" with vain persons, wherefore the bastardy rate was rising. In 1672, there was actually an attempt to supply Boston with a brothel (it was suppressed, but the synod was bearish about the future). Ninth, New Englanders were betraying a marked disposition to tell lies, especially when selling anything. In the tenth place, the business morality of even the most righteous left everything to be desired: the wealthy speculated in land and raised prices excessively; "Day-Labourers and Mechanicks are unreasonable in their demands." In the eleventh place, the people showed no disposition to reform, and in the twelfth, they seemed utterly destitute of civic spirit.

"The things here insisted on," said the synod, "have been oftentimes mentioned and inculcated by those whom the Lord hath set as Watchmen to the house of Israel." Indeed they had been, and thereafter they continued to be even more inculcated. At the end of the century, the synod's report was serving as a kind of handbook for preachers: they would take some verse of Isaiah or Jeremiah, set up the doctrine that God avenges the iniquities of a chosen people, and then run down the twelve heads, merely bringing the list up to date by inserting the new and still more depraved practices an ingenious people kept on devising. I suppose that in the whole literature of the world, including the satirists of imperial Rome, there is hardly such another uninhibited and unrelenting documentation of a people's descent into corruption.

I have elsewhere endeavored to argue[1] that, while the social or economic historian may read this literature for its contents—and so construct from the expanding catalogue of denunciations a record of social progress—the cultural anthropologist will look slightly askance at these jeremiads; he will exercise a methodological caution about taking them at face value. If you read them all through, the total effect, curiously enough, is not at all depressing: you come to the paradoxical realization that they do not bespeak a despairing frame of mind. There is something of a ritualistic incantation about them; whatever they may signify in the realm of theology, in that of psychology they are purgations of soul; they do not discourage but actually encourage the community to persist in its heinous conduct. The exhortation to a reformation which never materializes serves as a token payment upon the obligation, and so liberates the

[1] See *The New England Mind: From Colony to Province* (1952), Chapter II.

debtors. Changes there had to be: adaptations to environment, expansion of the frontier, mansions constructed, commercial adventures undertaken. These activities were not specifically nominated in the bond Winthrop had framed. They were thrust upon the society by American experience; because they were not only works of necessity but of excitement, they proved irresistible—whether making money, haunting taverns, or committing fornication. Land speculation meant not only wealth but dispersion of the people, and what was to stop the march of settlement? The covenant doctrine preached on the *Arbella* had been formulated in England, where land was not to be had for the taking; its adherents had been utterly oblivious of what the fact of a frontier would do for an imported order, let alone for a European mentality. Hence I suggest that under the guise of this mounting wail of sinfulness, this incessant and never successful cry for repentance, the Puritans launched themselves upon the process of Americanization.

However, there are still more pertinent or more analytical things to be said of this body of expression. If you compare it with the great productions of the founders, you will be struck by the fact that the second and third generations had become oriented toward the social, and only the social, problem; herein they were deeply and profoundly different from their fathers. The finest creations of the founders—the disquisitions of Hooker, Shepard, and Cotton—were written in Europe, or else, if actually penned in the colonies, proceeded from a thoroughly European mentality, upon which the American scene made no impression whatsoever. The most striking example of this imperviousness is the poetry of Anne Bradstreet: she came to Massachusetts at the age of eighteen, already two years married to Simon Bradstreet; there, she says, "I found a new world and new manners, at which my heart rose" in rebellion, but soon convincing herself that it was the way of God, she submitted and joined the church. She bore Simon eight children, and loved him sincerely, as her most charming poem, addressed to him, reveals:

> If ever two were one, then surely we;
> If ever man were loved by wife, then thee.

After the house burned, she wrote a lament about how her pleasant things in ashes lay and how no more the merriment of guests would sound in the hall; but there is nothing in the poem to suggest that the house stood in North Andover or that the things so tragically consumed were doubly precious because they had been transported across the ocean and were utterly irreplaceable in the wilderness. In between rearing children and keeping house she wrote her poetry; her brother-in-law carried the manuscript to London, and there published it in 1650 under the ambitious title, *The Tenth Muse Lately Sprung Up in America*. But the title is the only thing about the volume which shows any sense of America, and that little merely in order to prove that the plantations had something in the way of European wit and learning, that they had not receded into barbarism. Anne's flowers are English flowers, the birds, English birds, and the landscape is Lincolnshire. So also with the productions of immigrant scholarship: such a learned and acute work as Hooker's *Survey of the Summe of Church Discipline,* which is specifically about the regime set up in America, is written entirely within the logical patterns, and out of the religious experience, of Europe; it makes no concession to new and peculiar circumstances.

The titles alone of productions in the next generation show how concentrated have become emotion and attention upon the interest of New England, and none is more revealing than Samuel Danforth's conception of an errand into the wilderness. Instead of being able to compose abstract treatises like those of Hooker upon the soul's preparation, humiliation, or exultation, or such a collection of wisdom and theology as John Cotton's *The Way of Life* or Shepard's *The Sound Believer,* these later saints must, over and over again, dwell upon the specific sins of New England, and the more they denounce, the more they must narrow their focus to the provincial problem. If they write upon anything else, it must be about the halfway covenant and its manifold consequences—a development enacted wholly in this country—or else upon their wars with the Indians. Their range is sadly constricted, but every effort, no matter how brief, is addressed to the persistent question: what is the meaning of this society in the wilderness? If it does not mean what Winthrop said it must mean, what under Heaven is it? Who, they are forever asking themselves, who are we?— and sometimes they are on the verge of saying, who the Devil are we, anyway?

This brings us back to the fundamental ambiguity concealed in the word "errand," that *double entente* of which I am certain Danforth was aware when he published the words that give point to the exhibition. While it was true that in 1630, the covenant philosophy of a special and peculiar bond lifted the migration out of the ordinary realm of nature, provided it with a definite mission which might in the secondary sense be called its errand, there was always present in Puritan thinking the suspicion that God's saints are at best inferiors, despatched by their Superior upon particular assignments. Anyone who has run errands for other people, particularly for people of great importance with many things on their minds, such as army commanders, knows how real is the peril that, by the time he returns with the report of a message delivered or a bridge blown up, the Superior may be interested in something else; the situation at headquarters may be entirely changed, and the gallant errand boy, or the husband who desperately remembered to buy the ribbon, may be told that he is too late. This tragic pattern appears again and again in modern warfare: an agent is dropped by parachute and, after immense hardships, comes back to find that, in the shifting tactical or strategic situations, his contribution is no longer of value. If he gets home in time and his service proves useful, he receives a medal; otherwise, no matter what prodigies he has performed, he may not even be thanked. He has been sent, as the devastating phrase has it, upon a fool's errand, than which there can be a no more shattering blow to self-esteem.

The Great Migration of 1630 felt insured against such treatment from on high by the covenant; nevertheless, the God of the covenant always remained an unpredictable Jehovah, a *Deus Absconditus.* When God promises to abide by stated terms, His word, of course, is to be trusted; but then, what is man that he dare accuse Omnipotence of tergiversation? But if any such apprehension was in Winthrop's mind as he spoke on the *Arbella,* or in the minds of other apologists for the enterprise, they kept it far back and allowed it no utterance. They could stifle the thought, not only because Winthrop and his colleagues believed fully in the covenant, but because they could see in the pattern of history that their errand was not a mere scouting expedition: it was an essential maneuver in the drama of Christendom. The Bay Company was not a battered remnant of suffering Separatists thrown up on a rocky shore; it was an organized task force of Christians, executing a flank attack on the corruptions of Christendom. These Puritans did not flee to America; they went in order to work out that complete reformation which was not yet accomplished in England and Europe, but which would quickly be accomplished if only the saints back there had a working model to guide them. It is impossible to say that any who sailed from Southampton really expected to lay his bones in the new world; were it to come about—as all in their heart of hearts anticipated—that the forces of righteousness should prevail against Laud and Wentworth, that England after all should turn toward reformation, where else would the distracted country look for leadership except to those who in New England had perfected the ideal polity and who would know how to administer it? This was the large unspoken assumption in the errand of 1630: if the conscious intention were realized, not only would a federated Jehovah bless the new land, but He would bring back these temporary colonials to govern England.

In this respect, therefore, we may say that the migration was running an errand in the earlier and more primitive sense of the word—performing a job not so much for Jehovah as for history, which was the wisdom of Jehovah expressed through time. Winthrop was aware of this aspect of the mission—fully conscious of it. "For wee must Consider that wee shall be as a Citty upon a Hill, the eies of all people are uppon us." More was at stake than just one little colony. If we deal falsely with God, not only will He descend upon us in wrath, but even more terribly, He will make us "a story and a by-word through the world, wee shall open the mouthes of enemies to speake evill of the wayes of god and all professours for Gods sake." No less than John Milton was New England to justify God's ways to man, though not, like him, in the agony and confusion of defeat but in the confidence of approaching triumph. This errand was being run for the sake of Reformed Christianity; and while the first aim was indeed to realize in America the due form of government, both civil and ecclesiastical, the aim behind that aim was to vindicate the most rigorous ideal of the Reformation, so that ultimately all Europe would imitate New England. If we succeed, Winthrop told his audience, men will say of later plantations, "the lord make it like that of New England." There was an elementary prudence to be observed: Winthrop said that the prayer would arise from subsequent plantations, yet what was England itself but one of God's plantations? In America, he promised, we shall see, or may see, more of God's wisdom, power, and truth "then formerly wee have beene acquainted with." The situation was such that, for the moment, the model had no chance to be exhibited in England; Puritans could talk about it, theorize upon it, but they could not display it, could not prove that it would actually work. But if they had it set up in America—in a bare land, devoid of already established (and corrupt) institutions, empty of bishops and courtiers, where they could start *de novo,* and the eyes of the world were upon it—and if then it performed just as the saints had predicted of it, the Calvinist internationale would know exactly how to go about completing the already begun but temporarily stalled revolution in Europe.[2]

[2] See the perceptive analysis of Alan Heimert (*The New England Quarterly*, XXVI, September 1953) of the ingredients that ultimately went into the Puritans' metaphor of the "wilderness," all the more striking a concoction because they attached no significance a priori to their wilderness destination. To begin with, it was simply a void.

When we look upon the enterprise from this point of view, the psychology of the second and third generations becomes more comprehensible. We realize that the migration was not sent upon its errand in order to found the United States of America, nor even the New England conscience. Actually, it would not perform its errand even when the colonists did erect a due form of government in church and state: what was further required in order for this mission to be a success was that the eyes of the world be kept fixed upon it in rapt attention. If the rest of the world, or at least of Protestantism, looked elsewhere, or turned to another model, or simply got distracted and forgot about New England, if the new land was left with a polity nobody in the great world of Europe wanted—then every success in fulfilling the terms of the covenant would become a diabolical measure of failure. If the due form of government were not everywhere to be saluted, what would New England have upon its hands? How give it a name, this victory nobody could utilize? How provide an identity for something conceived under misapprehensions? How could a universal which turned out to be nothing but a provincial particular be called anything but a blunder or an abortion?

If an actor, playing the leading role in the greatest dramatic spectacle of the century, were to attire himself and put on his make-up, rehearse his lines, take a deep breath, and stride onto the stage, only to find the theater dark and empty, no spotlight working, and himself entirely alone, he would feel as did New England around 1650 or 1660. For in the 1640's, during the Civil Wars, the colonies, so to speak, lost their audience. First of all, there proved to be, deep in the Puritan movement, an irreconcilable split between the Presbyterian and Independent wings, wherefore no one system could be imposed upon England, and so the New England model was unserviceable. Secondly—most horrible to relate—the Independents, who in polity were carrying New England's banner and were supposed, in the schedule of history, to lead England into imitation of the colonial order, betrayed the sacred cause by yielding to the heresy of toleration. They actually welcomed Roger Williams, whom the leaders of the model had kicked out of Massachusetts so that his nonsense about liberty of conscience would not spoil the administrations of charity.

In other words, New England did not lie, did not falter; it made good everything Winthrop demanded—wonderfully good—and then found that its lesson was rejected by those choice spirits for whom the exertion had been made. By casting out Williams, Anne Hutchinson, and the Antinomians, along with an assortment of Gortonists and Anabaptists, into that cesspool then becoming known as Rhode Island, Winthrop, Dudley, and the clerical leaders showed Oliver Cromwell how he should go about governing England. Instead, he developed the utterly absurd theory that so long as a man made a good soldier in the New Model Army, it did not matter whether he was a Calvinist, an Antinomian, an Arminian, an Anabaptist or even—horror of horrors—a Socinian! Year after year, as the circus tours this country, crowds howl with laughter, no matter how many times they have seen the stunt, at the bustle that walks by itself: the clown comes out dressed in a large skirt with a bustle behind; he turns sharply to the left, and the bustle continues blindly and obstinately straight ahead, on the original course. It is funny in a circus, but not in history. There is nothing but tragedy in the realization that one was in the main path of events, and now is sidetracked and disregarded. One is always able, of course, to stand firm on his first resolution, and to condemn the clown of history for taking the wrong turning: yet this is a desolating sort of stoicism, because it always carries with it the recognition that history will never come back to the predicted path, and that with one's own demise, righteousness must die out of the world.

The most humiliating element in the experience was the way the English brethren turned upon the colonials for precisely their greatest achievement. It must have seemed, for those who came with Winthrop in 1630 and who remembered the clarity and brilliance with which he set forth the conditions of their errand, that the world was turned upside down and inside out when, in June 1645, thirteen leading Independent divines—such men as Goodwin, Owen, Nye, Burroughs, formerly friends and allies of Hooker and Davenport, men who might easily have come to New England and helped extirpate heretics—wrote the General Court that the colony's law banishing Anabaptists was an embarrassment to the Independent cause in England. Opponents were declaring, said these worthies, "that persons of our way, principall and spirit cannot beare with Dissenters from them, but Doe correct, fine, imprison and banish them wherever they have power soe to Doe." There were indeed people in England who admired the severities of Massachusetts, but we assure you, said the Independents, these "are utterly your enemyes and Doe seeke your extirpation from the face of the earth: those who now in power are your friends are quite otherwise minded, and doe professe they are much offended with your proceedings." Thus early commenced that chronic weakness in the foreign policy of Americans, an inability to recognize who in truth constitute their best friends abroad.

We have lately accustomed ourselves to the fact that there does exist a mentality which will take advantage of the liberties allowed by society in order to conspire for the ultimate suppression of those same privileges. The government of Charles I and Archbishop Laud had not, where that danger was concerned, been liberal, but it had been conspicuously inefficient; hence, it did not liquidate the Puritans (although it made halfhearted efforts), nor did it herd them into prison camps. Instead, it generously, even lavishly, gave a group of them a charter to Massachusetts Bay, and obligingly left out the standard clause requiring that the document remain in London, that the grantees keep their office within reach of Whitehall. Winthrop's revolutionaries availed themselves of this liberty to get the charter overseas, and thus to set up a regime dedicated to the worship of God in the manner they desired—which meant allowing nobody else to worship any other way, especially adherents of Laud and King Charles. All this was perfectly logical and consistent. But what happened to the thought processes of their fellows in England made no sense whatsoever. Out of the New Model Army came the fantastic notion that a party struggling for power should proclaim that, once it captured the state, it would recognize the right of dissenters to disagree and to have their own worship, to hold their own opinions. Oliver Cromwell was so far gone in this idiocy as to become a dictator, in order to impose toleration by force! Amid this shambles, the errand of New England collapsed. There was nobody left at headquarters to whom reports could be sent.

Many a man has done a brave deed, been hailed as a public hero, had honors and ticker tape heaped upon him—and then had to live, day after day, in the ordinary routine, eating breakfast and brushing his teeth, in what seems protracted anticlimax. A couple may win their way to each other across insuperable obstacles, elope in a blaze of passion and glory—and then have to learn that life is a matter of buying the groceries and getting the laundry done. This sense of the meaning having gone out of life, that all adventures are over, that no great days and no heroism lie ahead, is particularly galling when it falls upon a son whose father once was the public hero or the great lover. He has to put up with the daily routine without ever having known at first hand the thrill of danger or the ecstasy of passion. True, he has his own hardships—clearing rocky pastures, hauling in the cod during a storm, fighting Indians in a swamp —but what are these compared with the magnificence of leading an exodus of saints to found a city on a hill, for the eyes of all the world to behold? He might wage a stout fight against the Indians and one out of ten of his fellows might perish in the struggle, but the world was no longer interested. He would be reduced to writing accounts of himself and scheming to get a publisher in London, in a desperate effort to tell a heedless world, "Look, I exist!"

His greatest difficulty would be not the stones, storms, and Indians, but the problem of his identity. In something of this sort, I should like to suggest, consists the anxiety and torment that inform productions of the late seventeenth and early eighteenth centuries—and should I say, some thereafter? It appears most clearly in *Magnalia Christi Americana,* the work of that soul most tortured by the problem, Cotton Mather: "I write the Wonders of the Christian Religion, flying from the Depravations of Europe, to the American Strand." Thus he proudly begins, and at once trips over the acknowledgement that the founders had not simply fled from depraved Europe but had intended to redeem it. And so the book is full of lamentations over the declension of the children, who appear, page after page, in contrast to their mighty progenitors, about as profligate a lot as ever squandered a great inheritance.

And yet, the *Magnalia* is not an abject book; neither are the election sermons abject, nor is the inventory of sins offered by the synod of 1679. There is bewilderment, confusion, chagrin, but there is no surrender. A task has been assigned upon which the populace are in fact intensely engaged. But they are not sure any more for just whom they are working; they know they are moving, but they do not know where they are going. They seem still to be on an errand, but if they are no longer inferiors sent by the superior forces of the reformation, to whom they should report, then their errand must be wholly of the second sort, something with a purpose and an intention sufficient unto itself. If so, what is it? If it be not the due form of government, civil and ecclesiastical, that they brought into being, how otherwise can it be described?

The literature of self-condemnation must be read for meanings far below the surface, for meanings of which, we may be so rash as to surmise, the authors were not fully conscious, but by which they were troubled and goaded. They looked in vain to history for an explanation of themselves; more and more it appeared that the meaning was not to be found in theology, even with the help of the covenantal dialectic. Thereupon, these citizens found that they had no other place to search but within themselves—even though, at first sight, that repository appeared to be nothing but a sink of iniquity. Their errand having failed in the first sense of the term, they were left with the second, and required to fill it with meaning by themselves and out of themselves. Having failed to rivet the eyes of the world upon their city on the hill, they were left alone with America.

The Puritans and Sex

Edmund S. Morgan

INTRODUCTION

Discussing sex in relation to Puritan culture, a subject long freighted with sensationalism and stereotypes, in a way that reflects upon a broad spectrum of ideas and social practices is an important achievement. In his brief article, Morgan not only succeeds in demolishing the tired contention that our Puritan forebears were prudes; he also shows how the Puritans' ways of mitigating the tension between their moral code and their sexual practices acknowledged the reality of human nature without compromising their principles. Morgan's article provides a model of how a fresh and original treatment of a subject can bring about a new understanding of a culture. This subject can probably best be understood in its broad social context. For the English background M. M. Knappen, *Tudor Puritanism** (1939), and Christopher Hill, *Society and Puritanism in Pre-Revolutionary England** (1964), are useful. Two studies of family life are especially important: Edmund S. Morgan, *The Puritan Family*, rev. ed.* (1966), and John Demos, *A Little Commonwealth: Family Life in Plymouth Colony** (1970). Historical demography adds a further dimension as, for example, in Philip J. Greven, Jr., *Four Generations: Population, Land, and Family in Colonial Andover, Massachusetts* (1970), and Kenneth A. Lockridge, *A New England Town: The First Hundred Years, Dedham, Massachusetts, 1636–1736** (1970). The Puritans' ideas about sex were related to their ideas about nature; for a brilliant discussion of this matter, see Perry Miller, *The New England Mind: The Seventeenth Century** (1939, 1954). Further insight may be gained by studying a Puritan marriage; Edmund S. Morgan, *The Puritan Dilemma: The Story of John Winthrop** (1958), provides suggestive comments about a very successful one. Finally, the pioneering article by Charles F. Adams, "Some Phases of Sexual Morality and Church Discipline in Colonial New England," *Proceedings of the Massachusetts Historical Society*, XXVI (1891), 477–516, is still helpful.

32

HENRY Adams once observed that Americans have "ostentatiously ignored" sex. He could think of only two American writers who touched upon the subject with any degree of boldness—Walt Whitman and Bret Harte. Since the time when Adams made this penetrating observation, American writers have been making up for lost time in a way that would make Bret Harte, if not Whitman, blush. And yet there is still more truth than falsehood in Adams's statement. Americans, by comparison with Europeans or Asiatics, are squeamish when confronted with the facts of life. My purpose is not to account for this squeamishness, but simply to point out that the Puritans, those bogeymen of the modern intellectual, are not responsible for it.

At the outset, consider the Puritans' attitude toward marriage and the role of sex in marriage. The popular assumption might be that the Puritans frowned on marriage and tried to hush up the physical aspect of it as much as possible, but listen to what they themselves had to say. Samuel Willard, minister of the Old South Church in the latter part of the seventeenth century and author of the most complete textbook of Puritan divinity, more than once expressed his horror at "that Popish conceit of the Excellency of Virginity."[1] Another minister, John Cotton, wrote that

Women are Creatures without which there is no comfortable Living for man: it is true of them what is wont to be said of Governments, *That bad ones are better than none:* They are a sort of Blasphemers then who dispise and decry them, and call them *a necessary Evil,* for they are *a necessary Good.*[2]

These sentiments did not arise from an interpretation of marriage as a spiritual partnership, in which sexual intercourse was a minor or incidental matter. Cotton gave his opinion of "Platonic love" when he recalled the case of

one who immediately upon marriage, without ever approaching the *Nuptial Bed,* indented with the *Bride,* that by mutual consent they might both live such a life, and according did sequestring themselves according to the custom of those times, from the rest of mankind, and afterwards from one another too, in their retired Cells, giving themselves up to a Contemplative life; and this is recorded as an instance of no little or ordinary Vertue; but I must be pardoned in it, if I can account it no other than an effort of blind zeal, for they are the dictates of a blind mind they follow therein, and not of that Holy Spirit, which saith *It is not good that man should be alone.*[3]

FROM Edmund S. Morgan, "The Puritans and Sex," *The New England Quarterly,* XV, No. 4 (December 1942), 591–607. Reprinted by permission.

[1] Samuel Willard, *A Compleat Body of Divinity* (Boston, 1726), 125 and 608–613.
[2] John Cotton, *A Meet Help* (Boston, 1699), 14–15.   [3] *A Meet Help,* 16.

Here is as healthy an attitude as one could hope to find anywhere. Cotton certainly cannot be accused of ignoring human nature. Nor was he an isolated example among the Puritans. Another minister stated plainly that "the Use of the Marriage Bed" is "founded in mans Nature," and that consequently any withdrawal from sexual intercourse upon the part of husband or wife "Denies all relief in Wedlock vnto Human necessity: and sends it for supply vnto Beastiality when God gives not the gift of Continency."[4] In other words, sexual intercourse was a human necessity and marriage the only proper supply for it. These were the views of the New England clergy, the acknowledged leaders of the community, the most Puritanical of the Puritans. As proof that their congregations concurred with them, one may cite the case in which the members of the First Church of Boston expelled James Mattock because, among other offenses, "he denyed Coniugall fellowship vnto his wife for the space of 2 years together vpon pretense of taking Revenge upon himself for his abusing of her before marriage."[5] So strongly did the Puritans insist upon the sexual character of marriage that one New Englander considered himself slandered when it was reported, "that he Brock his deceased wife's hart with Greife, that he wold be absent from her 3 weeks together when he was at home, and wold never come nere her, and such Like."[6]

There was just one limitation which the Puritans placed upon sexual relations in marriage: sex must not interfere with religion. Man's chief end was to glorify God, and all earthly delights must promote that end, not hinder it. Love for a wife was carried too far when it led a man to neglect his God:

> . . . sometimes a man hath a good affection to Religion, but the love of his wife carries him away, a man may bee so transported to his wife, that hee dare not bee forward in Religion, lest hee displease his wife, and so the wife, lest shee displease her husband, and this is an inordinate love, when it exceeds measure.[7]

Sexual pleasures, in this respect, were treated like other kinds of pleasure. On a day of fast, when all comforts were supposed to be foregone in behalf of religious contemplation, not only were tasty food and drink to be abandoned but sexual intercourse, too. On other occasions, when food, drink, and recreation were allowable, sexual intercourse was allowable too, though of course only between persons who were married to each other. The Puritans were not ascetics; they never wished to prevent the enjoyment of earthly delights. They merely demanded that the pleasures of the flesh be subordinated to the greater glory of God: husband and wife must not become "so transported with affection, that they look at no higher end than marriage it self." "Let such as have wives," said the ministers, "look at them not for their own ends, but to be fitted for Gods service, and bring them nearer to God."[8]

Toward sexual intercourse outside marriage the Puritans were as frankly

---

[4] Edward Taylor, Commonplace Book (manuscript in the library of the Massachusetts Historical Society).

[5] Records of the First Church in Boston (manuscript copy in the library of the Massachusetts Historical Society), 12.

[6] Middlesex County Court Files, folder 42.

[7] John Cotton, *A Practical Commentary . . . upon the First Epistle Generall of John* (London, 1656), 126.

[8] *A Practical Commentary*, 126.

hostile as they were favorable to it in marriage. They passed laws to punish adultery with death, and fornication with whipping. Yet they had no misconceptions as to the capacity of human beings to obey such laws. Although the laws were commands of God, it was only natural—since the fall of Adam—for human beings to break them. Breaches must be punished lest the community suffer the wrath of God, but no offense, sexual or otherwise, could be occasion for surprise or for hushed tones of voice. How calmly the inhabitants of seventeenth-century New England could contemplate rape or attempted rape is evident in the following testimony offered before the Middlesex County Court of Massachusetts:

> The examination of Edward Wire taken the 7th of october and alsoe Zachery Johnson, who sayeth that Edward Wires mayd being sent into the towne about busenes meeting with a man that dogd hir from about Joseph Kettles house to goody marches. She came into William Johnsones and desired Zachery Johnson to goe home with her for that the man dogd hir. accordingly he went with her and being then as far as Samuell Phips his house the man over tooke them. which man caled himselfe by the name of peter grant would have led the mayd but she oposed itt three times: and coming to Edward Wires house the said grant would have kist hir but she refused itt: wire being at prayer grant dragd the mayd between the said wiers and Nathanill frothinghams house. hee then flung the mayd downe in the streete and got atop hir; Johnson seeing it hee caled vppon the fellow to be sivill and not abuse the mayd then Edward wire came forth and ran to the said grant and took hold of him asking him what he did to his mayd, the said grant asked whether she was his wife for he did nothing to his wife: the said grant swearing he would be the death of the said wire. when he came of the mayd; he swore he would bring ten men to pul down his house and soe ran away and they followed him as far as good[y] phipses house where they mett with John Terry and George Chin with clubs in their hands and soe they went away together. Zachy Johnson going to Constable Heamans, and wire going home. there came John Terry to his house to ask for beer and grant was in the streete but afterward departed into the towne, both Johnson and Wire both aferme that when grant was vppon the mayd she cryed out severall times.
>
> Deborah hadlocke being examined sayth that she mett with the man that cals himselfe peeter grant about good prichards that he dogd hir and followed hir to hir masters and there threw hir downe and lay vppon hir but had not the use of hir body but swore several othes that he would ly with hir and gett hir with child before she got home.
>
> Grant being present denys all saying he was drunk and did not know what he did.[9]

The Puritans became inured to sexual offenses, because there were so many. The impression which one gets from reading the records of seventeenth-century New England courts is that illicit sexual intercourse was fairly common. The testimony given in cases of fornication and adultery—by far the most numerous class of criminal cases in the records—suggests that many of the early New Englanders possessed a high degree of virility and very few inhibitions. Besides the case of Peter Grant, take the testimony of Elizabeth Knight about the manner of Richard Nevars's advances toward her:

[9] Middlesex Files, folder 48.

The last publique day of Thanksgiving (in the year 1674) in the evening as I was milking Richard Nevars came to me, and offered me abuse in putting his hand, under my coates, but I turning aside with much adoe, saved my self, and when I was settled to milking he agen took me by the shoulder and pulled me backward almost, but I clapped one hand on the Ground and held fast the Cows teatt with the other hand, and cryed out, and then came to mee Jonathan Abbot one of my Masters Servants, whome the said Never asked wherefore he came, the said Abbot said to look after you, what you doe unto the Maid, but the said Never bid Abbot goe about his businesse but I bade the lad to stay.[10]

One reason for the abundance of sexual offenses was the number of men in the colonies who were unable to gratify their sexual desires in marriage.[11] Many of the first settlers had wives in England. They had come to the new world to make a fortune, expecting either to bring their families after them or to return to England with some of the riches of America. Although these men left their wives behind, they brought their sexual appetites with them; and in spite of laws which required them to return to their families, they continued to stay, and more continued to arrive, as indictments against them throughout the seventeenth century clearly indicate.

Servants formed another group of men, and of women too, who could not ordinarily find supply for human necessity within the bounds of marriage. Most servants lived in the homes of their masters and could not marry without their consent, a consent which was not likely to be given unless the prospective husband or wife also belonged to the master's household. This situation will be better understood if it is recalled that most servants at this time were engaged by contract for a stated period. They were, in the language of the time, "covenant servants," who had agreed to stay with their masters for a number of years in return for a specified recompense, such as transportation to New England or education in some trade (the latter, of course, were known more specifically as apprentices). Even hired servants who worked for wages were usually single, for as soon as a man had enough money to buy or build a house of his own and to get married, he would set up in farming or trade for himself. It must be emphasized, however, that anyone who was not in business for himself was necessarily a servant. The economic organization of seventeenth-century New England had no place for the independent proletarian workman with a family of his own. All production was carried on in the household by the master of the family and his servants, so that most men were either servants or masters of servants; and the former, of course, were more numerous than the latter. Probably most of the inhabitants of Puritan New England could remember a time when they had been servants.

Theoretically no servant had a right to a private life. His time, day or night, belonged to his master, and both religion and law required that he obey his master scrupulously.[12] But neither religion nor law could restrain the sexual impulses of youth, and if those impulses could not be expressed in marriage,

[10] Middlesex Files, folder 71.

[11] Another reason was suggested by Charles Francis Adams in his scholarly article, "Some Phases of Sexual Morality and Church Discipline in Colonial New England," *Proceedings* of the Massachusetts Historical Society, xxvi, 477–516.

[12] On the position of servants in early New England see *More Books*, xvii (September, 1942), 311–328.

they had to be given vent outside marriage. Servants had little difficulty in finding the occasions. Though they might be kept at work all day, it was easy enough to slip away at night. Once out of the house, there were several ways of meeting with a maid. The simplest way was to go to her bedchamber, if she was so fortunate as to have a private one of her own. Thus Jock, Mr. Solomon Phipps's Negro man, confessed in court

> that on the sixteenth day of May 1682, in the morning, betweene 12 and one of the clock, he did force open the back doores of the House of Laurence Hammond in Charlestowne, and came in to the House, and went up into the garret to Marie the Negro.
>
> He doth likewise acknowledge that one night the last week he forced into the House the same way, and went up to the Negro Woman Marie and that the like he hath done at severall other times before.[13]

Joshua Fletcher took a more romantic way of visiting his lady:

> Joshua Fletcher . . . doth confesse and acknowledge that three severall nights, after bedtime, he went into Mr Fiskes Dwelling house at Chelmsford, at an open window by a ladder that he brought with him. the said windo opening into a chamber, whose was the lodging place of Gresill Juell servant to mr. Fiske. and there he kept company with the said mayd. she sometimes having her cloathes on, and one time he found her in her bed.[14]

Sometimes a maidservant might entertain callers in the parlor while the family were sleeping upstairs. John Knight described what was perhaps a common experience for masters. The crying of his child awakened him in the middle of the night, and he called to his maid, one Sarah Crouch, who was supposed to be sleeping with the child. Receiving no answer, he arose and

> went downe the stayres, and at the stair foot, the latch of doore was pulled in. I called severall times and at the last said if shee would not open the dore, I would breake it open, and when she opened the doore shee was all undressed and Sarah Largin with her undressed, also the said Sarah went out of doores and Dropped some of her clothes as shee went out. I enquired of Sarah Crouch what men they were, which was with them. Shee made mee no answer for some space of time, but at last shee told me Peeter Brigs was with them, I asked her whether Thomas Jones was not there, but shee would give mee no answer.[15]

In the temperate climate of New England it was not always necessary to seek out a maid at her home. Rachel Smith was seduced in an open field "about nine of the clock at night, being darke, neither moone nor starrs shineing." She was walking through the field when she met a man who

> asked her where shee lived, and what her name was and shee told him, and then shee asked his name, and he told her Saijing that he was old Good-man

13 Middlesex Files, folder 99.   14 Middlesex Files, folder 47.
15 Middlesex Files, folder 52.

Shepards man. Also shee saith he gave her strong liquors, and told her that it was not the first time he had been with maydes after his master was in bed.[16]

Sometimes, of course, it was not necessary for a servant to go outside his master's house in order to satisfy his sexual urges. Many cases of fornication are on record between servants living in the same house. Even where servants had no private bedroom, even where the whole family slept in a single room, it was not impossible to make love. In fact many love affairs must have had their consummation upon a bed in which other people were sleeping. Take for example the case of Sarah Lepingwell. When Sarah was brought into court for having an illegitimate child, she related that one night when her master's brother, Thomas Hawes, was visiting the family, she went to bed early. Later, after Hawes had gone to bed, he called to her to get him a pipe of tobacco. After refusing for some time,

> at the last I arose and did lite his pipe and cam and lay doune one my one bead and smoaked about half the pip and siting vp in my bead to giue him his pip my bead being a trundell bead at the sid of his bead he reached beyond the pip and Cauth me by the wrist and pulled me on the side of his bead but I biding him let me goe he bid me hold my peas the folks wold here me and if it be replyed come why did you not call out I Ansar I was posesed with fear of my mastar least my master shold think I did it only to bring a scandall on his brothar and thinking thay wold all beare witnes agaynst me but the thing is true that he did then begete me with child at that tim and the Child is Thomas Hauses and noe mans but his.

In his defense Hawes offered the testimony of another man who was sleeping "on the same side of the bed," but the jury nevertheless accepted Sarah's story.[17]

The fact that Sarah was intimidated by her master's brother suggests that maidservants may have been subject to sexual abuse by their masters. The records show that sometimes masters did take advantage of their position to force unwanted attentions upon their female servants. The case of Elizabeth Dickerman is a good example. She complained to the Middlesex County Court,

> against her master John Harris senior for profiring abus to her by way of forsing her to be naught with him: . . . he has tould her that if she tould her dame: what cariag he did show to her shee had as good be hanged and shee replyed then shee would run away and he sayd run the way is befor you: . . . she says if she should liwe ther shee shall be in fear of her lif.[18]

The court accepted Elizabeth's complaint and ordered her master to be whipped twenty stripes.

So numerous did cases of fornication and adultery become in seventeenth-century New England that the problem of caring for the children of extra-marital unions was a serious one. The Puritans solved it, but in such a way as to increase rather than decrease the temptation to sin. In 1668 the General Court of Massachusetts ordered:

[16] Middlesex Files, folder 44.   [17] Middlesex Files, folder 47.
[18] Middlesex Files, folder 94.

that where any man is legally convicted to be the Father of a Bastard childe, he shall be at the care and charge to maintain and bring up the same, by such assistance of the Mother as nature requireth, and as the Court from time to time (according to circumstances) shall see meet to Order: and in case the Father of a Bastard, by confession or other manifest proof, upon trial of the case, do not appear to the Courts satisfaction, then the Man charged by the Woman to be the Father, shee holding constant in it, (especially being put upon the real discovery of the truth of it in the time of her Travail) shall be the reputed Father, and accordingly be liable to the charge of maintenance as aforesaid (though not to other punishment) notwithstanding his denial, unless the circumstances of the case and pleas be such, on the behalf of the man charged, as that the Court that have the cognizance thereon shall see reason to acquit him, and otherwise dispose of the Childe and education thereof.[19]

As a result of this law a girl could give way to temptation without the fear of having to care for an illegitimate child by herself. Furthermore, she could, by a little simple lying, spare her lover the expense of supporting the child. When Elizabeth Wells bore a child, less than a year after this statute was passed, she laid it to James Tufts, her master's son. Goodman Tufts affirmed that Andrew Robinson, servant to Goodman Dexter, was the real father, and he brought the following testimony as evidence:

Wee Elizabeth Jefts aged 15 ears and Mary tufts aged 14 ears doe testyfie that their being one at our hous sumtime the last winter who sayd that thear was a new law made concerning bastards that If aney man wear aqused with a bastard and the woman which had aqused him did stand vnto it in her labor that he should bee the reputed father of it and should mayntaine it Elizabeth Wells hearing of the sayd law she sayed vnto vs that If shee should bee with Child shee would bee sure to lay it vn to won who was rich enough abell to mayntayne it wheather it wear his or no and shee farder sayed Elizabeth Jefts would not you doe so likewise If it weare your case and I sayed no by no means for right must tacke place: and the sayd Elizabeth wells sayed If it wear my Caus I think I should doe so.[20]

A tragic unsigned letter that somehow found its way into the files of the Middlesex County Court gives more direct evidence of the practice which Elizabeth Wells professed:

der loue i remember my loue to you hoping your welfar and i hop to imbras the but now i rit to you to let you nowe that i am a child by you and i wil ether kil it or lay it to an other and you shal have no blame at al for I haue had many children and none have none of them. . . . [i.e., none of their fathers is supporting any of them.][21]

In face of the wholesale violation of the sexual codes to which all these cases give testimony, the Puritans could not maintain the severe penalties which their laws provided. Although cases of adultery occurred every year, the death

[19] William H. Whitmore, editor, *The Colonial Laws of Massachusetts. Reprinted from the Edition of 1660* (Boston, 1889), 257.
[20] Middlesex Files, folder 52.   [21] Middlesex Files, folder 30.

penalty is not known to have been applied more than three times. The usual punishment was a whipping or a fine, or both, and perhaps a branding, combined with a symbolical execution in the form of standing on the gallows for an hour with a rope about the neck. Fornication met with a lighter whipping or a lighter fine, while rape was treated in the same way as adultery. Though the Puritans established a code of laws which demanded perfection—which demanded, in other words, strict obedience to the will of God, they nevertheless knew that frail human beings could never live up to the code. When fornication, adultery, rape, or even buggery and sodomy appeared, they were not surprised, nor were they so severe with the offenders as their codes of law would lead one to believe. Sodomy, to be sure, they usually punished with death; but rape, adultery, and fornication they regarded as pardonable human weaknesses, all the more likely to appear in a religious community, where the normal course of sin was stopped by wholesome laws. Governor Bradford in recounting the details of an epidemic of sexual misdemeanors in Plymouth, wrote resignedly:

> it may be in this case as it is with waters when their streames are stopped or damned up, when they gett passage they flow with more violence, and make more noys and disturbance, then when they are suffered to rune quietly in their owne chanels. So wickednes being here more stopped by strict laws, and the same more nerly looked unto, so at it cannot rune in a comone road of liberty as it would, and is inclined, it searches every wher, and at last breaks out wher it getts vente.[22]

The estimate of human capacities here expressed led the Puritans not only to deal leniently with sexual offenses but also to take every precaution to prevent such offenses, rather than wait for the necessity of punishment. One precaution was to see that children got married as soon as possible. The wrong way to promote virtue, the Puritans thought, was to "ensnare" children in vows of virginity, as the Catholics did. As a result of such vows, children, "not being able to contain," would be guilty of "unnatural pollutions, and other filthy practices in secret: and too oft of horrid Murthers of the fruit of their bodies," said Thomas Cobbett.[23] The way to avoid fornication and perversion was for parents to provide suitable husbands and wives for their children:

> Lot was to blame that looked not out seasonably for some fit matches for his two daughters, which had formerly minded marriage (witness the contract between them and two men in *Sodom,* called therfore for his Sons in Law, which had married his daughters, Gen. 19. 14.) for they seeing no man like to come into them in a conjugall way . . . then they plotted that incestuous course, whereby their Father was so highly dishonoured. . . .[24]

As marriage was the way to prevent fornication, successful marriage was the way to prevent adultery. The Puritans did not wait for adultery to appear; instead, they took every means possible to make husbands and wives live to-

22 William Bradford, *History of Plymouth Plantation* (Boston, 1912), II, 309.
23 Thomas Cobbett, *A Fruitfull and Usefull Discourse touching the Honour due from Children to Parents and the Duty of Parents toward their Children* (London, 1656), 174.
24 Cobbett, 177.

gether and respect each other. If a husband deserted his wife and remained within the jurisdiction of a Puritan government, he was promptly sent back to her. Where the wife had been left in England, the offense did not always come to light until the wayward husband had committed fornication or bigamy, and of course there must have been many offenses which never came to light. But where both husband and wife lived in New England, neither had much chance of leaving the other without being returned by order of the county court at its next sitting. When John Smith of Medfield left his wife and went to live with Patience Rawlins, he was sent home poorer by ten pounds and richer by thirty stripes. Similarly Mary Drury, who deserted her husband on the pretense that he was impotent, failed to convince the court that he actually was so, and had to return to him as well as to pay a fine of five pounds. The wife of Phillip Pointing received lighter treatment: when the court thought that she had over-stayed her leave in Boston, they simply ordered her "to depart the Towne and goe to Tanton to her husband." The courts, moreover, were not satisfied with mere cohabitation; they insisted that it be peaceful cohabitation. Husbands and wives were forbidden by law to strike one another, and the law was enforced on numerous occasions. But the courts did not stop there. Henry Flood was re-quired to give bond for good behavior because he had abused his wife simply by "ill words calling her whore and cursing of her." The wife of Christopher Collins was presented for railing at her husband and calling him "Gurley gutted divill." Apparently in this case the court thought that Mistress Collins was right, for although the fact was proved by two witnesses, she was discharged. On another occasion the court favored the husband: Jacob Pudeator, fined for strik-ing and kicking his wife, had the sentence moderated when the court was in-formed that she was a woman "of great provocation."[25]

Wherever there was strong suspicion that an illicit relation might arise between two persons, the authorities removed the temptation by forbidding the two to come together. As early as November, 1630, the Court of Assistants of Massachusetts prohibited a Mr. Clark from "cohabitacion and frequent keepeing company with Mrs. Freeman, vnder paine of such punishment as the Court shall thinke meete to inflict." Mr. Clark and Mrs. Freeman were both bound "in XX £ apeece that Mr. Clearke shall make his personall appear-ance att the nexte Court to be holden in March nexte, and in the meane tyme to carry himselfe in good behaviour towards all people and espetially towards Mrs. Freeman, concerning whome there is stronge suspicion of incontinency." Forty-five years later the Suffolk County Court took the same kind of measure to protect the husbands of Dorchester from the temptations offered by the daughter of Robert Spurr. Spurr was presented by the grand jury

> for entertaining persons at his house at unseasonable times both by day and night to the greife of theire wives and Relations &c The Court having heard what was alleaged and testified against him do Sentence him to bee admon-ish't and to pay Fees of Court and charge him upon his perill not to entertain any married men to keepe company with his daughter especially James Minott and Joseph Belcher.

[25] Samuel E. Morison and Zechariah Chafee, editors, *Records of the Suffolk County Court, 1671–1680, Publications* of the Colonial Society of Massachusetts, xxix and xxx, 121, 410, 524, 837–841, and 1158; George F. Dow, editor, *Records and Files of the Quarterly Courts of Essex County, Massachusetts* (Salem, 1911–1921), I, 274; and v, 377.

In like manner Walter Hickson was forbidden to keep company with Mary Bedwell, "And if at any time hereafter hee bee taken in company of the saide Mary Bedwell without other company to bee forthwith apprehended by the Constable and to be whip't with ten stripes." Elizabeth Wheeler and Joanna Peirce were admonished "for theire disorderly carriage in the house of Thomas Watts being married women and founde sitting in other mens Laps with theire Armes about theire Necks." How little confidence the Puritans had in human nature is even more clearly displayed by another case, in which Edmond Maddock and his wife were brought to court "to answere to all such matters as shalbe objected against them concerning Haarkwoody and Ezekiell Euerells being at their house at unseasonable tyme of the night and her being up with them after her husband was gone to bed." Haarkwoody and Everell had been found "by the Constable Henry Bridghame about tenn of the Clock at night sitting by the fire at the house of Edmond Maddocks with his wyfe a suspicious weoman her husband being on sleepe [sic] on the bedd." A similar distrust of human ability to resist temptation is evident in the following order of the Connecticut Particular Court:

> James Hallett is to returne from the Correction house to his master Barclyt, who is to keepe him to hard labor, and course dyet during the pleasure of the Court provided that Barclet is first to remove his daughter from his family, before the sayd James enter therein.

These precautions, as we have already seen, did not eliminate fornication, adultery, or other sexual offenses, but they doubtless reduced the number from what it would otherwise have been.[26]

In sum, the Puritan attitude toward sex, though directed by a belief in absolute, God-given moral values, never neglected human nature. The rules of conduct which the Puritans regarded as divinely ordained had been formulated for men, not for angels, and not for beasts. God had created mankind in two sexes; He had ordained marriage as desirable for all, and sexual intercourse as essential to marriage. On the other hand, He had forbidden sexual intercourse outside of marriage. These were the moral principles which the Puritans sought to enforce in New England. But in their enforcement they took cognizance of human nature. They knew well enough that human beings since the fall of Adam were incapable of obeying perfectly the laws of God. Consequently, in the endeavor to enforce those laws they treated offenders with patience and understanding, and concentrated their efforts on prevention more than on punishment. The result was not a society in which most of us would care to live, for the methods of prevention often caused serious interference with personal liberty. It must nevertheless be admitted that in matters of sex the Puritans showed none of the blind zeal or narrow-minded bigotry which is too often supposed to have been characteristic of them. The more one learns about these people, the less do they appear to have resembled the sad and sour portraits which their modern critics have drawn of them.

[26] *Records of the Suffolk County Court*, 442–443 and 676; John Noble, editor, *Records of the Court of Assistants of the Colony of Massachusetts Bay* (Boston, 1901–1928), II, 8; *Records of the Particular Court of Connecticut*, *Collections* of the Connecticut Historical Society, XXII, 20; and a photostat in the library of the Massachusetts Historical Society, dated March 29, 1653.

Indian–White Relations in Early America

A Review Essay

Bernard W. Sheehan

INTRODUCTION

The following essay not only asks important questions about the history of Indian–white relations in America, it also raises the issues of the historian's relationship to his culture and the purposes of his craft. As Sheehan demonstrates, the study of the American Indian has been filled with easy outrage, doubtful assumptions about race and culture, and a tendency to see the subject as one demanding moral judgments. This history of the study of the Indian and his relations with whites is closely examined in Sheehan's essay, and the question of the historian's task when he faces issues with striking contemporary and moral significance is considered from several different angles.

Anyone interested in further study should see William N. Fenton *et al., American Indian and White Relations to 1830: Needs and Opportunities for Study* (1957). The present editors share Sheehan's admiration for Wilbur R. Jacobs' *Wilderness Politics and Indian Gifts: The Northern Colonial Frontier, 1607–1763** (1966). Robert Berkhofer, Jr., *Salvation and the Savage: An Analysis of Protestant Missions and American Indian Response, 1787–1862* (1965) is important, though Sheehan's observations about it are telling. The most impressive book about American Indians published since Sheehan wrote is Anthony F. C. Wallace's *The Death and Rebirth of the Seneca* (1970).

THE white man is guilty. He has been charged with the destruction of the American Indian, the evidence has been presented, and the verdict returned for all to see. The sorry remnants of the American aborigine in our own day, beneficiaries and victims of the government's largess, testify to the overwhelming culpability of the civilized intruder in the Indian's domain. No doubt the objective fact is true: the modern Indian does, at least in the white man's mind, present a depressing contrast to his past eminence; and the occupation of the American continent by the European settler is surely the cause of his decline. The story has been recounted often enough to be part of the American folklore. Whether the settler out of sheer viciousness or unconquerable greed drove the native population from its ancestral home, decimating tribe after tribe until the pathetic survivors were herded on to reservations in the late nineteenth century, or merely brought to the new land the trappings of a foreign environment, liquor and disease, hostile to the Indian's continued existence, the result was the same. And the criminal was still the civilized European.

The archetypal historical definition of the white man's guilt was presented in 1881 by Helen Hunt Jackson in her *Century of Dishonor*. Though frankly polemical (the cover of the second edition in 1886 was stamped in red with a quotation from Benjamin Franklin: "Look upon your hands! They are stained with the blood of your relations."), the volume also made historical pretensions. But more important, it revealed the deep sense of guilt many white men felt at the fate of the Indian, and it contrived to formulate a scheme that would portray the native as a hapless victim and the white man as a merciless aggressor. In tone sentimental, it was in substance a moral tract whose purpose was to convict civilization of its crimes against the aborigine; and history was subordinate to this greater object.

Besides the melodrama of murder, robbery, cruelty, perfidy, and the white man's generally outrageous behavior, the burden of Mrs. Jackson's book conveyed a basic interpretation of Indian–white relations. In the first pages she spelled out her conviction that the Indians were organized into sovereign nations and that the whites were obliged under international law to treat them as such. The natives had a right to the soil that should have been honored and their agreements carried the force of sovereign contracts. In repeatedly violating treaties, the whites had set themselves outside the law and were thereby subject to arbitrary punishment by any civilized nation that should see fit to call them to account.[1] Indian negotiators behaved not in the manner of "ignorant barbarians" but as "clear-headed, statesman-like rulers, insisting on the rights

FROM Bernard W. Sheehan, "Indian–White Relations in Early America: A Review Essay," *William and Mary Quarterly*, XXVI (April 1969), 267–86. Reprinted by permission.

[1] Helen Hunt Jackson, *A Century of Dishonor: A Sketch of the United States Government's Dealings with Some of the Indian Tribes*, 2d ed. (Boston, 1886), 29.

of their nation."[2] The whites, especially on the frontier, were largely responsible for the violence that repeatedly flared between the two societies. And the conflict was not merely the fortuitous meeting of two groups of people with different interests. On the white man's side there was a measure of calculation. "Thus early in our history was the ingenious plan evolved of first maddening the Indians into war, and then falling upon them with exterminating punishment." Indian violence was the exception in the sum of frontier conflict and then it was either in response to the white man's aggression or instigated by the white for his own interests.[3] The Indian was depicted as the innocent victim of a hostile and unprincipled civilization and, adding pathos to his decline, as the possessor of a public order and private virtues not dissimilar to those supposedly characteristic of civilization.

To be sure, later historians, though deeply sympathetic to the Indian's cause, were neither so sentimental nor so one-sided in their treatment of Indian– white relations. Yet the Indian seemed consistently to manifest the qualities of national independence and most poignantly to suffer from the crass aggressiveness of the whites. For example, in her treatment of Indian removal, the culminating event of Indian–white relations in the early period, Annie H. Abel described with admirable detachment the process through which the Indians were induced to move west of the Mississippi.[4] Throughout the Indians performed as any other sovereign people, carrying on long and difficult negotiations with a power of equal independence. The other segment of the story was told by Grant Foreman in two studies, both dwelling on the actual process of removal.[5] Here the Indians "with bitter sorrow in their hearts, weakened by hardship and privation, decimated by disease, oppressed by penury, despondent and disheartened," struggled over their "trail of tears" to exile in the west.[6] In Annie Abel's account the native was scarcely recognizable as an Indian and in Foreman's two volumes, though solid and moderate works, the victimized aborigine could not but cast his shadow on the overwhelming guilt of the white man.

The white man's crime, however, was not an abrupt or even readily definable act. After all, whatever the Indian suffered as a consequence of the advent of the European on the American continent took a long time to reach its ghastly conclusion—has yet, in fact, to do so. In truth, as a historical phenomenon, the Indian disintegrated; as an Indian he was not annihilated but he faded culturally into another entity. The crime, if there was one, was the inexorable breakdown of the native's cultural integrity, in part the result of conscious policy and in part the inevitable consequence of competition between two disparate ways of life. Rather than the singular clarity of one despicable act, the American aborigine was the victim of a process. Perhaps process can be criminal but its natural complexity diffuses the locus of guilt. Criminality tends to be individual and guilt is much more easily imputed when the

---

[2] *Ibid.,* 41.   [3] *Ibid.,* 33–34, 40, 339, 405–406.
[4] Annie H. Abel, "The History of Events Resulting in Indian Consolidation West of the Mississippi River," American Historical Association, *Annual Report for the Year 1906* (Washington, 1908), I, 233–450.
[5] Grant Foreman, *Indian Removal: The Emigration of the Five Civilized Tribes of Indians,* new ed. (Norman [orig. pub., Norman, 1932], 1953); and Grant Foreman, *The Last Trek of the Indians* (Chicago, 1946).
[6] Foreman, *Indian Removal,* 386.

criminal and his victim can be seen apart from circumstance or the slow, dissolving force of cultural breakdown. The moralistic impact falls more exactingly when the demarcation between the opposing forces is set off clearly. When Indian and white meet on equal terms and the white man brazenly violates most of the rules, or when the Indian, helpless before the overpowering force of civilization, is portrayed as the pitiable victim of aggression, the simplistic duality makes the assignment of guilt an easy task; but when the conflict is submerged in the process of cultural intermingling, the moralistic dichotomy dissolves. If only because it is virtually impossible to declare a whole society guilty, the moralistic approach requires an implicit denial of the integrity of culture, in effect, a shattering of the wholeness of that complex of experience and rational judgment from which men inevitably construct a style of life peculiar to themselves.

As a formalizing conception, the notion of integral culture[7] is freighted with the dangers of moral relativism. Anthropologists, ethnologists, and sociologists have long argued the matter to no great satisfaction. Historians seem even more open to the apparent dilemma of scholarly detachment and moral involvement. Certainly the conflict between Indian and white, deeply associated with civilized man's misgivings in the face of his primitive antithesis, has always conjured in the historical mind oppression and hypocrisy and has demanded a moral accounting. Robert Berkhofer, in his recent study of missionary activities among the Indians, carries the relativist perspective beyond the subject perceived into the very eye of the perceiver. "Current indictments of past American conduct," he writes, "are on the same plane as earlier American condemnations of savage society. The Americans of the past were victims of their cultural values just as their latter-day judges are victims of today's beliefs."[8] We are all, one supposes, witting or not, in one degree or another, victims of our nurture, but at least we recognize it, thus saving the historian's capacity for judgment from the epistemological dead end of consistent relativism. The concept of integral culture should not reduce the historian to a mere recorder; it should only insure that judgments be qualified by the peculiar circumstances of a distinct cultural definition. Ethics, the imputing of guilt or innocence, must not be excluded from the process of historical judgment but it must become much less obtrusive. The issue of right or wrong must give way to an understanding of the process of cultural conflict that characterized the meeting of European and Indian in the New World. Cultural analysis should be relativist only in the sense that it is an inclusive conception, in the sense that it allows the historian to see all the intricate permeations of the intermeshing of disparate cultures rather than the one-to-one moral dichotomy of oppressor and oppressed.

Practically, it should be enough to refurbish William N. Fenton's plea in 1953 that Indian–white relations be treated as a common ground of history and ethnology. Little had been done when he wrote to combine the two sources of

[7] My own understanding of the concept is taken in part from: A. L. Kroeber and Clyde Kluckhohn, *Culture: A Critical Review of Concepts and Definitions,* Vintage ed. (New York, 1963); Robert K. Merton, *Social Theory and Social Structure,* 3d ed. (New York, 1968), Chap. III; A. R. Radcliffe-Brown, *Structure and Function in Primitive Society: Essays and Addresses* (New York, 1952), Introduction, Chap. IX; T. S. Eliot, *Notes Towards the Definition of Culture* (New York, 1949); Robert A. Nisbet, *The Sociological Tradition* (New York, 1966).
[8] Robert Berkhofer, Jr., *Salvation and the Savage: An Analysis of Protestant Missions and American Indian Response, 1787–1862* (Lexington, Ky., 1965), ix.

knowledge, that is, to examine Indian–white conflict as a clash of culture, and little has been done since. According to one historian of the frontier, recent work in anthropology and ethnology "has brought us much closer to a satisfactory understanding" of the character of native reaction to white intrusion. Another makes the determined pledge "to understand the life, the societies, the cultures, the thinking and feeling of the Indians."[9] The intentions are the best and even the performance is solid and enlightening. But it cannot be said in any broad sense that Fenton's hope has been fulfilled. We still await an account of Indian–white relations in the early period that will bring to bear the full weight of the knowledge of human culture.

The best of the recent literature does indeed make use of cultural analysis though not usually to the extent of excluding the moralistic disjunction. A notable exception is Wilbur R. Jacobs's examination of frontier diplomacy in the light of the native tradition of gift giving. By centering upon the major form of official contact between white and Indian and pointing out its ceremonial significance for the native society, Jacobs adds the sinews of culture to the bland confrontation between native and civilized negotiators. Though perhaps the broad subject of cultural conflict cannot be interpreted on the basis of so limited a theme, the volume remains one of the few recent efforts to lay out some of the intricacies of Indian–white relations while taking seriously the character of the native way of life. Surely, however, the most successful attempt in the past generation, describing the consequences of the infiltration of civilized manners into primitive America, is Anthony F. C. Wallace's biographical study of the Delaware leader Teedyuscung. Through a personality fatally undermined but rich in historical implications, Wallace examines the effect of civilization on the delicate structure of Indian culture.[10]

Of course there is much evidence in the recent literature that historians do take the integrity of the Indian's culture seriously. Reginald Horsman notes in more than one place the Indian's conscious determination to defend his own way of doing things against the inexorable push of advancing America. Louis De Vorsey, while conceding the rudimentary character of tribal political organization, maintains that "the Indians evinced a passionate desire to retain their territorial bases which they identified as vital to their continued existence as a people." In his account of the New England frontier, Alden Vaughan refers to the barriers of custom and language over which the Puritan missionaries could not prevail. But it is perhaps Berkhofer who sees most distinctly the Indian as a cultural entity. In perceiving that the cultural clash between missionary and native was total, that the missionary demanded nothing less from the Indian than a complete ethnic capitulation ("To become truly Christian was to become anti-Indian."), he broaches the question of the dynamics of cultural interplay. Though the white man's way of life operates, in this case as a culture-dissolving ideology, the Indian's manners and mores, in their gradual dissolution, are conceded a unique definition. The Indian and the white man

---

[9] William N. Fenton, *American Indian and White Relations to 1830: Needs & Opportunities for Study* (Chapel Hill, 1957), 17; Douglas Edward Leach, *The Northern Colonial Frontier, 1607–1763* (New York, 1966), 7; Louis De Vorsey, Jr., *The Indian Boundary in the Southern Colonies, 1763–1775* (Chapel Hill, 1966), 43.

[10] Wilbur R. Jacobs, *Wilderness Politics and Indian Gifts: The Northern Colonial Frontier, 1748–1763* (Lincoln, Neb., 1966); originally published as *Diplomacy and Indian Gifts: Anglo–French Rivalry Along the Ohio and Northwest Frontiers, 1748–1763* (Stanford, 1950); Anthony F. C. Wallace, *King of the Delawares: Teedyuscung, 1700–1763* (Philadelphia, 1949).

are different because their experience and historical adjustment to the surrounding world have been different. They come together in the inevitable clash and denouement and just as certain decline of the weaker, less resilient party. The totality of the conflict sharpens the conception of cultural differentiation.[11]

Paradoxically, the successes illustrate the failures. Though virtually every historian of Indian–white relations would agree to the need for a recognition of cultural distinctness as an essential part of his conceptual apparatus, few have been able to bring the idea into the actual complexities of cultural competition. It is virtually de rigueur for an author to make some formal pronouncement on the subject, but there seems to be no requirement that the idea reach fruition. What one comes to expect still is a history of Indian–white contact told from the white man's side, the Indian playing the role of anonymous opponent or victim. Disintegration or acculturation is often noted, and approved or regretted but there is seldom any deep analysis of the processes. Civilization simply sweeps across the pages in triumph or ignominy and the Indian fights or dies with no more identity than any other expendable resource. If the conceptualization need not produce an extensive ethnological examination, it should at least qualify the tendency for moralistic division and manifest some sense of the consequences of cultural conflict.

Berkhofer, having laid down the most solid base for cultural relativism, suffers most patently from the failure. As he writes, "psychologically speaking, there seemed to be no halfway point" for the Indians in their confrontation with civilization. The missionaries' ideology paid little heed to the complications of cultural transformation. They "did not know . . . that basic values change very slowly."[12] In taking his cue from the white man's mental disposition, Berkhofer never enters the arena in which the two societies meet. The missionaries try to supplant the native social order and fail because, as he aptly points out, their ideology takes no cognizance of the relative imperviousness of culture to change. Just so the historian, even though he is aware of the importance of cultural analysis, is unable to move beyond the sterile detachment of the white man's anti-cultural ideology. Cultural relativism, unless it leads to an analysis of the processes of societal transformation, will do no more than trace the outlines of a historiographical problem. It will not fill the empty space.

The older approach to Indian–white relations, which on principle paid little attention to cultural interplay, and portrayed the Indian as unwitting victim and the white man as conscienceless aggressor, apparently still has some steam

---

[11] Reginald Horsman, *Expansion and American Indian Policy, 1783–1812* (East Lansing, Mich., 1967), 38, 60; Reginald Horsman, *Matthew Elliott, British Indian Agent* (Detroit, 1964), 39; De Vorsey, *The Indian Boundary*, 44; Alden T. Vaughan, *New England Frontier: Puritans and Indians, 1620–1675* (Boston, 1965), 298, 304; Berkhofer, *Salvation and the Savage*, 69, 107, 122.

[12] *Ibid.*, 57, 111. Similarly, Roy Harvey Pearce, *The Savages of America: A Study of the Indian and the Idea of Civilization*, rev. ed. (Baltimore, 1965), in an often brilliant exposition of the content of the white man's mind on the subject of the Indian, is not able to stretch his account to cover the interplay of the two societies. Since his thesis is that the native was perceived mainly with reference to the white man's conception of himself, he does not step over and treat the Indian on his own ground. The validity of the thesis is not in question but the assumption that ideology can be so pristine and self-contained is another problem. The direct effect of the white man's conception, as Pearce admits, is the manipulation of the Indian and, therefore, even civilization's intellectual inversions concerning native society may be seen as part of the interplay of culture.

left in it. It is well enough that Leach should maintain that "we are now less interested in pointing the finger of guilt at one race or the other" or that Jacobs should caution us that in its own time the confrontation was not viewed "as the black-and-white moral issue which it often seems to us today." Wilcomb E. Washburn, however, will have none of such pussyfooting. In a vigorous and knowledgeable defense, he proclaims his strong sympathy for the American Indian and insists that historians must judge from the sources the relative weight of guilt or innocence in the story of Indian–white conflict. One cannot, as he says, "split the difference."[13]

The historian as distributor of censure has a far easier task if he may be permitted to abstract his subject from history and therefore from cultural analysis. And such has been the most frequently used method in assigning the burden of guilt to the white man. The Indian is enhanced in prestige by the simple expedient of being plucked from the cultural maelstrom. From the beginning of Indian–white contact the convention of the noble savage has acted primarily as a criterion of moral rectitude against which the transgressions of civilization might be judged. And it has always been an explicitly ahistorical concept, posited on a pre-Adamic definition of man. Washburn reveals a sympathy for just such an understanding of the Indian. He contends particularly that the natives manifested a natural hospitality toward the Europeans on first encounter and that violence was the fault of the whites. The Indian can be blamed only for retaliating against an original aggression. Indeed the noble savage convention itself stems from the first reports of his aboriginal good will.[14] In fact noble savagism had long been a part of the paradisaic strain in Western thought and did not grow out of the observations of early explorers and settlers. They brought the idea with them but were undoubtedly pleased for a new field in which to apply it.[15] At the same time it is entirely possible that European society had a higher violence quotient than the Indian's way of life; the white man was, after all, more adept. Of far more importance is the prognosis for historical understanding on the basis of a blatantly non-historical original assumption. A history of Indian–white relations must take its beginning in the admission of the Indian's peculiar cultural composition, itself the product of history. It can gain nothing, and it might well lose everything, by proposing a mythic natural innocence and proceeding to direct thunderbolts at those who supposedly despoiled it.

Despite his predilection for moral history, however, Washburn does not propose a consistent utilization of the noble savage theme in interpreting Indian–white relations. He defines noble savagery with a list of primitive attributes, "generosity, stoic bearing of pain, dignity, loftiness of speech in council," all of which are common properties of Edenic man. But for him they are

[13] Leach, *The Northern Colonial Frontier*, 7; Wilbur R. Jacobs, ed., *The Paxton Riots and the Frontier Theory* (Chicago, 1967), 1; Wilcomb E. Washburn, ed., *The Indian and the White Man* (Garden City, N.Y., 1964), xi.

[14] Wilcomb E. Washburn, "The Moral and Legal Justifications for Dispossessing the Indians," in James Morton Smith, ed., *Seventeenth Century America: Essays in Colonial History* (Chapel Hill, 1959), 22; Washburn, ed., *The Indian and the White Man*, xii, 415. Nancy Oestreich Lurie, "Indian Cultural Adjustment to European Civilization," in Smith, ed., *Seventeenth Century America*, 36–38, offers an explanation of the Indians' hospitable greeting of the Virginia settlers without recourse to any version of the noble savage theme.

[15] Henri Baudet, *Paradise on Earth: Some Thoughts on European Images of Non-European Man*, Elizabeth Wentholt, transl. (New Haven, 1965).

merely the norms of a noble Indian society.[16] He comes back finally to a cultural conception but his determination to assign moral blame leads him to impose on it the ends usually expected from the noble savage convention. The methodological ambiguity of such an approach can only cast doubt on the ultimate conclusions.

Though less abstracted than the primitivism of the noble savage concept, there has long been a tendency in Western thought to see human nature as a static, universal quality. Only the accidents of existence change; at the core of the human organism there remains a stable, predictable essence. Thus arguments for equality and human dignity usually have their basis in a timeless realm of moral value. In a practical sense, it is frequently difficult for the historian to see the complex of motive and action in a peculiar culture as in its root different from that of another style of existence. Besides the inhibitions of the historian's own ethnocentrism, he is usually forced to come to terms with a universalist ideology that constantly nudges him toward a static explanation of behavior.

In attempting to unravel the intricacies of the Indian–white relationship, therefore, the historian is tempted frequently to judge both sides against the same set of expectations. The Indian behaves as the white man does and for the same reasons. Of course there is some merit in the procedure. The Indian was far more affected by the white than the white by the Indian. He began absorbing the ways of civilization at first contact, sometimes even before a face-to-face meeting. But the Indian was not a blank tablet; even in the process of acculturation there remained a substratum of Indian character. He was always an Indian and the whites were frequently reminded of it. The truth of the matter will be out when the historian can tell at any given moment the level of Indianness in his subject—when, in effect, he can judge the extent of acculturation.

Doubtless such a demand is beyond the capacity of the historical science. Yet it is also questionable that analysis should be stopped at a mere recitation of the particular changes instituted in Indian society under the influence of civilization. If Berkhofer explained little about the processes of historical change in defining the totalism of the missionary ideology. Mary Young does not reveal more in listing the positive changes begun under missionary auspices. The introduction of civilized medicine, the discouragement of dancing and ball play, the elimination of elaborate and prolonged mourning, and the attack on polygamy, infanticide, whiskey drinking, and obscene conversation, all bore heavily on the alteration of native society, but, surely, not all to the same degree, and the cancellation of one white-induced habit, whiskey drinking, might well have meant a return to the old ways.[17] Breaking into a dynamic situation at a given point, without considering the subtle process of change, as in any still life, risks distortion. One is inclined, as a consequence, to weigh the quantity of change without detecting its vital quality.

---

[16] Wilcomb E. Washburn, "A Moral History of Indian–White Relations: Needs and Opportunities for Study," *Ethnohistory*, IV (1957), 55. An admirably perceptive treatment of relations between the Indian and one particular group of whites is in Lewis O. Saum, *The Fur Trader and the Indian* (Seattle, 1965). He contends that fur traders, frequently skirting the formulations of noble savagism (p. 80), managed to come up with a generally realistic conception of the native. "The more the trader saw of the Indian the greater were his misgivings" (p. 134).

[17] Mary Elizabeth Young, *Redskins, Ruffleshirts, and Rednecks: Indian Land Allotments in Alabama and Mississippi, 1830–1860* (Norman, 1961), 24–25.

Still more serious is the practice of imputing characteristics of the white man's culture to the Indians, as, for example, Francis Paul Prucha's contention that the "elemental question" between the two societies was "who was to own and control the land."[18] To be sure, the white man wanted the land and the Indian opposed him sometimes, but little has really been said about the nature of the conflict unless the position of land (even the concept takes its meaning from civilization) is laid out in the differing value systems of the two societies. The land can be accounted the basic point of conflict only if it can be shown that the Indian had a sense of spatial identity similar to the white man's. He did not, or at least there is no reason to think that he did. He did not do the same things to land that the white man did. If he sometimes manifested the jealous attachment to it that the whites were wont to expect, he certainly gave much of it up without more than a perfunctory struggle—assuming that he even understood what was meant by giving it up. Also, as the Indian came to see the white man's intense desire for the land and as he felt the effects of the civilized invasion of his own cultural sphere—which was, in effect, the white man taking the land—he came also to see that he had to preserve his territorial integrity. This, however, was more likely the consequence of acculturation than a primitive allegiance to a plot of soil. The issue was not so much the land as the disintegration of the native's culture which led finally to his sturdy defense of his territorial possessions. Whatever the explanation, it must avoid a formulation of values based on one culture without considering the interplay of different value systems.

Similarly Jacobs speaks of an Indian "war for independence" and of an essentially democratic government and individualist spirit. Allen Trelease uses such terms with reference to Indian society as "public opinion," "anarchy," and an "oligarchic body of sachems." Fenton seems to think it possible that the Iroquois federation served as archetype for the federal constitution. And Alvin M. Josephy, Jr., using Franklin's exasperated but quite conventional comparison of the supposed political accomplishments of the Indians and the ingrained divisiveness of the colonies, maintains that the Iroquois league had an "indirect" influence on the establishment of the union and the structure of the new government in 1789. Furthermore, he contends, these politically astute aborigines can be described with at least partial accuracy in the conventional wisdom of noble savagery. They believed in the "freedom and dignity of the individual" and relied on unanimous vote in their councils to preserve the "equality of individuals and respect for their rights." Such transference of the clichés of the white man's political rhetoric cannot but do violence to the Indian's cultural integrity. There is no dignity in the Indian impersonating the white man.[19]

More pertinent is the treatment of the Indian as warrior and diplomatist. Since a fair portion of the story of Indian–white relations is taken up with the proceedings of war and the making of peace, most authors are forced to com-

[18] Francis Paul Prucha, *American Indian Policy in the Formative Years: The Indian Trade and Intercourse Acts, 1790–1834* (Cambridge, Mass., 1962), 139; Horsman, *Expansion and American Indian Policy,* Introduction, makes the same point on the relation of land to Indian–white conflict.
[19] Jacobs, *Wilderness Politics and Indian Gifts,* 13–14, 185, n. 143; Allen W. Trelease, *Indian Affairs in Colonial New York: The Seventeenth Century* (Ithaca, 1960), 22; Fenton, *American Indian and White Relations to 1830,* 18, 27; Alvin M. Josephy, Jr., *The Indian Heritage of America* (New York, 1968), 34–35; see also Alvin M. Josephy, Jr., *The Patriot Chiefs: A Chronicle of American Indian Leadership* (New York, 1961), 28–29.

mit themselves, at least implicitly, to a rationale for dealing with the subject. Indeed no problems are more difficult of explanation than the motives which impelled the savages to violence and determined their objects in ending it. The great danger to the historian is in attributing to the Indian the rational detachment in external politics that would be expected from a civilized statesman. Perhaps the two best examples are Parkman's account of Pontiac as a potential builder of a forest empire and George T. Hunt's economic explanation of Iroquois belligerence.[20]

Trelease deals with the question of Iroquois motivation in his book on seventeenth-century Indian affairs in New York. A cautious historian, he approaches the matter with some trepidation. Though the Indians, he thinks, did not necessarily have the same motives as the whites, there is as much reason to attribute economic incentive to them as there is to civilized man. Before the arrival of the European, the Indians fought for various reasons, but with the beginning of the fur trade economics became paramount.[21] Without question, then, the European demand for furs and the Indian's willingness to supply them created a convenient barter nexus between the two societies—a decidedly economic relationship. But outside of Manchester there is no purely economic condition. The key is in the cultural context, the effect of the white man's artifacts on Indian society. The Indian's dependence was not economic, it was cultural. Any explanation must deal with the peculiar ecological and cultural changes induced by the spreading of the white man's wares through the forest.

The Iroquois portrayed by Trelease are far more self-contained than might be expected, though it is difficult to deny them their continued talent in wilderness politics even after their life had been seriously affected by the inroads of a foreign culture. The Five Nations prove their independence, writes Trelease, in choosing to move into the west for their own purposes; their attack on the Huron is a conscious tribal policy. (A similar calculation can be seen in the activities of the Algonquin Indians in the Peach War of 1655.) The Iroquois' prudence is illustrated in their determination not to expand the conflict to the Abenaki when they were already at war with the French; and their diplomatic nimbleness when, at least on one occasion, they were able to outmaneuver both the French and the British.[22] Now in any of its parts it is not really an unlikely story; Trelease tells a sensible tale and he writes from the sources. However, it is the accumulation, the piling up of evidence of native ability that tends finally to draw the two societies apart. The situation changes from the subtle intermingling of disparate cultures to the confrontation of two sovereign powers, both jealous of their independence, and both fully equipped to maintain it. The treatment of Indian–white relations through the medium of foreign policy leads invariably to the neglect of the cultural process.

But, even aside from the relative emphasis on the cultural approach, it seems that the white man's policy toward the Indian is in the throes of reinterpretation. There appear still such treatments as William T. Hagan's overview of the Indian in American history, more concerned with gratuitous slurs against

---

[20] Francis Parkman, *The Conspiracy of Pontiac* . . . (Boston [orig. pub., Boston, 1851], 1898), I, 190–198; for an alternate explanation, see Howard H. Peckham, *Pontiac and the Indian Uprising* (Chicago, 1961), 107–108, n. 12; George T. Hunt, *The Wars of the Iroquois: A Study of Intertribal Trade Relations* (Madison [orig. pub. Madison, 1940], 1960), 32–37; see the review by Fenton in *American Anthropologist*, New Ser., XLII (1940), 662–664.

[21] Trelease, *Indian Affairs in Colonial New York*, 53.

[22] *Ibid.*, 118–120, 141–142, 260, 266–267, 299.

the white than the thoughtful understanding of the meeting of the two societies, or R. S. Cotterill's essay in sarcasm on the five southern tribes.[23] In two recent volumes, however, the history of American Indian–white relations has taken an important step beyond the guilt-ridden accounts of the past. At one end of the period, Alden T. Vaughan on Puritan–Indian relations in the seventeenth century and, at the other end, Francis Paul Prucha on government Indian policy in the early national period, have provided the basis for a different perspective on the subject.

Vaughan's effort is a disarming defense of the Puritan treatment of the New England natives. On the whole the Puritans were "humane, considerate, and just," and "had a surprisingly high regard for the interests of a people who were less powerful, less civilized, less sophisticated, and—in the eyes of the New England colonists—less godly." Though doubtless their kind of violence was more intense, they employed it less frequently than the Indians. Rather than bringing chaos to New England, the Puritans were the only power capable of keeping the peace among the volatile tribes. In the two major Indian–white conflicts, with the Pequots and later against King Philip, the Puritans dealt devastating blows to Indian power but they did not cause the fighting. In the first, the Pequots, themselves intruders, must take the blame and in the second the impetus for war came not from the Puritans but from Philip in his fear for the loss of his prestige and power.[24]

Vaughan is not unsympathetic to the Indian. He simply believes that the Puritan attitude toward them was worthy of praise. The two societies did not really clash; it was merely that the one was "unified, visionary, disciplined, and dynamic" while the other was "self-satisfied, undisciplined, and static."[25] One knows, however, whose side he has chosen. The Puritans expanded, as was the European habit, into the sphere of the Indians. Since what the Indians did in a certain location cannot really be called occupying the land, at least not in the sense that the whites did, Puritan society gradually moved in and took over. It is not just a question of physical displacement though there was much of that; the Puritans did purchase land from the Indians. Rather the process was more an imperceptible cultural advance by the Puritans and recession by the Indians.

Thus in his conclusions Vaughan communicates a sense of the process of the Indian's cultural decline. But the bulk of his book contains no such impression. In overturning the critical view of the white man and in raising the estimation

---

[23] William T, Hagan, *American Indians* (Chicago, 1961), takes every opportunity to see the worst in the white man's action. "Traders employed any tactics to make an immediate profit" (p. 16); intermarriage was intended merely to further the economic and political objectives of the whites (p. 12); a "double standard of morality" was used by whites in dealing with Indians (p. 20); Indian students at William and Mary were "supported by charity and instructed in segregated classes" (pp. 10–11). Worse yet, during the Revolution "two Indians killed were partially flayed to provide boot tops for the troops as addicted to souvenir-hunting as their twentieth century counterparts" (p. 38). And Tecumseh, so the report goes, "was flayed and his skin made into souvenir razor strops by the representatives of the higher way of life" (p. 63). The Indian is merely victim and the white man only oppressor. R. S. Cotterill, *The Southern Indians: The Story of the Civilized Tribes Before Removal* (Norman, 1954), 124, 139–140, 153, 174, 224; a particularly cavalier and simplistic description of Jeffersonian policy may be found in Marshall Smelser, *The Democratic Republic, 1801–1815* (New York, 1968), 132–134.

[24] Vaughan, *New England Frontier*, vii–viii, 78, 136–137, 183–184, 312–313. Douglas Edward Leach, *Flintlock and Tomahawk: New England in King Philip's War* (New York [orig. pub., New York, 1958], 1966), 14–22, blames the conflict on the Puritan pressure for land.

[25] Vaughan, *New England Frontier*, 323.

of the Puritan's intentions, he dwells on the theme of positive policy. The Indian and Puritan, finally, are treated as equals, dealing with one another over the vital issues of war, peace, trade, religion, and social conviviality. The Indian, having a sound notion of the meaning of land possession, sells it, most often willingly, to the Puritan. The law of civilization is accepted by the native people as an equitable means of arranging for a mutually satisfactory juridical condition. The Puritans introduce themselves into a complex extra-tribal political situation as one more power among equals.[26] In his recounting of the story, Vaughan does not really break into the cultural interplay of Indian–white relations. It is not merely because he willingly uses only Puritan sources (all the historical sources, after all, are the white man's) but that he fails to take the Indian on his own terms. Indian society, as he notes, is "divided, self-satisfied, undisciplined, and static": all anti-virtues in Protestant civilization's hierarchy of value. The great defect of the Puritan in dealing with the Indian (with any other people, for that matter) was his inability to see the external world through any other glass but his own, and that darkly. If on the whole the Puritan did his best for the Indian, as a good Christian it was only expected of him, but he did not concede the Indian a cultural separateness and integrity. Vaughan has disposed of the guilty white man scheme, but just as the Puritans had, he does not act on the recognition that the two societies really were different.

Culminating with the removal policy and the revision of the trade and intercourse acts of 1834, Prucha presents a compelling account of the policy of the young nation toward the natives. His sympathy for the Indian is manifest, but he offers a rounded and perceptive portrayal of the white man's struggle to deal with the confrontation of the two societies. Though his perspective is dictated by his emphasis on policy, he is sensibly aware of the clash of culture, especially of the decline of the Indian under the influence of civilization, and he is chary of distributing blame. Perhaps the major revision in the volume is contained in chapter nine: "Civilization and Removal." The very title hurls defiance at an interpretation long accepted by historians. Removal, after all, has been considered the *locus classicus* of Indian–white relations as a "suffering situation." It was the last outrage heaped by the merciless white man on the heads of the much abused eastern Indians. Prucha's motive in coupling removal with the effort to civilize the Indian is clearly to metamorphose the argument from the one-level "trail of tears" to the complicated interplay of the white man's interest and conscience on the one side and the painful acculturation of a primitive society on the other. He admits, of course, that there was a sufficiency of nefarious motives behind the decision to drive the Indians west of the Mississippi but maintains that not enough attention has been paid to the good motives of those who made government policy in the second and third decades of the nineteenth century. The crucial point is the decision of such men as Thomas L. McKenney, Lewis Cass, and William Clark that the civilizing program had failed, that the major effect of the white man on the Indian was deleterious rather than improving, and that the native could be saved only by removing him from harm's way. Beyond the Mississippi, out of reach of the corrosive elements in the white man's way of life, he could be preserved and possibly civilized before the next advance of American society rolled over him. Re-

[26] *Ibid.,* 104–109, 155, 183, 210.

moval for many who approached the Indian from the highest philanthropy was "another program for the 'preservation and civilization' of the aborigines."[27]

Prucha's case is well taken; the oppressor–victim interpretation, after all, will not explain why men of generally laudable character favored removal. Placing it in the context of civilized philanthropy and Indian disintegration tells something of the way two disparate societies meet and come finally to terms with each other. But Prucha's intentions are limited. He is dealing with policy and the immediate motives leading to its formulation. Except for noting the dawning perception of the consequences of civilization on the Indian, he is not really concerned with the question of cultural interplay. And, indeed, a definition of policy without digging into the substratum of culture that rests beneath it will not yield an interpretation of Indian–white relations that brings together all the elements of cultural differentiation. Yet in showing that there was more to the white man's actions than viciousness, greed, and hypocrisy, he has opened a broad vista for historical imagination.

Horsman supplies the theme of American expansion as an introduction to his account of Indian–white relations in the early years of the nation. The Indian was overwhelmed by a new thriving people but not without a lingering sense of the wickedness of the proceeding. Americans were caught by the incompatibility of their interests (a growing population, the attraction of the fertile west, national feeling, and the need for strategic protection), and their conscience (the righteousness of the Revolution and the uniqueness of the American experiment) which in the face of Indian opposition could not produce a realistic policy.[28] The good will of the white man, then, as manifested in the civilizing program, appears as an inconsequential quirk, an aberration when the reality was removal. The pieces are all there but Horsman's division seems arbitrary. The thrust of the white man's culture, more likely, had an essential unity. The philanthropic determination to civilize the Indian was as much a part of an expanding America as greed for land and removal. The danger in assuming a contradiction between civilization and removal is that the first inevitably becomes a sham and the second merely positive evidence of the white man's callousness. Similarly, it tends to transpose the question out of the realm of cultural conflict. If the Indian was destroyed by the onrush of European culture then philanthropy must be seen as one instrument in the Indian's gradual demise. As Prucha so aptly puts it: "It was a question of civilization versus the savage state, and no one was ready to preach that savagism should be perpetuated."[29] Horsman's extension of the interpretation into an examina-

[27] Prucha, *American Indian Policy*, 224–227. But aside from Prucha, it is virtually impossible to find a treatment of removal that sees it as an extension of the civilizing effort. Most historians conceive of the two policies as contradictory and evidence of the hypocrisy or stupidity of the whites. See Horsman, *Expansion and American Indian Policy*, 109–111, 116–117, 140; Hagan, *American Indians*, 44, 54; Young, *Redskins, Ruffleshirts, and Rednecks*, 5–6, 9; R. Pierce Beaver, *Church, State, and the American Indians: Two and a Half Centuries of Partnership in Missions Between Churches and Government* (St. Louis, 1966), 90, 99–100, 117; Cotterill, *The Southern Indians*, 225–226. A recent Book-of-the-Month-Club Selection, Peter Farb, *Man's Rise to Civilization as Shown by the Indians of North America from Primeval Times to the Coming of the Industrial State* (New York, 1968), 250, calls the removal policy "genocide" and compares it to the Nuremburg Laws.

[28] Horsman, *Expansion and American Indian Policy*, Introduction, 172–173.

[29] Prucha, *American Indian Policy*, 239; Pearce, *Savages of America*, ix, 3–4, 41–42, 73–74, also emphasizes the division between savagism and civilization. He contends that after the middle of the eighteenth century the native was looked on mainly as an obstacle to civilization's advance.

tion of the forces of American expansion together with Prucha's association of removal with the civilizing program constitute a significant move towards the understanding of Indian–white relations as a problem in cultural conflict. Both the source of the white man's overpowering influence on the fragile structure of native society and the subtle operations of civilization's best intentioned philanthropy are thrown open to scrutiny.

Implicit in the suffering-Indian, wicked-white-man interpretation is the proposition that the American aborigine could have survived. The vague assumption is that things might have been different, that the white man should have been less pushy, that the Indian might have been better protected, that the treaties should have been kept, that, finally, the Indian could have endured as an Indian. As a moral injunction the idea takes on certain pristine clarity but it says little about the interplay of culture. Without drifting into the bog of historical inevitability, it must be said that any rearrangement of the forces of Indian–white relations in the early period does little to improve the native's chances. Perhaps a slowing of the white man's advance, some accommodation on median issues, even palliation of the native's suffering, a gentler demise, but whether the Indian was annihilated or transformed, he would no longer be an Indian. Short of abandoning the Mississippi Valley, says Horsman, there seems no reason to think that the problem could have been solved. The "stark realities," writes Leach, dictated that the native society had to submit. Even Hagan, speaking of the Cherokees, believes their case was hopeless.[30]

The consequences of Indian–white confrontation, the passing of a culture, are, however, too cosmic to be without a villain. The unruly frontiersman, fresh from years of Turnerian adulation, must now bear a major portion of the guilt for the Indian's destruction. As agent of American expansion, the wily and undisciplined pioneer, year after year, despite repeated governmental efforts to curb him, pushed the line of white settlement farther into the Indian country.[31] He was the practical surrogate of the white man's brash and aggressive society as it met and proceeded to accomplish the demolition of the native culture. The frontiersman could have been curbed only if the very nature of America could have been qualified; to stem the advance would have meant, conversely, to impair the very vitality of the white man's society. Besides attributing to the societal phenomenon an unrealistic level of rational discipline, the contention that order could have been imposed on the frontier assumes the existence of a bureaucratic and military establishment of far greater size and proficiency than circumstances would permit. The government could not have built a Chinese Wall, as Washington put it, to keep the whites and

---

And hence civilizing the Indian was one way of mastering him, of overcoming an obstacle to progress. Leslie A. Fiedler, *The Return of the Vanishing American* (New York, 1968), 76, offers a typically racy but apt version of the essential unity of the white man's treatment of the Indian: "Not quite destroying, really, for the act of genocide with which our nation began was inconclusive, imperfect, inhibited by a bad conscience, undercut by uncertainty of purpose. 'There's no good injun but a dead injun,' the really principled killers, which is to say, the soldiers, cried; but, 'The next best thing is a Christian Indian,' the softhearted castrators, which is to say, the Priests, reminded them; and, 'We can get along with *any* Indian, so long as he's on the Reservation,' the practical-minded ghetto-izers, which is to say, the bureaucrats and social workers, advised them both—having final say."

[30] Horsman, *Expansion and American Indian Policy*, 173; Leach, *The Northern Colonial Frontier*, 190; Hagan, *American Indians*, 76.

[31] Prucha, *American Indian Policy*, 3, 143–144, 147, 162.

Indians apart.[32] Even the supposed guilt of the frontiersman will not assuage the historiographical decisiveness of the situation; within the terms available for explanation, the Indian's transformation was inevitable.

As mere sentiment the hope for the Indian's survival removes the encounter between white and native from the dynamics of historical process, but it reveals also an unspoken rationalism which, when applied to history, supposes that society is capable of a self-articulation far beyond realistic expectation. A society manifesting such detachment, revealing fully its own inner workings, and thereby judging the effect it might have on another culture, would be a rare phenomenon. Doubtless, in every age there are some who are able to see a fair portion of the intricate patterns of their society and they are sometimes successful in convincing a fraction of their fellows of the accuracy of the vision. But the limitations of rational articulation and control are compounded when the society is as lacking in coherence as colonial and early national America. It was not merely a question of a shortage of governmental or philanthropic good will but of a booming white America bursting out of the constrictions of its social bounds, causing the decline of a native society virtually devoid of the resources for serious competition. The white man is guilty only if one supposes his society capable of a total transmogrification into an entity of mature social discipline, able to establish settled and well-defined relations with its fragile neighbor. There was as much possibility for such a cosmic alteration as there was that the Indian would suddenly develop the cultural muscle to withstand the effects of the white man's aggressiveness. Of course, neither the one nor the other was conceivable. The pattern of interrelation between white and Indian, at least in its limits, was set by the integral nature of the two cultures and its history can be written only by accepting its tragic implications for the Indian and proceeding to the business of analyzing the cultural clash between the two societies. One need not sanction the self-righteousness of the white man's society or see any merit in the disheveled individualism that underlay its rush for conquest to understand the Indian's desperate situation. The process of his decline derives no meaning from the assertion of the white man's guilt; without the context of cultural disintegration the accusation is gratuitous. Within that context, however, it takes on a fitting pathos.

To be sure, the concept of integral culture is at base ethnological, but it is also historical. In the deepest sense there is no history that is not cultural history. Any other conception separates man from his existential dimension. Though a wide knowledge of ethnology would be of incalculable value in the study of Indian–white confrontation, what is more important is the sensitive perception that the human condition, civilized or savage, is always a pattern of intricately connected elements, that the pattern has its limits, and that the limits set off one society from another. For historical research the concept is self-validating. The investigation of governmental policy toward the Indian will develop against the content of American society and its political organization. An account of the native's adjustment to the influx of civilized artifacts will unfold according to the aborigine's ability to absorb or repel them, or conversely, it will describe the eroding effects of the importation of such foreign elements. In the interweaving of the two, in the meeting of the two disparate

[32] George Washington to Timothy Pickering, July 1, 1796, John C. Fitzpatrick, ed., *The Writings of George Washington* . . . (Washington, 1931–1944), XXXV, 112.

social orders, the concept of integral culture is of supreme importance. A model of what may be done is Eric R. Wolfe's *Sons of the Shaking Earth,*[33] an account of the clash of Indian and Spanish culture in middle America. Though based on wide ethnological study, the volume is a perceptive combination of cultural analysis and historical evolution. From the very origins of the land and humankind in the New World, he carries the story to the ascendant warrior kingdoms at the arrival of the Spaniards in the sixteenth century. The native culture, tense and precarious in its grip on life, proved no match for the Europeans who came fully prepared to impose their own ways on the Indian population. Paradoxically, the Spaniards also came in search of a paradise that would fill an elusive deficiency in their own psychic makeup. In bringing together all the strands of competitive interplay between native and European culture and superimposing the anti-culture of the Spaniards paradisaic ideology, Wolfe goes to the heart of the dynamics of human development.[34]

Above all the Indian must be perceived as an Indian. Justice can be done him historically only if his special character is admitted. If he turns out to be only a vague reflection of the white man's wish for what he sees as best in himself—an idealized white man—or even if it is assumed that his behavior as a historical character can be judged by the objective definitions applied to civilized man, then the Indian will never be portrayed with the integrity he deserves. If his death is to be tragic, it must be the death of his real self, not of a white impostor.

[33] Eric R. Wolfe, *Sons of the Shaking Earth* (Chicago, 1959).
[34] *Ibid.,* Chap. VIII, IX, X.

From Coercion to Persuasion

Another Look at the Rise of Religious Liberty and the Emergence of Denominationalism

Sidney Mead

INTRODUCTION

Although the essays in this book insist upon the importance of ideas in history, they do not claim that the force of ideas can be understood apart from a particular set of social circumstances. The essay that follows, by a distinguished church historian, demonstrates the complex relationships that linked the ideology of religious toleration to the evolution of American colonial societies at a time when religious uniformity was still revered in Europe. While Mead does not deny that ideas of toleration and freedom affected colonial practice, he suggests that they gained acceptance in America out of a necessity composed of such disparate factors as the recruitment of settlers, the extent of physical space, the English policy of religious tolerance, and eighteenth-century revivalism.

Mead himself treats these matters in the essays published as *The Lively Experiment* (1963); his studies of the importance of denominationalism are especially important. For more on particular denominations see William G. McLoughlin, *Isaac Backus and the American Pietistic Tradition** (1967), on the Baptists; C. C. Goen, *Revivalism and Separatism in New England, 1740–1800* (1962), on the Congregationalists and Separate Baptists; and Leonard J. Trinterud, *The Forming of an American Tradition* (1949), on the Presbyterians. For church–state relationships, see Susan B. Reed, *Church and State in Massachusetts: 1691–1740* (1914), and the incisive discussion by L. K. Wroth and H. B. Zobel in *The Legal Papers of John Adams* (1965), Vol. 2, 20–46.

B Y the time English colonization got underway in the seventeenth century, the Reformation movement had shattered the once tangible unity of European Christendom. The spiritual reformation of the church was concurrent with the rising self-consciousness of the emerging nations. Quite naturally the reformation of the church found diverse expressions in the several countries—Lutheranism in the realms of the German princes and in the Scandinavian countries, Anglicanism in England, Reformed in Geneva and Scotland.

In general these right-wing Protestant groups agreed with Roman Catholics on the necessity for enforcing religious uniformity in doctrine and practice within a civil commonwealth. This view of many centuries' standing in Christendom the new churches accepted without question.

Meanwhile, in the social crevices created by universal upheaval, certain sects or left-wing groups were emerging as blades of grass spring up through the cracks once a cement sidewalk is broken. Throughout Europe, Catholics and Protestants alike tried to suppress these groups by force, branding them as heretics and schismatics who constituted a threat to the whole structure of Christian civilization.

All of the first settlements on that part of the continent that was to become the United States were made under the religious aegis of right-wing groups with the exception of Plymouth where a handful of separatists "made a small, bustling noise in an empty land." But Anglicans who were making a bigger noise on the James, as were Dutch Reformed on the Hudson, Swedes on the Delaware, and puritan Congregationalists on the Charles, all assumed that the pattern of religious uniformity would of necessity be transplanted and perpetuated in the colonies. And all took positive steps to insure this—even the Pilgrims. For as Plymouth colony prospered it made support of the church compulsory, demanded that voters be certified as "orthodox in the fundamentals of religion," and passed laws against Quakers and other heretics.[1]

The first Charter of Virginia of 1606 provided that "the true word and service of God and Christian faith be preached, planted, and used . . . according to the doctrine, rights, and religion now professed and established within our realm of England," and from the beginning laws provided for the maintenance of the church and clergy and for conformity.

Orthodox ministers of the Dutch church came early to New Netherlands, and the new charter of freedoms and exemptions of 1640 stated that

FROM Sidney Mead, "From Coercion to Persuasion: Another Look at the Rise of Religious Liberty and the Emergence of Denominationalism," *The Lively Experiment: The Shaping of Christianity in America,* New York: Harper & Row, 1963. Copyright © 1963 by Sidney E. Mead. Reprinted by permission of Harper & Row, Publishers, Inc. This article first appeared in *Church History,* XXV (December 1956).

[1] Evarts B. Greene, *Religion and the State: The Making and Testing of an American Tradition* (New York: New York University Press, 1941), p. 37. See also Joseph P. Thompson, *Church and State in the United States* (Boston: James R. Osgood & Co., 1873), p. 55.

no other religion shall be publicly admitted in New Netherlands except the Reformed, as it is at present preached and practiced by public authority in the United Netherlands; and for this purpose the Company shall provide and maintain good and suitable preachers, schoolmasters, and Comforters of the sick.

When John Prinz was sent as Governor to the struggling Swedish colony in 1643 he was specifically instructed to

labor and watch that he render in all things to Almighty God the true worship which is his due . . . and to take good measures that the divine service is performed according to the true confession of Augsburg, the Council of Upsala, and the ceremonies of the Swedish church . . .

After a brief stay he was happy to report that

Divine service is performed here in the good old Swedish tongue, our priest clothed in the vestments of the Mass on high festivals, solemn prayer-days, Sundays, and Apostles' days, precisely as in old Sweden, and differing in every respect from that of the sects around us.[2]

That the New England Puritans' experiment in the Bible Commonwealth required uniformity hardly needs documentation. "There is no Rule given by God for any State to give an Affirmative Toleration to any false Religion, or Opinion whatsoever; they must connive in some cases, but may not concede in any," was the dictum of their self-appointed spokesman, Nathaniel Ward. Although the forthright clarity of this lawyer-minister disguised as a "Simple Cobler" was not typical of the more discreet apologists for the New England way, nevertheless Ward's sentiment was one of the stones in the foundation of their "due forme of Government both ciuell & ecclesiastical."

Yet in spite of such beginnings the intention to perpetuate uniformity in the several Protestant colonies that were gathered under the broad wings and "salutary neglect" of mother England during the seventeenth and eighteenth centuries was everywhere frustrated. The tradition of thirteen-centuries' standing was given up in the relatively brief time of one hundred and eighty years. By around the middle of the eighteenth century toleration was universally, however reluctantly, accepted in all the English colonies. Within fifty years complete religious freedom was declared to be the policy of the new nation formed from these colonies.

The importance of this change can hardly be overestimated. Professor W. E. Garrison has rightly called it one of "the two most profound revolutions which have occurred in the entire history of the church . . . on the administrative side"—and so it was.

I

There have been many studies of the rise of religious freedom in America. They range all the way from the sentimental to the cynical with a large num-

---

[2] As quoted in Frederick J. Zwierlein, *Religion in New Netherlands* (Rochester, N.Y.: John P. Smith Printing Co., 1910), pp. 140–41, 117, 118–19.

ber of very substantial works by careful scholars in between. There seems to be fairly wide agreement with Professor Philip Schaff's thesis that the Constitutional Convention "was shut up to this course" by the previous history of the colonies and the situation existing at the time. In this essay I do not intend a detailed historical explanation of this "profound revolution," but wish only to raise two questions: What was the situation in 1787? and How had it come to be?

In order to answer the second question two factors have to be weighed and balanced: that of the positive ideological thrust for such freedom made, for example, by the Baptists as a group, and by individual leaders in most of the other churches, and that of practical necessity. The latter position is ably represented by Perry Miller, who argues that Protestants by and large "did not [willingly] contribute to religious liberty, they stumbled into it, they were compelled into it, they accepted it at last because they had to, or because they saw its strategic values."[3]

It is my impression that Protestant writers have commonly stressed the first factor, usually suggesting that religious freedom was a natural concomitant of the Reformation. If in this essay I stress the second factor, it is primarily to bring into the discussion what I hope will be a corrective emphasis.

This emphasis necessarily reduces the historical importance Protestants have placed upon the positive, self-conscious, and articulated aspiration for religious freedom expressed in our popular folklore through such gems as Felicia Heman's poem on the landing of the Pilgrims. It does not deny the existence of important seminal ideas among left-wingers and other outcasts such as the Roman Catholics who established Maryland or even among the respectable Puritans and Presbyterians. Nor does it underestimate the long-term symbolic value of the steps taken along this road by the Baltimores, by Roger Williams and that motley collection of the banished in Rhode Island, and by William Penn and his Quakers in the Jerseys and Pennsylvania. Still it should be kept in mind that Protestants connived in the freedom extended to all by Roman Catholics in Maryland only so long as was necessary for them to do so. Rhode Island was the scandal of respectable Massachusetts precisely because of its freedom and was commonly referred to by the Bay dignitaries as the sewer and loathsome receptacle of the land. They did not cleanse it because they could not. And by the time Penn launched his experiment with freedom in Pennsylvania, coerced uniformity had already broken down in the neighboring colonies, and England herself, having experimented extensively with toleration between 1648 and 1660 and unable to forget it during the Restoration, was trembling on the verge of toleration.

Accepting, then, the view that the original intention of the dominant and really powerful groups was to perpetuate the pattern of religious uniformity, I shall argue that this intention was frustrated by the unusual problems posed by the vast space with which the Planters had to deal, by a complex web of self-interest in which they were enmeshed, and by the practical necessity to connive at religious variety which both space and self-interest imposed. Finally, too, pressures from the motherland contributed to the process leading to religious freedom.

[3] Perry G. E. Miller, "The Contribution of the Protestant Churches to Religious Liberty in Colonial America," in *Church History,* IV (March, 1935), 57–66.

The web of self-interest was complex indeed, the strongest strands being Protestant, national, and personal. At a time when in England Protestant was synonymous with patriot, and the first feeble English settlements were encircled by the strong arms of French and Spanish Catholicism, whose fingers touched on the Mississippi, it is small wonder that all the early writings and charters stressed the planting of *Protestant* outposts of empire, and that a sentiment came to prevail that almost any kind of Protestantism was preferable to Catholicism. Perhaps this is why Dutch and English policy differed radically from French, in that the Protestant countries after a few random gestures such as the provision in the second Virginia Charter of 1609 that "none be permitted to pass in any Voyage . . . to be made into said Country but such as first shall have taken the Oath of Supremacy," let their dissenters go. Civil and ecclesiastical pressures ranging from slight disabilities to active persecution thus added an external push from the rear to the lure of land and of economic and social betterment operating in the colonists' minds. And this, coupled in many of them with a religious fervor that was always in danger of crossing the boundary into self-righteousness, pushed them out with the intention to become permanent settlers, to possess the land, and perchance to be an example for all mankind—as witness the Bay Puritans.

It is notable also that from the beginning the one outstanding Roman Catholic proprietor had to tolerate a majority of Protestants in his colony, and that eventually the heirs of the first Baltimore probably retained their lands and prerogatives only by becoming Protestants.

National self-interest mated easily with Protestant interests and spawned a desire for strong and profitable colonies that tended to overcome squeamishness about the religious complexion of the settlers. When Peter Stuyvesant came to New Netherlands in 1647 as Director General, he immediately took steps to put the religious house in order by limiting the sale of liquor on Sundays, instituting preaching twice rather than the former once a day, and compelling attendance thereon. When Lutherans, Jews, and Quakers arrived he tried to suppress them, finally shipping one notorious Quaker back to Holland. The Directors' reaction to this move is eloquent testimony to the mind that prevailed among them. They wrote in April 1663 that

> although it is our cordial desire that similar and other sectarians might not be found there, yet as the contrary seems to be the fact, we doubt very much if vigorous proceedings against them ought not to be discontinued, except you intend to check and destroy your population; which, however, in the youth of your existence ought rather to be encouraged by all possible means: Wherefore, it is our opinion, that some connivance would be useful; that the consciences of men, at least, ought ever to remain free and unshackled. Let everyone be unmolested, as long as he is modest; as long as his conduct in a political sense is irreproachable; as he does not disturb others, or oppose the government. This maxim of moderation has always been the guide of the magistrates of this city, and the consequence has been that, from every land, people have flocked to this asylum. Tread then in their steps, and, we doubt not, you will be blessed.[4]

---

[4] As quoted in W. W. Sweet, *Religion in Colonial America* (New York: Charles Scribner's Sons, 1942), pp. 151–52.

So on another occasion Stuyvesant argues that "to give liberty to the Jews will be very detrimental . . . because the Christians there will not be able at the same time to do business." And besides, "giving them liberty, we cannot refuse the Lutherans and Papists."[5]

At the time he was backed by the doughty Reformed minister, Megapolensis, who thought the situation was already bad enough since there were "Papists, Mennonites and Lutherans amongst the Dutch, also many Puritans or Independents, and various other servants of Baal among the English under this government," all of whom "conceal themselves under the name of Christians." Nevertheless, the desire of the Directors not to "check and destroy" the population overruled the desire of both magistrate and clergy for a semblance of religious uniformity and Jews had to be granted permission to reside and traffic in New Netherlands only "provided they shall not become a charge upon the deaconry or the Company."[6]

II

Finally, from the beginning the ruling geniuses of the new age of expansion managed to mingle strong personal self-interest with the more abstract Protestant and national goals by making trading companies and proprietaryships the instruments of planting. Dutch, Swedish, and English companies organized the plantings in Virginia, Plymouth, New Netherlands, Massachusetts Bay, and Delaware, while proprietors were instrumental in the founding of Maryland, New Hampshire, New Jersey, the Carolinas, Pennsylvania, and Georgia. It might further be argued that William Coddington and his commercial-minded cohorts were the real backbone of Rhode Island, while obviously Theophilus Eaton, the merchant, was hand in hand with John Davenport, the minister, in the founding of the ultratheocratic New Haven.

By 1685, says Greene, more territory along the seaboard than New England and Virginia combined was under proprietary control, and there "governmental policies in relation to religion were radically different from those prevailing either in New England or Virginia." From the viewpoint of the proprietors, he continues, "it was obviously not good business to set up religious tests to exclude otherwise desirable immigrants." "The proprietors tried to attract settlers," Greene explained, "by promising, if not full religious equality, at least greater tolerance than was allowed elsewhere."[7]

But if self-interest dictated in more or less subtle and devious ways a kind of connivance with religious diversity that helped to spell out toleration in the colonies, the efforts even of the most authoritarian groups to enforce uniformity on principle was dissipated in the vast spaces of the new land.

The Anglicans tried it in Virginia, even resorting to the savage "Lavves Diuine, Morall and Martiall &c." published in 1612 which threatened the death penalty for speaking "impiously or maliciously against the . . . Trinitie," or "against the knowne Articles of the Christian faith," or for saying or doing anything which might "tend to the derision or despight of Gods Holy Word," and threatened loss of the "dayes allowance," whipping, "a bodkin thrust through his tongue," six months in the "gallies," or other punishments for failing, among other things, in respect for the clergy, for not attending divine

---

[5] Zwierlein, *op. cit.,* p. 261.   [6] *Ibid.,* pp. 257, 256.   [7] Greene, *op. cit.,* pp. 52–53.

services twice daily, for breaking the "Sabboth by any gaming, publique or private, or refusing religious instruction."[8]

No one supposes that such laws were enforced during the horrendous years between 1607 and 1624 when thirteen thousand of the fourteen thousand people sent over died from exposure, disease, starvation, and the weapons of the savages. Meanwhile the economic awards in the cultivation of tobacco had been discovered and this scattered the families to plantations along the rivers. Even honest clergymen began to despair of conducting the routine affairs of the English church in parishes that might be one hundred miles in length. In 1661 an acute observer argues in *Virginia's Cure* . . . that the chief difficulty was due to the "scattered Planting" for which there was "no other Remedy . . . but by reducing her Planters into towns." His proposal to build towns in every county, and then to make the Planters bring their families and servants to these centers on weekends for catechetical instruction and church attendance was obviously the counsel of despairing, albeit ardent, churchmen who were beginning to realize that the snug parish life of settled England could not be duplicated in the wilderness.[9]

The Puritan theocrats on the Charles soon had one important aspect of the meaning of the great space available thrust upon them. They discovered that while they might protect their own religious uniformity by banishing all dissenters, they could neither keep the banished from settling in neighboring Rhode Island where "Justice did at greatest offenders wink,"[10] nor prevent every wind from the south carrying their contagious ideas back to the Puritan stronghold. They did not foresee that the same inscrutable Providence that gave Puritans the opportunity to build their kind of Bible commonwealth on Massachusetts soil would offer dissenters the equal opportunity to build whatever kind of commonwealth they wished on Rhode Island soil.

Meanwhile the zeal of the dissenters, far from being dissipated by banishment, was truly enlarged by the knowledge thus forced upon them that even the long arms of civil and ecclesiastical authority could not encompass the vast spaces of the new land. In rather short order, belief in the effectiveness of suppression by force and the will to use it to maintain religious uniformity were undermined by the obvious futility of trying to land solid blows on the subversive men and women who were seldom there when the blows fell. Samuel Gorton, compelled to attend church in the Bay, wrote that the sermonic fare seemed adapted to the digestive capacities of the ostrich. But in spite of such capacities, the residents were unable to stomach the savage proceedings against the Quakers, and finally even the magistrates and ministers had to connive in their existence.[11]

---

[8] *For the Colony in Virginea Britannia. Lavves Diuine, Moral and Martiall, &c.* (Printed at London for Walter Burre, 1612); in Peter Force, *Tracts and Other Papers* (Washington: Wm. Q. Force, 1844), III, #ii, pp. 10–11.

[9] *Virginia's Cure: Or an Advisive Narrative Concerning Virginia. Discovering the True Ground of That Unhappiness, and the Only True Remedy.* As it was presented to the Right Reverend Father in God *Gvilbert* Lord Bishop of London, September 2, 1661 (London: W. Godbid, 1662), reprinted in Force, *Tracts . . . , op. cit.,* III, #xv.

[10] Perry G. E. Miller and Thomas H. Johnson, eds., *The Puritans* (New York: American Book Co., 1938), p. 639.

[11] For the general factors at work, see Roland H. Bainton, "The Struggle for Religious Liberty," in *Church History,* X (June, 1941), 95–124. Professor Winthrop S. Hudson has argued that English Independents had developed a "denominational" conception of the church which, in spite of the rigors of the New England way, tended always to make its leaders inherently uncomfortable

There was of course another aspect of space—the distance from the motherland, which, relative to existing means of movement and communications, was immense. The Puritans began with the idea that

> God hath provided this place to be a refuge for many whome he meanes to save out of the generall callamity, and seeinge the Church hath noe place to flie into but the wildernesse, what better worke can there be, then to goe and provide tabernacles and foode for her against she comes thether.[12]

They early sensed the protection inherent in the great distance. Their ingenious idea of taking the Charter and the Company with them to New England is evidence of this. Thereafter they perfected a system of sanctified maneuvering within the time granted by distance that succeeded for three generations in frustrating the attempts of English courts and Crown to control them.

Distance also militated against effective control of the Church of England in the Southern colonies. From the beginning, oversight fell somewhat accidentally to the Bishop of London. During the last quarter of the seventeenth century, the Bishops sought to instrument their supervision of church activities in the colonies through representatives called Commissaries. But without resident Bishops, effective supervision proved to be impossible. The church languished under too many second-rate and even fraudulent clergymen. Increasingly the control passed to parochial vestries composed of local laymen.

Turmoil in Britain at times reinforced distance in frustrating effective ecclesiastical control of the colonies. In 1638, after a series of reports and proclamations beginning in 1632, Archbishop Laud made arrangements to send a bishop to New England with sufficient troops to enforce conformity and obedience if necessary. The outbreak of troubles in Scotland sidetracked this interesting project, however, and "no records of any official connection between the Anglican episcopate and the colonies during the period 1638–1663" exist.[13]

Meanwhile through revolution, Protectorate, and Restoration, England was moving toward its rendezvous with the kind of toleration made manifest in the famous Act of 1689. Already in 1652 Dr. John Clarke had published in London his *Ill Newes from Newe England or a Narrative of New England's Persecution,* protesting the fining and whipping of three Baptists in Massachusetts under the aegis of a law passed in 1644. His telling thesis was that in matters of religious tolerance, "while Old England is becoming new, New England is become Old."[14]

From about that time the mother country took definite steps to curb persecution in the colonies. When the King was reminded by Edward Burroughs that the execution of Quakers in Boston meant that there was *"a Vein of innocent Blood opened in his Dominions, which, if it were not stopt would overrun all,"* he declared, *"But I will stop that Vein,"* and he did. A Mandamus was granted and carried to New England by Samuel Shattock, a resident of

---

with persecution of dissenters; see his "Denominationalism as a Basis for Ecumenicity: A Seventeenth Century Conception," in *Church History,* XXIV (March, 1955), 32–50. This suggests a fruitful area for further exploration.

[12] As quoted in Charles M. Andrews, *The Colonial Period of American History* (New Haven: Yale University Press, 1934), I, 386.

[13] Arthur Lyon Cross, *The Anglican Episcopate and the American Colonies* (Cambridge: Harvard University Press, 1924), p. 22.

[14] In the *Massachusetts Historical Society Collections,* Ser. 4, II (1854), 1–113.

Salem who had been banished on pain of death. Shattock and his fellow Quakers made the most of the occasion, which resulted in a suspension of the laws against the Quakers as such in November, 1661.[15]

Meanwhile, John Clarke's *Ill Newes from Newe England* . . . had resulted in a protest to the Governor of Massachusetts from ten Congregational ministers in London, who, seeking for more toleration in England, were embarrassed by this show of intolerance on the part of their New England brethren. Sir Richard Saltonstall added his protest in a letter to Cotton and Wilson of Boston's First Church. The Puritans' reply that it was better to have "hypocrites than profane persons" in their churches sounded outmoded.[16]

In 1663 the Crown, in giving its consent to Rhode Island's "lively experiment" with "full liberty in religious concernm[ts]" in the new Charter,[17] gave official sanction to the scandal of Massachusetts Bay and forestalled all future attempts on the part of the Bay Puritans to impose their kind of theocratic order on the neighboring chaos.

The most spectacular case of royal interference that worked for the broadening of colonial toleration was the revocation of the Massachusetts Bay Charter in 1684 and the coming of Sir Edmund Andros as the Royal Governor in 1686. Andros brought an Anglican chaplain with him. Seeking a place for Anglican Services, he tried to persuade the Puritan ministers to provide a church. When this proved unsuccessful, he took over one of their meetinghouses by force and had the English services conducted therein while King's Chapel was being built. The new charter of 1691, in which the New Englanders themselves had a part through the person and work of Increase Mather, wrote "the end" to the Puritan chapter on the preservation of uniformity in the new land.

III

Thus the new century found the original intention to perpetuate religious uniformity almost universally frustrated by the strange rope of circumstances woven from various kinds of self-interest and the problems posed by the great space. Effective interference from the motherland in the interests of broader toleration served only to hasten the process. When the two Mathers, father and son, took part in the ordination of a Baptist minister in Boston in 1718, a new day was indeed dawning. But it is probably not to be wondered at that most of them adhered to the inherited standards and conceptions of the church with religious fervor sometimes bordering on desperation. It took the prolonged upheavals associated with the great revivals to break the dwindling hold of the old patterns and give the new an opportunity to grow, and, in the process, to scramble both inextricably with others emerging out of the immediate situation.

Once it was seen that uniformity was impracticable, two possible paths lay open before the churches: toleration, with a favored or established church and

15 Willem Sewel, *The History of the Rise, Increase, and Progress of the Christian People Called Quakers, Intermixed with Several Remarkable Occurrences,* written originally in Low-Dutch by Willem Sewel, and by himself translated into English, now rev. and published with some amendments (London: J. Sowle, 1722), p. 280.

16 See Sanford H. Cobb, *The Rise of Religious Liberty in America* (New York: The Macmillan Co., 1902), p. 69.

17 Andrews, *op. cit.,* II, 42.

dissenting sects—the path actually taken in England—or freedom, with complete equality of all religious groups before the civil law. Favoring the first solution was the fact that transplanted offshoots of Europe's state churches were clearly dominant in all but two of the colonies, and indeed remained so until after the Revolution. Nine of the colonies actually maintained establishments—Congregationalism in New England, Anglicanism in the South and, nominally, in part of New York. Presbyterians in the South and Anglicans in New England were willing to acknowledge the prerogatives of establishments by assuming the role of dissenters. On the eve of the great revivals, then, these dominant churches had not as yet rejected the principle of religious uniformity but were compelled to recognize the fact of religious variety.

Meanwhile in Rhode Island and the stronger middle colonies religious freedom prevailed—in New York practically, ambiguously, and largely because of necessity, in Rhode Island and Pennsylvania actually and more clearly on principle and experience. As intimated above, the factors that had confounded the uniformitarian intentions of the churches originally established in the new land had also encouraged the numerical growth, geographical expansion, and bumptious self-confidence of the dissenting and free groups in all the colonies. However, they were as yet largely unconscious of their real strength which was to lie in their success with persuasion alone for recruiting members and maintaining their institutions in competition with other groups. An entry in Henry M. Muhlenberg's *Journal*, November 28, 1742, suggests how rapidly a minister, transplanted from a European state church, might size up the realities of the new situation in America and come to terms with them. Sent over to bring some order into the scrambled Lutheran affairs, he immediately ran into a squabble in one of the churches, and recorded:

> The deacons and elders are unable to do anything about it, for in religious and church matters, each has the right to do what he pleases. The government has nothing to do with it and will not concern itself with such matters. Everything depends on the vote of the majority. A preacher must fight his way through with the sword of the Spirit alone and depend upon faith in the living God and His promises, if he wants to be a preacher and proclaim the truth in America.[18]

Such espousal of voluntaryism by these American offsprings of Europe's right-wing state churches meant that they accepted one aspect that had been common to the left-wing sectarian groups of Europe from their beginnings. But this was a triumph of a left-wing influence in America, as it is sometimes held, in a guilt-by-association sense only.

Much more important for the future than left-wing influence was the movement called Pietism. Originating in the European right-wing state churches during the last quarter of the seventeenth century, its leaders were seeking for more palatable spiritual food for the hungry souls of the common folk than current Protestant scholasticism and formalism afforded. Conceived and projected as a movement *within* churches aimed at the revitalization of the personal religious life of the members and a restoration of Christian unity, Pietism did tend to develop its own patterns of doctrine and polity. While as-

---

[18] Henry Melchior Muhlenberg, *The Journals,* trans. by Theodore G. Tappert and John W. Doberstein (Philadelphia: Muhlenberg Press, 1942), I, 67.

suming the validity and continuance of traditional standards and practices, Pietists tended to make personal religious experience more important than assent to correctly formulated belief and the observance of ecclesiastical forms. Here was an intimation that the essence of a church was the voluntary association of individuals who had had the experience.

Stress on the intuitive religion of the heart "strangely warmed" by "faith in Christ," as John Wesley was later to put it, became a possible seedbed for the dreaded religious "enthusiasm." However, in Europe the movement was always somewhat constrained by the sheer existence and accepted forms of the powerful state churches.

But, sprouting indigenously in America, or transplanted thereto by such leaders as Freylinghuysen, Muhlenberg, Zinzendorf, and the great Whitefield, where such constraining ecclesiastical forms were already weakened, Pietism, cross-fertilized by other movements, grew rankly and blossomed into the spectacular phenomena associated with the Great Awakenings. It swept the colonies from the 1720's to the Revolution, transforming the religious complexion of the land as it went.

Jonathan Edwards' experience in Northampton indicates how short was the step from preaching even the most traditional doctrines out of a heart "strangely warmed," to the outbreak of a surprising revival in the church that soon led to "strange enthusiastic delusions" which threatened to disrupt established parish customs.[19] To a modern student the emotional upheavals created by George Whitefield's preaching seem to be out of proportion to that noted evangelist's reputed powers that so impressed Benjamin Franklin.

Back of this was the peculiar religious situation that had been developing in the colonies for a century. Concurrent with the fracturing of uniformity had come the obvious decline of vital religion which concerned clergymen throughout the colonies during the twilight years of the seventeenth century and often turned their sermons into lamentations. The churches were not reaching the masses of the people, and they now confronted a greater proportion of unchurched adults than existed in any other Christian country. This grim statistic reflected the breakdown of the traditional pattern of church membership by birth into a commonwealth and baptism into a church that was coextensive with it, as well as the passing of support induced by coercion, at a time when no new, effective, and acceptable method for recruiting and holding members had emerged.

There was also the general cultural attrition associated with living on the frontier of western civilization where so much of the vital energy of the prosperous went into practical affairs—usually related to immediate profits—and of the poor in the even more engrossing problem of survival. The end of the seventeenth century has been called with reason the lowest ebb tide of the cultural amenities in America. Here was fertile soil for the growth of the kind of fearful and superstitious religiosity later so vividly pictured by Crèvecoeur in the twelfth of his *Letters from an American Farmer*. Hence, to change the figure, at the very time when the tried old dams of civil and ecclesiastical law and custom were crumbling, there was building up behind

---

[19] See Jonathan Edwards, "A Faithful Narrative of the Surprising Work of God in the Conversion of Many Hundred Souls, in Northampton . . . ," in his *The Works of President Edwards* (New York: Converse, 1830), IV, 70–71.

them a religious yearning waiting to be released in floods of religious enthusiasm. And the revivals came, doing just that.

Most of the early revivalists were pietistically inclined ministers who more or less unwittingly stumbled upon this technique. It so perfectly met the immediate needs of the churches that it seemed a direct answer to their prayers and a sign of the divine approbation of their doctrines.[20] The revivalists were obviously successful in carrying the gospel to the masses of indifferent people, in recruiting members from among the large body of the unchurched, and in filling the pews with convinced and committed Christians. The revivals demonstrated the spectacular effectiveness of persuasion alone to churches rapidly being shorn of coercive power.

In the context of our general interpretation it is important to note two things. The first is that the revivals took place largely within the entrenched and dominant churches of right-wing tradition. The second is that everywhere, whether among Dutch Reformed and Presbyterians in the middle colonies, Congregationalists in New England or Anglicans in the South, head-on clashes developed between the pietistic revivalists and the powerful defenders of the traditional authoritarian Protestant patterns of doctrine and polity. For the latter correctly sensed that the revivalists stressed religious experience and results—namely conversion—more than correctness of belief, adherence to creedal statements, and proper observance of traditional forms. They knew that in the long run this emphasis might undermine all standards.

When the revivals broke out, traditionalists were largely in control in all these churches. Their attitude is fairly reflected in the Old Side Presbyterian condemnation of the revivalists for

> preaching the terrors of the law in such a manner, and dialect as has no precedent in the Word of God . . . and so industriously working on the passions and affections of weak minds, as to cause them to cry out in a hideous manner, and fall down in convulsion-like fits, to the marring of the profiting both of themselves and others, who are so taken up in seeing and hearing these odd symptoms, that they cannot attend to or hear what the preacher says; and then, after all, boasting of these things as the work of God, which we are persuaded do proceed from an inferior or worse cause.[21]

As for the greatest of the revivalists, George Whitefield, the Rev. John Thompson wrote that he was almost fully persuaded that Whitefield was either "a downright Deceiver, or else under a dreadful Delusion," and condemned his publications as "nothing but mere confused inconsistent religious jargon, contrived to amuse and delude the simple."[22]

---

[20] As, e.g., Jonathan Edwards' words: "The Beginning of the late work of God in this Place was so circumstanced, that I could not but look upon it as a remarkable Testimony of God's Approbation of the Doctrine of Justification by Faith alone, here asserted and vindicated: . . . And at that time, while I was greatly reproached for defending this Doctrine in the Pulpit, and just upon my suffering a very open Abuse for it, God's Work wonderfully brake forth amongst us, and souls began to flock to Christ, as the Saviour in whose Righteousness alone they hoped to be justified; So that this was the Doctrine on which this work in its Beginning was founded, as it evidently was in the whole progress of it." *Discourses on Various Important Subjects, Nearly Concerning the Great Affair of the Soul's Eternal Salvation* (Boston: S. Kneeland & T. Green, 1738), p. ii.
[21] As quoted in Wesley M. Gewehr, *The Great Awakening in Virginia, 1740–1790* (Durham: Duke University Press, 1930), p. 16.
[22] In *ibid.*, p. 65.

Men like Thompson felt a strong sense of responsibility for order and decency in the churches. Still powerful in every colony, they used all available civil and ecclesiastical weapons against the revivalists.

The revivalists defended themselves primarily on the basic ground that personal religious experience was the important thing. They thought of course that the traditionalists neglected it. Gilbert Tennent struck their keynote in his sermon of March 8, 1740, which he called "The Danger of an Unconverted Ministry." Such ministers, he asserted, are "Pharisee-teachers, having no experience of a special work of the Holy Ghost, upon their own souls." They are merely "carnal," and have

> discover'd themselves too plainly to be so in the Course of their lives; some by Ignorance of the Things of God, and Errors about them, bantering and ridiculing of them; some by vicious Practices, some both Ways, all by a furious Opposition to the Work of God in the Land; and what need have we of further Witnesses?

Of course, he added, "God, as an absolute Sovereign, may use what Means he pleases to accomplish his Work by," *but* "we only assert this, that Success by unconverted Ministers Preaching is very improbable, and very seldom happens, so far as we can gather."[23]

Here was the revivalists' most telling argument—they were obviously more successful than their traditionalist brethren. The experience of the Presbyterian churches divided into traditional and revivalist groups between 1745 and 1758 amounted to a demonstration. At the time of the separation the Old Side party numbered twenty-five ministers, at its close only twenty-two. Meanwhile the New Side revivalist party, which began with twenty-two ministers, had seventy-two in 1758 with churches and members proportionately in keeping with these figures. The success of the revivalists could be made very tangible and nicely measured merely by counting ministers, churches, and converts. Thereafter the emphasis upon success in numbers was to play havoc with all tradition-rooted standards of doctrine and polity in the American churches. One hundred and fifty years later Dwight L. Moody was to declare that it makes no difference how you got a man to God, just so you got him there. Moody's outlook was a natural culmination of the emphasis originating with his eighteenth-century forebears.

At this point it is worthwhile to note specifically that the battle was not one between tolerant left-wing sectarian revivalists riding the wave of the democratic future and anachronistic right-wing chairmen stubbornly defending the past and their own present prerogatives. It is important to stress this, because even Professor William Warren Sweet, dean of the historians of Christianity in America, gave the prestige of his name to the thesis that "it was the triumph of left-wing Protestantism in eighteenth century colonial America which underlay the final achievement of the separation of church and state."[24] This thesis has difficulties, chief of which is the plain fact that the left wing, whether defined institutionally or ideologically, never "triumphed" during the colonial

---

[23] From Leonard J. Trinterud, *The Forming of an American Tradition, A Re-examination of Colonial Presbyterianism* (Philadelphia: The Westminster Press, 1944), pp. 89–91.
[24] W. W. Sweet, *The American Churches, an Interpretation* (New York: Abingdon-Cokesbury Press, 1948), pp. 30–31.

period in America.[25] Colonial revivalism was largely a righ-wing church affair.

To be sure, the pietistic revivalists everywhere belabored what Tennent had called "The Danger of an Unconverted Ministry," and Jonathan Edwards was dismissed from his Northampton church in 1750 primarily for insisting, in that stronghold of right-wing sentiment locally known as "Stoddardeanism," that a conversion experience was the prime requisite for full communion in a Christian church—something he had perhaps learned in the revivals. The revivalists—harassed by traditionalists—naturally developed a kind of anticlericalism and antiecclesiasticism that helped to blur the lines between them and those of more authentic left-wing origin. Compounding this confusion between the revivalists and authentic left wingers was the fact that ever since the time of Munster, every departure from accepted order in the Protestant churches was apt to conjure up visions of an imminent upsurge of familism, antinomianism, anabaptism, and enthusiasm. These were terms that the traditionalists used freely but loosely during the heat of the controversies over revivalism.

Actually all the outstanding revivalists belonged to churches or right-wing tradition, and it might cogently be argued that what growth accrued to left-wing groups as a result of the revivals came largely through their ability to reap where others had sown. Thus, for example, the Baptists in New England apparently took little part in the Awakenings there, looking upon them as a movement within the churches of their Congregational oppressors.[26] But when conflict led to a separatist movement, and Separate Congregationalists were treated even more harshly than Baptists by their erstwhile Congregational brethren, many separatists became Baptists.

Once this point is clear, we see that during the clash between traditionalists and revivalists, the latter were thrown willy-nilly—but somewhat incidentally —on the side of greater toleration and freedom. It was not that they developed clearly formulated theories about religious freedom. In fact the striking thing about the whole pietistic movement, as A. N. Whitehead pointed out, was that it "was singularly devoid of new ideas." Rather it appears that the revivalists were prompted by a practical desire for freedom from the immediate restraints imposed by the dominant churchmen. They fought for the right to promote their own point of view in their own ways unmolested by traditional civil and ecclesiastical customs and laws.

Simultaneously the rationalist permeation of the intellectual world during the eighteenth century led to a situation where any man or group that appeared to be fighting for wider toleration of religious differences would attract the sympathetic attention of "enlightened" men in positions of social and political leadership. Furthermore, these men, unlike the Pietists, were interested in giving religious freedom rational, theoretical justification. However much they might abhor "enthusiasm," they could take a sympathetic view of the practical moral application of the revivalist's gospel and the concomitant pietistic appeal to the teachings and simple religion of Jesus. As these rationalists observed the controversies in and between the religious "sects" occasioned

[25] See, e.g., Winthrop S. Hudson's review of Sweet's *The American Churches, an Interpretation* (*ibid.*), in *The Crozer Quarterly*, XXV (October, 1948), 358–60.

[26] Isaac Backus, *A History of New England, with Particular Reference to the Denomination of Christians Called Baptists*, 2d ed., with notes by David Weston (Newton, Mass.: The Backus Historical Society, 1871), II, 41. See also C. C. Goen, *Revivalism and Separatism in New England, 1740–1800* (New Haven: Yale University Press, 1962).

by the revivals, along with the attempts of entrenched traditionalists to preserve order through the use of power, their sympathies were with the revivalists who appeared to be on the side of freedom.

Hence came that apparently strange coalition of rationalists with pietistic-revivalistic sectarians during the last quarter of the eighteenth century. Together, they provided much of the propelling energy behind the final thrust for the religious freedom that was written into the constitution of the new nation. This coalition seems less strange if we keep in mind that, at the time, religious freedom was for both more a practical and legal problem than a theoretical one. They agreed on the practical goal.

IV

Now to hark back to my guiding questions. Having suggested how it had come to be, we may briefly describe the situation in 1787 that necessitated the declaration for religious freedom in the new nation.

First, the churches of right-wing background were still dominant in every area. But no one of them, and no possible combination of them, was in a position to make a successful bid for a national establishment even if those of the Calvinistic tradition were numerous and powerful enough to give Jefferson reason to fear the possibility.[27] Meanwhile the sweep of pietistic sentiments through these right-wing churches during the revivals had undermined much of their desire for establishment. On the question of religious freedom for all, there were many shades of opinion in these churches, but all were practically unanimous on one point: each wanted freedom for itself. And by this time it had become clear that the only way to get it for themselves was to grant it to all others.

Second, the situation had actually made all previous distinctions between established churches and sects, between right- and left-wing groups, practically meaningless. In the South all but the Anglican Church were dissenting sects, as in New England were all but Congregational churches. In this respect, there was no difference between historically right-wing groups such as Presbyterians, Lutherans, and Anglicans and historically left-wing groups such as Quakers and Baptists. The latter, of course, had traditionally held for religious freedom on principle, while the former had recently come to accept it of necessity. But since the immediate problem of such freedom was practical and legal, all worked together for it—each for his own complete freedom to publish his own point of view in his own way.

Hence the true picture is not that of the "triumph" in America of right-wing or left-wing, of churches or sects, but rather a mingling through frustration, controversy, confusion, and compromise of all the diverse ecclesiastical patterns transplanted from Europe, with other patterns improvised on the spot. The result was a complex pattern of religious thought and institutional life that was peculiarly "American," and is probably best described as "denominationalism."

Most of the effectively powerful intellectual, social, and political leaders were rationalists, and these men made sense theoretically out of the actual, practical situation which demanded religious freedom. They gave it tangible

[27] Ralph Barton Perry, *Puritanism and Democracy* (New York: The Vanguard Press, 1944), p. 80.

form and legal structure. This the churches, each intent on its own freedom, accepted in practice but without reconciling themselves to it intellectually by developing theoretical defenses of religious freedom that were legitimately rooted in their professed theological positions. And they never have. Anson Phelps Stokes' massive three-volume work on *Church and State in the United States,* proceeding over the historical evidence like a vacuum cleaner over a rug, is notable for the paucity of positive Protestant pronouncements on religious freedom that it sweeps up.

The religious groups that were everywhere dominant in America throughout the colonial period seem to have placed their feet unwittingly on the road to religious freedom. Rather than following the cloud and pillar of articulated aspiration in that direction, they granted it (insofar as any can be said to have "granted" it) not as the kind of cheerful givers their Lord is said to love, but grudgingly and of necessity.

Meanwhile, by the time that the original intention to preserve religious uniformity was seen to be impossible of fulfillment in the new land, there had been incubated, largely within the dissenting groups (which were not necessarily left wing), ideas, theories, and practices that pointed the way toward a new kind of "church" consistent with the practice of religious freedom. During the colonial upheavals of the Great Awakenings, these dissenters' patterns of thought and practice infiltrated the dominant churches, and through the misty atmosphere of confusion and compromise, there began that historical merging of the traditional European patterns of "church" and "sect," "right" and "left" wings into a new kind of organization combining features of both plus features growing out of the immediate situation. The resulting organizational form was unlike anything that had preceded it in Christendom, and for purposes of distinctive clarity it is best known as the "denomination."

Popular Uprisings and Civil Authority in Eighteenth-Century America

Pauline Maier

INTRODUCTION

In the last decade, historians have become interested once more in the history of the anonymous, of ordinary people, of common men and their roles in great and small events. Family studies and historical demography have renewed such interest and are themselves evidence of such concerns. Crowd behavior, mobs and riots, and popular insurrections have also provided subjects for study of the anonymous. Pauline Maier's article deals with these last categories and raises important questions about the relationship of popular uprisings to the political process in eighteenth-century America. Of particular interest are the questions of the part played by mobs in the American Revolution and of whether crowd activity differed significantly before and during the Revolution. Maier revives questions that were asked in the eighteenth century about violence and how it affected the form of the Constitution. In considering these matters, we should also consider what mob participation suggests about the character of the American Revolution. The issue of whether the Revolution was truly a popular movement has preoccupied historians for years.

Historians of Europe have written suggestive books and essays on popular upheavals. Among the best are E. J. Hobsbawm, *Primitive Rebels: Studies in Archaic Forms of Social Movement in the 19th and 20th Centuries,* 2nd ed.* (1963), and George Rudé, *The Crowd in the French Revolution** (1959) and *Wilkes and Liberty: A Social Study of 1763 to 1774* (1962). Rudé and Hobsbawm have collaborated on *Captain Swing* (1968), which, though it deals with a later period, is fascinating and useful. For the social setting of much urban violence in the eighteenth-century American colonies, students should see Carl Bridenbaugh's distinguished studies, *Cities in the Wilderness** (1938, 1971) and *Cities in Revolt** (1955, 1971). Edmund S. and Helen M. Morgan, *The Stamp Act Crisis:*

Prologue to Revolution, rev. ed.* (1963), deals compellingly with the mobs and riots of 1765–66; Hiller B. Zobel, *The Boston Massacre* (1970), is a useful and thorough treatment of that incident; and Benjamin Labaree, *The Boston Tea Party** (1964), gives a fine account of the mob making tea in Boston's harbor. An older book, Arthur M. Schlesinger, *The Colonial Merchants and the American Revolution** (1918), contains much information on popular uprisings and merchant attitudes toward them. Finally, Niel J. Smelser, *Theory of Collective Behavior* (1963), is an excellent theoretical study of mass activity.

I is only natural that the riots and civil turbulence of the past decade and a half have awakened a new interest in the history of American mobs. It should be emphasized, however, that scholarly attention to the subject has roots independent of contemporary events and founded in long-developing historiographical trends. George Rudé's studies of pre-industrial crowds in France and England, E. J. Hobsbawm's discussion of "archaic" social movements, and recent works linking eighteenth-century American thought with English revolutionary tradition have all, in different ways, inspired a new concern among historians with colonial uprisings.[1] This discovery of the early American mob promises to have a significant effect upon historical interpretation. Particularly affected are the Revolutionary struggle and the early decades of the new nation, when events often turned upon well-known popular insurrections.

Eighteenth-century uprisings were in some important ways different than those of today—different in themselves, but even more in the political context within which they occurred. As a result they carried different connotations for the American Revolutionaries than they do today. Not all eighteenth-century mobs simply defied the law: some used extralegal means to implement official demands or to enforce laws not otherwise enforceable, others in effect extended the law in urgent situations beyond its technical limits. Since leading eighteenth-century Americans had known many occasions on which mobs took on the defense of the public welfare, which was, after all, the stated purpose of government, they were less likely to deny popular upheavals all legitimacy than are modern leaders. While not advocating popular uprisings, they could still grant such incidents an established and necessary role in free societies, one that made them an integral and even respected element of the political order. These attitudes, and the tradition of colonial insurrections on which they drew, not only shaped political events of the Revolutionary era, but also lay behind

FROM Pauline Maier, "Popular Uprisings and Civil Authority in Eighteenth-Century America," *William and Mary Quarterly,* XXVIII (January 1970), 3–35. Reprinted by permission.

[1] See the following by George Rudé: *The Crowd in the French Revolution* (Oxford, 1959); "The London 'Mob' of the Eighteenth Century," *The Historical Journal,* II (1959), 1–18; *Wilkes and Liberty: A Social Study of 1763 to 1774* (Oxford, 1962); *The Crowd in History: A Study of Popular Disturbances in France and England, 1730–1848* (New York, 1964). See also E. J. Hobsbawm, *Primitive Rebels: Studies in Archaic Forms of Social Movement in the 19th and 20th Centuries* (New York, 1959), esp. "The City Mob," 108–125. For recent discussions of the colonial mob see: Bernard Bailyn, *Pamphlets of the American Revolution* (Cambridge, Mass., 1965), I, 581–584; Jesse Lemisch, "Jack Tar in the Street: Merchant Seamen in the Politics of Revolutionary America," *William and Mary Quarterly,* 3d Ser., XXV (1968), 371–407; Gordon S. Wood, "A Note on Mobs in the American Revolution," *Wm. and Mary Qtly.,* 3d Ser., XXIII (1966), 635–642, and more recently Wood's *Creation of the American Republic, 1776–1787* (Chapel Hill, 1969), *passim,* but esp. 319–328. Wood offers an excellent analysis of the place of mobs and extralegal assemblies in the development of American constitutionalism. Hugh D. Graham and Ted R. Gurr, *Violence in America: Historical and Comparative Perspectives* (New York, 1969) primarily discusses uprisings of the 19th and 20th centuries, but see the chapters by Richard M. Brown, "Historical Patterns of Violence in America," 45–84, and "The American Vigilante Tradition," 154–226.

many laws and civil procedures that were framed during the 1780's and 1790's, some of which still have a place in the American legal system.

<h1 style="text-align:center">I</h1>

Not all colonial uprisings were identical in character or significance. Some involved no more than disorderly vandalism or traditional brawls such as those that annually marked Pope's Day on November 5, particularly in New England. Occasional insurrections defied established laws and authorities in the name of isolated private interests alone—a set of Hartford County, Connecticut, landowners arose in 1722, for example, after a court decision imperiled their particular land titles. Still others—which are of interest here—took on a broader purpose, and defended the interests of their community in general where established authorities failed to act.[2] This common characteristic linked otherwise diverse rural uprisings in New Jersey and the Carolinas. The insurrectionists' punishment of outlaws, their interposition to secure land titles or prevent abuses at the hands of legal officials, followed a frustration with established institutions and a belief that justice and even security had to be imposed by the people directly.[3] The earlier Virginia tobacco insurrection also illustrates this common pattern well: Virginians began tearing up young tobacco plants in 1682 only after Governor Thomas Culpeper forced the quick adjournment of their assembly, which had been called to curtail tobacco planting during an economic crisis. The insurrections in Massachusetts a little over a century later represent a variation on this theme. The insurgents in Worcester, Berkshire, Hampshire, Middlesex, and Bristol counties—often linked together as members of "Shays's Rebellion"—forced the closing of civil courts, which threatened to send a major portion of the local population to debtors' prison, only until a new legislature could remedy their pressing needs.[4]

This role of the mob as extralegal arm of the community's interest emerged, too, in repeated uprisings that occurred within the more densely settled coastal areas. The history of Boston, where by the mid-eighteenth century "public order . . . prevailed to a greater degree than anywhere else in England or America," is full of such incidents. During the food shortage of 1710, after the governor rejected a petition from the Boston selectmen calling for a temporary embargo on the exportation of foodstuffs one heavily laden ship found its

---

[2] Carl Bridenbaugh, *Cities in the Wilderness: The First Century of Urban Life in America, 1625–1742* (New York, 1964), 70–71, 223–224, 382–384; and Carl Bridenbaugh, *Cities in Revolt: Urban Life in America, 1743–1776* (New York, 1964), 113–118; Charles J. Hoadly, ed., *The Public Records of the Colony of Connecticut* . . . (Hartford, 1872), VI, 332–333, 341–348.

[3] See particularly Richard M. Brown, *The South Carolina Regulators* (Cambridge, Mass., 1963). There is no published study of the New Jersey land riots, which lasted over a decade and were due above all to the protracted inability of the royal government to settle land disputes stemming from conflicting proprietary grants made in the late 17th century. See, however, "A State of Facts concerning the Riots and Insurrections in New Jersey, and the Remedies Attempted to Restore the Peace of the Province," William A. Whitehead *et al.*, eds., *Archives of the State of New Jersey* (Newark, 1883), VII, 207–226. On other rural insurrections see Irving Mark, *Agrarian Conflicts in Colonial New York, 1711–1775* (New York, 1940), Chap. IV, V; Staughton Lynd, "The Tenant Rising at Livingston Manor," *New-York Historical Society Quarterly*, XLVIII (1964), 163–177; Matt Bushnell Jones, *Vermont in the Making, 1750–1777* (Cambridge, Mass., 1939), Chap. XII, XIII; John R. Dunbar, ed., *The Paxton Papers* (The Hague, 1957), esp. 3–51.

[4] Richard L. Morton, *Colonial Virginia* (Chapel Hill, 1960), I, 303–304; Jonathan Smith, "The Depression of 1785 and Daniel Shays' Rebellion," *Wm. and Mary Qtly.*, 3d Ser., V (1948), 86–87, 91.

rudder cut away, and fifty men sought to haul another outward bound vessel back to shore. Under similar circumstances Boston mobs again intervened to keep foodstuffs in the colony in 1713 and 1729. When there was some doubt a few years later whether or not the selectmen had the authority to seize a barn lying in the path of a proposed street, a group of townsmen, their faces blackened, levelled the structure and the road went through. Houses of ill fame were attacked by Boston mobs in 1734, 1737, and 1771; and in the late 1760's the *New York Gazette* claimed that mobs in Providence and Newport had taken on responsibility for "disciplining" unfaithful husbands. Meanwhile in New London, Connecticut, another mob prevented a radical religious sect, the Rogerenes, from disturbing normal Sunday services, "a practice they . . . [had] followed more or less for many years past; and which all the laws made in that government, and executed in the most judicious manner could not put a stop to."[5]

Threats of epidemic inspired particularly dramatic instances of this community oriented role of the mob. One revealing episode occurred in Massachusetts in 1773–1774. A smallpox hospital had been built on Essex Island near Marblehead "much against the will of the multitude" according to John Adams. "The patients were careless, some of them wantonly so; and others were suspected of designing to spread the smallpox in the town, which was full of people who had not passed through the distemper." In January 1774 patients from the hospital who tried to enter the town from unauthorized landing places were forcefully prevented from doing so; a hospital boat was burned; and four men suspected of stealing infected clothes from the hospital were tarred and feathered, then carted from Marblehead to Salem in a long cortege. The Marblehead town meeting finally won the proprietors' agreement to shut down the hospital; but after some twenty-two new cases of smallpox broke out in the town within a few days "apprehension became general," and some "Ruffians" in disguise hastened the hospital's demise by burning the nearly evacuated building. A military watch of forty men were needed for several nights to keep the peace in Marblehead.[6]

A similar episode occurred in Norfolk, Virginia, when a group of wealthy residents decided to have their families inoculated for smallpox. Fears arose that the lesser disease brought on by the inoculations would spread and necessitate a general inoculation, which would cost "more money than is circulating in Norfolk" and ruin trade and commerce such that "the whole colony would feel the effects." Local magistrates said they could not interfere because "the law was silent in the matter." Public and private meetings then sought to negotiate the issue. Despite a hard-won agreement, however, the pro-inoculation faction persisted in its original plan. Then finally a mob drove the newly inoculated women and children on a five-mile forced march in darkness and

[5] Bridenbaugh, *Cities in Revolt,* 114; Bridenbaugh, *Cities in the Wilderness,* 196, 383, 388–389; Edmund S. and Helen M. Morgan, *The Stamp Act Crisis,* rev. ed. (New York, 1963), 159; Anne Rowe Cunningham, ed., *Letters and Diary of John Rowe, Boston Merchant, 1759–1762, 1764–1779* (Boston, 1903), 218. On the marriage riots, see *New-York Gazette* (New York City), July 11, 1765—and note, that when the reporter speaks of persons "concern'd in such unlawful Enterprises" he clearly is referring to the husbands, not their "Disciplinarians." On the Rogerenes, see item in *Connecticut Gazette* (New Haven), Apr. 5, 1766, reprinted in Lawrence H. Gipson, *Jared Ingersoll* (New Haven, 1920), 195, n. 1.
[6] John Adams, "Novanglus," in Charles F. Adams, ed.. *The Works of John Adams* (Boston, 1850–1856), IV, 76–77; Salem news of Jan. 25 and Feb. 1, 1774, in *Providence Gazette* (Rhode Island), Feb. 5, and Feb. 12, 1774.

rain to the common Pest House, a three-year-old institution designed to isolate seamen and others, particularly Negroes, infected with smallpox.[7]

These local incidents indicate a willingness among many Americans to act outside the bounds of law, but they cannot be described as anti-authoritarian in any general sense. Sometimes in fact—as in the Boston bawdy house riot of 1734, or the Norfolk smallpox incident—local magistrates openly countenanced or participated in the mob's activities. Far from opposing established institutions, many supporters of Shays's Rebellion honored their leaders "by no less decisive marks of popular favor than elections to local offices of trust and authority."[8] It was above all the existence of such elections that forced local magistrates to reflect community feelings and so prevented their becoming the targets of insurrections. Certainly in New England, where the town meeting ruled, and to some extent in New York, where aldermen and councilmen were annually elected, this was true; yet even in Philadelphia, with its lethargic closed corporation, or Charleston, which lacked municipal institutions, authority was normally exerted by residents who had an immediate sense of local sentiment. Provincial governments were also for the most part kept alert to local feelings by their elected assemblies. Sometimes, of course, uprisings turned against domestic American institutions—as in Pennsylvania in 1764, when the "Paxton Boys" complained that the colony's Quaker assembly had failed to provide adequately for their defense against the Indians. But uprisings over local issues proved *extra-institutional* in character more often than they were anti-institutional; they served the community where no law existed, or intervened beyond what magistrates thought they could do officially to cope with a local problem.

The case was different when imperial authority was involved. There legal authority emanated from a capital an ocean away, where the colonists had no integral voice in the formation of policy, where governmental decisions were based largely upon the reports of "king's men" and sought above all to promote the king's interests. When London's legal authority and local interest conflicted, efforts to implement the edicts of royal officials were often answered by uprisings, and it was not unusual in these cases for local magistrates to participate or openly sympathize with the insurgents. The colonial response to the White Pines Acts of 1722 and 1729 is one example. Enforcement of the acts was difficult in general because "the various elements of colonial society . . . seemed inclined to violate the pine laws—legislatures, lumbermen, and merchants were against them, and even the royal governors were divided." At Exeter, New Hampshire, in 1734 about thirty men prevented royal officials from putting the king's broad arrow on some seized boards; efforts to enforce the acts in Connecticut during the 1750's ended after a deputy of the surveyor-general was thrown in a pond and nearly drowned; five years later logs seized in Massachusetts and New Hampshire were either "rescued" or destroyed.[9]

[7] Letter from "Friend to the Borough and county of Norfolk," in Purdie and Dixon's *Virginia Gazette Postscript* (Williamsburg), Sept. 8, 1768, which gives the fullest account. This letter answered an earlier letter from Norfolk, Aug. 6, 1768, available in Rind's *Va. Gaz. Supplement* (Wmsbg.), Aug. 25, 1768. See also letter of Cornelius Calvert in Purdie and Dixon's *Va. Gaz.* (Wmsbg.), Jan. 9, 1772. Divisions over the inoculation seemed to follow more general political lines. See Patrick Henderson, "Smallpox and Patriotism, The Norfolk Riots, 1768–1769," *Virginia Magazine of History and Biography*, LXXIII (1965), 413–424.

[8] James Madison to Thomas Jefferson, Mar. 19, 1787, in Julian P. Boyd, ed., *The Papers of Thomas Jefferson* (Princeton, 1950–), XI, 223.

[9] Bernhard Knollenberg, *Origin of the American Revolution: 1759–1766* (New York, 1965),

Two other imperial issues that provoked local American uprisings long before 1765 and continued to do so during the Revolutionary period were impressment and customs enforcement.

As early as 1743 the colonists' violent opposition to impressment was said to indicate a "Contempt of Government." Some captains had been mobbed, the Admiralty complained, "others emprisoned, and afterwards held to exorbitant Bail, and are now under Prosecutions carried on by Combination, and by joint Subscription towards the expense." Colonial governors, despite their offers, furnished captains with little real aid either to procure seamen or "even to protect them from the Rage and Insults of the People." Two days of severe rioting answered Commodore Charles Knowles's efforts to sweep Boston harbor for able-bodied men in November 1747. Again in 1764 when Rear Admiral Lord Alexander Colville sent out orders to "procure" men in principal harbors between Casco Bay and Cape Henlopen, mobs met the ships at every turn. When the St. John sent out a boat to seize a recently impressed deserter from a Newport wharf, a mob protected him, captured the boat's officer, and hurled stones at the crew; later fifty Newporters joined the colony's gunner at Fort George in opening fire on the king's ship itself. Under threat to her master the Chaleur was forced to release four fishermen seized off Long Island, and when that ship's captain went ashore at New York a mob seized his boat and burned it in the Fields. In the spring of 1765 after the Maidstone capped a six-month siege of Newport harbor by seizing "all the Men" out of a brigantine from Africa, a mob of about five hundred men similarly seized a ship's officer and burned one of her boats on the Common. Impressment also met mass resistance at Norfolk in 1767 and was a major cause of the famous Liberty riot at Boston in 1768.[10]

Like the impressment uprisings, which in most instances sought to protect or rescue men from the "press," customs incidents were aimed at impeding the customs service in enforcing British laws. Tactics varied, and although incidents occurred long before 1764—in 1719, for example, Caleb Heathcote reported a "riotous and tumultuous" rescue of seized claret by Newporters—their frequency, like those of the impressment "riots," apparently increased after the Sugar Act was passed and customs enforcement efforts were tightened. The 1764 rescue of the Rhoda in Rhode Island preceded a theft in Dighton, Massachusetts, of the cargo from a newly seized vessel, the Polly, by a mob of some forty men with blackened faces. In 1766 again a mob stoned a customs official's

126, 129. See also Robert G. Albion, Forests and Sea Power (Cambridge, Mass., 1926), 262–263, 265. Joseph J. Malone, Pine Trees and Politics (Seattle, 1964), includes less detail on the forceful resistance to the acts.

[10] Admiralty to Gov. George Thomas, Sept. 26, 1743, in Samuel Hazard et al., eds., Pennsylvania Archives (Philadelphia, 1852–1949), I, 639. For accounts of the Knowles riot, see Gov. William Shirley to Josiah Willard, Nov. 19, 1747, Shirley's Proclamation of Nov. 21, 1747, and his letter to the Board of Trade, Dec. 1, 1747, in Charles H. Lincoln, ed., The Correspondence of William Shirley . . . 1731–1760 (New York, 1912), I, 406–419; see also Thomas Hutchinson, History of the Province of Massachusetts Bay, ed. Lawrence S. Mayo (Cambridge, Mass., 1936), II, 330–333; and Reports of the Record Commissioners of Boston (Boston, 1885), XIV, 127–130. David Lovejoy, Rhode Island Politics and the American Revolution, 1760–1776 (Providence, 1958), 36–39, and on the Maidstone in particular see "O. G." in Newport Mercury (Rhode Island), June 10, 1765. Bridenbaugh, Cities in Revolt, 309–311; documents on the St. John episode in Records of the Colony of Rhode Island and Providence Plantations (Providence, 1856–1865), VI, 427–430. George G. Wolkins, "The Seizure of John Hancock's Sloop 'Liberty,'" Massachusetts Historical Society, Proceedings (1921–1923), LV, 239–284. See also Lemisch, "Jack Tar," Wm. and Mary Qtly., 3d Ser., XXV (1968), 391–393; and Neil R. Stout, "Manning the Royal Navy in North America, 1763–1775," American Neptune, XXIII (1963), 179–181.

home in Falmouth (Portland), Maine, while "Persons unknown and disguised" stole sugar and rum that had been impounded that morning. The intimidation of customs officials and of the particularly despised customs informers also enjoyed a long history. In 1701 the South Carolina attorney general publicly attacked an informer "and struck him several times, crying out, this is the Informer, this is he that will ruin the country." Similar assaults occurred decades later, in New Haven in 1766 and 1769, and New London in 1769, and were then often distinguished by their brutality. In 1771 a Providence tidesman, Jesse Saville, was seized, stripped, bound hand and foot, tarred and feathered, had dirt thrown in his face, then was beaten and "almost strangled." Even more thorough assaults upon two other Rhode Island tidesmen followed in July 1770 and upon Collector Charles Dudley in April 1771. Finally, customs vessels came under attack: the *St. John* was shelled at Newport in 1764 where the customs ship *Liberty* was sunk in 1769—both episodes that served as prelude to the destruction of the *Gaspée* outside Providence in 1772.[11]

Such incidents were not confined to New England. Philadelphia witnessed some of the most savage attacks, and even the surveyor of Sassafras and Bohemia in Maryland—an office long a sinecure, since no ships entered or cleared in Sassafras or Bohemia—met with violence when he tried to execute his office in March 1775. After seizing two wagons of goods being carried overland from Maryland toward Duck Creek, Delaware, the officer was overpowered by a "licentious mob" that kept shouting "Liberty and Duck Creek forever" as it went through the hours-long rituals of tarring and feathering him and threatening his life. And at Norfolk, Virginia, in the spring 1766 an accused customs informer was tarred and feathered, pelted with stones and rotten eggs, and finally thrown in the sea where he nearly drowned. Even Georgia saw customs violence before independence, and one of the rare deaths resulting from a colonial riot occurred there in 1775.[12]

[11] Heathcote letter from Newport, Sept. 7, 1719, *Records of the Colony of Rhode Island*, IV, 259–260; Lovejoy, *Rhode Island Politics*, 35–39. There is an excellent summary of the *Polly* incident in Morgan, *Stamp Act Crisis*, 59, 64–67; and see also *Providence Gaz.* (R.I.), Apr. 27, 1765. On the Falmouth incident see the letter from the collector and comptroller of Falmouth, Aug. 19, 1766, Treasury Group 1, Class 453, Piece 182, Public Records Office. Hereafter cited as T. 1/453, 182. See also the account in Appendix I of Josiah Quincy, Jr., *Reports of the Cases Argued and Adjudged in the Superior Court of Judicature of the Province of Massachusetts Bay, between 1761 and 1772* (Boston, 1865), 446–447. W. Noel Sainsbury *et al.*, eds. *Calendar of State Papers, Colonial Series, America and the West Indies* (London, 1910), *1701*, no. 1042, xi, a. A summary of one of the New Haven informer attacks is in Willard M. Wallace, *Traitorous Hero: The Life and Fortunes of Benedict Arnold* (New York, 1954), 20–23. Arnold's statement on the affair which he led is in Malcolm Decker, *Benedict Arnold, Son of the Havens* (Tarrytown, N.Y., 1932), 27–29. Gipson, in *Jared Ingersoll*, 277–278, relates the later incidents. For the New London informer attacks, see documents of July 1769 in T. 1/471. On the Saville affair see Saville to collector and comptroller of customs in Newport, May 18, 1769. T. 1/471, and *New York Journal* (New York City), July 6, 1769. On later Rhode Island incidents see Dudley and John Nicoll to governor of Rhode Island, Aug. 1, 1770, T. 1/471. Dudley to commissioners of customs at Boston, Newport, Apr. 11, 1771, T. 1/482. On the destruction of the *Liberty* see documents in T. 1/471, esp. comptroller and collector to the governor, July 21, 1769.

[12] On Philadelphia violence see William Sheppard to commissioners of customs, Apr. 21, 1769, T. 1/471; Deputy Collector at Philadelphia John Swift to commissioners of customs at Boston, Oct. 13, 1769, *ibid.*; and on a particularly brutal attack on the son of customsman John Hatton, see Deputy Collector John Swift to Boston customs commissioners, Nov. 15, 1770, and related documents in T. 1/476. See also Alfred S. Martin, "The King's Customs: Philadelphia, 1763–1774," *Wm. and Mary Qtly.*, 3d Ser., V (1948), 201–216. Documents on the Maryland episode are in T. 1/513, including the following: Richard Reeve to Grey Cooper, Apr. 19, 1775; extracts from a Council meeting. Mar. 16, 1775; deposition of Robert Stratford Byrne, surveyor of His Majesty's Customs at Sassafras and Bohemia, and Byrne to customs commissioners, Mar. 17, 1775. On the Virginia incident see William Smith to Jeremiah Morgan, Apr. 3, 1766. Colonial

White Pines, impressment, and customs uprisings have attracted historians' attention because they opposed British authority and so seemed to presage the Revolution. In fact, however, they had much in common with many exclusively local uprisings. In each of the incidents violence was directed not so much against the "rich and powerful"[13] as against men who—as it was said after the Norfolk smallpox incident—"in every part of their conduct . . . acted very inconsistently as good neighbors or citizens." The effort remained one of safeguarding not the interests of isolated groups alone, but the community's safety and welfare. The White Pines Acts need not have provoked this opposition had they applied only to trees of potential use to the Navy, and had they been framed and executed with concern for colonial rights. But instead the acts reserved to the Crown all white pine trees including those "utterly unfit for masts, yards, or bowsprits," and prevented colonists from using them for building materials or lumber exportation even in regions where white pine constituted the principal forest growth. As a result the acts "operated so much against the convenience and even necessities of the inhabitants," Surveyor John Wentworth explained, that "it became almost a general interest of the country" to frustrate the acts' execution. Impressment offered a more immediate effect, since the "press" could quickly cripple whole towns. Merchants and masters were affected as immediately as seamen: the targeted port, as Massachusetts' Governor William Shirley explained in 1747, was drained of mariners by both impressment itself and the flight of navigation to safer provinces, driving the wages for any remaining seamen upward. When the press was of long duration, moreover, or when it took place during a normally busy season, it could mean serious shortages of food or firewood for winter, and a general attrition of the commercial life that sustained all strata of society in trading towns. Commerce seemed even more directly attacked by British trade regulations, particularly by the proliferation of customs procedures in the mid-1760's that seemed to be in no American's interest, and by the Sugar Act with its virtual prohibition of the trade with the foreign West Indies that sustained the economies of colonies like Rhode Island. As a result even when only a limited contingent of sailors participated in a customs incident officials could suspect—as did the deputy collector at Philadelphia in 1770—that the mass of citizens "in their Hearts" approved of it.[14]

Because the various uprisings discussed here grew out of concerns essential

Office Group, Class 5, Piece 1331, 80, Public Record Office. Hereafter cited as C. O. 5/1331, 80. W. W. Abbot, *The Royal Governors of Georgia, 1754–1775* (Chapel Hill, 1959), 174–175. These customs riots remained generally separate from the more central intercolonial opposition to Britain that emerged in 1765. Isolated individuals like John Brown of Providence and Maximilian Calvert of Norfolk were involved in both the organized intercolonial Sons of Liberty and in leading mobs against customs functionaries or informers. These roles, however, for the most part were unconnected, that is, there was no radical program of customs obstruction *per se*. Outbreaks were above all local responses to random provocations and, at least before the Townshend duties, usually devoid of explicit ideological justifications.

13 Hobsbawm, *Primitive Rebels*, 111. For a different effort to see class division as relevant in 18th century uprisings, see Lemisch, "Jack Tar," *Wm. and Mary Qtly.*, 3d Ser., XXV (1968), 387.

14 "Friends to the borough and county of Norfolk," Purdie and Dixon's *Va. Gaz. Postscrpt.* (Wmsbg.), Sept. 8, 1768. Wentworth quoted in Knollenberg, *Origin of American Revolution*, 124–125. Lemisch, "Jack Tar," *Wm. and Mary Qtly.*, 3d Ser., XXV (1968), 383–385. Shirley to Duke of New Castle, Dec. 31, 1747, in Lincoln, ed., *Shirley Correspondence*, I, 420–423. Dora Mae Clark, "The Impressment of Seamen in the American Colonies," *Essays in Colonial History Presented to Charles McLean Andrews* (New Haven, 1931), 199–200; John Swift to Boston customs commissioners, Nov. 15, 1770, T. 1/476.

to wide sections of the community, the "rioters" were not necessarily confined to the seamen, servants, Negroes, and boys generally described as the staple components of the colonial mob. The uprising of Exeter, New Hampshire, townsmen against the king's surveyor of the woods in 1754 was organized by a member of the prominent Gillman family who was a mill owner and a militia officer. Members of the upper classes participated in Norfolk's smallpox uprising, and Cornelius Calvert, who was later attacked in a related incident, protested that leading members of the community, doctors and magistrates, had posted securities for the good behavior of the "Villains" convicted of mobbing him. Captain Jeremiah Morgan complained about the virtually universal participation of Norfolkers in an impressment incident of 1767, and "all the principal Gentlemen in Town" were supposedly present when a customs informer was tarred and feathered there in 1766. Merchant Benedict Arnold admitted leading a New Haven mob against an informer in 1766; New London merchants Joseph Packwood and Nathaniel Shaw commanded the mob that first accosted Captain William Reid the night the *Liberty* was destroyed at Newport in 1769, just as John Brown, a leading Providence merchant, led that against the *Gaspée*. Charles Dudley reported in April 1771 that the men who beat him in Newport "did not come from the . . . lowest class of Men," but were "stiled Merchants and the Masters of their Vessels"; and again in 1775 Robert Stratford Byrne said many of his Maryland and Pennsylvania attackers were "from Appearance . . . Men of Property." It is interesting, too, that during Shays's Rebellion—so often considered a class uprising—"men who were of good property and owed not a shilling" were said to be "involved in the train of desperado's to suppress the courts."[15]

Opposition to impressment and customs enforcement in itself was not, moreover, the only cause of the so-called impressment or customs "riots." The complete narratives of these incidents indicate again not only that the crowd acted to support local interests, but that it sometimes enforced the will of local magistrates by extralegal means. Although British officials blamed the *St. John* incident upon that ship's customs and impressment activities, colonists insisted that the confrontation began when some sailors stole a few pigs and chickens from a local miller and the ship's crew refused to surrender the thieves to Newport officials. Two members of the Rhode Island council then ordered the gunner of Fort George to detain the schooner until the accused seamen were delivered to the sheriff, and "many People went over the Fort to assist the Gunner in the Discharge of his Duty." Only after this uprising did the ship's officers surrender the accused men.[16] Similarly, the 1747 Knowles impressment

    [15] Malone, *White Pines,* 112. "Friends to the borough and county of Norfolk," Purdie and Dixon's *Va. Gaz. Postscript.* (Wmsbg.), Sept. 8, 1768; Calvert letter, *ibid.,* Jan. 9, 1772. Capt. Jeremiah Morgan, quoted in Lemisch, "Jack Tar," *Wm. and Mary Qtly.,* 3d Ser., XXV (1968), 391; and William Smith to Morgan, Apr. 3, 1766, C. O. 5/1331, 80. Decker, *Benedict Arnold,* 27–29; deposition of Capt. William Reid on the *Liberty* affair, July 21, 1769, T. 1/471; Ephraim Bowen's narrative on the *Gaspée* affair, *Records of the Colony of Rhode Island,* VII, 68–73; Charles Dudley to Boston customs commissioners, Apr. 11, 1771, T. 1/482, and deposition by Byrne, T. 1/513. Edward Carrington to Jefferson, June 9, 1787, Boyd, ed., *Jefferson Papers,* XI, 408; and see also Smith, "Depression of 1785," *Wm. and Mary Qtly.,* 3d Ser., V (1948), 88—of the 21 men indicted for treason in Worcester during the court's April term 1787, 15 were "gentlemen" and only 6 "yeomen."

    [16] Gov. Samuel Ward's report to the Treasury lords, Oct. 23, 1765, Ward Manuscripts, Box 1, fol. 58, Rhode Island Historical Society, Providence. See also deposition of Daniel Vaughn of Newport—Vaughn was the gunner at Fort George—July 8, 1764, Chalmers Papers, Rhode Island, fol. 41, New York Public Library, New York City. For British official accounts of the affair, see

riot in Boston and the 1765 *Maidstone* impressment riot in Newport broke out after the governors' request for the release of impressed seamen had gone unanswered, and only after the outbreaks of violence were the governors' requests honored. The crowd that first assembled on the night the *Liberty* was destroyed in Newport also began by demanding the allegedly drunken sailors who that afternoon had abused and shot at a colonial captain, Joseph Packwood, so they could be bound over to local magistrates for prosecution.[17]

In circumstances such as these, the "mob" often appeared only after the legal channels of redress had proven inadequate. The main thrust of the colonists' resistance to the White Pines Acts had always been made in their courts and legislatures. Violence broke out only in local situations where no alternative was available. Even the burning of the *Gaspée* in June 1772 was a last resort. Three months before the incident a group of prominent Providence citizens complained about the ship's wanton severity with all vessels along the coast and the colony's governor pressed their case with the fleet's admiral. The admiral, however, supported the *Gaspée's* commander, Lieutenant William Dudingston; and thereafter, the *Providence Gazette* reported, Dudingston became "more haughty, insolent and intolerable, . . . personally ill treating every master and merchant of the vessels he boarded, stealing sheep, hogs, poultry, etc. from farmers round the bay, and cutting down their fruit and other trees for firewood." Redress from London was possible but time-consuming, and in the meantime Rhode Island was approaching what its governor called "the deepest calamity" as supplies of food and fuel were curtailed and prices, especially in Newport, rose steeply. It was significant that merchant John Brown finally led the Providence "mob" that seized the moment in June when the *Gaspée* ran aground near Warwick, for it was he who had spearheaded the effort in March 1772 to win redress through the normal channels of government.[18]

II

There was little that was distinctively American about the colonial insurrections. The uprisings over grain exportations during times of dearth, the attacks on brothels, press gangs, royal forest officials, and customsmen, all had their counterparts in seventeenth- and eighteenth-century England. Even the Americans' hatred of the customs establishment mirrored the Englishman's traditional loathing of excise men. Like the customsmen in the colonies, they seemed

---

Lieut. Hill's version in James Munro, ed., *Acts of the Privy Council of England, Colonial Series* (London, 1912), VI, 374–376, and the report of John Robinson and John Nicoll to the customs commissioners, Aug. 30, 1765, Privy Council Group, Class I, Piece 51, Bundle 1 (53a), Public Record Office. Hill, whose report was drawn up soon after the incident, does not contradict Ward's narrative, but seems oblivious of any warrant-granting process on shore; Robinson and Nicoll—whose report was drawn up over a year later, and in the midst of the Stamp Act turmoil—claimed that a recent customs seizure had precipitated the attack upon the *St. John*.

[17] On the Knowles and *Maidstone* incidents see above, n. 10. On the *Liberty* affair see documents in T. 1/471, esp. the deposition of Capt. William Reid, July 21, 1769, and that of John Carr, the second mate, who indicates that the mob soon forgot its scheme of delivering the crew members to the magistrates.

[18] Malone, *White Pines*, 8–9, and *passim*. *Records of the Colony of Rhode Island*, VII, 60, 62–63, 174–175, including the deposition of Dep. Gov. Darius Sessions, June 12, 1772, and Adm. Montagu to Gov. Wanton, Apr. 8, 1772. Also, Wanton to Hillsborough, June 16, 1772, and Ephraim Bowen's narrative, *ibid.*, 63–73, 90–92. *Providence Gaz.* (R.I.), Jan. 9, 1773.

to descend into localities armed with extraordinary prerogative powers. Often, too, English excisemen were "thugs and brutes who beat up their victims without compunction or stole or wrecked their property" and against whose extravagances little redress was possible through the law.[19] Charges of an identical character were made in the colonies against customsmen and naval officials as well, particularly after 1763 when officers of the Royal Navy were commissioned as deputy members of the customs service,[20] and a history of such accusations lay behind many of the best-known waterfront insurrections. The Americans' complaints took on particular significance only because in the colonies those officials embodied the authority of a "foreign" power. Their arrogance and abritrariness helped effect "an estrangement of the Affections of the People from the Authority under which they act," and eventually added an emotional element of anger against the Crown to the revolutionary conflict otherwise carried on in the language of law and right.[21]

The focused character of colonial uprisings also resembled those in England and even France where, Rudé has pointed out, crowds were remarkably single-minded and discriminating.[22] Targets were characteristically related to grievances: the Knowles rioters sought only the release of the impressed men; they set free a captured officer when assured he had nothing to do with the press, and refrained from burning a boat near Province House for fear the fire would spread. The Norfolk rioters, driven by fear of smallpox, forcefully isolated the inoculated persons where they would be least dangerous. Even the customs rioters vented their brutality on customs officers and informers alone, and the Shaysite "mobs" dispersed after closing the courts which promised most immediately to effect their ruin. So domesticated and controlled was the Boston mob that it refused to riot on Saturday and Sunday nights, which were considered holy by New Englanders.[23]

When colonists compared their mobs with those in the Mother Country they were struck only with the greater degree of restraint among Americans. "These People bear no Resemblance to an English Mob," John Jay wrote of the Shaysites in December 1786, "they are more temperate, cool and regular in their Conduct—they have hitherto abstained from Plunder, nor have they that I know of committed any outrages but such as the accomplishment of their

---

[19] Max Beloff, *Public Order and Popular Disturbances, 1660–1714* (London, 1938), *passim;* Albion, *Forests and Sea Power,* 263; J. H. Plumb, *England in the Eighteenth Century* (Baltimore, 1961 [orig. publ., Oxford, 1950]), 66.

[20] See, for example, "A Pumkin" in the *New London Gazette* (Connecticut), May 14, 18, 1773; "O. G." in *Newport Merc.* (R.I.), June 10, 1765; *New London Gaz.* (Conn.), Sept. 22, 1769; complaints of Marylander David Bevan, reprinted in Rind's *Va. Gaz.* (Wmsbg.), July 27, 1769, and *New London Gaz.* (Conn.), July 21, 1769. Stout, "Manning the Royal Navy," *American Neptune,* XXIII (1963), 174. For a similar accusation against a surveyor-general of the king's woods, see Albion, *Forests and Sea Power,* 262.

[21] Joseph Reed to the president of Congress, Oct. 21, 1779, in Hazard *et al.,* eds. *Pennsylvania Archives,* VII, 762. Five years earlier Reed had tried to impress upon Lord Dartmouth the importance of constraining Crown agents in the colonies if any reconciliation were to be made between Britain and the colonies. See his letter to Earl of Dartmouth, Apr. 4, 1774, in William B. Reed, *Life and Correspondence of Joseph Reed* (Philadelphia, 1847), I, 56–57. For a similar plea, again from a man close to the American Revolutionary leadership, see Stephen Sayre to Lord Dartmouth, Dec. 13, 1766, Dartmouth Papers, D 1778/2/258, William Salt Library, Stafford, England.

[22] Rudé, *Crowd in History,* 60, 253–254. The restraint exercised by 18th century mobs has often been commented upon. See, for example, Wood, "A Note on Mobs," *Wm. and Mary Qtly.,* 3d Ser., XXIII (1966), 636–637.

[23] Joseph Harrison's testimony in Wolkins, "Seizure of Hancock's Sloop 'Liberty,' " Mass. Hist. Soc., *Proceedings,* LV, 254.

Purpose made necessary." Similar comparisons were often repeated during the Revolutionary conflict, and were at least partially grounded in fact. When Londoners set out to "pull down" houses of ill fame in 1688, for example, the affair spread, prisons were opened, and disorder ended only when troops were called out. But when eighteenth-century Bostonians set out on the same task, there is no record that their destruction extended beyond the bordellos themselves. Even the violence of the customs riots—which contrast in that regard from other American incidents—can sometimes be explained by the presence of volatile foreign seamen. The attack on the son of customsman John Hatton, who was nearly killed in a Philadelphia riot, occurred, for example, when the city was crowded by over a thousand seamen. His attackers were apparently Irish crew members of a vessel he and his father had tried to sieze off Cape May, and they were "set on," the Philadelphia collector speculated, by an Irish merchant in Philadelphia to whom the vessel was consigned. One of the most lethal riots in the history of colonial America, in which rioters killed five people, occurred in a small town near Norfolk, Virginia, and was significantly perpetrated entirely by British seamen who resisted the local inhabitants' efforts to reinstitute peace.[24] During and immediately after the Revolutionary War some incidents occurred in which deaths are recorded; but contemporaries felt these were historical aberrations, caused by the "brutalizing" effect of the war itself. "Our citizens, from a habit of putting . . . [the British] to death, have reconciled their minds to the killing of each other," South Carolina Judge Aedanus Burke explained.[25]

To a large extent the pervasive restraint and virtual absence of bloodshed in American incidents can best be understood in terms of social and military circumstance. There was no large amorphous city in America comparable to London, where England's worst incidents occurred. More important, the casualties even in eighteenth-century British riots were rarely the work of rioters. No deaths were inflicted by the Wilkes, Anti-Irish, or "No Popery" mobs, and only single fatalities resulted from other upheavals such as the Porteous riots of 1736. "It was authority rather than the crowd that was conspicuous for its violence to life and limb": all 285 casualties of the Gordon riots, for example, were rioters.[26] Since a regular army was less at the ready for use against colonial mobs, casualty figures for American uprisings were naturally much reduced.

To some extent the general tendency toward a discriminating purposefulness was shared by mobs throughout western Europe, but within the British Em-

[24] Jay to Jefferson, Dec. 14, 1786, Boyd, ed., *Jefferson Papers*, X, 597. Beloff, *Public Order*, 30. John Swift to Boston customs commissioners, Nov. 15, 1770, Gov. William Franklin's Proclamation Nov. 17, 1770, and John Hatton to Boston custom commissioners, Nov. 20, 1770, T. 1/476. The last mentioned riot occurred in November 1762. A cartel ship from Havana had stopped for repairs in October. On Nov. 21 a rumor spread that the Spaniards were murdering the inhabitants, which drew seamen from His Majesty's ship, *Arundel*, also in the harbor, into town, where the seamen drove the Spaniards into a house, set fire to it, and apparently intended to blow it up. A dignitary of the Spanish colonial service, who had been a passenger on the cartel ship, was beaten and some money and valuables were stolen from him. Local men tried to quell the riot without success. It was eventually put down by militiamen from Norfolk. See "A Narrative of a Riot in Virginia in November 1762," T. 1/476.
[25] Burke and others to the same effect, quoted in Jerome J. Nadelhaft, "The Revolutionary Era in South Carolina, 1775–1788" (unpubl. Ph.D. diss., University of Wisconsin, 1965), 151–152. See also account of the "Fort Wilson" riot of October 1779 in J. Thomas Scharf and Thompson Westcott, *History of Philadelphia, 1609–1884* (Philadelphia, 1884), I, 401–403.
[26] Rudé, *Crowd in History*, 255–257.

pire the focused character of popular uprisings and also their persistence can be explained in part by the character of law enforcement procedures. There were no professional police forces in the eighteenth century. Instead the power of government depended traditionally upon institutions like the "hue and cry," by which the community in general rose to apprehend felons. In its original medieval form the "hue and cry" was a form of summary justice that resembled modern lynch law. More commonly by the eighteenth century magistrates turned to the *posse commitatus,* literally the "power of the country," and in practice all able-bodied men a sheriff might call upon to assist him. Where greater and more organized support was needed, magistrates could call out the militia.[27] Both the *posse* and the militia drew upon local men, including many of the same persons who made up the mob. This was particularly clear where these traditional mechanisms failed to function effectively. At Boston in September 1766 when customsmen contemplated breaking into the house of merchant Daniel Malcom to search for contraband goods, Sheriff Stephen Greenleaf threatened to call for support from members of the very crowd suspected of an intent to riot; and when someone suggested during the Stamp Act riots that the militia be raised Greenleaf was told it had already risen. This situation meant that mobs could naturally assume the manner of a lawful institution, acting by habit with relative restraint and responsibility. On the other hand, the militia institutionalized the practice of forcible popular coercion and so made the formation of extralegal mobs more natural that J. R. Western has called the militia "a relic of the bad old days," and hailed its passing as "a step towards . . . bringing civilization and humanity into our [English] political life."[28]

These law enforcement mechanisms left magistrates virtually helpless whenever a large segment of the population was immediately involved in the disorder, or when the community had a strong sympathy for the rioters. The Boston militia's failure to act in the Stamp Act riots, which was repeated in nearly all the North American colonies, recapitulated a similar refusal during the Knowles riot of 1747.[29] If the mob's sympathizers were confined to a single locality, the governor could try to call out the militias of surrounding areas, as Massachusetts Governor William Shirley began to do in 1747, and as, to some extent, Governor Francis Bernard attempted after the rescue of the *Polly* in 1765.[30] In the case of sudden uprisings, however, these peace-keeping mecha-

27 On the "hue and cry" see Frederick Pollock and Frederic W. Maitland, *The History of English Law before the Time of Edward I* (Cambridge, Eng., 1968 [orig. publ., Cambridge, Eng., 1895]), II, 578–580, and William Blackstone, *Commentaries on the Laws of England* (Philadelphia, 1771), IV, 290–291. John Shy, *Toward Lexington: The Role of the British Army in the Coming of the American Revolution* (Princeton, 1965), 40. The English militia underwent a period of decay after 1670 but was revived in 1757. See J. R. Western, *The English Militia in the Eighteenth Century* (London, 1965).

28 Greenleaf's deposition, T. 1/446; *Providence Gaz.* (R.I.), Aug. 24, 1765. Western, *English Militia,* 74.

29 Gov. William Shirley explained the militia's failure to appear during the opening stages of the Knowles riot by citing the militiamen's opposition to impressment and consequent sympathy for the rioters. See his letter to the Lords of Trade, Dec. 1, 1747, in Lincoln, ed., *Shirley Correspondence,* I, 417–418. The English militia was also unreliable. It worked well against invasions and unpopular rebellions, but was less likely to support the government when official orders "clashed with the desires of the citizens" or when ordered to protect unpopular minorities. Sir Robert Walpole believed "that if called on to suppress smuggling, protect the turnpikes, or enforce the gin act, the militia would take the wrong side." Western, *English Militia,* 72–73.

30 Shirley to Josiah Willard, Nov. 19, 1747, Lincoln, ed., *Shirley Correspondence,* I, 407; Bernard's orders in *Providence Gaz.* (R.I.), Apr. 27, 1765.

nisms were at best partially effective since they required time to assemble strength, which often made the effort wholly pointless.

When the disorder continued and the militia either failed to appear or proved insufficient, there was, of course, the army, which was used periodically in the eighteenth century against rioters in England and Scotland. Even in America peacetime garrisons tended to be placed where they might serve to maintain law and order. But since all Englismen shared a fear of standing armies the deployment of troops had always to be a sensitive and carefully limited recourse. Military and civil spheres of authority were rigidly separated, as was clear to Lord Jeffrey Amherst, who refused to use soldiers against anti-military rioters during the Seven Years' War because that function was "entirely foreign to their command and belongs of right to none but the civil power." In fact troops could be used against British subjects, as in the suppression of civil disorder, only upon the request of local magistrates. This institutional inhibition carried, if anything, more weight in the colonies. There royal governors had quickly lost their right to declare martial law without the consent of the provincial councils that were, again, usually filled with local men.[31]

For all practical purposes, then, when a large political unit such as an entire town or colony condoned an act of mass force, problems were raised "almost insoluble without rending the whole fabric of English law." Nor was the situation confined to the colonies. After describing England's institutions for keeping the peace under the later Stuarts, Max Beloff suggested that no technique for maintaining order was found until nineteenth-century reformers took on the task of reshaping urban government. Certainly by the 1770's no acceptable solution had been found—neither by any colonists, nor "anyone in London, Paris, or Rome, either," as Carl Bridenbaugh has put it. To even farsighted contemporaries like John Adams the weakness of authority was a fact of the social order that necessarily conditioned the way rulers could act. "It is vain to expect or hope to carry on government against the universal bent and genius of the people," he wrote, "we may whimper and whine as much as we will, but nature made it impossible when she made man."[32]

The mechanisms of enforcing public order were rendered even more fragile since the difference between legal and illegal applications of mass force was distinct in theory, but sometimes indistinguishable in practice. The English common law prohibited riot, defined as an uprising of three or more persons who performed what Blackstone called an "unlawful act of violence" for a private purpose. If the act was never carried out or attempted the offense became unlawful assembly; if some effort was made toward its execution, rout; and if the purpose of the uprising was public rather than private—tearing down whore houses, for example, or destroying all enclosures rather than just those personally affecting the insurgents—the offense became treason since it constituted a usurpation of the king's function, a "levying war against the King." The precise legal offense lay not so much in the purpose of the uprising as in its use of force and violence "wherein the Law does not allow the Use of such Force." Such unlawful assumptions of force were carefully distinguished by commentators upon the common law from other occasions on which the law

<hr />

[31] Shy, *Toward Lexington*, 39–40, 44, 47, 74. Amherst, quoted in J. C. Long, *Lord Jeffery Amherst* (New York, 1933), 124.

[32] Shy, *Toward Lexington*, 44; Beloff, *Public Order*, 157–158; Bridenbaugh, *Cities in Revolt*, 297; C. F. Adams, ed., *Works of Adams*, IV, 74–75, V, 209.

authorized a use of force. It was, for example, legal for force to be used by a sheriff, constable, "or perhaps even . . . a private Person" who assembled "a competent Number of People, in Order with Force to suppress Rebels, or Enemies, or Rioters"; for a justice of the peace to raise the *posse* when opposed in detaining lands, or for Crown officers to raise "a Power as may effectually enable them to over-power any . . . Resistance" in the execution of the King's writs.[33]

In certain situations these distinctions offered at best a very uncertain guide as to who did or did not exert force lawfully. Should a *posse* employ more force than was necessary to overcome overt resistance, for example, its members acted illegally and were indictable for riot. And where established officials supported both sides in a confrontation, or where the legality of an act that officials were attempting to enforce was itself disputed, the decision as to who were or were not rioters seemed to depend upon the observer's point of view. Impressment is a good example. The colonists claimed that impressment was unlawful in North America under an act of 1708, while British authorities and some—but not all—spokesmen for the government held that the law had lapsed in 1713. The question was settled only in 1775, when Parliament finally repealed the "Sixth of Anne." Moreover, supposing impressment could indeed be carried on, were press warrants from provincial authorities still necessary? Royal instructions of 1697 had given royal governors the "sole power of impressing seamen in any of our plantations in America or in sight of them." Admittedly that clause was dropped in 1708, and a subsequent parliamentary act of 1746, which required the full consent of the governor and council before impressment could be carried on within their province, applied only to the West Indies. Nonetheless it seems that in 1764 the Lords of the Admiralty thought the requirement held throughout North America.[34] With the legality of impressment efforts so uncertain, especially when opposed by local authorities, it was possible to see the press gangs as "rioters" for trying *en masse* to perpetuate an unlawful act of violence. In that case the local townsmen who opposed them might be considered lawful defenders of the public welfare, acting much as they would in a *posse*. In 1770 John Adams cited opposition to press gangs who acted without warrants as an example of the lawful use of force; and when the sloop of war *Hornet* swept into Norfolk, Virginia, in September 1767 with a "bloody riotous plan . . . to impress seamen, without consulting the Mayor, or any other magistrate," the offense was charged to the pressmen. Roused by the watchman, who called out *"a riot by man of war's men,"* the inhabitants rose to back the magistrates, and not only secured the release of the impressed men but also imprisoned ten members of the press gang. The ship's captain, on the other hand, condemned the townsmen as "Rioters." Ambiguity was present, too, in Newport's *St. John* clash, which involved both impressment and criminal action on the part of royal seamen and culminated with Newporters firing on the king's ship. The Privy Council in England promptly classified the incident as a riot, but the Rhode Island governor's report boldly maintained that "the

---

[33] The definition of the common law of riot most commonly cited—for example, by John Adams in the Massacre trials—was from William Hawkins, *A Treatise of the Pleas of the Crown* (London, 1716), I, 155–159. See also Blackstone, *Commentaries*, IV, 146–147, and Edward Coke, *The Third Part of the Institutes of the Laws of England* (London, 1797), 176.

[34] Clark, "Impressment of Seamen," *Essays in Honor of Andrews*, 198–224; Stout, "Manning the Royal Navy," *American Neptune*, XXIII (1963), 178–179; and Leonard W. Labaree, ed., *Royal Instructions to British Colonial Governors, 1670–1776* (New York, 1935), 442–443.

people meant nothing but to assist [the magistrates] in apprehending the Offenders" on the vessel, and even suggested that "their Conduct be honored with his Majesty's royal Approbation."[35]

The enforcement of the White Pines Acts was similarly open to legal dispute. The acts seemed to violate both the Massachusetts and Connecticut charters; the meaning of provisions exempting trees growing within townships (act of 1722) and those which were "the property of private persons" (act of 1729) was contested, and royal officials tended to work on the basis of interpretations of the laws that Bernhard Knollenberg has called farfetched and, in one case, "utterly untenable." The Exeter, New Hampshire, "riot" of 1734, for example, answered an attempt of the surveyor to seize boards on the argument that the authorization to seize logs from allegedly illegally felled white pine trees in the act of 1722 included an authorization to seize processed lumber. As a result, Knollenberg concluded, although the surveyors' reports "give the impression that the New Englanders were an utterly lawless lot, . . . in many if not most cases they were standing for what they believed, with reason, were their legal and equitable rights in trees growing on their own lands."[36]

Occasions open to such conflicting interpretations were rare. Most often even those who sympathized with the mobs' motives condemned its use of force as illegal and unjustifiable. That ambiguous cases did arise, however, indicates that legitimacy and illegitimacy, *posses* and rioters, represented but poles of the same spectrum. And where a mob took upon itself the defense of the community, it benefited from a certain popular legitimacy even when the strict legality of its action was in doubt, particularly among a people taught that the legitimacy of law itself depended upon its defense of the public welfare.

Whatever quasi-legal status mobs were accorded by local communities was reinforced, moreover, by formal political thought. "Riots and rebellions" were often calmly accepted as a constant and even necessary element of free government. This acceptance depended, however, upon certain essential assumptions about popular uprisings. With words that could be drawn almost verbatim from John Locke or any other English author of similar convictions, colonial writers posited a continuing moderation and purposefulness on the part of the mob. "Tho' innocent Persons may sometimes suffer in popular Tumults," observed a 1768 writer in the *New York Journal,* "yet the general Resentment of the People is principally directed according to Justice, and the greatest Delinquent feels it most." Moreover, upheavals constituted only occasional interruptions in well-governed societies. "Good Laws and good Rulers will always be obey'd and respected"; "the Experience of all Ages proves, that Mankind are much more likely to submit to bad Laws and wicked Rulers, than to resist good ones." "Mobs and Tumults," it was often said, "never happen but thro' Oppression and a scandalous Abuse of Power."[37]

35 L. Kinvin Wroth and Hiller B. Zobel, eds., *Legal Papers of John Adams* (Cambridge, Mass., 1965), III, 253. Account of the Norfolk incident by George Abyvon, Sept. 5, 1767, in Purdie and Dixon's *Va. Gaz.* (Wmsbg.), Oct. 1, 1767. Capt. Morgan quoted in Lemisch, "Jack Tar," *Wm. and Mary Qtly.,* 3d Ser., XXV (1968), 391. Munro, ed., *Acts of the Privy Council, Colonial Series,* VI, 374; Gov. Samuel Ward to Treasury lords Oct. 23, 1765, Ward MSS, Box 1, fol. 58.

36 Knollenberg, *Origin of the Revolution,* 122–130; Albion, *Forests and Sea Power,* 255–258.

37 *N.Y. Jour.* (N.Y.C.), Aug. 18, 1768 (the writer was allegedly drawing together arguments that had recently appeared in the British press); and *N.Y. Jour. Supplement* (N.Y.C.), Jan. 4, 1770. Note also that Jefferson accepted Shays's rebellion as a sign of health in American institutions only after he had been assured by men like Jay that the insurgents had acted purposefully and moderately, and after he had concluded that the uprising represented no continuous threat to

In the hands of Locke such remarks constituted relatively inert statements of fact. Colonial writers, however, often turned these pronouncements on their heads such that observed instances of popular disorder became *prima facie* indictments of authority. In 1747, for example, New Jersey land rioters argued that "from their Numbers, Violences, and unlawful Actions" it was to be "inferred that . . . they are wronged and oppressed, or else they would never *rebell agt. the Laws."* Always, a New York writer said in 1770, when "the People of any Government" become "turbulent and uneasy," it was above all "a certain Sign of Maladministration." Even when disorders were not directly levelled against government they provided "strong proofs that something is much amiss in the state" as William Samuel Johnson put it; that—in Samuel Adams's words—the "wheels of good government" were "somewhat clogged." Americans who used this argument against Britain in the 1760's continued to depend upon it two decades later when they reacted to Shays's Rebellion by seeking out the public "Disease" in their own independent governments that was indicated by the "Spirit of Licentiousness" in Massachusetts.[38]

Popular turbulence seemed to follow so naturally from inadequacies of government that uprisings were often described with similes from the physical world. In 1770 John Adams said that there were "Church-quakes and state-quakes in the moral and political world, as well as earthquakes, storms and tempests in the physical." Two years earlier a writer in the *New York Journal* likened popular tumults to "Thunder Gusts" which "commonly do more Good than Harm." Thomas Jefferson continued the imagery in the 1780's, particularly with his famous statement that he liked "a little rebellion now and then" for it was "like a storm in the atmosphere." It was, moreover, because of the "imperfection of all things in this world," including government, that Adams found it "vain to seek a government in all points free from a possibility of civil wars, tumults and seditions." That was "a blessing denied to this life and preserved to complete the felicity of the next."[39]

If popular uprisings occurred "in all governments at all times," they were nonetheless most able to break out in free governments. Tyrants imposed order and submission upon their subjects by force, thus dividing society, as Jefferson said, into wolves and sheep. Only under free governments were the people "nervous," spirited, jealous of their rights, ready to react against unjust provocations; and this being the case, popular disorders could be interpreted as "Symptoms of a strong and healthy Constitution" even while they indicated some lesser shortcoming in administration. It would be futile, Josiah Quincy, Jr., said in 1770, to expect "that pacific, timid, obsequious, and servile temper, so pre-

---

established government. "An insurrection in one of the 13. states in the course of 11. years that they have subsisted amounts to one in any particular state in 143 years, say a century and a half," he calculated. "This would not be near as many as has happened in every other government that has ever existed," and clearly posed no threat to the constitutional order as a whole. To David Hartley, July 2, 1787, Boyd, ed., *Jefferson Papers*, XI, 526.

[38] John Locke, *The Second Treatise of Government*, paragraphs 223–225. "A State of Facts Concerning the Riots . . . in New Jersey," *New Jersey Archives*, VII, 217. N.Y. *Jour., Supp.* (N.Y.C.), Jan. 4, 1770. Johnson to Wm. Pitkin, Apr. 29, 1768, Massachusetts Historical Society, *Collections*, 5th Ser., IX (1885), 275. Adams as "Determinus" in *Boston Gazette*, Aug. 8, 1768; and Harry A. Cushing, ed., *The Writings of Samuel Adams* (New York, 1904–1908), I, 237. Jay to Jefferson, Oct. 27, 1786, Boyd, ed., *Jefferson Papers*, X, 488.

[39] Wroth and Zobel, eds., *Adams Legal Papers*, III, 249–250; N.Y. *Jour. Supp.* (N.Y.C.), Aug. 18, 1768; Jefferson to Abigail Adams, Feb. 22, 1787, Boyd, ed. *Jefferson Papers*, XI, 174. C. F. Adams, ed., *Works of Adams*, IV, 77, 80 (quoting Algernon Sydney).

dominant in more despotic governments" from those who lived under free British institutions. From "our happy constitution," he claimed, there resulted as "very natural Effects" an "impatience of injuries, and a strong resentment of insults."[40]

This popular impatience constituted an essential force in the maintenance of free institutions. "What country can preserve it's [sic] liberties if their rulers are not warned from time to time that their people preserve the spirit of resistance?" Jefferson asked in 1787. Occasional insurrections were thus "an evil . . . productive of good": even those founded on popular error tended to hold rulers "to the true principles of their institution" and generally provided "a medicine necessary for the sound health of government." This meant that an aroused people had a role not only in extreme situations, where revolution was requisite, but in the normal course of free government. For that reason members of the House of Lords could seriously argue—as A. J. P. Taylor has pointed out—that "rioting is an essential part of our constitution"; and for that reason, too, even Massachusetts's conservative Lieutenant Governor Thomas Hutchinson could remark in 1768 that "mobs a sort of them at least are constitutional."[41]

III

It was, finally, the interaction of this constitutional role of the mob with the written law that makes the story of eighteenth-century popular uprisings complexity itself.[42] If mobs were appreciated because they provided a check on power, it was always understood that, insofar as upheavals threatened "running to such excesses, as will overturn the whole system of government," "strong discouragements" had to be provided against them. For eighteenth-century Americans, like the English writers they admired, liberty demanded the rule of law. In extreme situations where the rulers had clearly chosen arbitrary power over the limits of law, men like John Adams could prefer the risk of anarchy to

[40] Jefferson to Edward Carrington, Jan. 16, 1787, Boyd, ed., *Jefferson Papers*, XI, 49, and Rev. James Madison to Jefferson, Mar. 28, 1787, *ibid.*, 252. Wroth and Zobel, eds., *Adams Legal Papers*, III, 250. Quincy's address to the jury in the soldiers' trial after the Boston Massacre in Josiah Quincy, *Memoir of the Life of Josiah Quincy, Junior, of Massachusetts Bay, 1744–1775*, ed. Eliza Susan Quincy, 3d ed. (Boston, 1875), 46. See also Massachusetts Assembly's similar statement in its address to Gov. Hutchinson, Apr. 24, 1770, Hutchinson, *History of Massachusetts Bay*, ed. Mayo, III, 365–366. This 18th century devotion to political "jealousy" resembles the doctrine of "vigilance" that was defended by 19th century vigilante groups. See Graham and Gurr, *Violence in America*, 179–183.

[41] Jefferson to William Stephen Smith, Nov. 13, 1787, Boyd, ed., *Jefferson Papers*, XII, 356, Jefferson to Carrington, Jan. 16, 1787, *ibid.*, XI, 49, Jefferson to James Madison, Jan. 30, 1787, *ibid.*, 92–93. Taylor's remarks in "History of Violence," *The Listener*, CXXIX (1968), 701. ("Members of the House of Lords . . . said . . . if the people really don't like something, then they wreck our carriages and tear off our wigs and throw stones through the windows of our town-houses. And this is an essential thing to have if you are going to have a free country.") Hutchinson to [John or Robert] Grant, July 27, 1768, Massachusetts Archives, XXVI, 317, State House, Boston. See also the related story about John Selden, the famous 17th century lawyer, told to the House of Commons in Jan. 1775 by Lord Camden and recorded by Josiah Quincy, Jr., in the "Journal of Josiah Quincy, Jun., During his Voyage and Residence in England from September 28th, 1774, to March 3d, 1775," Massachusetts Historical Society, *Proceedings*, L (1916–1917), 462–463. Selden was asked what lawbook contained the laws for resisting tyranny. He replied he did not know, "but I'll tell [you] what is most certain, that it has always been the custom of England—and the Custom of England is the *Law* of the *Land*."

[42] On the developing distinction Americans drew between what was legal and constitutional, see Wood, *Creation of the American Republic*, 261–268.

continued submission because "anarchy can never last long, and tyranny may be perpetual," but only when "there was any hope that the fair order of liberty and a free constitution would arise out of it." This desire to maintain the orderly rule of law led legislatures in England and the colonies to pass antiriot statutes and to make strong efforts—in the words of a 1753 Massachusetts law— to discountenance "a mobbish temper and spirit in . . . the inhabitants" that would oppose "all government and order."[43]

The problem of limiting mass violence was dealt with most intensely over a sustained period by the American Revolutionary leadership, which has perhaps suffered most from historians' earlier inattention to the history of colonial uprisings. So long as it could be maintained—as it was only fifteen years ago— that political mobs were "rare or unknown in America" before the 1760's, the Revolutionaries were implicitly credited with their creation. American patriots, Charles McLean Andrews wrote, were often "lawless men who were nothing more than agitators and demagogues" and who attracted a following from the riffraff of colonial society. It now seems clear that the mob drew on all elements of the population. More important, the Revolutionary leaders had no need to create mob support. Instead they were forced to work with a "permanent entity," a traditional crowd that exerted itself before, after, and even during the Revolutionary struggle over issues unrelated to the conflict with Britain, and that, as Hobsbawm has noted, characteristically aided the Revolutionary cause in the opening phases of conflict but was hard to discipline thereafter.[44]

In focusing popular exuberance the American leaders could work with long-established tendencies in the mob toward purposefulness and responsibility. In doing so they could, moreover, draw heavily upon the guidelines for direct action that had been defined by English radical writers since the seventeenth century. Extralegal action was justified only when all established avenues to redress had failed. It could not answer casual errors or private failings on the part of the magistrates, but had to await fundamental public abuses so egregious that the "whole people" turned against their rulers. Even then, it was held, opposition had to be measured so that no more force was exerted than was necessary for the public good. Following these principles colonial leaders sought by careful organization to avoid the excesses that first greeted the Stamp Act. Hutchinson's query after a crowd in Connecticut had forced the resignation of stampman Jared Ingersoll—whether "such a public regular assembly can be called a mob"—could with equal appropriateness have been repeated

[43] *N.Y. Jour. Supp.* (N.Y.C.), Jan. 4, 1770; Wroth and Zobel, eds., *Adams Legal Papers*, III, 250, and C. F. Adams, ed., *Works of Adams*, VI, 151. Adams's views were altered in 1815, *ibid.*, X, 181. It is noteworthy that the Boston town meeting condemned the Knowles rioters not simply for their method of opposing impressment but because they insulted the governor and the legislature and the Massachusetts Assembly acted against the uprising only after Gov. Shirley had left Boston and events seemed to be "tending to the destruction of all government and order." Hutchinson, *History of Massachusetts Bay,* ed. Mayo, II, 332–333. *Acts and Resolves of the Province of Masachusetts Bay,* III, 647. (Chap. 18 of the Province laws, 1752–1753, "An Act for Further Preventing all Riotous, Tumultuous and Disorderly Assemblies or Companies of Persons. . . .") This act, which was inspired particularly by Pope's Day violence, was renewed after the Boston Massacre in 1770 even though the legislature refused to renew its main Riot Act of 1751. *Ibid.,* IV, 87.

[44] Arthur M. Schlesinger, "Political Mobs and the American Revolution, 1765–1776," *Proceedings of the American Philosophical Society,* XCIX (1955), 246; Charles M. Andrews, *The Colonial Background of the American Revolution,* rev. ed. (New Haven, 1939), 176; Charles M. Andrews, "The Boston Merchants and the Non-Importation Movement," Colonial Society of Massachusetts, *Transactions,* XIX (1916–1917), 241; Hobsbawm, *Primitive Rebels,* 111, 123–124.

during the tea resistance, or in 1774 when Massachusetts *mandamus* councillors were forced to resign.[45]

From the first appearance of an organized resistance movement in 1765, moreover, efforts were made to support the legal magistrates such that, as John Adams said in 1774, government would have "as much vigor then as ever" except where its authority was specifically under dispute. This concern for the maintenance of order and the general framework of law explains why the American Revolution was largely free from the "universal tumults and all the irregularities and violence of mobbish factions [that] naturally arise when legal authority ceases." It explains, too, why old revolutionaries like Samuel Adams or Christopher Gadsden disapproved of those popular conventions and committees that persisted after regular independent state governments were established in the 1770's. "Decency and Respect [are] due to Constitutional Authority," Samuel Adams said in 1784, "and those Men, who under any Pretence or by any Means whatever, would lessen the Weight of Government lawfully exercised must be Enemies to our happy Revolution and the Common Liberty."[46]

In normal circumstances the "strong discouragements" to dangerous disorder were provided by established legislatures. The measures enacted by them to deal with insurrections were shaped by the eighteenth-century understanding of civil uprisings. Since turbulence indicated above all some shortcoming in government, it was never to be met by increasing the authorities' power of suppression. The "weakness of authority" that was a function of its dependence upon popular support appeared to contemporary Americans as a continuing virtue of British institutions, as one reason why rulers could not simply dictate to their subjects and why Britain had for so long been hailed as one of the freest nations in Europe. It was "far less dangerous to the Freedom of a State" to allow "the laws to be trampled upon, by the licence among the rabble . . . than to dispence with their force by an act of power." Insurrections were to be answered by reform, by attacking the "Disease"—to use John Jay's term of 1786—that lay behind them rather than by suppressing its "Symptoms." And ultimately, as William Samuel Johnson observed in 1768, "the only effectual way to prevent them is to govern with wisdom, justice, and moderation."[47]

In immediate crises, however, legislatures in both England and America resorted to special legislation that supplemented the common law prohibition of riot. The English Riot Act of 1714 was passed when disorder threatened to disrupt the accession of George I; a Connecticut act of 1722 followed a rash of incidents over land title in Hartford County; the Massachusetts act of 1751 answered "several tumultuous assemblies" over the currency issue and another

[45] Hutchinson to Thomas Pownall [Sept. or Oct. 1765], Mass. Archives, XXVI, 157. Pauline Maier, "From Resistance to Revolution: American Radicals and the Development of Intercolonial Opposition to Britain, 1765–1776" (unpubl. Ph.D. diss., Harvard University, 1968), I, 37–45, 72–215.

[46] C. F. Adams, ed., *Works of Adams*, IV, 51; Rev. Samuel Langdon's election sermon to third Massachusetts Provincial Congress, May 31, 1775, quoted in Richard Frothingham, *Life and Times of Joseph Warren* (Boston, 1865), 499; Samuel Adams to Noah Webster, Apr. 30, 1784, Cushing, ed., *Writings of Samuel Adams*, IV, 305–306. On Gadsden see Richard Walsh, *Charleston's Sons of Liberty* (Columbia, 1959), 87.

[47] N.Y. *Jour. Supp.* (N.Y.C.), Jan. 4, 1770; Jay to Jefferson, Oct. 27, 1786, Boyd, ed., *Jefferson Papers*, X, 488; Johnson to William Pitkin, July 23, 1768, Massachusetts Historical Society, *Collections*, 5th Ser., IX, 294–295.

of 1786 was enacted at the time of Shays's Rebellion. The New Jersey legislature passed an act in 1747 during that colony's protracted land riots; Pennsylvania's Riot Act of 1764 was inspired by the Paxton Boys; North Carolina's of 1771 by the Regulators; New York's of 1774 by the "land wars" in Charlotte and Albany Counties.[48] Always the acts specified that the magistrates were to depend upon the *posse* in enforcing their provisions, and in North Carolina on the militia as well. They differed over the number of people who had to remain "unlawfully, riotously, and tumultuously assembled together, to the Disturbance of the Publick Peace" for one hour after the reading of a prescribed riot proclamation before becoming judicable under the act. Some colonies specified lesser punishments than the death penalty provided for in the English act, but the American statutes were not in general more "liberal" than the British. Two of them so violated elementary judicial rights that they were subsequently condemned—North Carolina's by Britain, and New York's act of 1774 by a later, Revolutionary state legislature.[49]

In one important respect, however, the English Riot Act was reformed. Each colonial riot law, except that of Connecticut, was enacted for only one to three years, whereas the British law was perpetual. By this provision colonial legislators avoided the shortcoming which, it was said, was "more likely to introduce *arbitrary Power* than even an *Army* itself," because a perpetual riot act meant that "in all future time" by "reading a Proclamation" the Crown had the power "of hanging up their Subjects wholesale, or of picking out Those, to whom they have the greatest Dislike." If the death penalty was removed, the danger was less. When, therefore, riot acts without limit of time were finally enacted— as Connecticut had done in 1722, Massachusetts in 1786, New Jersey in 1797— the punishments were considerably milder, providing, for example, for imprisonment not exceeding six months in Connecticut, one year in Massachusetts, and three years in New Jersey.[50]

Riot legislation, it is true, was not the only recourse against insurgents, who throughout the eighteenth century could also be prosecuted for treason. The colonial and state riot acts suggest, nonetheless, that American legislators recognized the participants in civil insurrections as guilty of a crime peculiarly complicated because it had social benefits as well as damages. To some degree, it appears, they shared the idea expressed well by Jefferson in 1787; that "honest republican governors" should be "so mild in their punishments of rebellions, as not to discourage them too much."[51] Even in countering riots the legislators seemed as intent upon preventing any perversion of the forces of law and order by established authorities as with chastising the insurgents. Reform of the English Riot Act thus paralleled the abolition of constituent treasons—a

---

[48] *The Statutes at Large* [of Great Britain] (London, 1786), V, 4–6; Hoadly, ed., *Public Records of Connecticut*, VI, 346–348 for the law, and see also 332–333, 341–348; *Acts and Resolves of Massachusetts Bay*, III, 544–546, for the Riot Act of 1751, and see also Hutchinson, *History of Massachusetts Bay*, ed. Mayo, III, 6–7; and *Acts and Laws of the Commonwealth of Massachusetts* (Boston, 1893), 87–88, for Act of 1786; "A State of Facts Concerning the Riots . . . in New Jersey," *N.J. Archives*, VII, 211–212, 221–222; *The Statutes at Large of Pennsylvania* . . . (n.p., 1899), VI, 325–328; William A. Saunders, ed., *The Colonial Records of North Carolina* (Raleigh, 1890), VIII 481–486; *Laws of the Colony of New York in the Years 1774 and 1775* (Albany, 1888), 38–43.
[49] See additional instruction to Gov. Josiah Martin, Saunders, ed., *Colonial Records of North Carolina*, VIII, 515–516; and *Laws of the State of New York* (Albany, 1886), I, 20.
[50] *The Craftsman* (London, 1731), VI, 263–264. Connecticut and Massachusetts laws cited in n. 45; and *Laws of the State of New Jersey* (Trenton, 1821), 279–281.
[51] Jefferson to Madison, Jan. 30, 1787, Boyd, ed., *Jefferson Papers*, XI, 93.

traditional recourse against enemies of the Crown—in American state treason acts of the Revolutionary period and finally in Article III of the Federal Constitution.[52] From the same preoccupation, too, sprang the limitations placed upon the regular army provided for in the Constitution in part to assure the continuation of republican government guaranteed to the states by Article IV, Section IV. Just as the riot acts were for so long limited in duration, appropriations for the army were never to extend beyond two years (Article I, Section viii, 12); and the army could be used within a state against domestic violence only after application by the legislature or governor, if the legislature could not be convened (Article IV, Section iv).

A continuing desire to control authority through popular action also underlay the declaration in the Second Amendment that "a well regulated Militia being necessary to the security of a free State," citizens were assured the "right . . . to keep and bear Arms." The militia was meant above all "to prevent the establishment of a standing army, the bane of liberty"; and the right to bear arms—taken in part from the English Bill of Rights of 1689—was considered a standing threat to would-be tyrants. It embodied "a public allowance, under due restrictions, of the *natural right of resistance and self preservation,* when the sanctions of society and laws are found *insufficient* to restrain the *violence of oppression.*" And on the basis of their eighteenth-century experience, Americans could consider that right to be "perfectly harmless. . . . If the government be equitable; if it be reasonable in its exactions; if proper attention be paid to the education of children in knowledge, and religion," Timothy Dwight declared, "few men will be disposed to use arms, unless for their amusement, and for the defence of themselves and their country."[53]

The need felt to continue the eighteenth-century militia as a counterweight to government along with the efforts to outlaw rioting and to provide for the use of a standing army against domestic insurrections under carefully defined circumstances together illustrate the complex attitude toward peacekeeping that prevailed among the nation's founders. The rule of law had to be maintained, yet complete order was neither expected nor even desired when it could be purchased, it seemed, only at the cost of forcefully suppressing the spirit of a free people. The constant possibility of insurrection—as institutionalized in the militia—was to remain an element of the United States Constitution, just as it had played an essential role in Great Britain's.

This readiness to accept some degree of tumultuousness depended to a large degree upon the lawmakers' own experience with insurrections in the eighteenth century, when "disorder" was seldom anarchic and "rioters" often acted to defend law and justice rather than to oppose them. In the years after independence this toleration declined, in part because mass action took on new dimensions. Nineteenth-century mobs often resembled in outward form those of the previous century, but a new violence was added. Moreover, the literal assumption of popular rule in the years after Lexington taught many thoughtful Revolutionary partisans what was for them an unexpected lesson—that the

---

[52] See Bradley Chapin, "Colonial and Revolutionary Origins of the American Law of Treason," *Wm. and Mary Qtly.,* 3d Ser., XVII (1960), 3–21.

[53] Elbridge Gerry in Congressional debates, quoted in Irving Brant, *The Bill of Rights, Its Origin and Meaning* (Indianapolis, 1965), 486; Samuel Adams, quoting Blackstone, as "E. A." in *Boston Gaz.,* Feb. 27, 1769, and Cushing, ed., *Writings of Samuel Adams,* I, 317. Timothy Dwight, quoted in Daniel J. Boorstin, *The Americans: The Colonial Experience* (New York, 1958), 353.

people were "as capable of despotism as any prince," that "public liberty was no guarantee after all of private liberty."[54] With home rule secured, attention focused more exclusively upon minority rights, which mob action had always to some extent imperiled. And the danger that uprisings carried for individual freedom became ever more egregious as mobs shed their former restraint and burned Catholic convents, attacked nativist speakers, lynched Mormons, or destroyed the presses and threatened the lives of abolitionists.

Ultimately, however, changing attitudes toward popular uprisings turned upon fundamental transformations in the political perspective of Americans after 1776. Throughout the eighteenth century political institutions had been viewed as in a constant evolution: the colonies' relationship with Britain and with each other, even the balance of power within the governments of various colonies, remained unsettled. Under such circumstances the imputations of governmental shortcoming that uprisings carried could easily be accepted and absorbed. But after Independence, when the form and conduct of the Americans' governments were under their exclusive control, and when those governments represented, moreover, an experiment in republicanism on which depended their own happiness and "that of generations unborn," Americans became less ready to endure domestic turbulence or accept its disturbing implications. Some continued to argue that "distrust and dissatisfaction" on the part of the multitude were "always the consequence of tyranny or corruption." Others, however, began to see domestic turbulence not as indictments but as insults to government that were likely to discredit American republicanism in the eyes of European observers. "Mobs are a reproach to Free Governments," where all grievances could be legally redressed through the courts or the ballot box, it was argued in 1783. They originated there "not in Oppression, but in Licentiousness," an "ungovernable spirit" among the people. Under republican governments even that distrust of power colonists had found so necessary for liberty, and which uprisings seemed to manifest, could appear outmoded. "There is some consistency in being jealous of power in the hands of those who assume it by birth . . . and over whom we have no controul . . . as was the case with the Crown of England over America," another writer suggested. "But to be jealous of those whom we chuse, the instant we have chosen them" was absurd: perhaps in the transition from monarchy to republic Americans had "bastardized" their ideas by placing jealousy where confidence was more appropriate.[55] In short, the assumptions behind the Americans' earlier toleration of the mob were corroded in republican America. Old and new attitudes coexisted in the 1780's and even later. But the appropriateness of popular uprisings in the United States became increasingly in doubt after the Federal Constitution came to be seen as the final product of long-term institutional experimentation, "a momentous contribution to the history of politics" that rendered even that most glorious exertion of popular force, revolution itself, an obsolete resort for Americans.[56]

Yet this change must not be viewed exclusively as a product of America's

[54] Wood, *Creation of the American Republic,* 410.

[55] Judge Aedanus Burke's Charge to the Grand Jury at Charleston, June 9, 1783, in *South-Carolina Gazette and General Advertiser* (Charleston), June 10, 1783; "A Patriot," *ibid.,* July 15, 1783; and "Another Patriot," *ibid.,* July 29, 1783; and on the relevance of jealousy of power, see a letter to Virginia in *ibid.,* Aug. 9, 1783. "Democratic Gentle-Touch," *Gazette of the State of South Carolina* (Charleston), May 13, 1784.

[56] Wood, *Creation of the American Republic,* 612–614.

distinctive Revolutionary achievement. J. H. Plumb has pointed out, that a century earlier, when England passed beyond her revolutionary era and progressed toward political "stability," radical ideology with its talk of resistance and revolution was gradually left behind. A commitment to peace and permanence emerged from decades of fundamental change. In America as in England this stability demanded that operative sovereignty, including the right finally to decide what was and was not in the community's interest, and which laws were and were not constitutional, be entrusted to established governmental institutions. The result was to minimize the role of the people at large, who had been the ultimate arbiters of those questions in English and American Revolutionary thought. Even law enforcement was to become the task primarily of professional agencies. As a result in time all popular upheavals alike became menacing efforts to "pluck up law and justice by the roots," and riot itself gradually became defined as a purposeless act of anarchy, "a blind and misguided outburst of popular fury," of "undirected violence with no articulated goals."[57]

[57] J. H. Plumb, *The Origins of Political Stability, England 1675–1725* (Boston, 1967), xv, 187; John Adams on the leaders of Shays's Rebellion in a letter to Benjamin Hitchborn, Jan. 27, 1787, in C. F. Adams, ed., *Works of Adams*, IX, 551; modern definitions of riot in "Riot Control and the Use of Federal Troops," *Harvard Law Review*, LXXXI (1968), 643.

The Ritualization of the American Revolution

Robert Middlekauff

INTRODUCTION

Historians of the American Revolution have appropriately given much of their attention to the political and constitutional issues which defined it from beginning to end. They have not, however, ignored the economic and religious issues that accompanied the Revolution, nor the culture—especially the political culture—that yielded the Revolution. But for the most part the way the Revolutionaries expressed themselves in symbol and ritual has gone unstudied. Middlekauff's essay attempts to open up this area of study by concentrating on the self-conscious creation of a Revolutionary tradition by the Americans who shaped the resistance to Britain.

This essay is indebted to E. J. Hobsbawm's *Primitive Rebels: Studies in Archaic Forms of Social Movement in the 19th and 20th Centuries,* 2nd ed.* (1963) for its method and focus. A pioneering study of a major Revolutionary symbol is Arthur M. Schlesinger's "Liberty Tree: A Genealogy," *New England Quarterly,* XXV (1952), 435–58. Alan Heimert, *Religion and the American Mind* (1966), gives much information about the religious themes in the ritualization of the Revolution. A related emphasis appears in Perry Miller, "From the Covenant to the Revival," in J. W. Smith and A. L. Jamison, eds., *Religion in American Life,* Vol. 1: *The Shaping of American Religion* (4 vols., 1961), 322–68. Paul C. Nagel, *One Nation Indivisible: The Union in American Thought, 1776–1861** (1961), gives an excellent account of the changing aspects of the Union as a symbol. Two other books aid in understanding the intellectual background of the Revolution: Caroline Robbins, *The Eighteenth-Century Commonwealthman* (1959), and Bernard Bailyn, *The Ideological Origins of the American Revolution* (1967).

100

S HORTLY after the United States Senate convened for the first time in April 1789, it engaged in one of those farces which have enlivened its proceedings ever since. The Senate held in its hands the inaugural address of the President, and it believed that it had to reply. Framing the response proved less troublesome than sending it with proper address to the President. What was he to be called, anyway? Vice-President Adams, presiding energetically over the Senate, plumped for "His Highness the President of the United States and Protector of their Liberties." Over in the House of Representatives, James Madison averted his gaze from this pseudo-monarchism and quietly addressed the House reply "to George Washington, President of the United States." The Senate eventually agreed that republican simplicity was the only appropriate guide and adopted the practice of the House, but not until it had listened to the Vice-President's pleas for giving the President high-sounding titles and not until it had coaxed the House into sending representatives to a Conference Committee which thrashed about and decided nothing. The only title that emerged from this episode was tagged to John Adams, thereafter celebrated as His Rotundity.[1]

John Adams appears ridiculous in this episode: his insensitivity to the American revulsion against anything smacking of monarchy was monumental. But in his concern for form, his feeling that even a simple republic required conventions and symbols, he was sound. Americans had felt this need for a very long time, and acutely, ever since they began resisting Parliamentary attempts to tax them in 1764.

Almost all people have experienced at various times the need to express their values and intentions in some sort of forms—especially in symbol and ritual. The need seems to be an essential part of human nature, related to aesthetic and even religious concerns. Ritual and symbol permit expression of the highest values, and they satisfy impulses for order in relationships among human beings and their ideals.

The formalism of social movements may have several uses, of course. In primitive social movements—that is, in premodern and preindustrial movements, form assumes a far more important role than content, at least in providing the essential unity holding participants together. The failure of a medieval king to be crowned and anointed in the correct ritual-way might seriously compromise his claims to the allegiance of his subjects, and today in many religious groups baptism, or any sacramental observance including marriage, that is not celebrated according to prescribed form lacks authority Baptism is of course an initiatory rite in many Christian groups—by it men ire admitted

FROM Robert Middlekauff, "The Ritualization of the American Revolution," in Stanley Coben and Lorman Ratner, eds., *The Development of an American Culture*, © 1970, 31–43. Reprinted by permission of Prentice-Hall, Inc., Englewood Cliffs, N.J.

[1] For a good brief account of this affair see Irving Brant, *James Madison: Father of the Constitution, 1787–1800* (Indianapolis and New York, 1950), pp. 255–57.

to the church, or as one group of Congregationalists used to insist, by it their membership was confirmed. Besides bringing men together, a joint act of worship, or any ritualistic act performed in a group, may impart a sense of community, a kind of emotion common to the group, and may discipline it and give it a sense of purpose. Symbols may contribute similar kinds of emotion, summing up in themselves the leading desires and impulses of a group. For more than a century in the American colonies, the church building, from the New England meeting house to southern Georgian churches, must have performed this function, evoking the most important values and aspirations of their members.[2]

Apart from religion, colonial life was not especially rich in symbol and ritual. Politics began in factions and remained factionalized until the Revolution was well advanced. If they opposed the representatives of the Crown, colonial factions had to tread a narrow line between legitimacy and disloyalty, a situation which discouraged the invention of formalistic observance. Membership in the Empire supplied all the forms British subjects could ask for anyway—a King still carrying a faint whiff of divine origin, a structure of administrative officials all conscious of their place in the apparatus of empire, and the conventions regulating the relationship of Crown and commons. If the factions organized themselves along other lines, as in Rhode Island, where Wards opposed Hopkinses and where force, knavery, and nastiness probably repelled any attempts at ritualization, the transitory character of the groups never permitted symbolic forms to develop.[3]

Where organization intruded into other areas of colonial affairs ritualization of function appeared only casually. Merchants joined one another in colonial cities but interest overruled everything else; guild and artisan organizations developed late in the colonial period and assumed few of the forms marking comparable nineteenth-century organizations. The absence of guilds seems startling; as pale as they are, modern unions in the United States have succeeded in perpetuating a more colorful ritualistic life. The difference in styles lies partly in the differences in class. Eighteenth-century artisans in cities were usually aspiring merchants and often engaged in some kind of mercantile activity. Though this activity was usually only a sideline that contributed to their main efforts, it blurred their economic interests and they experienced difficulty in locating themselves socially. Their lack of a clear sense of who they were inhibited the ritualistic expression so characteristic of guilds in the next century, which usually were composed of members beset with no such doubts.[4]

Not even the violence that filled colonial life supplied much ritual. There were rebellions before the Revolution in all the colonies; none aimed at independence, or at separation from Britain; and none lasted long enough to develop their own forms. Rather, almost all clung to the fiction that they represented legitimacy and its forms. Rebels uniformly professed loyalty to

[2] This paragraph owes much to E. J. Hobsbawn, *Primitive Rebels*, 2nd ed. (New York, 1963), pp. 150–74.

[3] For the Ward–Hopkins contest, see David S. Lovejoy, *Rhode Island Politics and the American Revolution, 1760–1776* (Providence, R.I., 1958), and Mack Thompson, "The Ward-Hopkins Controversy and the American Revolution in Rhode Island: An Interpretation," *William and Mary Quarterly,* 3d Ser., 16 (1959), 363–75.

[4] For information about artisans see Carl Bridenbaugh, *The Colonial Craftsman* (New York, 1950), and *Cities in Revolt: Urban Life in America, 1743–1776* (New York, 1955).

Britain—and believed it. A profession of loyalty imposed the use of a ritual already long established; as in Nathaniel Bacon's "Manifesto," which proclaimed that the Rebellion of 1676 in Virginia aimed "at his Majesties Honour and the Publick good."[5]

Of all the crude movements in the colonies preceding the Revolution, only the revivals—and in particular the Great Awakening—created their own ritualism. Revivals of religion depend upon meetings, and even the simplest of these meetings usually offered a ritualized performance which created relationships between revivalist and listeners, among the participants themselves, and hopefully between the initiates and some higher being. The first such gatherings began in New England as a communal exercise in renewing the church covenant. After a brief sermon by the minister explaining what was required of the church, the members were asked to rise silently as a token of their devotion. This simple ceremony held possibilities for extension which did not escape the ministers who soon enlisted the congregation and then non-members as participants; sermons grew more hortatory and the purposes of the ritual assumed larger proportions. By the time of the explosions of the 1740's a highly structured ritual had developed, the climax of which saw the mass undergo conversion, an initiation which sealed them to God and to one another. The progress of awakening enthusiasm from community to community also followed a ritualistic path, with a minister making his way from one community to the next, holding meetings, confronting the Devil and his agents, and bringing the populace to the faith.

The Revolutionary movement that began in the 1760's and that carried through to independence displayed many of the characteristics of a revival. It was larger and more complex, of course, and it was defined primarily by its substantive issues. (The Revolutionary movement was value-oriented, to use the jargon of sociologists, in a way the Great Awakening was not.) Before 1776 the movement gained its cohesion at the top, in particular from groups which took a name rich with symbolic meaning, the Sons of Liberty. The Sons had a variety of tactical objectives throughout this period: at times they simply wished to force the resignation of Crown officials—the Stamp Distributors in 1765, for example. As they grew in sophistication, they managed boycotts and joined merchants and artisan groups in enforcing non-importation agreements. They also collected arms, drilled their followers in military tactics, and prepared for war. All these activities contributed to the resistance to Parliamentary measures of imperial reform and to the development of a revolutionary tradition.[6]

The Sons chose to develop resistance and to create a Revolutionary tradition in still other ways: most importantly by ritualizing the movement against Britain and giving it symbolic expression. Here their activities approached in technique those of the revivalists. Just as the revivalists did, the Sons of Liberty depended upon the public meeting. Although these meetings occurred in various places, the favorite spot up and down the eastern seaboard came to be around a liberty tree or, in many cases, a liberty pole. The first tree seems to have been designated the representative of liberty on August 14, 1765. The place was near the Boston Common, the tree a stately elm, and the occasion an attempt to bring Andrew Oliver to resign his Stamp Distributorship. Oliver

[5] Robert Middlekauff, ed., *Bacon's Rebellion* (Chicago, 1964), p. 20.
[6] For the Sons of Liberty and their activities see Edmund S. and Helen M. Morgan, *The Stamp Act Crisis: Prologue to Revolution,* rev. ed. (New York, 1963).

gave up his office, and the tree gained the fame that was to make it an emblem of liberty—and the model for dozens of others in all the colonies.[7]

There is no need to pause too long over the meaning of the liberty tree or the liberty pole as a symbol. By themselves they symbolized freedom and evoked the strong emotions of resistance to attempts to subvert freedom. The historical origin of the poles doubtless was the maypole of English country life (perhaps the first to appear in America was at Merrymount in Plymouth Colony). The maypole had served first as the emblem of the lower classes' disaffection from their social betters; and it soon took on the obvious sexual connotations a later age, which has gone to the school of Freud, has seen in it. (The sexual significance of the liberty tree was suggested long before Freud, of course; Joel Barlow in the eighteenth century traced the liberty tree to phallic symbols common to ancient mythologies). As a symbol the liberty tree expressed a subtle meaning dependent upon the context in which it was used. In part what was attached to it was even more important for meanings, one suspects, than the Americans were aware of. Liberty Tree in Boston, for example, was usually adorned with effigies of the Devil and his local representatives, the assorted officials of the crown.[8] The confrontation intended may have been good against evil, the tree of course in this case representing the forces of good. At the grand celebration of the repeal of the Stamp Act in the spring of 1766 the symbolism was even more explicit. A large obelisk of oiled paper was to decorate the tree (it burned up before it could be placed). It was to be illuminated by several hundred lamps; and on its sides were pictures of the tree, with an angel hovering over it, and an eagle in the branches.[9]

Any Protestant would have recognized the meaning of this tableau: the struggle between imperial and colonial powers was the age-old conflict of the forces of dark and light. Good was arrayed against evil in the American resistance to illegal taxation. The theme was honestly felt in a culture that still retained its Protestant cast and that instinctively thought of politics, as of all else, in moral terms. Something of the same meaning surely was implicit in the series of ceremonial burials of liberty which occurred in the 1760's and the 1770's. The religious significance of this ceremony is plain; the ritualized manner of the performance, with truth, liberty, and evil taking allegorical forms, could not escape anyone.

Numerology was employed in much the same way, for example in the episode of the Massachusetts circular letter. Sent by the Massachusetts Assembly in 1768, the circular letter called the attention of the other colonial assemblies to the Townshend Acts. Its phrasing and tone were moderate, but the Grafton ministry thought it seditious and saw in it an opportunity to smash the colonial opposition. The ministry ordered the Massachusetts assembly to rescind the letter and the Governor to dissolve them if they refused. They refused, of course. The vote was 92 to 17; and the Sons of Liberty under Sam Adams' tutelage began to celebrate the glorious 92 and to execrate the cowardly 17. At this time John Wilkes in England was trying to stay in the House of Commons; his slogan was "45," the number of the newspaper which the English

---

[7] Arthur M. Schlesinger, "Liberty Tree: A Genealogy," *New England Quarterly*, 25 (1952), 435–58.

[8] *Ibid., passim;* Esther Forbes, *Paul Revere and the World He Lived In* (Cambridge, Mass.), pp. 101–2.

[9] Forbes, *Revere*, pp. 115–17.

government had suppressed. The Sons of Liberty in Boston sent him two turtles, one weighing 45 pounds, the other 47 pounds, for a total of 92 pounds— the number synonymous with patriotism in Massachusetts. The number 92 was celebrated in other ways too: Paul Revere fashioned a silver punch bowl dedicated to the "Immortal 92" and engraved with slogans and symbols, among them "Wilkes & Liberty" and "No. 45." Here the technique—which may seem strained today—may have derived from the Protestant fascination with eschatological numerology which sometimes expressed the opposition of good and evil in numbers.[10]

Even the simple act of wearing homespun as a part of the boycott of British goods, which seems empty of anything except economic coercion, was freighted with Protestant concern. Homespun was one part of the general repudiation of English corruption, and the resolve to wear it was testimony in favor of purity in thought and action. The Association, the large-scale boycott and non-importation agreement adopted by the First Continental Congress in 1774, pledged Americans to a wholesale reform:

> we will, in our several stations encourage frugality, economy, and industry, and promote agriculture, arts and the manufactures of this country, especially that of wool; and will discountenance and discourage every species of extravagance and dissipation, especially of horse-racing, and all kinds of gaming, cock-fighting, exhibitions of shews, plays, and other expensive diversions and entertainments . . . .[11]

In this context homespun became emblematic of Protestant values.

The Congress also called upon Americans to repent and reform before invoking divine aid against the British government. It suggested that Parliament's oppression was punishment for the Americans' sins, and could be lifted only by an act of national self-purification. This theme was also featured in countless sermons of the 1760's and 70's; such preaching employed a device much older than the colonies; employed in the Revolutionary situation, it explained current griefs and offered a way out of them.[12] In a peculiar way this sort of

ritualization, playing on old, conventional themes in a familiar tone, probably offered some reassurance. The problems it implied only seemed new; in reality

[10] See Arthur M. Schlesinger, *Prelude to Independence: The Newspaper War on Britain 1764–1776* (New York, 1958), pp. 36–37, and the newspapers cited there. The Sons of Liberty in Petersham trimmed the town's Liberty Tree so that 92 branches remained. In South Carolina, the number 26 was celebrated because 26 members of the Assembly defied the Governor and passed resolves supporting the Circular Letter. For an example of Protestant numerology see Elisha Rich, *The Number of the Beast Found Out By Spiritual Arithmetic* (Chelmsford, Mass., 1775). Rich says (on p. 23) of the Antichrist: "Observe, that although it [Antichrist] numbers so many: yet the number seven, or sevens is never once brought into the reckoning, but it lacks one of that number by which GOD would have the true CHURCH distinguished from the false. For the BEAST comes to six hundred and sixty six, but not seven or sevens, and so the Beast lacks one in each number."

[11] Samuel E. Morison, *Sources and Documents Illustrating the American Revolution, 1764–1788* (2nd ed. Oxford, Eng., 1953), p. 124. Since this essay was written, Edmund S. Morgan's "The Puritan Ethic and the American Revolution," *William and Mary Quarterly*, 3d Ser., 24 (1967), 3–43, has appeared, which provides an excellent discussion of the relationship between Protestant values and the Revolutionary movement.

[12] Perry Miller, "From the Covenant to the Revival," in *Religion in American Life*, Vol. 1: *The Shaping of American Religion*, James Ward Smith and A. Leland Jamison, eds. (4 vols., Princeton, N.J., 1961), pp. 326–34.

they were the old ones of good against evil; their form was new but the old remedies were sure. All in all, this was a masterful, if instinctive, formulation of Revolutionary affairs.

If the revivalistic impulse contributed so much to the Revolutionary movement and if Protestant values inescapably found expression there, so also did Protestant expectations about the future of America. Although the American sense of order curbed "enthusiasm," there were unspoken millennial hints in American Revolutionary thinking. Any revolution rests on the assumption that things can be made better—this one seemed to Americans to forecast the New Jerusalem, the new heavens and the new earth of the thousand years. Despite their concern for property and taxes, the Americans were not what their fathers called "carnal chiliasts," seekers only of earthly abundance. Their utopianism was in some measure a response to the evils they perceived in English life—bribery in politics, decadence in manners, and infidelity in religion—and hence was committed to a general reformation of morals and institutions.

Politics demanded reform more than anything else, and it began with the resistance to Parliamentary measures and royal officials in the 1760's. Americans hesitated for years about open attack on the monarchy, but that reluctance vanished early in 1776 with Thomas Paine's *Common Sense*. With his delicate ability to read public sentiment, Paine sensed that the monarchy was a kind of image, or idol, of Americans, and his role was the iconoclast. He played the part with great skill, treating the monarchy as a remnant of heathenish and Jewish superstition which had been transformed into modern despotism. His conclusion must have seemed obvious in this context: monarchy was the enemy of freedom in religion as well as in politics, "For monarchy in every instance is the Popery of government."[13]

The Revolutionaries' concern for reform had yet another source: evangelical Protestantism, which had been preoccupied with social reformation as a fulfillment of history. Thus the calls for Americans to attain a purified society, with simple and sinless institutions. In this millennial state, bliss would be enjoyed as long as purity and simplicity lasted. Even the "life, liberty, and pursuit of happiness" of the Declaration of Independence gained resonance in this context of millennial expectation.

During the period before independence, millennialism proved to have great allegorical utility which could be elaborated and extended as the conflict with the English government developed. At the beginning of the Revolutionary movement the Americans applied the symbols of millennialism to specific men and measures. By the end in 1776, when American purposes had expanded from resistance to independence, they gave these millennial symbols broader, even typological meanings. Such development can be seen by comparing sermons preached in 1766 with those of 1776. For example, on February 14, 1766, a sermon was preached around the Liberty Tree in Boston, in which the doctrine was inspired by the thirteenth chapter of Revelation, "where the wolves

---

[13] Thomas Paine, *Common Sense and the Crisis* (Garden City, N.Y., 1965), p. 22. Americans in New York City carried out another kind of iconoclasm when they pulled down an equestrian statue of George III in Bowling Green in 1776. Had there been more such statues, there surely would have been more such iconoclasm. For similar episodes in the French Revolution see the account by Stanley J. Idzerda, "Iconoclasm During the French Revolution," *American Historical Review*, 60 (Oct., 1954), 13–26.

of our day are so plainly pointed out . . . ."[14] This chapter describes two terrible beasts: the first, with seven heads and ten horns, "sets before our eyes the wicked Earl of Bute." The seven heads represent the offices he held; the crowns on them indicate that he was royally appointed; the horns he soon fixed on the heads of "honester men." This beast continued in power for forty-two months, and so, by the calculation of the minister preaching this sermon, did Bute. The second beast had two horns like a lamb and spoke like a dragon; this monster was George Grenville, whose mark was the Stamp Act. Thus the crisis of the Stamp Act was put in an old prophetic scheme: the beast, or the Antichrist, and its creation, the Stamp Act, opposed Christ and his own, the Americans in the wilderness. This design appeared clear to all a month before the Stamp Act was repealed. The end of the prophecy could not be doubted; just as the beast was slain, so also would the Stamp Act be killed.[15]

How this symbolic representation could be extended to give larger meaning may be seen in a sermon preached in New York almost exactly ten years later, in January 1776. In this sermon the American struggle with Britain was completely absorbed into Biblical prophecy. It pictures the church in the American wilderness, with the emphasis on God's commitment to America, where the church, and Christian liberty, will survive. It is an optimistic statement idenfying the American cause with "the Protestant cause in general." The "American quarter of the globe," it announces, is reserved by Providence for the church free of tyranny, and free to enjoy "right of rule and government, so as not to be controll'd and oppressed by the tyrannical powers . . . represented by the Great Red Dragon." The war of Britain upon America is described as a war on God, and God's support of America is not doubted:

> we have incontestible evidence, that God Almighty, with all the powers of heaven, are on our side. Great numbers of Angels no doubt, are encamped round our coast, for our defense and protection. Michael stands ready, with all the artillery of heaven, to encounter the dragon, and vanquish this black host.[16]

As in 1766, victory awaits the powers of good: the good in the New World where liberty "has been planted. . . . These commotions and convulsions in the British empire, may be leading to the fulfillment of such prophecies as relate to his [the Devil's] downfal and overthrow, and to the future glory and prosperity of Christ's church."[17] In this formulation the purpose of the American struggle has been broadened so as to coincide with the final epic conflict with sin in defense of Christian liberty.

This exalted expression of the meaning of the war with Britain spoke to the deepest impulses in Americans. It defined liberty and union in Christian terms; it reconciled the defense of property with the defense of good (they were inseparable, it suggested). It posed the struggle in the terms most congenial to Americans—in moral terms, with America serving as the instrument of Provi-

---

[14] *A Discourse, Addressed To The Sons of Liberty, At A Solemn Assembly, Near Liberty-Tree in Boston, February 14, 1766* (Providence, R.I., 1766), p. 3.

[15] The quotations are in the *Discourse*, pp. 4–5.

[16] Samuel Sherwood, *The Church's Flight Into The Wilderness: An Address on the Times Containing Some Very Interesting and Important Observations on Scripture Prophecies* (New York, 1776). The quotations are from pp. 18, 24, 46n.

[17] *Ibid.*, p. 49.

dence. In the next eight bloody years, it invested sacrifice with Christian meaning and thereby released those energies of Americans which would sustain them to the end of the war.

Independence did not bring Americans to a repudiation of these old Protestant values. But it did begin a fresh tendency towards a secular culture. Historians of religion in America have taught us that the secularization in America began in the seventeenth century, perhaps almost simultaneously with the founding. Secularization, they urge, expressed itself institutionally: in church organization that saw laymen progressively assume authority in discipline, in management of church affairs, and even in the definition of doctrine; and in the altering of church–state relationships in favor of the voluntary principle. Secularization also expressed itself in values: in the decline of traditional piety or its conversion into ethical and humanitarian impulses; and in the indifference which found men taking their definitions of life's purposes and concerns from other authorities than religion: from reason and science, for example, and from business and politics.

The Revolution contributed to this process by redirecting American energies, and by wrenching American thought and feeling into some new forms. The ritualization of the Revolution helped both to create new values and, more importantly, to express them, for their sources lay, to a large extent, outside the forms themselves.

With independence, the Revolution itself became a symbol, evocative of a complex tradition of liberty and sacrifice. Perhaps in the incantations to American sacrifices during the war lies the strongest link to the Protestant past, with its emphasis on sin and affliction. As a symbol, the Revolution was celebrated through the means of other symbols and an intricate ritualization drawing on the familiar devices of meetings, holidays (the Fourth of July was pre-eminent), medals, paintings, statues, and hero-worship. A part of this process was plainly deliberate and self-conscious. Thus in ordering medals struck in France, Congress declared their purposes to be "grateful to the illustrious personages for whom they are designed, worthy the dignity of the sovereign power by whom they are presented, and calculated to perpetuate the remembrance of those great events which they are intended to consecrate to immortality."[18] During the Confederation period fifteen medals were authorized by Congress commemorating such events as the evacuation of Boston by the British, the surrender of Burgoyne at Saratoga, the engagements at Stony Point, Cowpens, Eutaw Springs, the capture of Major André, and the victory of the *Bonhomme Richard* over the *Serapis*.

Although medals and meetings espoused a simple patriotism calculated to strengthen national feeling, they also presented the Revolution as an event having transcendent meaning. No doubt the connections between this conception of the Revolution and the remnants of the eschatological vision lie here. The connection may be seen in a proclamation of 1776 commemorating the Battle of Lexington which stated "from this day will be dated the liberty of the world." In the same year a Massachusetts minister compared the robust liberty

---

[18] Julian Boyd, ed., *The Papers of Thomas Jefferson* (17 vols. to date, Princeton, N.J., 1950–), XVI, p. 53.

in Revolutionary America to other benighted parts of the world where it was "gasping for life." America's Revolution was described in 1780 as being in the service of such less happy areas: "Our contest is not merely for our own families, friends, and posterity, but for the rights of humanity, for the civil and religious privileges of mankind." And David Ramsey, the historian of the Revolution who watched its course, agreed with foreign opinion that the Revolution marked a new age in history.[19]

The Revolution as a symbol of promise and prophecy pervaded every attempt of the Revolutionary generation to understand what they had done. This tendency is especially apparent in the symbolic meanings attached to the Union. Although after 1776 the Union remained "elusive in its form and function," it commanded emotional and intellectual attachment as the means for the American experiment.[20] There was resistance to this concept, of course, and opposition to what it meant when it was translated into power relationships in government. Those who persisted in seeing the Union as America's hope wished to strengthen it; and those who valued the states or other local authority opposed attempts to add to its power. Advocates of state sovereignty proved as fully aware of the connections of form and function as any devotee of the Union. As the freeholders of Fairfax County, Virginia, expressed their fears in 1783, about the encroaching union: "We like not the language of the late address from Congress to the different States [urging that Congress be given powers to tax] . . . . The very style is alarming. . . . Forms generally imply substance."[21] This last point—"Forms generally imply substance"—probably put the matter too strongly for the exponents of the Union. Their conception, the prevailing one, was of the Union as a means by which Revolutionary ends might be achieved, not as an end in itself. In the most frequently used language the Union was the "foundation," or the "tie," the "bounds," the "remedy" for political diseases—it was not an end, nor an absolute. As a means the Union would ensure happiness and peace. It would, in Hamilton's phrase, serve as a barrier to faction and insurrection; Madison in the Tenth Federalist conceived of it as an agency by which the worst effects of political faction might be controlled. Useful in domestic politics, it would serve American interests abroad by focusing power, which had been tending to fragment among the new states, against European enemies.[22]

For some Americans the Union evoked the Revolution's dedication to the principle of democratic consent as the basis of government. After all, the early resistance to Britain rested on the right of men to be taxed only by political bodies in which their representatives sat; and the Constitution, in the procedure by which it was drafted and ratified and in its substantive commitment to popular interest and the general welfare, institutionalized a broadly based government. Other Americans resisted these propositions and urged that the states alone could be relied upon both for the protection of rights and as the

[19] The quotations and the citation from Ramsey are from Wesley Frank Craven, *The Legend of the Founding Fathers* (New York, 1956), pp. 59–60.
[20] Paul C. Nagel, *One Nation Indivisible: The Union in American Thought, 1776–1861* (New York, 1961), p. 15.
[21] Quoted in Alpheus Thomas Mason, *The States Rights Debate* (Englewood Cliffs, N.J., 1964), p. 22.
[22] For language describing the Union I have relied on *The Federalist;* see in particular numbers 2–10, 39, 84.

mechanisms through which popular consent should be registered. But in either case the culture was explicitly pledged to a political process that took its power and its limits from the people.

Form did not control substance in 1789, when the new government commenced its operations, and would not begin to until the great romantic outpouring of the nineteenth century, when a secular cult would grow up around the Union. In the eighteenth century, as a symbol the Union was unavailable to those who would have made it the basis for a secular ideology because it was still imprecise in meaning. Yet even though it was an inexact symbol, and seemingly invited only experimentalism, the Union contributed to secularization, as indeed it expressed it. For its very character as a means opened the way to new centers of thought and purpose. It permitted, for example, the development of a national politics. In time such new purposes would find ritualized expression.

Yet a Protestant culture survived the Revolution intact, committed to traditional purposes and means but also in a subtle way liberated from them, and prepared for further revolutionary change. With disestablishment accomplished in several colonies and threatened in all, the church as an institution seemed less self-contained and more dependent upon popular desires if it were to perpetuate itself. By itself, this new condition of financial precariousness did not impose a greater sensitivity to secular purposes. But considered with the strengthened authority of laymen and the increased authority of the national state, disestablishment inevitably resulted in renewed secularization. Revivals would break out again at the end of the century, but despite their familiar incantations to original sin and human depravity, Protestantism would have to accommodate itself increasingly to non-religious values.

The proclivity to see things in moral terms persisted; it is one of the enduring American characteristics. Many of the old symbols survived too, with undiminished evocative capacity, though they were susceptible to fresh interpretations. The liberty tree, for example, took on meanings defined more by politics than by morals. The problems of the society offered further promise of secularization—especially the need to ease sectional tensions. And the questions surrounding the national government's role in economic life, which would receive a neo-mercantilist resolution under Hamilton's careful tuition, carried the state far away from any religious issues.

The ritualization of the Revolution in the eighteenth century remained faithful then to Revolutionary values, clarifying and expressing them. Revolutionary experience itself was so evocative of the colonial past, and still so promising of the future, that in some measure it acted to check for a time the extravagant ritualization of the intense sense of American destiny, and the absolutist conceptions of America, which would appear in the nineteenth century. Yet by the end of the Revolution, ritualistic and symbolic expression had taken on an ambiguous character, still indebted to the past and yet holding promise of development.

2 The Developing National Temper

American Schoolbooks
and "Culture"
in the Nineteenth Century

Ruth Miller Elson

INTRODUCTION

The persistent moralism of nineteenth-century Americans, their devotion to utility in contrast to an indifference to esthetics, and their self-regarding nationalism continue to fascinate historians concerned with understanding and defining the national temper. Elson's discussion may not explain the origins of these cultural traits, but it goes a long way toward explaining how they were perpetuated and how they were modified over time. This article also deserves attention for still another reason: its meticulous examination of children's textbooks, a source of information about the American mentality that is usually ignored by cultural historians. Elson's comments on these textbooks, studied in conjunction with the discussions of folk heroes and manifest destiny, will reveal much about the development of American values.

Students may wish to consult any of the great studies of American character from Tocqueville on; they should also see Ruth Miller Elson, *Guardians of Tradition: American Schoolbooks of the Nineteenth Century* (1964). For the colonial background of Elson's subject, see Lawrence A. Cremin, *American Education: The Colonial Experience, 1607–1763* (1970), a monumental account. Cremin's *The American Common School: An Historic Conception* (1951) is valuable for study of the nineteenth century. See also Michael Katz, *The Irony of Early School Reform: Educational Innovation in Mid-Nineteenth Century Massachusetts* (1968); Neil G. McCluskey, *Public Schools and Moral Education: The Influence of Horace Mann, William Torrey Harris, and John Dewey* (1958); J. Merton England, "The Democratic Faith in American Schoolbooks, 1783–1860," *American Quarterly*, XV (1963), 191–99.

Does America have a culture of its own? Has America contributed to that concept of culture which Noah Webster and the nineteenth century defined as "the enlightenment and refinement of taste acquired by intellectual and aesthetic training"?[1] This issue has been lightly and hotly debated across the Atlantic for a century and a half, and European criticisms of our contributions to scholarship and the fine arts made Americans painfully sensitive to any trans-Atlantic discussions in these areas. But the discussion in the United States was continuous; it reached points of egocentric frenzy at times when Americans were particularly proud of themselves in other respects vis-à-vis Europe, as in the periods after the American Revolution, the War of 1812, and World War II. The discussion has generally revolved around two questions: Has the United States produced art and scholarship of a quality comparable to that of Europe? Has the United States a literary and aesthetic culture of its own?

After the Revolution these issues were posed by American writers and intellectuals when they called for the development of a distinctively American culture. Immediately after the achievement of American political independence, Noah Webster hoped to separate America from Britain culturally by the creation of a distinctive American system of spelling. Charles Brockden Brown called on American literary men to use the resources of the American scene and, in his novel *Wieland,* illustrated his point by transposing the Gothic novel from the ruined castle of Europe to the American forest. In 1837 Ralph Waldo Emerson issued his famous declaration of independence for American scholars in an address at Harvard. The activities of James Fenimore Cooper, William Cullen Bryant, and others in calling for an American art as well as in creating one are well known.

That the American intellectual in the first part of our national existence wished to encourage American creativity in the fine arts and in scholarship cannot be questioned. But was the ordinary American aware of this? Was he encouraged to consider these fields worth cultivating in America? Was the intellectual climate in which the Americans lived favorable to the development of American scholars, or were potential scholars generally turned into the more useful field of schoolteaching? Was the American public encouraged to consider the fine arts an important element in national development?

What the a-verbal man of the past thought about anything is probably forever lost to historical research. But by examining the books that most Americans read one can at least discover those ideas to which they were exposed. In the nineteenth century, apart from the Bible, the books most widely read were not those written by intellectuals, but schoolbooks written by printers, journal-

FROM Ruth Miller Elson, "American Schoolbooks and 'Culture' in the Nineteenth Century," *Mississippi Valley Historical Review,* XLVI (December 1959), 411–34. Reprinted by permission.

[1] *Webster's New International Dictionary* (2nd ed., Springfield, Mass., 1946).

ists, future lawyers earning their way through college, teachers, and ministers.[2] However ill-qualified to do so, the authors of schoolbooks both created and solidified American traditions. The selective process by which they decided what political, economic, social, cultural, and moral concepts should be presented to American youth undoubtedly helped to form the average American's view of the past, the present, and the possible future of man. The choice of what was to be admired in the past and present and preserved for the future was likely to be the first formal evaluation of man and his works to which the child was exposed, and it came to him from authority. The schoolbooks also delineated for the American child an idealized image of himself and of the history that had produced the much-admired American type. These books, then, were a kind of compendium of ideas popularly approved at the time, and they are an excellent index of concepts considered proper for the nineteenth-century American.[3] And while their nationalism demanded pride in American productions of any sort, they were far from encouraging to the potential artist or scholar. In these schoolbooks, scholarship and the fine arts were considered fields unfit for the American.

The primary intellectual value embodied in these books is that the only important knowledge is that which is "useful." The word "knowledge" is so often preceded by the word "useful" that it is clear only such knowledge is approved, and it is this kind of knowledge that is provided by a sound education. Useful knowledge is presumed to be uniquely characteristic of American education. The best definition of this "useful knowledge" as used in nineteenth-century schoolbooks comes from an 1807 reader, and was acceptable throughout the century:

> Our government and habits are republican; they cherish equal rights and tend to an equal distribution of property. Our mode of education has the same tendency to promote an equal distribution of knowledge, and to make us emphatically a "republic of letters." I would not be understood adept in the fine arts, but participants of useful knowledge. . . . We are all scholars in the useful; and employed in improving the works of nature, rather than in imitating them.[4]

And because of our special preparation in this kind of knowledge, the useful arts have become the peculiar province of the American. A reader of the 1850's notes: "In the arts which contribute to domestic culture and national aggrandizement, the American states will sustain no unfavorable comparison with Europe."[5] By the latter part of the century American achievements in this area have been recognized by all: "The ingenuity of the people of the United States has passed into a proverb. To them are due many of the inventions

---

[2] By the end of the century experts such as Arnold H. Guyot and Matthew F. Maury in geography and John Fiske and Edward Channing in history were used. But the books most read—the spellers and readers—continued to be turned out by those who were apparently learning by doing.

[3] This paper is part of a larger study of the social and cultural concepts in nineteenth-century schoolbooks. It is based on an analysis of 1,050 of the most popular readers, spellers, geographies, histories, and some arithmetics used in American schools from 1776 to 1900. Most of them are available in the Plimpton Collection in the Columbia University Library.

[4] Caleb Bingham, *The Columbian Orator* (Boston, 1807), 299.

[5] Epes Sargent, *The Standard Fourth Reader* (Boston, 1856), 167. See also William Swinton, *Swinton's Fifth Reader and Speaker* (New York, 1883), 411–13; Joel D. Steele and Esther B. Steele, *A Brief History of the United States* (New York, 1898), 307–08.

which have contributed most to the comfort and improvement of the race."[6] Thus useful knowledge is interpreted in a narrow sense; those arts that are functional to a more comfortable material life are equated to republicanism and to Americanism. Talents in these fields are inherent in the Americans and unique to them: "While many other nations are wasting the brilliant efforts of genius in monuments of ingenious folly, to perpetuate their pride, the Americans, according to the true spirit of republicanism, are employed almost entirely in works of public and private utility."[7]

In all of these books the fact that we have not produced scholars is noted with pride as a sign that knowledge is democratically diffused instead of being concentrated in the hands of an upper class:

> In the monarchical and aristocratic governments of Europe . . . a few privileged orders monopolize not only the wealth and honors, but the knowledge of their country. They produce a few profound scholars, who make study the business of their lives; we acquire a portion of science as a necessary instrument of livelihood, and deem it absurd to devote our whole lives to the acquisition of implements without having it in our power to make them useful to ourselves or others.[8]

Our institutions of higher learning are not designed to produce scholars; they are institutions

> Where homebred freemen seize the solid prize;
> Fixt in small spheres with safer beams to shine.
> They reach the useful and refuse the fine,
> Found on its proper base, the social plan,
> The broad plain truths, the common sense of man.[9]

Another book notes happily: "There are none of those splendid establishments such as Oxford and Cambridge in which immense salaries maintain the professors of literature in monastic idleness. . . . The People of this country have not yet been inclined to make much literary display—They have rather aimed at works of general utility."[10] Instead of such aristocratic institutions, public schools and small libraries have been set up in towns and villages all over the United States, "which serve a more valuable purpose, in the general diffusion of knowledge."[11] Instead of an isolated group of scholars toiling away in useless labor we produce educated men whose minds are bent to the improvement of society. "The greatest scholars of the country . . . have not deemed the latter [schoolbooks] an unworthy labor."[12] Most of our learned men "are so devoted to the instruction of youth, or the active employments of life, as to leave little opportunity for the prosecution of literary research, or scientific discovery."[13] And indeed the actual situation described here was

[6] George P. Quackenbos, *American History for Schools* (New York, 1879), 305.
[7] Jedidiah Morse, *Geography Made Easy* (Boston, 1791), 87. See also William H. McGuffey, *McGuffey's New Juvenile Speaker* (Cincinnati, 1860), 55–56.
[8] Bingham, *Columbian Orator*, 299.
[9] Rodolphus Dickinson, *The Columbian Reader* (Boston, 1815), 188, quoted from Joel Barlow.
[10] John L. Blake, *A Geographical, Chronological, and Historical Atlas* (New York, 1826), 165.
[11] William C. Woodbridge and Emma Willard, *Universal Geography, Ancient and Modern* (Hartford, 1824), 205.
[12] William H. Venable, *A School History of the United States* (Cincinnati, 1872), 183.
[13] William C. Woodbridge, *System of Modern Geography* (Hartford, 1866), 339.

sometimes elevated and abstracted into a principle of virtuous behavior for scholars: "It is not in literary production only, or chiefly, that the educated mind finds fit expression, and fulfills its mission in honor and beneficence. In the great theatre of the world's affairs there is a worthy and sufficient sphere."[14] Even on an elementary level scholarship was associated with Europe rather than with America. A delightful illustration of this occurs in an 1828 reader. Next to a picture entitled "German with Book" is the sentence: "The Germans read, write, and think a great deal."[15] Such activities were evidently not to be regarded by the child as part of the ordinary life of man, but were worthy of note as functions of a particular foreign culture.

Besides reserving education for the elite and sponsoring useless knowledge, the European universities have another serious disadvantage which it corrected in American institutions of higher learning. "The colleges and universities of Europe differ materially from those of the United States. They are rather places of study for such as wish to acquire knowledge. Scarcely any control or care is exercised over the character and conduct of the students, and their efforts are purely voluntary."[16] As a result, although the European university produced serious scholars it also produced men learned in the ways of drink, gambling, dissipation, and vice—activities that aroused transports of horror in the schoolbooks.[17]

The picture of the American college in these schoolbooks is one of an institution designed to inculcate moral values rather than intellectual ones; it should instill useful knowledge in the sense of principles useful to the maintenance of Christianity (Protestant, except in those books written for the parochial schools), the American form of government, and the American society. The colleges were firmly founded on the principle stated by Webster in a most popular 1805 reader: "How little of our peace and security depends on REASON and how much on *religion* and *government*."[18] The function of the American college was to produce men who were prepared to uphold the values already dominant in society rather than to examine them critically. It was the formation of character and sound principles rather than the pursuit of truth that was to engage the university student. This conception of the function of higher education in America has interesting implications for the principle of academic freedom. If the primary duty of the professor is to train the student in principles accepted as good by American society, then it is logical to contend that American society has the right to investigate the beliefs held by college teachers.

It was not the university, however, that was regarded in American schoolbooks as the most effective carrier of civilization; it was rather the common school that was to perpetuate what the authors considered most important in American civilization. Every author pointed with pride to the public school system as one of the most distinctive features of American civilization. A typical statement, emphasizing spread rather than depth, is the following: "Edu-

[14] Floyd B. Wilson, *Wilson's Book of Recitations and Dialogues* (New York, 1869), 159, quoted from George R. Putnam.
[15] [Eliza Robbins], *American Popular Lessons* (New York, 1828), 22.
[16] Woodbridge, *System of Modern Geography*, 345.
[17] For an example of this see Lucius Osgood, *Osgood's American Fifth Reader* (New York, 1872), 170–73.
[18] Noah Webster, *An American Selection of Lessons in Reading and Speaking* (Salem, Mass., 1805), 147.

cation is more widely diffused in this than in any other country in the world."[19] And America's devotion to universal education is old: "The idea of popular education was brought to the new world by our forefathers. Even in the wilderness, while the wolf prowled about the log-house, and the cry of the wild-cat was still heard, the school and even the college, were established."[20]

But it is clear from the books used in these schools that the purpose of the common school as well as of the university was to train the heart rather than the head. Emma Willard's preface to her 1868 history was quite explicit: "We have, indeed, been desirous to cultivate the memory, the intellect and the taste. But much more anxious have we been to sow the seeds of virtue by showing the good in such amicable lights that the youthful heart shall kindle into desires of imitation."[21] That virtue is superior to knowledge or even to wisdom was stressed, as in this admonition by Alice Cary: "Little children, you must seek Rather to be good than wise";[22] or, on a more advanced level, "Man's intellect is not man's sole nor best adorning."[23] It has often been stated in histories of American education that the American public school system was instituted to train citizens, native and immigrant, and to equalize classes, but the evidence of the schoolbooks would seem to indicate that this was to be accomplished by training character as well as by imparting knowledge. The "useful knowledge" offered in the school was useful to success in the material world, but it was also aimed to produce those qualities of character that we associate both with Puritanism and with the self-made man: thrift, hard work, and the rejection of frivolity.

In the early readers and spellers most of the literary excerpts are taken from *The Tatler* and *The Spectator,* from the writings of Franklin, Pope, Sterne, Dryden, Swift, and from various religious tracts. From the 1820's on the contemporary literature of Romanticism became dominant, and remained so throughout the century, disregarding newer trends in literature. Bryant, Longfellow, Whittier, Emerson, and watered down versions of these were fed to the child in a steady diet. Heroism, death, illness, decay, a mystical nationalism, a transcendental approach to nature, and the process of winning success against great odds were the popular subjects. But underlying all of these was the premise that the heart was more important than the head. The nearest approach to realism in the late nineteenth century was in the very large literature of the self-made man; here, although the head was important in achieving success, yet success came only to the pure in heart.

In the schoolbook characterizations of the great men of America some of the same attitudes are evident. All assumed that the function of American society was to produce men great in character as well as in achievements. And all were confident that America was peculiarly distinguished by these virtuous

---

[19] Francis McNally, *An Improved System of Geography* (New York, 1875), 54.

[20] [Joel D. Steele], *A Brief History of the United States* (New York, 1889 [?]), 307.

[21] Emma Willard, *Abridged History of the United States or Republic of America* (New York, 1868), preface.

[22] H. I. Gourley and J. N. Hunt, *The Modern Third Reader* (New York, 1882), 196.

[23] Richard G. Parker and J. Madison Watson, *The National Fifth Reader* (New York, 1867), 338. See also William H. McGuffey, *McGuffey's New Fourth Eclectic Reader* (Cincinnati, 1866), 79–80; Epes Sargent, *Sargent's Standard Second Reader* ([1866?], title page missing), 101; Charles W. Sanders, *Sanders' Union Fourth Reader* (New York, 1870), 314–15; William H. McGuffey, *McGuffey's Fourth Eclectic Reader* (New York, [189?], 1879 copyright), 151–53.

heroes; the United States "has already produced some of the greatest and best men who have ever lived."[24] And in the future:

> But why may not Columbia's soil
> Rear men as great as Britain's isle;
> Exceed what Greece and Rome have done,
> Or any land beneath the sun?[25]

The distinction between the great men of Europe and those of America was a sharp one in the schoolbooks. American heroes were distinguished for their virtue; European heroes were remembered for their vices as soldiers, or as "great scholars who were pensioned flatterers of power, and poets, who profaned the high gift of genius, to pamper the vices of a corrupted court."[26]

The two men who appeared most often and most emphatically as heroes were George Washington and Benjamin Franklin. In words attributed to John Quincy Adams: "What other two men, whose lives belong to the eighteenth century of Christendom, have left a deeper impression of themselves upon the age in which they lived, and upon all after time?"[27] The heroic stature of Washington was unique; he appeared rather as divinity than as man. As a Christlike liberator the contrast between Washington and European heroes was sharp indeed. That this greatest of all men appeared in the United States is sufficient justification for American civilization:

> At the grand and soothing idea that this greatest instance of human perfectibility, this conspicuous phenomenon of human elevation and grandeur should have been permitted to rise first on the horizon of America, every citizen of these states must feel his bosom beat with rapturous and honest pride, tempered with reverential gratitude to the great author and source of all perfection. . . . He will be penetrated with astonishment, and kindled into thanksgiving when he reflects that our globe had existed six thousand years before a Washington appeared on the theatre of the world; and that he was then destined to appear in America—to be the ornament, the deliverer, the protector, the delight![28]

The same idea is contained in an excerpt from Daniel Webster's oration at Bunker Hill in 1843, which appears in many books: "America has furnished to the world the character of Washington! And if our American institutions had done nothing else, that alone would have entitled them to the respect of mankind."[29]

[24] John L. Blake, *A Geography for Children* (Boston, 1831), 16–17.
[25] Bingham, *Columbian Orator,* 58.
[26] John Goldsbury and William Russell, *The American Common-School Reader and Speaker* (Boston, 1844), 94–95. See also Sargent, *Standard Fourth Reader,* 313–16; Anon., *Fourth Progressive Reader* (New York, c. 1873), 239–41 (for Catholic schools); Noah Webster, *The Elementary Spelling Book* (New York, 1857), 50, 52.
[27] Goldsbury and Russell, *Common-School Reader,* 419–20; Swinton, *Fifth Reader and Speaker,* 318; [William H. McGuffey], *McGuffey's Alternate Fifth Reader* (Cincinnati, 1888), 299. See also Jesse Torrey, Jr., *Familiar Spelling Book* (Philadelphia, 1825), frontispiece; Epes Sargent, *The Standard Speller* (Boston, 1856), 157; John J. Anderson, *The United States Reader* (New York, 1873), 237–38.
[28] Ignatius Thomson, *The Patriot's Monitor, for New Hampshire* (Randolph, Vt., 1810), 70. See also George S. Hillard, *The Franklin Fifth Reader* (Boston, 1871), 342; Swinton, *Fifth Reader and Speaker,* 372.
[29] Goldsbury and Russell, *Common School Reader,* 386–88; Marcus Smith, *The Boston Speaker* (Boston, 1844), 19–23; Salem Town, *The Grammar School Reader* (Portland, Me., 1852), 351–53;

As they did with all hero-figures, the textbook authors attach to Washington's prestige-giving figure the virtues that they expect the child to emulate, whether these bear any resemblance to the hero's life or not. He is brave, charitable, industrious, religious, courteous, and a paragon of the domestic virtues. The best qualities of the self-made man are his, and from the 1840's on he is exalted as such in many books.[30] But in no instance are intelligence, learning, or disinterested inquiry associated with Washington. Indeed, in some of the later books he is specifically shown as a practical man who rejected the intellectual life. It is said that "He was more solid than brilliant, and had more judgment than genius. He had great dread of public life, cared little for books, and possessed no library."[31] As a child Washington "was fonder of playing out of doors than study in school, for he was a strong, manly boy, who could best all his school-mates in their sports."[32] This would seem to imply an unbridgeable abyss between the physically active boy and the student, between the successful man of affairs and the scholar. Manliness and scholarship would seem to be antithetical. And manliness was for the American, scholarship for the effete European.

Nor are intellectual qualities attached, as in this case they might logically be, to the second hero-figure of these books—Benjamin Franklin. It is not Franklin the scientist, cosmopolite, and democrat who appears here; it is rather Franklin the apotheosis of the self-made man. His temperance, industry, and thrift are praised to the highest degree as ends in themselves rather than as the conveniences that they seem to be to Franklin himself. His biography appears many times, and almost every schoolbook contains some of his adages with or without acknowledgment of their source. Washington is the hero of great actions and virtue; Franklin is the typical American writ large. But in both cases it is moral and patriotic rather than intellectual stature that elevates these Americans.

The only public figure to whom scholarship is ever a sign of distinction is Thomas Jefferson, but he is a quite minor figure in these books, only occasionally noted as a scholar. He is more than offset by Daniel Boone, a figure with obvious appeal to school-children, and one who was "ignorant of books, but versed in the forest and forest life."[33] The American hero-figure was

Epes Sargent, *The Standard Third Reader* (Boston, 1859), 81–82; William H. McGuffey, *McGuffey's New Fifth Eclectic Reader* (Cincinnati, 1866), 273; Anderson, *United States Reader*, 307–08.

[30] Daniel Adams, *The Monitorial Reader* (Concord, N.H., 1845), 210; American Society for the Diffusion of Useful Knowledge, *The English Spelling Book* (New York, 1847), 120; Epes Sargent, *The First Class Standard Reader* (Boston, 1854), 249–51; Joseph B. Burleigh, *The Thinker: A Moral Reader, Part I* (Philadelphia, 1855), 41–43; Charles W. Sanders, *The School Reader, Third Book* (New York, 1864), 233–34; Epes Sargent and Amasa May, *The New American Fifth Reader* (Philadelphia, 1871), 65–66; Mrs. Lewis B. Monroe, *The Story of Our Country* (Boston, 1889), 179–80.

[31] Steele and Steele, *Brief History of the United States* (1898 edition), 150 (same in 1881 and 1889 editions); William T. Harris, Andrew J. Rickoff, and Mark Bailey, *The Fifth Reader* (New York, 1879), 367–69. See also *McGuffey's Alternate Fifth Reader*, 242–44; Monroe, *Story of Our Country*, 180; M. E. Thalheimer, *The Eclectic History of the United States* (Cincinnati, 1881 [actually probably 1888]), 187.

[32] Charles Morris, *Primary History of the United States* (Philadelphia, 1899 [actually includes material to 1904]), 131.

[33] James Baldwin, *School Reading by Grades: Fifth Year* (New York, 1897), 102. See also William T. Harris, Andrew J. Rickoff, and Mark Bailey, *The Fourth Reader* (New York, 1880), 165–68; Eliza H. Morton, *Potter's Advanced Geography* (Philadelphia, 1891), 78; George F. Holmes and Frank A. Hill, *Holmes' Fourth Reader* (New York, 1899), 221; Morris, *Primary History of the United States*, 172.

stereotyped, then, as a practical, moral, hard-working man who needs "useful knowledge" to get ahead in the world, but finds scholarship unnecessary and even demeaning.

Was the child specifically encouraged to read on his own? He was exhorted to apply the Franklin virtues to his school work and to the acquisition of "useful knowledge" as a part of his struggle for success in the world. But doubts were frequently expressed as to both the quantity and the quality of books that he should read. He must be careful not to read too much: "She is a strange child. She will take a book and read it while the boys and girls run and play near her. I fear she reads and thinks too much. The brain must have rest."[34] Furthermore the frequent appearance of excerpts from the writings of Emerson and Wordsworth, shorn in this context of transcendental qualities, seems to recommend the achievement of the good life only by the rejection of the intellectual life in favor of direct experience. The following are typical examples:

> Up! up! my friend and quit your books
> Or surely you'll grow double;
> Books! 'Tis a dull and endless strife. . . .[35]

> I laugh at the lore and the pride of man,
> At the sophists' schools, and the learned clan;
> For what are they all in their high conceit,
> When man in the bush with God may meet.[36]

Taken out of context in this way, Wordsworth (more popular in the first half of the century) and Emerson (popular in the second half of the century) seem to stand for anti-intellectualism rather than awareness of the insufficiency of reason. There are countless tales of the value of direct experience over the value of book experience. A typical case is the tale of a boy forced by family difficulties to go to work rather than to go on with school. A merchant about to hire him gives him this advice: "Manhood is better than Greek. Self-reliance is worth more to a man than Latin."[37] Here, obviously, it is the self-reliance of self-support in a financial, not a spiritual, sense that is considered desirable. Emerson has been adapted to the market place.

Apart from the question of quantity, it was thought that reading must be carefully limited in quality to those books that impart "useful knowledge" and that strengthen character. William H. McGuffey, for example, believed that only "good" books are to be used—books that will inspire the reader with "love of what is right and useful." He continued: "Next to the fear of God, implanted in the heart nothing is a better safeguard to character, than the love of good books. They are the handmaids of virtue and religion."[38] Conversely:

---

[34] Richard Soule and William Wheeler, *First Lessons in Reading* (Boston, 1866), 41. See also Marcius Willson, *The Fifth Reader* (New York, 1872), 163; George S. Hillard, *The Franklin Advanced Fourth or Intermediate Reader* (New York, 1874), 53; A. J. Demarest and William M. Van Sickle, *New Education Readers: Book Two* (New York, 1900), 132.

[35] From Wordsworth's "Vacation Song," quoted in Loomis J. Campbell, *The New Franklin Fourth Reader* (New York, 1884), 215–16.

[36] From Emerson's "Goodby," quoted in Campbell, *The New Franklin Fifth Reader* (New York, 1884), 109–10.

[37] Mrs. Lewis B. Monroe, *The Fifth Reader* (Philadelphia, 1871), 58–59.

[38] *McGuffey's New Fifth Eclectic Reader*, 92.

"Bad books are the public fountains of vice."[39] The reading of novels (and few distinctions are made among them) was almost always condemned in the first half of the century, and frequently in the latter half. An 1868 reader, in seeking the cause of the complete deterioration of a character under discussion, asks: "Is it the bottle or the betting book? Is it the billiard table or the theatre? Is it smoking? Is it laziness? Is it novel-reading?"[40] So the child was cautioned to read with great selectivity—a selectivity based not on training one's taste by wide reading but by canons laid down by authority. He was not only warned not to read too much, but his purpose in reading was to be censored. To read for pleasure was frowned upon: "A book which is torn and mutilated is abused, but one which is merely read for enjoyment is misused."[41]

It is clear from this evidence that anti-intellectualism is not only not new in American civilization, but that it is thoroughly embedded in the schoolbooks that have been read by generations of pupils since the beginning of the republic. The rejection of the intellectual required the rejection of an intellectual past—that of the Puritans and of the founders of the republic—as part of the American tradition. The frontier did not need scholarship, whereas "useful knowledge" was essential to survival. And the needs of the frontier were probably reinforced by the needs of expanding business. Thus an 1875 speller records current attitudes in saying: "We do not blame a man who is proud of his success, so much as one who is vain of his learning."[42]

To these schoolbook writers the concept of "usefulness" was perhaps even more important for the fine arts than for the intellectual elements of American culture. Historically, the arts occupied a quite different position from that of scholarship in American development. In undertaking to determine what was to be considered the American tradition it was possible to draw upon an actual scholarly heritage; but the arts had always been held in a distinctly subservient position in America. In the colonial period literary labors were made to serve theology and politics, but the visual and auditory arts were regarded with suspicion by New Englanders as being inconsistent with Puritan precautions against the seductiveness of the senses. It was also true that in a frontier environment relatively few had the leisure or the opportunity to participate, either as creator or as audience, in the fine arts and belles-lettres. Yet by the nineteenth century America had produced many creative artists whose art was not designed to serve some other cause; and the fact that their work was too important to be ignored raises questions as to how the schoolbooks evaluated their contributions. Was the American child in this period, for example, taught to regard the arts as worthy of serious attention? To what extent were they

39 Henry N. Day, *The American Speller* (New York, 1869), 163. See also M. J. Kerney, *The First Class Book of History* (Baltimore, 1868), 216 (for Catholic schools); Sherman Williams, *Choice Literature: Book I for Grammar Grades* (New York, 1898), 330, 334; Sherman Williams, *Choice Literature: Book I for Primary Grades* (New York, 1898), pref., p. 3; George L. Aldrich and Alexander Forbes, *The Progressive Course in Reading, Fifth Book* (New York, 1900), Part I, 18–19.
40 Richard G. Parker and J. Madison Watson, *The National Third Reader* (New York, 1868), 118. See also Sargent and May, *New American Fifth Reader*, 146–49; Sherman Williams, *Choice Literature: Book II for Grammar Grades* (New York, 1898), 136. Actually, certain "moral" novels were recommended, such as those by Scott and Cooper.
41 Lillian Kupfer, *The Natural Speller and Word Book* (New York, 1890), 58. See also Epes Sargent, *The Standard Third Reader*, Part II (Boston, 1866), 129; Baldwin, *School Reading by Grades: Fifth Year*, 7–9; S. W. Black, *Fifth Reader* (Chicago, 1898), 7–12.
42 Lewis B. Monroe, *The Practical Speller* (Philadelphia, 1875), 144.

considered to be essential or, at the least, important to national development?

Music and the fine arts appeared in these schoolbooks primarily in discussions of three subjects: the self-made artist, national monuments, and evaluations of American art. Those paintings and sculptures that glorified American heroes and the American past were frequently noted. For example, the statues of Washington in Richmond, Baltimore, and Raleigh were almost always mentioned in the sections of the geographies devoted to those cities. But discussions of the aesthetic qualities of such works are absent; they are to be observed for nationalistic rather than for aesthetic reasons.

Discussions of the fine arts appear mainly in the examples of self-made men in the field of the arts, and it is evident that in these tales their self-achieved success is more important than their art. The career of the Italian sculptor, Antonio Canova, for example, is described in the same terms as those used to describe the career of a successful businessman of the nineteenth century. The story of his boyhood act of carving a lion out of butter to provide a substitute for a centerpiece which had not been delivered was frequently told. He was praised, however, not as a man of artistic achievement but as one who "was diligent and regular in his habits," and who saw an opportunity for success and used it.[43] A similar tale that appeared more often in the schoolbooks was that the American painter, Benjamin West, too poor as a boy to buy paint brushes, made them of hairs plucked from his cat's tail and taught himself to paint. "Thus we see," runs the moral, "that, by industry, ingenuity, and perseverance, a little American boy became the most distinguished painter of his day in England."[44] Obviously, these are not discussions of talented artists but of self-made men who happened to be artists. Their success was accomplished by diligence combined with the ability to recognize opportunity.

The aesthetic theories held in these books necessarily settled the fine arts into a position inferior to that of literature. The statement that "statues and pictures are pleasing representations of nature"[45] expressed their attitude throughout the century, and Longfellow's aphorism, "Nature is a revelation of God, art is a revelation of man,"[46] was quoted to show that as imitations of nature works of art could never approach nature itself. According to this theory a landscape is of necessity more beautiful than a pleasing representation of it, and God, who is manifest through nature itself, can be discerned but dimly, if at all, through an imperfect imitation. Consequently in the schoolbooks painting and sculpture acquire importance only for extra-artistic qualities. Sculpture was useful to commemorate the dead, and the schoolbooks were not alone in the nineteenth century in recommending tours of the cemeteries

[43] Sargent, *Standard Second Reader*, 146–47. See also Richard G. Parker and J. Madison Watson, *The National Fourth Reader* ([1867?], title page missing), 73–77; Monroe, *Fifth Reader*, 156–57; Gourley and Hunt, *Modern Third Reader*, 225–27; *McGuffey's Alternate Fifth Reader*, 170–74; Black, *Fifth Reader*, 21–25.

[44] Josiah F. Bumstead, *Third Reading-Book in the Primary School* (Boston, 1844), 137–42. See also Bela B. Edwards, *The Eclectic Reader* (Boston, 1832), 297; Adams, *The Monitorial Reader*, 213; Sargent, *Standard Second Reader*, 76–78; Hillard, *Franklin Advanced Fourth or Intermediate Reader*, 156; Joseph E. Worcester, *Pronouncing Spelling-Book of the English Language* (Boston, 1874), 123.

[45] B. Brandreth, *A New System for the Instruction of Youth* (New York, 1836), 98. See also Charles Peirce, *The Arts and Sciences Abridged, with a Selection of Pieces from Celebrated Modern Authors* (Portsmouth, N.H., 1806), 48; Harris, Rickoff, and Bailey, *Fifth Reader*, 397–99; Kupfer, *Natural Speller and Word Book*, 63.

[46] Quoted in Samuel T. Dutton, *The Morse Speller* (New York, 1896), 114.

of Philadelphia and Boston. But more important than this, the fine arts were useful in engendering nationalism by portraying American heroes and historical events. This is made quite clear in what purports to be an aesthetic judgment of the field of painting: "Q. What are the most esteemed paintings? A. Those representing historical events."[47]

The most curious argument in favor of encouraging the fine arts in the United States, and indeed the only argument for encouraging them on any grounds, was presented in an 1826 reader under the heading "Usefulness of the Fine Arts."[48] In this article the fine arts are recommended partly because they would produce a new class of people to be fed and, in the case of sculpture, would stimulate the marble and granite industries. Furthermore, those artists who did not succeed in the fine arts would then turn their talents to the useful arts of the clay, glass, and cotton industries. This process of failure in the fine arts had given England her lead in manufacturing. So, concluded this ingenious author, America should encourage the fine arts not for their own sakes, but that they may be transmuted into the useful arts and so stimulate American industry.

When the arts serve no useful project, however, they are often looked on with suspicion. In statement and by implication the schoolbooks fear that too much concentration on the arts is unhealthy and indeed dangerous to civilization. An excerpt from the writings of Hannah More as quoted in an 1876 text specifically warns of the possibility of such subversion:

> It will be prudent to reflect, that in all polished countries an entire devotedness to the fine arts has been one grand source of the corruption of women. . . . And while corruption brought on by an excessive cultivation of the arts has contributed its full share to the decline of states, it has always furnished an infallible symptom of their impending fall.[49]

Art and the decadence of the individual and society are regarded as natural companions in many of these books. In a frequently quoted poem by Bayard Taylor, "Napoleon at Gotha," for example, the following lines describe a German duke:

> A handsome prince and courtly, of light and shallow heart,
> No better than he should be, but with a taste for art.

And when Napoleon invaded his country:

> But while the German people were silent in despair,
> Duke August painted pictures, and curled his yellow hair.[50]

In the geographies which survey the state of civilization in every country, Europe is always introduced as the seat of the arts and sciences. But the Europe that has produced great art is also the Europe of rigid class distinctions, vice,

---

[47] Peirce, *The Arts and Sciences Abridged*, 48.
[48] John Frost, *The Class Book of American Literature* (Boston, 1826), 43–44.
[49] Anon., *The Young Ladies' Progressive Reader* (New York, 1876), 203 (for Catholic schools).
[50] Lewis B. Monroe, *Monroe's New Fifth Reader* (New York, 1884), 380. See also Parker and Watson, *National Fifth Reader*, 247; Wilson, *Book of Recitations and Dialogues*, 118–20; Thalheimer, *Eclectic History of the United States*, 96.

and degeneracy. In particular, "The Italians are celebrated for their musical skill and perfection in the fine arts";[51] but the descriptions of Italian national character and Italian morals would hardly be a recommendation for accomplishments in the arts. Italy is generally described as a land of beggars, filth, and poverty, and the Italians as a degenerate, superstitious, revengeful, effeminate, and immoral people. This unfavorable view of the Italians was undoubtedly the result of a strong anti-Catholic bias in American schoolbooks, but the conjunction of such a national character with the greatest talents in the fine arts of any country in the world would hardly persuade the Americans that the cultivation of the fine arts was necessary for national development.

On the other hand, in the view of these schoolbooks art can and should have a moral purpose. It should show that virtue inevitably leads to beauty, and that the only true beauty is that which is equated to goodness:

> Would'st behold beauty
> Near thee, all round?
> Only hath duty
> Such a sight found.[52]

But it was to literature rather than to painting and sculpture that the schoolbooks turned for their discussion of the relationship between beauty and goodness. The literary man, according to one of them, "thinks beautiful thoughts, and tells them in beautiful words, and he helps to make people better by showing how beautiful goodness is."[53] Even here, however, it was content, not artistic form, that determined the merit of a literary production. The same piece (a comment on Henry Wadsworth Longfellow) goes on to say: "But it is not the way it is written that makes a poem, but rather the beautiful thought in it." Indeed it is clear from the literary excerpts in the spellers and readers (most of these, beyond the primer, are anthologies) that style was considered in the nature of a clever trick and was of very little importance to the authors and editors of these books. Wordsworth, Emerson, Irving, and Dickens are there, but they are outspaced by Alcott, Longfellow, Mrs. Hemans, Mrs. Sigourney, and Lydia Maria Child. Longfellow's poem "The Day Is Done" was taken to heart by these authors and editors, especially the passage in which the poet asks to have poetry read to him:

> Not from the grand old masters,
> Not from the bards sublime. . . .
>
> Read from some humbler poet,
> Whose songs gushed from his heart,
> As showers from the clouds of summer
> Or tears from the eyelids start.[54]

[51] McNally, *Improved System of Geography*, 75.

[52] Monroe, *Monroe's New Fifth Reader*, 366. See also Parker and Watson, *National Third Reader*, 46; Hillard, *Franklin Advanced Fourth or Intermediate Reader*, 155–56; William B. Watkins, *McGuffey's Alternate Spelling Book* (Cincinnati, 1888), 24; William H. McGuffey, *McGuffey's Third Eclectic Reader* (New York, 1896), 65; James Baldwin, *School Reading by Grades: Third Year* (New York, 1897), 208; Harry Pratt Judson and Ida C. Bender, *Graded Literary Readers: Third Book* (New York, 1900), 127.

[53] Sarah L. Arnold and Charles B. Gilbert, *Stepping Stones to Literature: A Reader for Seventh Grades* (New York, 1897), 29–30.

[54] Baldwin, *School Reading by Grades: Fourth Year*, 65–66.

That good literature is thought to be moral, and to engender morality in its readers is evident in the following samples of the adjectives used in literary criticism in the schoolbooks: Bryant—"Lofty moral tone";[55] Alcott—"Healthy tone";[56] Whittier—"His verse is distinguished by vigor and a certain moral sweetness";[57] Scott—"Healthfulness of tone."[58] And because moral qualities should be paramount in his writings, it was considered entirely proper to inquire into the author's moral behavior in life. Scott comes out very well in this respect. More attention is given in several books to his labors to pay back creditors than to his writings: "The sterling integrity of the man shown forth in this dark hour."[59] This portrayal of an honest and industrious man was used as an introduction to and an evaluation of his writings. Byron, on the other hand, is to be read with caution. His poems are of "startling power on new and original themes. The principles inculcated in some of these shocked his countrymen, and still offend the moral sense of readers."[60] Coleridge's use of opium[61] and the dissipation of Burns[62] interfered with and marred the work of these two writers And ironically, Poe, the American writer of whom they could have been the most proud because of his European reputation, also falls into this category. Although his writings showed "marked ability, [they] are marred by their morbid subjects and their absence of moral feeling."[63] "He was intemperate, quarrelsome and without business ability. . . . Nothing that he has written can fairly be called of a high class. His chief fame rests on his cleverness in constructing plots, and his use of the grotesque and weird."[64] Only one book admits that although he led a dissipated life and died young in consequence, still "He left behind him some of the choicest treasures of American Literature."[65] Frequently the introduction to a literary excerpt, and its moral evaluation of the author, is more extensive than the piece of literature itself. Literature was to be interpreted according to its moral tone; should it lack moral qualities or embody the wrong ones it was not good literature.

It should be noted that the selectivity used in discarding improper pieces from the schoolbooks did not operate as effectively in some of the books published before 1820. Excerpts from Shakespeare and Molière used in that period did not always embody the "lofty moral tone" that later became standard in the schoolbooks. On the other hand, these pieces were often taken out of context in such peculiar ways that they made no sense, moral or otherwise. Pedagogical improvement changed the books in the latter respect, but also eliminated some subjects that had heretofore appeared.

From the 1820's on, all gambling, drinking, and laziness are condemned. All women are virtuous, or wish they had been as they sink into a miserable

---

[55] Hillard, *Franklin Fifth Reader*, 155.   [56] *Ibid.*, 294.   [57] Monroe, *Fifth Reader*, 314.
[58] George F. Holmes and Frank A. Hill, *Holmes' Fifth Reader* (New York, 1896), 161.
[59] Black, *Fifth Reader*, 162–65. See also *McGuffey's Alternate Fifth Reader*, 95; Williams, *Choice Literature: Book I for Grammar Grades*, 17–18.
[60] Campbell, *New Franklin Fifth Reader*, 238. See also Williams, *Choice Literature: Book II for Grammar Grades*, 289–94; Aldrich and Forbes, *Progressive Course in Reading, Fifth Book*, Part II, 76.
[61] *McGuffey's Alternate Fifth Reader*, 227.
[62] Williams, *Choice Literature: Book II for Grammar Grades*, 315.
[63] Aldrich and Forbes, *Progressive Course in Reading, Fifth Book*, Part II, 78.
[64] Williams, *Choice Literature: Book I for Grammar Grades*, 223. See also Swinton, *Fifth Reader and Speaker*, 120.
[65] Arnold and Gilbert, *Stepping Stones to Literature*, 193.

death; all widows are poor and honest; all married women are mothers with the virtues thereof; all self-respecting men try for financial success; there are no physical relations between the sexes even if hallowed by marriage. Yet this does not indicate a general denial of the material world, for the acquisition of goods by the individual and the nation is regarded as a national blessing. But just as Whitman is conspicuously absent from the anthologies, so the physical nature of man is a subject to be subdued if mentioned at all.

Throughout the century all of the schoolbooks were sensitive to such European criticisms as those of the Abbé Raynal, who had taken America to task for producing no important artists. Those published before 1830 responded by a simple rejection of Raynal's evaluation and by catalogues of the artists America had produced, such as Trumbull, Copley, West, Barlowe, and others. Many of the lists of American artists culminated with the name of George Washington![66] This would seem to indicate that the textbook authors were not arguing that America had produced better artists than those of Europe, but that she had produced greater men; and one Washington would obviously outweigh any number of artists or scholars. A typical early evaluation of American arts asserted that "Printing, engraving and architecture among the fine arts, as well as the mechanic arts, exhibit as much native genius in the United States as in any part of the world. This genius has been cultivated for the last few years to such a degree as, in some instances, to rival the most splendid and useful exhibitions of art in Europe."[67] A few of the authors at the beginning of the century complained, however, that the American artist found it hard to make a living by his art. They ascribed this situation to the snobbish attitude of some Americans who believed that the only good art was European and refused to give any attention to art produced by an American.

After 1830 the textbook writers changed the grounds for their defense of American art. Abandoning their simple refusal to accept the low evaluation of our arts by European critics, they admitted our inferiority in the arts with an explanation. This inferiority, they said proudly, came from the fact that we had deliberately neglected the fine arts in favor of the arts that produce a comfortable and happy life for everyone. If the founders of America produced no great music, painting, sculpture, architecture, or literature, "It was enough for them to lay the foundation of that noble fabric of civil liberty."[68] McGuffey in 1858 lists freedom, useful knowledge, and patriotism as American gifts to the world which more than make up for our lack of artistic contributions.[69] Our monuments are not Gothic cathedrals, said another commentary, but "an active, vigorous, intelligent, moral population."[70] Thus the American answer to European critics from 1830 through the Civil War held that although American artists might not be equal to those of Europe, America had been engaged in producing something of far greater significance to the world—a superior society.

[66] Alexander Thomas, *The Orator's Assistant* (Worcester, 1797), 211–13; William Biglow, *The Youth's Library* (2 vols., Salem, 1803), I, 164–65; Abner Alden, *The Speaker* (Boston, 1810), 127–30.
[67] William Darby, *Ewing's Geography* (New York, 1820), 91. See also Bingham, *Columbian Orator*, 296–99; Thomas, *Orator's Assistant*, 211–12.
[68] George B. Cheever, *The American Common-Place Book of Prose* (Boston, 1831), 417.
[69] William H. McGuffey, *McGuffey's New Eclectic Speaker* (Cincinnati, 1858), 259–60.
[70] Goldsbury and Russell, *Common-School Reader*, 119–20.

After the Civil War, however, American schoolbooks aggressively placed American artists and writers on a level with those of Europe. Bolstered by a newly proved nationalism and backed by solid accomplishments in American literature they were ready to refute European criticisms. "It is not long," one of them said, "since it was asked 'Who reads an American book?' Now the question is, who does not cherish as household words the names of our charming fiction writers, Irving, Cooper and Hawthorne—our historians, Bancroft, Prescott and Motley—our poets, Bryant and Longfellow, Halleck and Whittier, Lowell and Holmes?" The same author, however, evidently had some slight doubt about the status of American belles-lettres, because he added: "In magazines and school-books especially, the United States has nothing to fear from a comparison with the most cultivated of the older nations."[71] By the 1870's there was general and confident agreement that America had her own literary culture. America has produced many authors, "some of whom have acquired a reputation even in the Old World, and whose works have now become sufficiently numerous and important to form an American literature."[72] Two late-nineteenth-century authors admit that in the past "The greatest triumphs achieved in the United States have been in the direction of mechanical ingenuity; and American literature, science, and art have not yet won the applause of the world quite so thoroughly as have American sewing machines and agricultural implements."[73] But both say that this is much less true in their day, and they are confident that it will be even less so in the future.

In rating American artists, the major criterion used in the schoolbooks is whether they compare favorably to European artists and whether they have been accepted abroad. Gilbert Stuart is proudly put into the first category: "Some critics think he is the best portrait painter of the age except for Joshua Reynolds."[74] And American historiography comes out well by comparison to that of Europe: "Bancroft, Hildreth, Prescott and Motley stand among the best writers of history the world has ever produced."[75] The great landmark in American literature came with its first recognition abroad. The distinction of being the first to achieve this is variously accorded to Irving and Cooper. The author who has brought greatest acclaim to American literature in the eyes of Europe is Emerson, and he is placed even above European writers. McGuffey records Matthew Arnold's opinion that Emerson's work was "the most important work done in prose" in the nineteenth century.[76] At the end of the century this was reaffirmed: "Abroad, Emerson was recognized as a master-mind."[77]

What made American literature American in the eyes of schoolbook writers? Was it part of American literature because it was produced by American citizens, or did it have characteristics of its own? Most of the schoolbooks echo

[71] Quackenbos, *American History for Schools*, 305–06. See also Charles Morris, *An Elementary History of the United States* (Philadelphia, 1890), 192.

[72] Mary L. Hall, *Our World: No. II, A Second Series of Lessons in Geography* (Boston, 1872), 49. See also John J. Anderson, *A Junior Class History of the United States* (New York, 1874), 236.

[73] Thomas Wentworth Higginson, *Young Folks' History of the United States* (Boston, 1875), 328; Morris, *Elementary History of the United States*, 223.

[74] John A. Doyle, *History of the United States* (New York, 1876), 224 (an English work adapted for American schools). See also Parker and Watson, *National Fourth Reader*, 82–84; Samuel Eliot, *History of the United States from 1492 to 1872* (Boston, 1881), 487.

[75] Anderson, *Junior Class History of the United States*, 237.

[76] *McGuffey's Alternate Fifth Reader*, 229.

[77] Arnold and Gilbert, *Stepping Stones to Literature*, 223.

the opinion of Noah Webster in 1783 that America must be culturally independent of Europe:

> While the Americans stand astonished at their former delusion and enjoy the pleasure of a final separation from their insolent sovereigns, it becomes their duty to attend to the *arts of peace*, and particularly to the interests of literature to see if there be not some error to be corrected, some defects to be supplied, and some improvements to be introduced into our systems of education, as well as into those of civil policy. We find Englishmen practising upon very erroneous maxims in politics and religion: and possibly we shall find, upon careful examination, that their methods of education are equally erroneous and defective. . . . Europe is grown old in folly, corruption and tyranny—in that country laws are perverted, manners are licentious, literature is declining and human nature is debased. For America in her infancy to adopt the present maxims of the Old World, would be to stamp the wrinkles of decrepid [*sic*] age upon the bloom of youth and to plant the seeds of decay in a vigorous constitution.[78]

To implement his desire for cultural reform Webster himself engaged in a famous attempt to differentiate American from English spelling. Other authors of schoolbooks suggest that the American artist should find his inspiration in American landscape rather than in the Alps or Westminster Abbey. The American literary man should use American scenes and situations to illustrate American virtues.[79] In this way he will improve on European literature by teaching self-control, initiative, honesty, industry, and other characteristics that differentiate the American from the European. Just as European literature reflects the vices and crimes of Europe, so American literature should reflect the virtues of America, and should then be supported for moral as well as nationalistic reasons.[80] Bryant is frequently used as the ideal American man of letters. "We find in his pages all the most obvious and all the most retiring graces of our native landscapes, but nothing borrowed from books—nothing transplanted from a foreign soil."[81] A lofty moral tone is regarded as characteristic of American authors; it is this that makes American literature unique. Lacking this quality an American author is not considered to be a part of American literature. The most obvious case in point is Edgar Allan Poe. According to the major canon of literary eminence used in these books, European recognition, Poe should have replaced Emerson as our greatest writer by the end of the century. He was not only seriously read abroad, but he influenced the development of French literature. This accolade could not be transferred from the virtuous Emerson to the immoral Poe. Although Poe lived in America, it was said, he did not write American literature.

Whatever might be said of the past, American nationalism demanded that the future of American art be assured. With the establishment of our political and social foundations, our intellectual and artistic prospects were seen to be boundless and unprecedented. To achieve this one need not sponsor or even

[78] Noah Webster, *A Grammatical Institute of the English Language* (Hartford, 1783), Part I, Introduction.
[79] Goldsbury and Russell, *Common-School Reader*, 222–24.
[80] Ebenezer R. Porter, *The Rhetorical Reader* (New York, 1835), 218–19.
[81] George S. Hillard, *A First Class Reader* (Boston, 1856), 96.

encourage the arts; in fact, this is to be avoided. But it is our manifest destiny, when the time comes, to reach such eminence naturally. America is "ordained, we believe, to be the chosen seat of intelligence, of literature, of arts, and of science."[82] It shall be "The first in letters, as the first in arms."[83] Furthermore, American efforts, freed from class limitations, will provide a larger audience for the arts than Europe can afford: "The universal diffusion of knowledge, which distinguishes the United States from the rest of the world, by exciting a literary thirst among the people in general, must also render the patrons of ingenuity and taste infinitely more numerous than they can possibly be in those nations, where the means, the pleasures, and the advantages of information are confined within the limited circles of nobility and wealth."[84] This confidence in the future of America was apparently based on nationalistic optimism, but also on the assumption that a superior political and social system will inevitably breed great art. Since America has the former she will inevitably develop the latter in time:

> Be just, Columbians, and assert your name,
> Avow your genius, and protect your fame.
> The clime which gave a WASHINGTON to you,
> May give an OTWAY and a SHAKESPEARE too.[85]

Thus, although the future of American art was to be as glorious as were all things American, yet no preparation whatever was made in the schoolbooks to encourage the development either of future artists or of a public for art. The American was not expected to accept art, let alone sponsor it for its own sake. This was the attitude of an effete and declining Europe whose civilization the schoolbooks specifically and carefully reject. Only when art becomes propaganda for good morals, or nationalism, or when it is in the service of the useful arts is it worthy of serious attention. According to the schoolbooks it is this kind of art that Americans have produced and will continue to produce.

The child was of course influenced by things other than schoolbooks. But the latter came from authority, and laid a careful foundation particularly important in those areas of thought in which the child might have little personal experience. The nineteenth-century schoolbook, as compared to that of the twentieth century, had relatively little competition from outside sources of information, and poorly trained teachers were often entirely dependent on the text adopted for use in their schools. The method of the classroom in most schools consisted primarily in memorizing the schoolbook.

And the child who accepted the meaning of the words that he memorized would consider scholarship and the fine arts mere embellishments identified with Europe and therefore with a civilization that he was taught to reject as inferior to his own. He would expect men of talent in the arts to serve their nationality consciously in their art. He would think it a waste of time to engage himself in these fields; American creativity was and should be directed

[82] John Pierpont, *Introduction to the National Reader* (Boston, 1828), 167.
[83] Noah Webster, *Instructive and Entertaining Lessons for Youth* (New Haven, 1835), 246. See also Bingham, *Columbian Orator*, 30–34; Herman Mann, *The Material Creation* . . . (Dedham, 1818), ix–xii; Sargent, *Standard Fourth Reader*, 238; Parker and Watson, *National Fifth Reader*, 164–65.
[84] Thomas, *Orator's Assistant*, 211–13.
[85] Joseph Chandler, *The Young Gentleman and Lady's Museum* (Hallowell, Me., 1811), 82.

to the immediately practical. Only when the artist or the scholar used his talents for the extension of good morals, for the development of a comfortable material existence, or for the propagation of nationalism was his work to be respected as good art or scholarship. Guided by his schoolbooks the nineteenth-century American child would grow up to be honest, industrious, religious, and moral. He would be a useful citizen untouched by the effeminate and perhaps even dangerous influence of the arts or scholarship. The concept of American culture presented in these schoolbooks, therefore, had prepared him for a life devoted to the pursuit of material success and a perfected character, but a life in which intellectual and artistic achievements would seem important only when they could be made to subserve some useful purpose.

The Mountain Man as Jacksonian Man

William H. Goetzmann

INTRODUCTION

One of the many virtues of this intriguing article is the questions it raises about the character of Americans in the first half of the nineteenth century. With Richard Hofstadter, Marvin Meyers, and Alexis de Tocqueville, Goetzmann is impressed by these Americans' energetic pursuit of work and profit, whereas other commentators have regarded them as simple and romantic democrats. Goetzmann's article is also distinguished by its use of a statistical technique, employed to discover the occupations entered by mountain men once they left the fur trade. Goetzmann argues that the character and variety of these occupations suggest how quickly the West was transformed into a mercantile and semi-urban society. But if Goetzmann's article is impressive for its suggestiveness and its method, it also adds to our understanding by its reconsiderations of the myths we have long entertained about the American West—and about Jacksonian democracy.

To gain a sense of the way historians have interpreted Jacksonian democracy, students might start with Arthur M. Schlesinger, Jr., *The Age of Jackson** (1945), which emphasizes conflict between eastern workingmen and businessmen. Richard Hofstadter's essay on Jackson in *The American Political Tradition** (1948) argues that Jacksonians were entrepreneurs. See also John W. Ward, *Andrew Jackson: Symbol for an Age** (1955); Marvin Meyers, *The Jacksonian Persuasion: Politics and Belief** (1957); Thomas P. Abernethy, *From Frontier to Plantation in Tennessee* (1932); Lee Benson, *The Concept of Jacksonian Democracy** (1961). The fur trade has been discussed in Hiram M. Chittenden, *The American Fur Trade of the Far West* (3 vols., rev. ed., 1935), and Robert Glass Cleland, *This Reckless Breed of Men: The Trappers and Fur Traders of the Southwest* (1950). There is a good brief discussion of mountain men in Ray A. Billington, *The Far Western Frontier** (1956). Finally, all students of this subject should read Henry Nash Smith, *Virgin Land: The American West as Symbol and Myth** (1950).

132

ONE of the most often studied and least understood figures in American history has been the Mountain Man. Remote, so it would seem, as Neanderthal, and according to some almost as inarticulate, the Mountain Man exists as a figure of American mythology rather than history. As such he has presented at least two vivid stereotypes to the public imagination. From the first he has been the very symbol for the romantic banditti of the forest, freed of the artificial restrictions of civilization —a picturesque wanderer in the wilderness whose very life is a constant and direct association with Nature.

"There is perhaps, no class of men on the face of the earth," said Captain Bonneville [and through him Washington Irving], "who lead a life of more continued exertion, peril, and excitement, and who are more enamoured of their occupations, than the free trappers of the west. No toil, no danger, no privation can turn the trapper from his pursuit. His passionate excitement at times resembles a mania. In vain may the most vigilant and cruel savages beset his path; in vain may rocks, and precipices, and wintry torrents oppose his progress; let but a single track of a beaver meet his eye, and he forgets all dangers and defies all difficulties. At times, he may be seen with his traps on his shoulder, buffeting his way across rapid streams amidst floating blocks of ice: at other times, he is to be found with his traps on his back clambering the most rugged mountains, scaling or descending the most frightening precipices, searching by routes inaccessible to the horse, and never before trodden by white man, for springs and lakes unknown to his comrades, and where he may meet with his favorite game. Such is the mountaineer, the hardy trapper of the west; and such as we have slightly sketched it, is the wild, Robin Hood kind of life,

[*Author's note:*] The term "Jacksonian Man" is used throughout this essay in a general rather than a particular sense. It is intended to describe a fictional composite, the average man of the period under consideration regardless of whether or not he was a follower of Andrew Jackson and his party. Those qualities which I take to be general enough to characterize the average man are defined in my quotations from Richard Hofstadter, Marvin Meyers and Alexis de Tocqueville. It should not be inferred from this that I seek to portray the Mountain Men as members of Andrew Jackson's political party nor that I mean to suggest that the particular objectives of the Democratic Party were necessarily those described by Hofstadter, Meyers and Tocqueville. Rather their terms seem to characterize to some extent men of all political persuasions in this period. Lee Benson in his recent book, *The Concept of Jacksonian Democracy*, has shown that in New York State, at least, the Jackson party had no particular monopoly on such terms as "egalitarianism" and "democracy," and that indeed most parties in the state including the Whigs actually preceded the Jackson men in their advocacy of these views. He thus demonstrates that there were certain values and goals common to all men of the day. Benson then concludes that instead of calling the period "The Age of Jackson," it should properly be called "The Age of Egalitarianism." His evidence indicates to me, however, that a still more precise term for the period might well be "The Age of Expectant Capitalism," and following Hofstadter and Meyers, and before them Frederick Jackson Turner, I have seen this as the most generally applicable descriptive concept for the period. Thus it forms the basis for my definition of "Jacksonian Man," or *Genus Homo Americanus* during the years of the presidency of Andrew Jackson and his successor Martin Van Buren.

FROM William H. Goetzmann, "The Mountain Man as Jacksonian Man," *American Quarterly*, XV, No. 3 (Fall 1963), 402–15. Copyright, 1963, Trustees of the University of Pennsylvania. Reprinted by permission.

with all its strange and motley populace, now existing in full vigor among the Rocky mountains."[1]

To Irving in the nineteenth century the Mountain Man was Robin Hood, a European literary convention. By the twentieth century the image was still literary and romantic but somewhat less precise. According to Bernard De Voto, "For a few years Odysseus Jed Smith and Siegfried Carson and the wing-shod Fitzpatrick actually drew breath in this province of fable," and Jim Beckwourth "went among the Rockies as Theseus dared the wine-dark seas. Skirting the rise of a hill, he saw the willows stirring; he charged down upon them, while despairing Blackfeet sang the death-song—and lo, to the clear music of a horn, Roland had met the pagan hordes. . . ."[2]

On the other hand, to perhaps more discerning eyes in his own day and down through the years, the Mountain Man presented another image—one that was far less exalted. Set off from the ordinary man by his costume of greasy buckskins, coonskin cap and Indian finery, not to mention the distinctive odor that went with bear grease and the habitual failure to bathe between one yearly rendezvous and the next, the Mountain Man seemed a forlorn and pathetic primitive out of the past. "They are stared at as though they were bears," wrote Rudolph F. Kurz, a Swiss artist who traveled the Upper Missouri.[3]

The Mountain Man, so it was said, was out of touch with conventional civilization and hence not quite acceptable.[4] Instead in his own time and even more today he has been viewed as a purely hedonistic character who lived for the year's end rendezvous where he got gloriously drunk on diluted rot-gut company alcohol, gave his beaver away for wildly inflated company trade goods and crawled off into the underbrush for a delirious orgy with some unenthusiastic Indian squaw. In this view the romantic rendezvous was nothing more than a modern company picnic, the object of which was to keep the employees docile, happy and ready for the company year's task.

Pacified, satisfied, cheated, impoverished and probably mortified the next day, the Mountain Man, be he free trapper or not, went back to his dangerous work when the rendezvous was over. He was thus to many shrewd observers not a hero at all but a docile and obedient slave of the company. By a stretch of the imagination he might have seemed heroic, but because of the contrast between his daring deeds and his degraded status he seemed one of the saddest heroes in all history. Out of date before his time was up, he was a wild free spirit who after all was not free. He was instead an adventurer who was bringing about his own destruction even as he succeeded in his quest to search out the beaver in all of the secret places of the mountain West. A dependent of the London dandy and his foppish taste in hats, the Mountain Man was Caliban. He was a member of a picturesque lower class fast vanishing from the face of America. Like the Mohican Indian and quaint old Leatherstocking he

[1] Washington Irving, *The Rocky Mountains: or, Scenes, Incidents, and Adventures in the Far West* (2 vols.; Philadelphia, 1837), I, 27.

[2] Bernard De Voto, "Introduction," *The Life and Adventures of James P. Beckwourth*, ed. T. D. Bonner (New York, 1931), p. xxvii.

[3] Quoted in Dorothey O. Johansen, "Introduction," *Robert Newell's Memoranda* (Portland, Ore., 1959), p. 2.

[4] *Ibid.*, pp. 2–3; see also Ray A. Billington, *The Far Western Frontier* (New York, 1956), p. 44.

was a vanishing breed, forlorn and permanently class-bound in spite of all his heroics.[5]

Both of these stereotypes embody, as do most effective stereotypes, more than a measure of reality. The Mountain Man traveled far out ahead of the march of conventional civilization, and the job he did required him to be as tough, primitive and close to nature as an Indian. Moreover, it was an out-of-doors life of the hunt and the chase that he often grew to like. By the same token because he spent much of his time in primitive isolation in the mountains, he very often proved to be a poor businessman ignorant of current prices and sharp company practices. Even if aware of his disadvantageous position he could do nothing to free himself until he had made his stake.

The fact is, however, that many Mountain Men lived for the chance to exchange their dangerous mountain careers for an advantageous start in civilized life. If one examines their lives and their stated aspirations one discovers that the Mountain Men, for all their apparent eccentricities, were astonishingly similar to the common men of their time—plain republican citizens of the Jacksonian era.

Jacksonian Man, according to Richard Hofstadter, "was an expectant capitalist, a hardworking ambitious person for whom enterprise was a kind of religion."[6] He was "the master mechanic who aspired to open his own shop, the planter, or farmer who speculated in land, the lawyer who hoped to be a judge, the local politician who wanted to go to Congress, the grocer who would be a merchant. . . ."[7] To this list one might well add, the trapper who hoped some day, if he hit it lucky and avoided the scalping knife, to be one or all of these, or perhaps better still, a landed gentleman of wealth and prestige.

"Everywhere," writes Hofstadter, the Jacksonian expectant capitalist "found conditions that encouraged him to extend himself."[8] And there were many like William Ashley or Thomas James who out of encouragement or desperation looked away to the Rocky Mountains, teeming with beaver and other hidden resources, and saw a path to economic success and rapid upward mobility. In short, when he went out West and became a Mountain Man the Jacksonian Man did so as a prospector. He too was an expectant capitalist.

Marvin Meyers has added a further characterization of Jacksonian Man. He was, according to Meyers, the "venturous conservative,"[9] the man who desired relative freedom from restraint so that he might risk his life and his fortune, if not his sacred honor, on what appeared to be a long-term, continent-wide boom. Yet at the same time he wished to pyramid his fortune within the limits of the familiar American social and economic system, and likewise to derive his status therefrom. Wherever he went, and especially on the frontier, Jacksonian Man did not wish to change the system. He merely wished to throw it open as much as possible to opportunity, with the hope that by so doing he could place himself at the top instead of at the bottom of the conven-

---

[5] Billington, pp. 46–47; Robert Glass Cleland, *This Reckless Breed of Men* (New York, 1950), pp. 24–25; Bernard De Voto, *Across the Wide Missouri* (Boston, 1947), pp. 96–104. See also Henry Nash Smith, *Virgin Land* (Boston, 1950), pp. 59–70, 81–89. My portrait is a composite derived, but not quoted from the above sources.
[6] Richard Hofstadter, *The American Political Tradition* (New York, 1955), p. 57.
[7] *Ibid.*, p. 59.   [8] *Ibid.*, p. 57.
[9] Marvin Meyers, *The Jacksonian Persuasion* (New York, 1957), pp. 33–56.

tional social and economic ladder. "They love change," wrote Tocqueville, "but they dread revolutions."[10] Instead of a new world the Jacksonian Man wished to restore the old where the greatest man was the independent man—yeoman or mechanic, trader or ranchero—the man who basked in comfort and sturdy security under his own "vine and fig tree."

The structure of the Rocky Mountain fur trade itself, the life stories of the trappers and on rare occasions their stated or implied aspirations all make it clear that if he was not precisely the Meyers-Hofstadter Jacksonian Man, the Mountain Man was most certainly his cousin once removed, and a clearly recognizable member of the family.

It is a truism, of course, to state that the Rocky Mountain fur trade was a business, though writers in the Mountain Man's day and since have sometimes made it seem more like a sporting event. The Mountain Man himself often put such an ambiguous face on what he was doing. "Westward! Ho!" wrote Warren Ferris, an American Fur Company trapper.

> It is the sixteenth of the second month A.D. 1830, and I have joined a trapping, trading, hunting expedition to the Rocky Mountains. Why, I scarcely know, for the motives that induced me to this step were of a mixed complexion,—something like the pepper and salt population of this city of St. Louis. Curiosity, a love of wild adventure, and perhaps also a hope of profit,—for times *are* hard, and my best coat has a sort of sheepish hang-dog hesitation to encounter fashionable folk—combined to make me look upon the project with an eye of favor. The party consists of some thirty men, mostly Canadian; but a few there are, like myself, from various parts of the Union. Each has some plausible excuse for joining, and the aggregate of disinterestedness would delight the most ghostly saint in the Roman calendar. Engage for money! no, not they;—health, and the strong desire of seeing strange lands, of beholding nature in the savage grandeur of her primeval state,—these are the only arguments that *could* have persuaded such independent and high-minded young fellows to adventure with the American Fur Company in a trip to the mountain wilds of the great west.[11]

Ambiguous though the Mountain Man's approach to it may have been, it is abundantly clear that the Rocky Mountain fur trade was indeed a *business,* and not an invariably individualistic enterprise at that. The unit of operation was the company, usually a partnership for the sake of capital, risk and year-round efficiency. Examples of the company are The Missouri Fur Company, Gantt and Blackwell, Stone and Bostwick, Bean and Sinclair, and most famous of all, the Rocky Mountain Fur Company and its successors, Smith, Jackson, and Sublette, Sublette & Campbell, and Sublette, Fitzpatrick, Bridger, Gervais and Fraeb. These were the average company units in the Rocky Mountain trade and much of the story of their existence is analogous to Jackson's war on "Monster Bank" for they were all forced to contend against John Jacob Astor's "Monster Monopoly," the American Fur Co., which was controlled and financed by eastern capitalists.

Perhaps the most interesting aspect of the independent fur companies was their fluid structure of leadership. There was indeed, "a baton in every knap-

10 Quoted in *ibid.,* p. 43.
11 W. A. Ferris, *Life in the Rocky Mountains,* ed. Paul C. Phillips (Denver, Colo., 1940), p. 1.

sack" or more accurately, perhaps, in every "possibles" bag. William Ashley, owner of a gun powder factory, and Andrew Henry, a former Lisa lieutenant and lead miner, founded the Rocky Mountain Fur Company.[12] After a few years of overwhelming success, first Henry, and then Ashley, retired, and they were succeeded by their lieutenants, Jedediah Smith, David Jackson and William Sublette, three of the "enterprising young men" who had answered Ashley's advertisement in the St. Louis *Gazette and Public Advertiser* in 1823. When Smith and Jackson moved on to more attractive endeavors first William Sublette and Robert Campbell, then Tom "Broken Hand" Fitzpatrick, James "Old Gabe" Bridger, Henry Fraeb, Milton "Thunderbolt" Sublette and Jean Baptiste Gervais moved up to fill their entrepreneurial role.

In another example Etienne Provost was successively an employee of Auguste Chouteau, partner with LeClair and leader of his own Green River brigade, and servant of American Fur.[13] Sylvestre Pattie became a Santa Fe trader, then an independent trapper, then manager of the Santa Rita (New Mexico) Copper Mines and ultimately leader of an independent trapping venture into the Gila River country of the far Southwest—a venture that ended in disaster when he was thrown into a Mexican prison in California and there left to die.[14] Most significant is the fact that few of the trappers declined the responsibility of entrepreneurial leadership when it was offered them. On the contrary, the usual practice was to indenture oneself to an established company for a period of time, during which it was possible to acquire the limited capital in the way of traps, rifle, trade goods, etc., that was needed to become independent and a potential brigade leader. Referring to his arrangement with the old Missouri Fur Company in 1809, Thomas James wrote,

> We Americans were all private adventurers, each on his own hook, and were led into the enterprise by the promises of the Company, who agreed to subsist us to the trapping grounds, we helping to navigate the boats, and on our arrival there they were to furnish us each with a rifle and sufficient ammunition, six good beaver traps and also four men of their hired French, to be under our individual commands for a period of three years.
>
> By the terms of the contract each of us was to divide one-fourth of the profits of our joint labor with the four men thus to be appointed to us.[15]

James himself retired when he could from the upper Missouri trade and eventually became an unsuccessful storekeeper in Harrisonville, Illinois.[16]

In addition to the fact of rapid entrepreneurial succession within the structure of the independent fur companies, a study of 446 Mountain Men (perhaps 45 per cent of the total engaged in this pursuit between 1805 and 1845) indicates that their life-patterns could be extremely varied. One hundred seventeen Mountain Men definitely turned to occupations other than trapping subsequent to their entering the mountain trade. Of this number 39 followed more than

---

[12] Harrison C. Dale, *The Ashley-Smith Explorations and the Discovery of a Central Route to the Pacific, 1822–1829*, rev. ed. (Glendale, Calif., 1941), pp. 57–61.
[13] Dale L. Morgan, *Jedediah Smith* (Indianapolis and New York, 1953), pp. 145–48; Ferris, pp. 150, 156, 158.
[14] James Ohio Pattie, *Personal Narrative*, ed. Timothey Flint (Cincinnati, 1831), *passim*.
[15] Thomas James, *Three Years Among the Indians and Mexicans*, ed. Milo M. Quaife (Chicago, 1953), pp. 9–10.
[16] *Ibid.*, p. 100. When his store failed, Thomas James set out in May 1821 on a trading venture to Sante Fe. By July of 1822 he had returned to his home in Illinois.

one pursuit. As such they often worked at as many as four or five different callings.[17]

Moreover beyond the 117 definite cases of alternative callings, 32 others were found to have indeterminate occupations that were almost certainly not connected with the fur trade,[18] making a total of 149 out of 154 men for whom some occupational data exists who had turned away from the trapping fraternity before 1845. Of the remaining men in the study, 110 men yielded nothing to investigation beyond the fact that they had once been trappers, 182 can be listed as killed in the line of duty and only five men out of the total stayed with the great out-of-doors life of the free trapper that according to the myth they were all supposed to love.

TABLE I

Total Number of Cases	446
Persons whose other occupations are known	117
Persons whose other occupations are probable	32
Persons with more than one other occupation	39
Persons who stayed on as trappers	5
Persons whose status is unknown	110
Persons killed in the fur trade	182

[17] This study is based upon the lives of the Mountain Men whose entrance into the Rocky Mountain fur trade during the period 1805–45 can be proven, and who fit the criteria listed below. As anyone who has worked in the field will undoubtedly understand, the estimated one-thousand-man total given for those who would possibly qualify for consideration under these criteria represents merely an informed guess, since it is impossible with present-day evidence to determine with accuracy *all* of the Mountain Men who entered the West during this period. The data upon which this study is based is the sum total of men and careers that the extensive investigation described below has yielded. The author believes this to be the most extensive such investigation undertaken to date and also the largest number of such Mountain Men and careers located as of this time. However, in presenting this statistical analysis, the author wishes to stress the tentativeness of the conclusions herein reached. Further study of those whose "other occupations were indeterminable," and those "whose other occupations are probable" quite obviously might alter the present statistical results to a significant degree, and though the attempt was made to determine the occupations of as many men as possible, the author wishes specifically to acknowledge this possibility.

The basic sources for this sample study were: 1) General histories of the western states. In this respect the pioneer register in H. H. Bancroft's *History of California* proved to be particularly useful. 2) Original and modern editions of the relevant fur trade classics listed in Henry Raup Wagner and Charles Camp, *Plains and Rockies.* 3) The many available monographs and biographies relating to the fur trade such as those by Hiram M. Chittenden, Paul C. Phillips, Dale L. Morgan and John E. Sunder. 4) The files of historical journals containing materials on the fur trade of the Far West. 5) Reports submitted to the United States Government and published in the House and Senate document series. 6) Newspapers and periodicals for the fur trade period. In this latter category the author's research was by no means complete, nor was it possible to carry out the research project to the extent of consulting the multitude of local and county histories that almost certainly would have yielded further information. Enough research was conducted in these latter two categories of materials, however, to indicate the probable extent of their utility, which the author deemed insufficient for the present purposes.

The criteria for selecting the men to be included in the study are relatively simple. 1) They must have been associated with the fur trapping enterprise during the period 1805–45. 2) They must have pursued their trapping activities in the Rocky Mountains, northern or southern; hence the term Mountain Man. 3) They could not be employees of the American Fur Company, nor engagées at any of the Missouri River trading posts. The American Fur Company men are excluded from this study for two reasons: first, because the majority of them were river traders, not Mountain Men and they have never been classified under the old stereotyped images; secondly, of those few American Fur men who did go into the mountains in this period a large percentage were killed. Further study of the survivors, however, indicates that they too changed occupations much as did the Mountain Men. (See for example the career of Warren A. Ferris.)

[18] This conclusion is deduced by the author primarily upon the basis of their residence during this period in places far removed from fur trapping or trading activities.

The list of alternative callings pursued by the trappers is also revealing. Twenty-one became ranchers, fifteen farmers, seventeen traders (at stationary trading posts), eight miners, seven politicians, six distillers, five each storekeepers and army scouts, four United States Indian agents, three carpenters, two each bankers, drovers and hatters and at least one pursued each of the following occupations, sheepherder, postman, miller, medium, ice dealer, vintner, fancy fruit grower, baker, saloon keeper, clockmaker, cattle buyer, real estate speculator, newspaper editor, lawyer, lumberman, superintendent of schools, tailor, blacksmith, and supercargo of a trading schooner. Moreover many of these same individuals pursued secondary occupations such as that of hotel keeper, gambler, soldier, health resort proprietor, coal mine owner, tanner, sea captain, horse thief and opera house impresario.

TABLE 2

LIST OF OCCUPATIONS

A. *Primary*

1. Farmer	15	17. Blacksmith	1
2. Rancher	21	18. Tailor	1
3. Politician	7	19. Supercargo	1
4. Sheepherder	1	20. Superintendent of Schools	1
5. Scout [For Govt.]	5	21. Lumberman	2
6. Trader	17	22. Newspaper Editor	1
7. Miner	8	23. Carpenter	3
8. Postman	1	24. Cattle Buyer	1
9. Distiller	6	25. Clockmaker	1
10. Miller	1	26. Saloon Keeper	1
11. Storekeeper	5	27. Baker	1
12. Medium	1	28. Fruit Grower	1
13. Banker	2	29. Vintner	1
14. Drover	2	30. Ice Dealer	1
15. Hatter	2	31. Real Estate Speculator	1
16. Indian Agent	4	32. Lawyer	1

B. *Secondary*

1. Trader	4	12. Lumberman	2
2. Transportation	2	13. Gambler	3
3. Scout	5	14. Blacksmith	1
4. Hotel Keeper	1	15. Soldier	1
5. Miner	2	16. Spa Keeper	1
6. Farmer	5	17. Coal Mine Operator	1
7. Politician	3	18. Tanner	1
8. Rancher	5	19. Opera House Impresario	1
9. Storekeeper	4	20. Sea Captain	1
10. Miller	3	21. Carpenter	1
11. Real Estate	3	22. Horse Thief	1

From this it seems clear that statistically at least the Mountain Man was hardly the simple-minded primitive that mythology has made him out to be. Indeed it appears that whenever he had the chance, he exchanged the joys of the rendezvous and the wilderness life for the more civilized excitement of "getting ahead." In many cases he achieved this aim, and on a frontier where able men were scarce he very often became a pillar of the community, and even of the nation. From the beginning, as Ashley's famous advertisement implied, the Mountain Men were men of "enterprise" who risked their lives for something more than pure romance and a misanthropic desire to evade civilization. The picturesqueness and the quaintness were largely the creation of what was the literary mentality of an age of artistic romanticism. For every "Cannibal Phil" or Robert Meldrum or "Peg-Leg" Smith there was a Sarchel Wolfskill (vintner), a George Yount (rancher) and a William Sublette (banker-politician).

Two further facts emerge in part from this data. First, it is clear that though the Jeffersonian agrarian dream of "Arcadia" bulked large in the Mountain Man's choice of occupations, it by no means obscured the whole range of "mechanical" or mercantile pursuits that offered the chance for success on the frontier. Indeed, if it suggests anything a statistical view of the Mountain Man's "other life" suggests that almost from the beginning the Far Western frontier took on the decided aspect of an urban or semi-urban "industrial" civilization. Secondly, though it is not immediately apparent from the above statistics, a closer look indicates that a surprising number of the Mountain Men succeeded at their "other" tasks to the extent that they became regionally and even nationally prominent.

William H. Ashley became Congressman from Missouri and a spokesman for the West, Charles Bent an ill-fated though famed governor of New Mexico. "Doc" Newell was a prominent figure in the organization of Oregon Territory. Elbridge Gerry, William McGaa and John Simpson Smith were the founders and incorporators of Denver. Lucien Maxwell held the largest land grant in the whole history of the United States.

Joshua Pilcher was a famous superintendent of Indian Affairs. William Sublette, pursuing a hard money policy, saved the Bank of Missouri in the panic of 1837 and went on to be a Democratic elector for "young hickory" James K. Polk in 1844. Benjamin Wilson was elected first mayor of Los Angeles. James Clyman and his Napa Valley estate were famous in California as were the ranches of George Yount and J. J. Warner, while Sarchel Wolfskill was a co-founder of the modern California wine industry. James Waters built the first opera house in Southern California, and Kit Carson, in his later years a silver miner, received the supreme tribute of finding a dime novel dedicated to his exploits in plunder captured from marauding Apache Indians who had recently attacked and massacred a wagon train.[19]

Many of the Mountain Men achieved fame and national status through works that they published themselves, or, as in the case of Carson, through works that immortalized correctly, or as was more usual, incorrectly, their exploits. Here one need only mention Kit Carson's *Autobiography* and his favorable treatment at the hands of Jessie Benton Frémont, T. D. Bonner's *Life and Adventures of James Beckwourth*, Francis Fuller Victor's *River of the West* (about Joe Meek), James Ohio Pattie's *Personal Narrative*, Thomas James' *Three Years Among the Indians and Mexicans*, H. L. Conard's *Uncle Dick Wooton*, David Coyner's *The Lost Trappers* (about Ezekial Williams), Irv-

<hr>

[19] Kit Carson, *Autobiography*, ed. Milo M. Quaife (Chicago, 1935), p. 135.

ing's portrait of Joseph Reddeford Walker in *The Adventures of Captain Bonneville*. Zenas Leonard's *Narrative*, Peg-Leg Smith's "as told to" exploits in *Hutchings' California Magazine*, Stephen Meek's *Autobiography*, Warren Ferris' letters to the Buffalo, New York, *Western Literary Messenger*, John Hatcher's yarns in Lewis H. Garrard's *Wah To Yah and The Taos Trail* and perhaps most interesting of all, trapper John Brown's pseudo-scientific *Mediumistic Experiences*, to realize the extent and range of the Mountain Man's communication with the outside world in his own day. Not only was he a typical man of his time, he was often a conspicuous success and not bashful about communicating the fact in somewhat exaggerated terms to his fellow countrymen.

Direct evidence of the Mountain Men's motives is scarce, but it is clear their intentions were complex.

"Tell them that I have no heirs and that I hope to make a fortune," wrote Louis Vasquez ("Old Vaskiss" to Bernard De Voto) in 1834 from "Fort Convenience" somewhere in the Rockies.[20] Later as he set out on one last expedition in 1842 he added somewhat melodramatically, "I leave to make money or die."[21] And finally Colonel A. G. Brackett, who visited Fort Bridger (jointly owned by Bridger and Vasquez), described him as "a Mexican, who put on a great deal of style, and used to ride about the country in a coach and four."[22]

"It is, that I may be able to help those who stand in need, that I face every danger," wrote Jedediah Smith from the Wind River Mountains in 1829, "most of all, it is for this, that I deprive myself of the privilege of Society and the satisfaction of the Converse of My Friends! but I shall count all this pleasure, if I am allowed by the Alwise Ruler the privilege of Joining my Friends. . . ." And he added "let it be the greatest pleasure that we can enjoy, the height of our ambition, now, when our Parents are in the decline of Life, to smooth the Pillow of their age, and as much as in us lies, take from them all cause of Trouble."[23] So spoke Jedediah Smith of his hopes and ambitions upon pursuing the fur trade. No sooner had he left the mountains, however, than he was killed by Plains Indians before he could settle down in business with his brothers as he had intended.[24] Noble and ignoble were the motives of the Mountain Men. Colonel John Shaw, starting across the southern plains and into the Rockies in search of gold; Thomas James, desperate to recoup his failing fortunes; the Little Rock *Gazette* of 1829 "confidently" believing "that this enterprise affords a prospect of great profit to all who may engage in it"; the St. Louis *Enquirer* in 1822 labeling the Rocky Mountains "the Shining Mountains," and innocently declaring, "A hunter pursuing his game found the silver mines of Potosi, and many others have been discovered by the like accidents, and there is no reason to suppose that other valuable discoveries may not be

[20] Quoted in Leroy Hafen, "Louis Vasquez," *The Colorado Magazine*, X (1933), 17. De Voto's nickname for Vasquez appears in *Across the Wide Missouri*, p. xxvi. 351–54.

[21] *Ibid.*, p. 19.   [22] *Ibid.*, p. 20.

[23] Jedediah Smith to Ralph Smith, Wind River, East Side of the Rocky Mountains, December 24, 1829. MS. Kansas State Historical Society. Also reproduced in Morgan, *Jedediah Smith*, pp. 351–54.

[24] Jedediah S. Smith to Ralph Smith, Blue River, fork of Kansas, 30 miles from the Ponnee Villages, September 10, 1830. MS. Kansas State Historical Society. Also reproduced in Morgan, *Jedediah Smith*, pp. 355–56.

made";[25] Ashley calling clearly and unmistakably for men of "enterprise," all added up to the fact that the Mountain Man when he went West was a complex character. But in his complexity was a clearly discernible pattern—the pattern of Jacksonian Man in search of respectability and success in terms recognized by the society he had left behind. His goal was, of course, the pursuit of happiness. But happiness, contrary to Rousseauistic expectations, was not found in the wilderness; it was an integral product of society and civilization.

If the Mountain Man was indeed Jacksonian Man, then there are at least three senses in which this concept has importance. First, more clearly than anything else a statistical and occupational view of the various callings of the Mountain Man tentatively indicates the incredible rate and the surprising *nature* of social and economic change in the West. In little more than two decades most of the surviving enterprising men had left the fur trade for more lucrative and presumably more useful occupations. And by their choice of occupations it is clear that in the Far West a whole step in the settlement process had been virtually skipped. They may have dreamed of "Arcadia," but when they turned to the task of settling the West as fast as possible, the former Mountain Men and perhaps others like them brought with them all the aspects of an "industrial," mercantile and quasi-urban society. The opera house went up almost simultaneously with the ranch, and the Bank of Missouri was secured before the land was properly put into hay.

Secondly, as explorers—men who searched out the hidden places in the western wilderness—the Mountain Men as Jacksonian Men looked with a flexible eye upon the new land. Unlike the Hudson's Bay explorer who looked only for beaver and immediate profit, the Mountain Man looked to the future and the development of the West, not as a vast game preserve, but as a land like the one he had known back home. "Much of this vast waste of territory belongs to the Republic of the United States," wrote Zenas Leonard from San Francisco Bay in 1833.

> What a theme to contemplate its settlement and civilization. Will the jurisdiction of the federal government ever succeed in civilizing the thousands of savages now roaming over these plains, and her hardy freeborn population here plant their homes, build their towns and cities, and say here shall the arts and sciences of civilization take root and flourish? Yes, here, even in this remote part of the Great West before many years will these hills and valleys be greeted with the enlivening sound of the workman's hammer, and the merry whistle of the ploughboy . . . we have good reason to suppose that the territory *west* of the mountains will some day be equally as important to the nation as that on the east.[26]

In 1830 in a famous letter to John H. Eaton, the Secretary of War, Jedediah S. Smith, David E. Jackson and William L. Sublette aired their views on the possibilities of the West. Smith made clear that a wagon road route suitable for settlers existed all the way to Oregon, and Sublette dramatized the point

---

[25] St. Louis *Enquirer* quoted in Donald McKay Frost, *Notes on General Ashley* (Barre, Mass., 1960), p. 67. Little Rock *Gazette* quoted in Leroy R. Hafen, "The Bean-Sinclair Party of Rocky Mountain Trappers, 1830–32," *The Colorado Magazine*, XXXI (1954), 163.

[26] Zenas Leonard, *Narrative of the Adventures of Zenas Leonard*, ed. John C. Ewers (Norman, Okla., 1959), pp. 94–95.

when he brought ten wagons and two dearborns and even a milch cow over the mountains as far as the Wind River rendezvous. Their report made abundantly clear that in their opinion the future of the West lay with settlers rather than trappers. Indeed they were worried that the English at Fort Vancouver might grasp this fact before the American government.[27] In short, as explorers and trappers theirs was a broad-ranging, flexible, settler-oriented, public view of the Far West.

Tied in with this and of the greatest significance is a third and final point. Not only did they *see* a settler's future in the West, but at least some of the Mountain Men were most eager to see to it that such a future was *guaranteed* by the institutions of the United States Government which must be brought West and extended over all the wild new land to protect the settler in the enjoyment of his own "vine and fig tree." The Mexican Government, unstable, and blown by whim or caprice, could not secure the future, and the British Government, at least in North America, was under the heel of monopoly. France was frivolous and decadent. Russia was a sinister and backward despotism. Only the free institutions of Jacksonian America would make the West safe for enterprise. So strongly did he feel about this that in 1841 the Mountain Man Moses "Black" Harris sent a letter to one Thornton Grimsley offering him the command of 700 men, of which he was one, who were eager to "join the standard of their country, and make a clean sweep of what is called the Oregon [sic] Territory; that is clear it of British and Indians." Outraged not only at British encroachments, he was also prepared to "march through to California" as well.[28] It may well have been this spirit that settled the Oregon question and brought on the Mexican War.[29]

Settlement, security, stability, enterprise, free enterprise, a government of laws which, in the words of Jackson himself, confines "itself to equal *protection,* and as Heaven does its rains, showers its favors alike on the high and the low, the rich and the poor,"[30] all of these shaped the Mountain Man's vision of the West and his role in its development. It was called Manifest Destiny. But long before John L. O'Sullivan nicely turned the phrase in the *Democratic Review,*[31] the Mountain Man as Jacksonian Man—a "venturous conservative"— was out in the West doing his utmost to lend the Almighty a helping hand. James Clyman perhaps put it most simply:

> Here lies the bones of old Black Harris
> who often traveled beyond the far west
> and for the freedom of Equal rights
> He crossed the snowy mountain Hights
> was free and easy kind of soul
> Especially with a Belly full.[32]

[27] Reproduced in Morgan, *Jedediah Smith,* pp. 343–48.
[28] Quoted in Charles L. Camp, ed. *James Clyman Frontiersman* (Portland, Ore., 1960), pp. 61–62.
[29] Ray Allen Billington, *The Far Western Frontier,* pp. 154–73. See also Frederick Merk, *Manifest Destiny and Mission in American History* (New York, 1963).
[30] James D. Richardson, ed. *A Compilation of the Messages and Papers of the Presidents 1789–1897* (1900), II, 590–91. Italics mine.
[31] John L. O'Sullivan, "Annexation," unsigned article, *United States Magazine and Democratic Review,* XVII (July–August 1845), 797–98. See also his more popular statement in the New York *Morning News,* December 27, 1845.
[32] Camp, *James Clyman Frontiersman,* p. 64.

The Cult of True Womanhood
1820–1860

Barbara Welter

INTRODUCTION

How men viewed women and how women were taught to understand themselves in the ante-bellum United States are the subjects of this essay. Although Welter does not develop the idea fully, she explains that the cult of True Womanhood provided a stable set of values in a society in flux. The American woman in this set of myths purveyed by magazines, books, and sermons was a safe "hostage in the home"—pious, pure, submissive, and loyally domestic—while the American man labored in a materialistic society. Historians of America, (prodded by women far different from those described by the cult of True Womanhood), are beginning to realize that the history of women has been badly neglected. Welter's article at least begins to correct that neglect. Students might consider what other sorts of questions might be asked about the history of women in America. Of particular concern, of course, is the need to place women's history within the context of American history.

Studies of women are few and scattered, but a good place for the student of American history to begin is Julia Cherry Spruill, *Women's Life and Work in the Southern Colonies* (1938). Edmund S. Morgan's *The Puritan Family** (1966) and *Virginians at Home: Family Life in the Eighteenth Century** (1952) are excellent studies. Robert Middlekauff, *Ancients and Axioms: Secondary Education in Eighteenth-Century New England* (1963) gives an account of the education of girls. Two recent books, William L. O'Neill, *Everyone Was Brave: The Rise and Fall of Feminism in America* (1969), and Page Smith, *Daughters of the Promised Land* (1970), are useful. For a fascinating comparative view of English ideas and attitudes about women, see Walter E. Houghton, *The Victorian Frame of Mind** (1957).

THE nineteenth-century American man was a busy builder of bridges and railroads, at work long hours in a materialistic society. The religious values of his forebears were neglected in practice if not in intent, and he occasionally felt some guilt that he had turned this new land, this temple of the chosen people, into one vast countinghouse. But he could salve his conscience by reflecting that he had left behind a hostage, not only to fortune, but to all the values which he held so dear and treated so lightly. Woman, in the cult of True Womanhood[1] presented by the women's magazines, gift annuals and religious literature of the nineteenth century, was the hostage in the home.[2] In a society where values changed frequently, where fortunes rose and fell with frightening rapidity, where social and economic mobility provided instability as well as hope, one thing at least remained the same—a true woman was a true woman, wherever she was found. If anyone, male or female, dared to tamper with the complex of virtues which made up True Womanhood, he was damned immediately as an enemy of God, of civilization and of the Republic. It was a fearful obligation, a solemn responsibility, which the nineteenth-century American woman had—to uphold the pillars of the temple with her frail white hand.

The attributes of True Womanhood, by which a woman judged herself and was judged by her husband, her neighbors and society, could be divided into four cardinal virtues—piety, purity, submissiveness and domesticity. Put them all together and they spelled mother, daughter, sister, wife—woman.

FROM Barbara Welter, "The Cult of True Womanhood: 1820–1860," *American Quarterly*, XVIII, No. 2, Pt. 1 (Summer 1966), 151–74. Copyright, 1966, Trustees of the University of Pennsylvania. Reprinted by permission.

[1] Authors who addressed themselves to the subject of women in the mid-nineteenth century used this phrase as frequently as writers on religion mentioned God. Neither group felt it necessary to define their favorite terms; they simply assumed—with some justification—that readers would intuitively understand exactly what they meant. Frequently what people of one era take for granted is most striking and revealing to the student from another. In a sense this analysis of the ideal woman of the mid-nineteenth century is an examination of what writers of that period actually meant when they used so confidently the vague phrase True Womanhood.

[2] The conclusions reached in this article are based on a survey of almost all of the women's magazines published for more than three years during the period 1820–60 and a sampling of those published for less than three years; all the gift books cited in Ralph Thompson, *American Literary Annuals and Gift Books, 1825–1865* (New York, 1936) deposited in the Library of Congress, the New York Public Library, the New-York Historical Society, Columbia University Special Collections, Library of the City College of the University of New York, Pennsylvania Historical Society, Massachusetts Historical Society, Boston Public Library, Fruitlands Museum Library, the Smithsonian Institution and the Wisconsin Historical Society; hundred of religious tracts and sermons in the American Unitarian Society and the Galatea Collection of the Boston Public Library; and the large collection of nineteenth-century cookbooks in the New York Public Library and the Academy of Medicine of New York. Corroborative evidence not cited in this article was found in women's diaries, memoirs, autobiographies and personal papers, as well as in all the novels by women which sold over 75,000 copies during this period, as cited in Frank Luther Mott, *Golden Multitudes: The Story of Best Sellers in the United States* (New York, 1947) and H. R. Brown, *The Sentimental Novel in America, 1789–1860* (Durham, N.C., 1940). This latter information also indicated the effect of the cult of True Womanhood on those most directly concerned.

Without them, no matter whether there was fame, achievement or wealth, all was ashes. With them she was promised happiness and power.

Religion or piety was the core of woman's virtue, the source of her strength. Young men looking for a mate were cautioned to search first for piety, for if that were there, all else would follow.[3] Religion belonged to woman by divine right, a gift of God and nature. This "peculiar susceptibility" to religion was given her for a reason: "the vestal flame of piety, lighted up by Heaven in the breast of woman," would throw its beams into the naughty world of men.[4] So far would its candle power reach that the "Universe might be Enlightened, Improved, and Harmonized by WOMAN!!"[5] She would be another, better Eve, working in cooperation with the Redeemer, bringing the world back "from its revolt and sin."[6] The world would be reclaimed for God through her suffering, for "God increased the cares and sorrows of woman, that she might be sooner constrained to accept the terms of salvation."[7] A popular poem by Mrs. Frances Osgood, "The Triumph of the Spiritual Over the Sensual," expressed just this sentiment, woman's purifying passionless love bringing an erring man back to Christ.[8]

Dr. Charles Meigs, explaining to a graduating class of medical students why women were naturally religious, said that "hers is a pious mind. Her confiding nature leads her more readily than men to accept the proffered grace of the Gospel."[9] Caleb Atwater, Esq., writing in *The Ladies' Repository,* saw the hand of the Lord in female piety: "Religion is exactly what a woman needs, for it gives her that dignity that best suits her dependence."[10] And Mrs. John Sandford, who had no very high opinion of her sex, agreed thoroughly: "Religion is just what woman needs. Without it she is ever restless or unhappy. . . ."[11] Mrs. Sandford and the others did not speak only of that restlessness of the human heart, which St. Augustine notes, that can only find its peace in God. They spoke rather of religion as a kind of tranquilizer for the many undefined longings which swept even the most pious young girl, and about which it was better to pray than to think.

One reason religion was valued was that it did not take a woman away from her "proper sphere," her home. Unlike participation in other societies or movements, church work would not make her less domestic or submissive, less a

---

[3] As in "The Bachelor's Dream," in *The Lady's Gift: Souvenir for All Seasons* (Nashua, N.H., 1849), p. 37.

[4] *The Young Ladies' Class Book: A Selection of Lessons for Reading in Prose and Verse,* ed. Ebenezer Bailey, Principal of Young Ladies' High School, Boston (Boston, 1831), p. 168.

[5] A Lady of Philadelphia, *The World Enlightened, Improved, and Harmonized by WOMAN! ! !* A lecture, delivered in the City of New York, before the Young Ladies' Society for Mutual Improvement, on the following question, proposed by the society, with the offer of $100 for the best lecture that should be read before them on the subject proposed;—What is the power and influence of woman in moulding the manners, morals and habits of civil society? (Philadelphia, 1840), p. 1.

[6] *The Young Lady's Book: A Manual of Elegant Recreations, Exercises, and Pursuits* (Boston, 1830), p. 29.

[7] *Woman As She Was, Is, and Should Be* (New York, 1849), p. 206.

[8] "The Triumph of the Spiritual Over the Sensual: An Allegory," in *Ladies' Companion: A Monthly Magazine Embracing Every Department of Literature, Embellished With Original Engravings and Music,* XVII (New York, 1842), 67.

[9] *Lecture on Some of the Distinctive Characteristics of the Female,* delivered before the class of the Jefferson Medical College, Jan. 1847 (Philadelphia, 1847), p. 13.

[10] "Female Education," *Ladies' Repository and Gatherings of the West: A Monthly Periodical Devoted to Literature and Religion,* I (Cincinnati), 12.

[11] *Woman, in Her Social and Domestic Character* (Boston, 1842), pp. 41–42.

True Woman. In religious vineyards, said the *Young Ladies' Literary and Missionary Report,* "you may labor without the apprehension of detracting from the charms of feminine delicacy." Mrs. S. L. Dagg, writing from her chapter of the Society in Tuscaloosa, Alabama, was equally reassuring: "As no sensible woman will suffer her intellectual pursuits to clash with her domestic duties," she should concentrate on religious work "which promotes these very duties."[12]

The women's seminaries aimed at aiding women to be religious, as well as accomplished. Mt. Holyoke's catalogue promised to make female education "a handmaid to the Gospel and an efficient auxiliary in the great task of renovating the world."[13] The Young Ladies' Seminary at Bordentown, New Jersey, declared its most important function to be "the forming of a sound and virtuous character."[14] In Keene, New Hampshire, the Seminary tried to instill a "consistent and useful character" in its students, to enable them in this life to be "a good friend, wife and mother" but more important, to qualify them for "the enjoyment of Celestial Happiness in the life to come."[15] And Joseph M' D. Mathews, Principal of Oakland Female Seminary in Hillsborough, Ohio, believed that "female education should be preeminently religious."[16]

If religion was so vital to a woman, irreligion was almost too awful to contemplate. Women were warned not to let their literary or intellectual pursuits take them away from God. Sarah Josepha Hale spoke darkly of those who, like Margaret Fuller, threw away the "One True Book" for others, open to error. Mrs. Hale used the unfortunate Miss Fuller as fateful proof that "the greater the intellectual force, the greater and more fatal the errors into which women fall who wander from the Rock of Salvation, Christ the Saviour. . . ."[17]

One gentleman, writing on "Female Irreligion," reminded his readers that "Man may make himself a brute, and does so very often, but can woman brutify herself to his level—the lowest level of human nature—without exerting special wonder?" Fanny Wright, because she was godless, "was no woman, mother though she be." A few years ago, he recalls, such women would have been whipped. In any case, "woman never looks lovelier than in her reverence for religion" and, conversely, "female irreligion is the most revolting feature in human character."[18]

Purity was as essential as piety to a young woman, its absence as unnatural and unfeminine. Without it she was, in fact, no woman at all, but a member of some lower order. A "fallen woman" was a "fallen angel," unworthy of the celestial company of her sex. To contemplate the loss of purity brought tears; to be guilty of such a crime, in the women's magazines at least, brought madness or death. Even the language of the flowers had bitter words for it: a dried white rose symbolized "Death Preferable to Loss of Innocence."[19] The marriage

[12] *Second Annual Report of the Young Ladies' Literary and Missionary Association of the Philadelphia Collegiate Institution* (Philadelphia, 1840), pp. 20, 26.

[13] *Mt. Holyoke Female Seminary: Female Education. Tendencies of the Principles Embraced, and the System Adopted in the Mt. Holyoke Female Seminary* (Boston, 1839), p. 3.

[14] *Prospectus of the Young Ladies' Seminary at Bordentown, New Jersey* (Bordentown, 1836), p. 7.

[15] *Catalogue of the Young Ladies' Seminary in Keene, New Hampshire* (n.p., 1832), p. 20.

[16] "Report to the College of Teachers, Cincinnati, October, 1840" in *Ladies' Repository,* I (1841), 50.

[17] *Woman's Record: or Sketches of All Distinguished Women from The Beginning Till A. D. 1850* (New York, 1853), pp. 665, 669.

[18] "Female Irreligion," *Ladies' Companion,* XIII (May–Oct. 1840), 111.

[19] *The Lady's Book of Flowers and Poetry,* ed. Lucy Hooper (New York, 1842), has a "Floral Dictionary" giving the symbolic meaning of floral tributes.

night was the single great event of a woman's life, when she bestowed her greatest treasure upon her husband, and from that time on was completely dependent upon him, an empty vessel,[20] without legal or emotional existence of her own.[21]

Therefore all True Women were urged, in the strongest possible terms, to maintain their virtue, although men, being by nature more sensual than they, would try to assault it. Thomas Branagan admitted in *The Excellency of the Female Character Vindicated* that his sex would sin and sin again, they could not help it, but woman, stronger and purer, must not give in and let man "take liberties incompatible with her delicacy." "If you do," Branagan addressed his gentle reader, "You will be left in silent sadness to bewail your credulity, imbecility, duplicity, and premature prostitution."[22]

Mrs. Eliza Farrar, in *The Young Lady's Friend,* gave practical logistics to avoid trouble: "Sit not with another in a place that is too narrow; read not out of the same book; let not your eagerness to see anything induce you to place your head close to another person's."[23]

If such good advice was ignored the consequences were terrible and inexorable. In *Girlhood and Womanhood: or, Sketches of My Schoolmates,* by Mrs. A. J. Graves (a kind of mid-nineteenth-century *The Group*), the bad ends of a boarding school class of girls are scrupulously recorded. The worst end of all is reserved for "Amelia Dorrington: The Lost One." Amelia died in the almshouse "the wretched victim of depravity and intemperance" and all because her mother had let her be "high-spirited not prudent." These girlish high spirits had been misinterpreted by a young man, with disastrous results. Amelia's "thoughtless levity" was "followed by a total loss of virtuous principle" and Mrs. Graves editorializes that "the coldest reserve is more admirable in a woman a man wishes to make his wife, than the least approach to undue familiarity."[24]

A popular and often-reprinted story by Fanny Forester told the sad tale of "Lucy Dutton." Lucy "with the seal of innocence upon her heart, and a roseleaf on her cheek" came out of her vine-covered cottage and ran into a city slicker. "And Lucy was beautiful and trusting, and thoughtless, and he was gay, selfish and profligate. Needs the story to be told? . . . Nay, censor, Lucy was a child—consider how young, how very untaught—oh! her innocence was no match for the sophistry of a gay, city youth! Spring came and shame was stamped upon the cottage at the foot of the hill." The baby died; Lucy went mad at the funeral and finally died herself. "Poor, poor Lucy Dutton! The grave is a blessed couch and pillow to the wretched. Rest thee there, poor

[20] See, for example, Nathaniel Hawthorne, *The Blithedale Romance* (Boston, 1852), p. 71, in which Zenobia says: "How can she be happy, after discovering that fate has assigned her but one single event, which she must contrive to make the substance of her whole life? A man has his choice of innumerable events."

[21] Mary R. Beard, *Woman As Force in History* (New York, 1946) makes this point at some length. According to common law, a woman had no legal existence once she was married and therefore could not manage property, sue in court, etc. In the 1840s and 1850s laws were passed in several states to remedy this condition.

[22] *Excellency of the Female Character Vindicated: Being an Investigation Relative to the Cause and Effects on the Encroachments of Men Upon the Rights of Women, and the Too Frequent Degradation and Consequent Misfortunes of The Fair Sex* (New York, 1807), pp. 277, 278.

[23] By a Lady (Eliza Ware Rotch Farrar), *The Young Lady's Friend* (Boston, 1837), p. 299.

[24] *Girlhood and Womanhood: or, Sketches of My Schoolmates* (Boston, 1844), p. 140.

Lucy!"[25] The frequency with which derangement follows loss of virtue suggests the exquisite sensibility of woman, and the possibility that, in the women's magazines at least, her intellect was geared to her hymen, not her brain.

If, however, a woman managed to withstand man's assults on her virtue, she demonstrated her superiority and her power over him. Eliza Farnham, trying to prove this female superiority, concluded smugly that "the purity of women is the everlasting barrier against which the tides of man's sensual nature surge."[26]

A story in *The Lady's Amaranth* illustrates this dominance. It is set, improbably, in Sicily, where two lovers, Bianca and Tebaldo, have been separated because her family insisted she marry a rich old man. By some strange circumstance the two are in a shipwreck and cast on a desert island, the only survivors. Even here, however, the rigid standards of True Womanhood prevail. Tebaldo unfortunately forgets himself slightly, so that Bianca must warn him: "We may not indeed gratify our fondness by caresses, but it is still something to bestow our kindest language, and looks and prayers, and all lawful and honest attentions on each other." Something, perhaps, but not enough, and Bianca must further remonstrate: "It is true that another man is my husband, but you are my guardian angel." When even that does not work she says in a voice of sweet reason, passive and proper to the end, that she wishes he wouldn't but "still, if you insist, I will become what you wish; but I beseech you to consider, ere that decision, that debasement which I must suffer in your esteem." This appeal to his own double standards holds the beast in him at bay. They are rescued, discover that the old husband is dead, and after "mourning a decent season" Bianca finally gives in, legally.[27]

Men could be counted on to be grateful when women thus saved them from themselves. William Alcott, guiding young men in their relations with the opposite sex, told them that "Nothing is better calculated to preserve a young man from contamination of low pleasures and pursuits than frequent intercourse with the more refined and virtuous of the other sex." And he added, one assumes in equal innocence, that youths should "observe and learn to admire, that purity and ignorance of evil which is the characteristic of well-educated young ladies, and which, when we are near them, raises us above those sordid and sensual considerations which hold such sway over men in their intercourse with each other."[28]

The Rev. Jonathan F. Stearns was also impressed by female chastity in the face of male passion, and warned women never to compromise the source of her power: "Let her lay aside delicacy, and her influence over our sex is gone."[29]

Women themselves accepted, with pride but suitable modesty, this priceless virtue. *The Ladies' Wreath,* in "Woman the Creature of God and the Manufacturer of Society," saw purity as her greatest gift and chief means of discharging her duty to save the world: "Purity is the highest beauty—the true

[25] Emily Chubbuck, *Alderbrook* (Boston, 1847), 2nd. ed., II, 121, 127.
[26] *Woman and Her Era* (New York, 1864), p. 95.
[27] "The Two Lovers of Sicily," *The Lady's Amaranth: A Journal of Tales, Essays, Excerpts— Historical and Biographical Sketches, Poetry and Literature in General* (Philadelphia), II (Jan. 1839), 17.
[28] *The Young Man's Guide* (Boston, 1833), pp. 229, 231.
[29] *Female Influence: and the True Christian Mode of Its Exercise; a Discourse Delivered in the First Presbyterian Church in Newburyport, July 30, 1837* (Newburyport, 1837), p. 18.

pole-star which is to guide humanity aright in its long, varied, and perilous voyage."[30]

Sometimes, however, a woman did not see the dangers to her treasure. In that case, they must be pointed out to her, usually by a male. In the nineteenth century any form of social change was tantamount to an attack on woman's virtue, if only it was correctly understood. For example, dress reform seemed innocuous enough and the bloomers worn by the lady of that name and her followers were certainly modest attire. Such was the reasoning only of the ignorant. In another issue of *The Ladies' Wreath* a young lady is represented in dialogue with her "Professor." The girl expresses admiration for the bloomer costume—it gives freedom of motion, is healthful and attractive. The "Professor" sets her straight. Trousers, he explains, are "only one of the many manifestations of that wild spirit of socialism and agrarian radicalism which is at present so rife in our land." The young lady recants immediately: "If this dress has any connexion with Fourierism or Socialism, or fanaticism in any shape whatever, I have no disposition to wear it at all . . . no true woman would so far compromise her delicacy as to espouse, however unwittingly, such a cause."[31]

America could boast that her daughters were particularly innocent. In a poem on "The American Girl" the author wrote proudly:

> Her eye of light is the diamond bright,
> Her innocence the pearl,
> And these are ever the bridal gems
> That are worn by the American girl.[32]

Lydia Maria Child, giving advice to mothers, aimed at preserving that spirit of innocence. She regretted that "want of confidence between mothers and daughters on delicate subjects" and suggested a woman tell her daughter a few facts when she reached the age of twelve to "set her mind at rest." Then Mrs. Child confidently hoped that a young lady's "instinctive modesty" would "prevent her from dwelling on the information until she was called upon to use it."[33] In the same vein, a book of advice to the newly-married was titled *Whisper to a Bride*.[34] As far as intimate information was concerned, there was no need to whisper, since the book contained none at all.

A masculine summary of this virtue was expressed in a poem "Female Charms":

> I would have her as pure as the snow on the mount—
> As true as the smile that to infamy's given—
> As pure as the wave of the crystalline fount,
> Yet as warm in the heart as the sunlight of heaven.

[30] W. Tolles, "Woman the Creature of God and the Manufacturer of Society," *Ladies' Wreath* (New York), III (1852), 205.

[31] Prof. William M. Heim, "The Bloomer Dress," *Ladies' Wreath*, III (1852), 247.

[32] *The Young Lady's Offering: or Gems of Prose and Poetry* (Boston, 1853), p. 283. The American girl, whose innocence was often connected with ignorance, was the spiritual ancestress of the Henry James heroine. Daisy Miller, like Lucy Dutton, saw innocence lead to tragedy.

[33] *The Mother's Book* (Boston, 1831), pp. 151, 152.

[34] Mrs. L. H. Sigourney, *Whisper to a Bride* (Hartford, 1851), in which Mrs. Sigourney's approach is summed up in this quotation: "Home! Blessed bride, thou art about to enter this sanctuary, and to become a priestess at its altar.," p. 44.

With a mind cultivated, not boastingly wise,
I could gaze on such beauty, with exquisite bliss;
With her heart on her lips and her soul in her eyes—
What more could I wish in dear woman than this.[35]

Man might, in fact, ask no more than this in woman; but she was beginning to ask more of herself, and in the asking was threatening the third powerful and necessary virtue, submission. Purity, considered as a moral imperative, set up a dilemma which was hard to resolve. Woman must preserve her virtue until marriage and marriage was necessary for her happiness. Yet marriage was, literally, an end to innocence. She was told not to question this dilemma, but simply to accept it.

Submission was perhaps the most feminine virtue expected of women. Men were supposed to be religious, although they rarely had time for it, and supposed to be pure, although it came awfully hard to them, but men were the movers, the doers, the actors. Women were the passive, submissive responders. The order of dialogue was, of course, fixed in Heaven. Man was "woman's superior by God's appointment, if not in intellectual dowry, at least by official decree." Therefore, as Charles Elliott argued in *The Ladies' Repository*, she should submit to him "for the sake of good order at least."[36] In *The Ladies Companion* a young wife was quoted approvingly as saying that she did not think woman should "feel and act for herself" because "When, next to God, her husband is not the tribunal to which her heart and intellect appeals—the golden bowl of affection is broken."[37] Women were warned that if they tampered with this equality they tampered with the order of the Universe.

The Young Lady's Book summarized the necessity of the passive virtues in its readers' lives: "It is, however, certain, that in whatever situation of life a woman is placed from her cradle to her grave, a spirit of obedience and submission, pliability of temper, and humility of mind, are required from her."[38]

Woman understood her position if she was the right kind of woman, a true woman. "She feels herself weak and timid. She needs a protector," declared George Burnap, in his lectures on *The Sphere and Duties of Woman*.

She is in a measure dependent. She asks for wisdom, constancy, firmness, perseverance, and she is willing to repay it all by the surrender of the full treasure of her affections. Woman despises in man every thing like herself except a tender heart. It is enough that she is effeminate and weak; she does not want another like herself.[39]

Or put even more strongly by Mrs. Sandford: "A really sensible woman feels her dependence. She does what she can, but she is conscious of inferiority, and therefore grateful for support."[40]

Mrs. Sigourney, however, assured young ladies that although they were sep-

[35] S. R. R. "Female Charms," *Godey's Magazine and Lady's Book* (Philadelphia), XXXIII (1846), 52.
[36] Charles Elliott, "Arguing With Females," *Ladies' Repository*, I (1841), 25.
[37] *Ladies' Companion*, VIII (Jan. 1838), 147.
[38] *The Young Lady's Book* (New York, 1830), American edition, p. 28. (This is a different book than the one of the same title and date of publication cited in note 6.)
[39] *Sphere and Duties of Woman* (5th ed., Baltimore, 1854), p. 47.
[40] *Woman*, p. 15.

arate, they were equal. This difference of the sexes did not imply inferiority, for it was part of that same order of Nature established by Him "who bids the oak brave the fury of the tempest, and the alpine flower lean its cheek on the bosom of eternal snows."[41] Dr. Meigs had a different analogy to make the same point, contrasting the anatomy of the Apollo of the Belvedere (illustrating the male principle) with the Venus de Medici (illustrating the female principle). "Woman," said the physician, with a kind of clinical gallantry, "has a head almost too small for intellect but just big enough for love."[42]

This love itself was to be passive and responsive. "Love, in the heart of a woman," wrote Mrs. Farrar, "should partake largely of the nature of gratitude. She should love, because she is already loved by one deserving her regard."[43]

Woman was to work in silence, unseen, like Wordsworth's Lucy. Yet, "working like nature, in secret" her love goes forth to the world "to regulate its pulsation, and send forth from its heart, in pure and temperate flow, the life-giving current."[44] She was to work only for pure affection, without thought of money or ambition. A poem, "Woman and Fame," by Felicia Hemans, widely quoted in many of the gift books, concludes with a spirited renunciation of the gift of fame:

> Away! to me, a woman, bring
> Sweet flowers from affection's spring.[45]

"True feminine genius," said Grace Greenwood (Sara Jane Clarke) "is ever timid, doubtful, and clingingly dependent; a perpetual childhood." And she advised literary ladies in an essay on "The Intellectual Woman"—"Don't trample on the flowers while longing for the stars."[46] A wife who submerged her own talents to work for her husband was extolled as an example of a true woman. In *Women of Worth: A Book for Girls,* Mrs. Ann Flaxman, an artist of promise herself, was praised because she "devoted herself to sustain her husband's genius and aid him in his arduous career."[47]

Caroline Gilman's advice to the bride aimed at establishing this proper order from the beginning of a marriage: "Oh, young and lovely bride, watch well the first moments when your will conflicts with his to whom God and society have given the control. Reverence his *wishes* even when you do not his *opinions.*"[48]

Mrs. Gilman's perfect wife in *Recollections of a Southern Matron* realizes that "the three golden threads with which domestic happiness is woven" are "to repress a harsh answer, to confess a fault, and to stop (right or wrong) in the midst of self-defense, in gentle submission." Woman could do this, hard though it was, because in her heart she knew she was right and so could afford

[41] *Letters to Young Ladies* (Hartford, 1835), p. 179.
[42] *Lecture*, p. 17.   [43] *The Young Lady's Friend*, p. 313.
[44] Maria J. McIntosh, *Woman in America: Her Work and Her Reward* (New York, 1850), p. 25.
[45] *Poems and a Memoir of the Life of Mrs. Felicia Hemans* (London, 1860), p. 16.
[46] Letter "To an Unrecognized Poetess, June, 1846" (Sara Jane Clarke), *Greenwood Leaves* (2nd ed.; Boston, 1850), p. 311.
[47] "The Sculptor's Assistant: Ann Flaxman," in *Women of Worth: A Book for Girls* (New York, 1860), p. 263.
[48] Mrs. Clarissa Packard (Mrs. Caroline Howard Gilman), *Recollections of a Housekeeper* (New York, 1834), p. 122.

to be forgiving, even a trifle condescending. "Men are not unreasonable," averred Mrs. Gilman. "Their difficulties lie in not understanding the moral and physical nature of our sex. They often wound through ignorance, and are surprised at having offended." Wives were advised to do their best to reform men, but if they couldn't, to give up gracefully. "If any habit of his annoyed me, I spoke of it once or twice, calmly, then bore it quietly."[49]

A wife should occupy herself "only with domestic affairs—wait till your husband confides to you those of a high importance—and do not give your advice until he asks for it," advised the *Lady's Token*. At all times she should behave in a manner becoming a woman, who had "no arms other than gentleness." Thus "if he is abusive, never retort,"[50] *A Young Lady's Guide to the Harmonious Development of a Christian Character* suggested that females should "become as little children" and "avoid a controversial spirit."[51] *The Mother's Assistant and Young Lady's Friend* listed "Always Conciliate" as its first commandment in "Rules for Conjugal and Domestic Happiness." Small wonder that these same rules ended with the succinct maxim: "Do not expect too much."[52]

As mother, as well as wife, woman was required to submit to fortune. In *Letters to Mothers* Mrs. Sigourney sighed: "To bear the evils and sorrows which may be appointed us, with a patient mind, should be the continual effort of our sex. . . . It seems, indeed, to be expected of us; since the passive and enduring virtues are more immediately within our province." Of these trials "the hardest was to bear the loss of children with submission," but the indomitable Mrs. Sigourney found strength to murmur to the bereaved mother: "The Lord loveth a cheerful giver."[53] *The Ladies' Parlor Companion* agreed thoroughly in "A Submissive Mother," in which a mother who had already buried two children and was nursing a dying baby saw her sole remaining child "probably scalded to death. Handing over the infant to die in the arms of a friend, she bowed in sweet submission to the double stroke." But the child "through the goodness of God survived, and the mother learned to say 'Thy will be done.' "[54]

Woman then, in all her roles, accepted submission as her lot. It was a lot she had not chosen or deserved. As *Godey's* said, "the lesson of submission is forced upon woman." Without comment or criticism the writer affirms that "To suffer and to be silent under suffering seems the great command she has to obey."[55] George Burnap referred to a woman's life as "a series of suppressed emotions."[56] She was, as Emerson said, "more vulnerable, more infirm, more

---

[49] *Recollections of a Southern Matron* (New York, 1838), pp. 256, 257.

[50] *The Lady's Token: or Gift of Friendship*, ed. Colesworth Pinckney (Nashua, N.H., 1848), p. 119.

[51] Harvey Newcomb, *Young Lady's Guide to the Harmonious Development of Christian Character* (Boston, 1846), p. 10.

[52] "Rules for Conjugal and Domestic Happiness," *Mother's Assistant and Young Lady's Friend*, III (Boston), (April 1843), 115.

[53] *Letters to Mothers* (Hartford, 1838), p. 199. In the diaries and letters of women who lived during this period the death of a child seemed consistently to be the hardest thing for them to bear and to occasion more anguish and rebellion, as well as eventual submission, than any other event in their lives.

[54] "A Submissive Mother," *The Ladies' Parlor Companion: A Collection of Scattered Fragments and Literary Gems* (New York, 1852), p. 358.

[55] "Woman," *Godey's Lady's Book*, II (Aug. 1831), 110.

[56] *Sphere and Duties of Woman*, p. 172.

mortal than man."[57] The death of a beautiful woman, cherished in fiction, represented woman as the innocent victim, suffering without sin, too pure and good for this world but too weak and passive to resist its evil forces.[58] The best refuge for such a delicate creature was the warm and safety of her home.

The true woman's place was unquestionably by her own fireside—as daughter, sister, but most of all as wife and mother. Therefore domesticity was among the virtues most prized by the women's magazines. "As society is constituted," wrote Mrs. S. E. Farley, on the "Domestic and Social Claims on Woman," "the true dignity and beauty of the female character seem to consist in a right understanding and faithful and cheerful performance of social and family duties."[59] Sacred Scripture re-enforced social pressure: "St. Paul knew what was best for women when he advised them to be domestic," said Mrs. Sandford. "There is composure at home; there is something sedative in the duties which home involves. It affords security not only from the world, but from delusions and errors of every kind."[60]

From her home woman performed her great task of bringing men back to God. *The Young Ladies' Class Book* was sure that "the domestic fireside is the great guardian of society against the excesses of human passions."[61] *The Lady at Home* expressed its convictions in its very title and concluded that "even if we cannot reform the world in a moment, we can begin the work by reforming ourselves and and our households—It is woman's mission. Let her not look away from her own little family circle for the means of producing moral and social reforms, but begin at home."[62]

Home was supposed to be a cheerful place, so that brothers, husbands and sons would not go elsewhere in search of a good time. Woman was expected to dispense comfort and cheer. In writing the biography of Margaret Mercer (every inch a true woman) her biographer (male) notes: "She never forgot that it is the peculiar province of woman to minister to the comfort, and promote the happiness, first, of those most nearly allied to her, and then of those, who by the Providence of God are placed in a state of dependence upon her."[63] Many other essays in the women's journals showed woman as comforter: "Woman, Man's Best Friend," "Woman, the Greatest Social Benefit," "Woman, A Being to Come Home To," "The Wife: Source of Comfort and the Spring of Joy."[64]

---

[57] Ralph Waldo Emerson, "Woman," *Complete Writings of Ralph Waldo Emerson* (New York, 1875), p. 1180.

[58] As in Donald Fraser, *The Mental Flower Garden* (New York, 1857). Perhaps the most famous exponent of this theory is Edgar Allen Poe who affirms in "The Philosophy of Composition" that "the death of a beautiful woman is unquestionably the most poetical topic in the world. . . ."

[59] "Domestic and Social Claims on Woman," *Mother's Magazine*, VI (1846), 21.

[60] *Woman*, p. 173.   [61] *The Young Ladies' Class Book*, p. 166.

[62] T. S. Arthur, *The Lady at Home: or, Leaves from the Every-Day Book of an American Woman* (Philadelphia, 1847), pp. 177, 178.

[63] Caspar Morris, *Margaret Mercer* (Boston, 1840), quoted in *Woman's Record*, p. 425.

[64] These particular titles come from: *The Young Ladies' Oasis: or Gems of Prose and Poetry*, ed. N. L. Ferguson (Lowell, 1851), pp. 14, 16; *The Genteel School Reader* (Philadelphia, 1849), p. 271; and *Magnolia*, I (1842), 4. A popular poem in book form, published in England, expressed very fully this concept of woman as comforter: Coventry Patmore, *The Angel in the Home* (Boston, 1856 and 1857). Patmore expressed his devotion to True Womanhood in such lines as:

> The gentle wife, who decks his board
> And makes his day to have no night,
> Whose wishes wait upon her Lord,
> Who finds her own in his delight. (p. 94)

One of the most important functions of woman as comforter was her role as nurse. Her own health was probably, although regrettably, delicate.[65] Many homes had "little sufferers," those pale children who wasted away to saintly deaths. And there were enough other illnesses of youth and age, major and minor, to give the nineteenth-century American woman nursing experience. The sickroom called for the exercise of her higher qualities of patience, mercy and gentleness as well as for her housewifely arts. She could thus fulfill her dual feminine function—beauty and usefulness.

The cookbooks of the period offer formulas for gout cordials, ointment for sore nipples, hiccough and cough remedies, opening pills and refreshing drinks for fever, along with recipes for pound cake, jumbles, stewed calves head and currant wine.[66] *The Ladies' New Book of Cookery* believed that "food prepared by the kind hand of a wife, mother, sister, friend" tasted better and had a "restorative power which money cannot purchase."[67]

A chapter of *The Young Lady's Friend* was devoted to woman's privilege as "ministering spirit at the couch of the sick." Mrs. Farrar advised a soft voice, gentle and clean hands, and a cheerful smile. She also cautioned against an excess of female delicacy. That was all right for a young lady in the parlor, but not for bedside manners. Leeches, for example, were to be regarded as "a curious piece of mechanism . . . their ornamental stripes should recommend them even to the eye, and their valuable services to our feelings." And she went on calmly to discuss their use. Nor were women to shrink from medical terminology, since "If you cultivate right views of the wonderful structure of the body, you will be as willing to speak to a physician of the bowels as the brains of your patient."[68]

Nursing the sick, particularly sick males, not only made a woman feel useful and accomplished, but increased her influence. In a piece of heavy-handed humor in *Godey's* a man confessed that some women were only happy when their husbands were ailing that they might have the joy of nursing him to recovery, "thus gratifying their medical vanity and their love of power by making him more dependent upon them."[69] In a similar vein a husband sometimes suspected his wife "almost wishes me dead—for the pleasure of being utterly inconsolable."[70]

In the home women were not only the highest adornment of civilization, but they were supposed to keep busy at morally uplifting tasks. Fortunately most of housework, if looked at in true womanly fashion, could be regarded as uplifting. Mrs. Sigourney extolled its virtues: "The science of housekeeping

---

[65] The women's magazines carried on a crusade against tight lacing and regretted, rather than encouraged, the prevalent ill health of the American woman. See, for example, *An American Mother, Hints and Sketches* (New York, 1839), pp. 28 ff. for an essay on the need for a healthy mind in a healthy body in order to better be a good example for children.

[66] The best single collection of nineteenth-century cookbooks is in the Academy of Medicine of New York Library, although some of the most interesting cures were in hand-written cookbooks found among the papers of women who lived during the period.

[67] Sarah Josepha Hale, *The Ladies' New Book of Cookery: A Practical System for Private Families in Town and Country* (5th ed.; New York, 1852), p. 409. Similar evidence on the importance of nursing skills to every female is found in such books of advice as William A. Alcott, *The Young Housekeeper* (Boston, 1838), in which, along with a plea for apples and cold baths, Alcott says "Every female should be trained to the angelic art of managing properly the sick," p. 47.

[68] *The Young Lady's Friend*, pp. 75–77, 79.

[69] "A Tender Wife," *Godey's*, II (July 1831), 28.

[70] "MY WIFE! A Whisper," *Godey's*, II (Oct. 1831), 231.

affords exercise for the judgment and energy, ready recollection, and patient self-possession, that are the characteristics of a superior mind."[71] According to Mrs. Farrar, making beds was good exercise, the repetitiveness of routine tasks inculcated patience and perseverance, and proper management of the home was a surprisingly complex art: "There is more to be learned about pouring out tea and coffee, than most young ladies are willing to believe."[72] *Godey's* went so far as to suggest coyly, in "Learning vs. Housewifery" that the two were complementary, not opposed: chemistry could be utilized in cooking, geometry in dividing cloth, and phrenology in discovering talent in children.[73]

Women were to master every variety of needlework, for, as Mrs. Sigourney pointed out, "Needle-work, in all its forms of use, elegance, and ornament, has ever been the appropriate occupation of woman."[74] Embroidery improved taste; knitting promoted serenity and economy.[75] Other forms of artsy-craftsy activity for her leisure moments included painting on glass or velvet, Poonah work, tussy-mussy frames for her own needlepoint or water colors, stands for hyacinths, hair bracelets or baskets of feathers.[76]

She was expected to have a special affinity for flowers. To the editors of *The Lady's Token,* "A Woman never appears more truly in her sphere, than when she divides her time between her domestic avocations and the culture of flowers."[77] She could write letters, an activity particularly feminine since it had to do with the outpourings of the heart,[78] or practice her drawingroom skills of singing and playing an instrument. She might even read.

Here she faced a bewildering array of advice. The female was dangerously addicted to novels, according to the literature of the period. She should avoid them, since they interfered with "serious piety." If she simply couldn't help herself and read them anyway, she should choose edifying ones from lists of morally acceptable authors. She should study history since it "showed the depravity of the human heart and the evil nature of sin." On the whole, "religious biography was best."[79]

The women's magazines themselves could be read without any loss of concern for the home. *Godey's* promised the husband that he would find his wife "no less assiduous for his reception, or less sincere in welcoming his return" as a result of reading their magazine.[80] *The Lily of the Valley* won its right to be admitted to the boudoir by confessing that it was "like its namesake humble

---

[71] *Letters to Young Ladies*, p. 27. The greatest exponent of the mental and moral joys of housekeeping was the *Lady's Annual Register and Housewife's Memorandum Book* (Boston, 1838), which gave practical advice on ironing, hair curling, budgeting and marketing, and turning cuffs —all activities which contributed to the "beauty of usefulness" and "joy of accomplishment" which a woman desired (I, 23).

[72] *The Young Lady's Friend*, p. 230.

[73] "Learning vs. Housewifery," *Godey's*, X (Aug. 1839), 95.

[74] *Letters to Young Ladies*, p. 25. W. Thayer, *Life at the Fireside* (Boston, 1857), has an idyllic picture of the woman of the house mending her children's garments, the grandmother knitting and the little girl taking her first stitches, all in the light of the domestic hearth.

[75] "The Mirror's Advice," *Young Maiden's Mirror* (Boston, 1858), p. 263.

[76] Mrs. L. Maria Child, *The Girl's Own Book* (New York, 1833).

[77] P. 44.

[78] T. S. Arthur, *Advice to Young Ladies* (Boston, 1850), p. 45.

[79] R. C. Waterston, *Thoughts on Moral and Spiritual Culture* (Boston, 1842), p. 101. Newcomb's *Young Lady's Guide* also advised religious biography as the best reading for women (p. 111).

[80] *Godey's*, I (1828), 1. (Repeated often in *Godey's* editorials.)

and unostentatious, but it is yet pure, and, we trust, free from moral imperfections."[81]

No matter what later authorities claimed, the nineteenth century knew that girls *could* be ruined by a book. The seduction stories regard "exciting and dangerous books" as contributory causes of disaster. The man without honorable intentions always provides the innocent maiden with such books as a prelude to his assault on her virtue.[82] Books which attacked or seemed to attack woman's accepted place in society were regarded as equally dangerous. A reviewer of Harriet Martineau's *Society in America* wanted it kept out of the hands of American women. They were so suspectible to persuasion, with their "gentle yielding natures," that they might listen to "the bold ravings of the hard-featured of their own sex." The frightening result: "such reading will unsettle them for their true station and pursuits, and they will throw the world back again into confusion."[83]

The debate over women's education posed the question of whether a "finished" education detracted from the practice of housewifely arts. Again it proved to be a case of semantics, for a true woman's education was never "finished" until she was instructed in the gentle science of homemaking.[84] Helen Irving, writing on "Literary Women," made it very clear that if women invoked the muse, it was as a genie of the household lamp. "If the necessities of her position require these duties at her hands, she will perform them nonetheless cheerfully, that she knows herself capable of higher things." The literary woman must conform to the same standards as any other woman: "That her home shall be made a loving place of rest and joy and comfort for those who are dear to her, will be the first wish of every true woman's heart."[85] Mrs. Ann Stephens told women who wrote to make sure they did not sacrifice one domestic duty. "As for genius, make it a domestic plant. Let its roots strike deep in your house. . . ."[86]

The fear of "blue stockings" (the eighteenth-century male's term of derision for educated or literary women) need not persist for nineteenth-century American men. The magazines presented spurious dialogues in which bachelors were convinced of their fallacy in fearing educated wives. One such dialogue took place between a young man and his female cousin. Ernest deprecates learned ladies ("A *Woman* is far more lovable than a *philosopher*") but Alice refutes him with the beautiful example of their Aunt Barbara who "although she *has* perpetrated the heinous crime of writing some half dozen folios" is still a model of "the spirit of feminine gentleness." His memory prodded, Ernest concedes that, by George, there was a woman: "When I last had a cold she not only made me a bottle of cough syrup, but when I complained of nothing new to read, set to work and wrote some twenty stanzas on consumption."[87]

[81] *The Lily of the Valley*, n. v. (1851), p. 2.

[82] For example, "The Fatalist," *Godey's*, IV (Jan. 1834), 10, in which Somers Dudley has Catherine reading these dangerous books until life becomes "a bewildered dream. . . . O passion, what a shocking perverter of reason thou art."

[83] Review of *Society in America* (New York, 1837) in *American Quarterly Review* (Philadelphia), XXII (Sept. 1837), 38.

[84] "A Finished Education," *Ladies' Museum* (Providence), I (1825), 42.

[85] Helen Irving, "Literary Women," *Ladies' Wreath*, III (1850), 93.

[86] "Women of Genius," *Ladies' Companion*, XI (1839), 89.

[87] "Intellect vs. Affection in Woman," *Godey's*, XVI (1846), 86.

The magazines were filled with domestic tragedies in which spoiled young girls learned that when there was a hungry man to feed French and china painting were not helpful. According to these stories many a marriage is jeopardized because the wife has not learned to keep house. Harriet Beecher Stowe wrote a sprightly piece of personal experience for *Godey's*, ridiculing her own bad housekeeping as a bride. She used the same theme in a story, "The Only Daughter," in which the pampered beauty learns the facts of domestic life from a rather difficult source, her mother-in-law. Mrs. Hamilton tells Caroline in the sweetest way possible to shape up in the kitchen, reserving her rebuke for her son: "You are her husband—her guide—her protector—now see what you can do," she admonishes him. "Give her credit for every effort: treat her faults with tenderness; encourage and praise whenever you can, and depend upon it, you will see another woman in her." He is properly masterful, she properly domestic and in a few months Caroline is making lumpless gravy and keeping up with the darning. Domestic tranquillity has been restored and the young wife moralizes: "Bring up a girl to feel that she has a responsible part to bear in promoting the happiness of the family, and you make a reflecting being of her at once, and remove that lightness and frivolity of character which makes her shrink from graver studies."[88] These stories end with the heroine drying her hands on her apron and vowing that *her* daughter will be properly educated, in piecrust as well as Poonah work.

The female seminaries were quick to defend themselves against any suspicion of interfering with the role which nature's God had assigned to women. They hoped to enlarge and deepen that role, but not to change its setting. At the Young Ladies' Seminary and Collegiate Institute in Monroe City, Michigan, the catalogue admitted few of its graduates would be likely "to fill the learned professions." Still, they were called to "other scenes of usefulness and honor." The average woman is to to be "the presiding genius of love" in the home, where she is to "give a correct and elevated literary taste to her children, and to assume that influential station that she ought to possess as the companion of an educated man."[89]

At Miss Pierce's famous school in Litchfield, the students were taught that they had "attained the perfection of their characters when they could combine their elegant accomplishments with a turn for solid domestic virtues."[90] Mt. Holyoke paid pious tribute to domestic skills: "Let a young lady despise this branch of the duties of woman, and she despises the appointments of her existence." God, nature and the Bible "enjoin these duties on the sex, and she cannot violate them with impunity." Thus warned, the young lady would have to seek knowledge of these duties elsewhere, since it was not in the curriculum at Mt. Holyoke. "We would not take this privilege from the mother."[91]

One reason for knowing her way around a kitchen was that America was "a land of precarious fortunes," as Lydia Maria Child pointed out in her book *The Frugal Housewife: Dedicated to Those Who Are Not Ashamed of Economy*. Mrs. Child's chapter "How To Endure Poverty" prescribed a combina-

[88] "The Only Daughter," *Godey's*, X (Mar. 1839), 122.
[89] *The Annual Catalogue of the Officers and Pupils of the Young Ladies' Seminary and Collegiate Institute* (Monroe City, 1855), pp. 18, 19.
[90] *Chronicles of a Pioneer School* from 1792 to 1833: Being the History of Miss Sarah Pierce and Her Litchfield School, Compiled by Emily Noyes Vanderpoel; ed. Elizabeth C. Barney Buel (Cambridge, 1903), p. 74.
[91] *Mt. Holyoke Female Seminary*, p. 13.

tion of piety and knowledge—the kind of knowledge found in a true woman's education, "a thorough religious *useful* education."[92] The woman who had servants today, might tomorrow, because of a depression or panic, be forced to do her own work. If that happened she knew how to act, for she was to be the same cheerful consoler of her husband in their cottage as in their mansion.

An essay by Washington Irving, much quoted in the gift annuals, discussed the value of a wife in case of business reverses:

> I have observed that a married man falling into misfortune is more apt to achieve his situation in the world than a single one . . . it is beautifully ordained by providence that woman, who is the ornament of man in his happier hours, should be his stay and solace when smitten with sudden calamity.[93]

A story titled simply but eloquently "The Wife" dealt with the quiet heroism of Ellen Graham during her husband's plunge from fortune to poverty. Ned Graham said of her: "Words are too poor to tell you what I owe to that noble woman. In our darkest seasons of adversity, she has been an angel of consolation—utterly forgetful of self and anxious only to comfort and sustain me." Of course she had a little help from "faithful Dinah who absolutely refused to leave her beloved mistress," but even so Ellen did no more than would be expected of any true woman.[94]

Most of this advice was directed to woman as wife. Marriage was the proper state for the exercise of the domestic virtues. "True Love and a Happy Home," an essay in *The Young Ladies' Oasis*, might have been carved on every girl's hope chest.[95] But although marriage was best, it was not absolutely necessary. The women's magazines tried to remove the stigma from being an "Old Maid." They advised no marriage at all rather than an unhappy one contracted out of selfish motives.[96] Their stories showed maiden ladies as unselfish ministers to the sick, teachers of the young, or moral preceptors wtih their pens, beloved of the entire village. Usually the life of single blessedness resulted from the premature death of a fiancé, or was chosen through fidelity to some high mission. For example, in "Two Sisters," Mary devotes herself to Ellen and her abandoned children, giving up her own chance for marriage. "Her devotion to her sister's happiness has met its reward in the consciousness of having fulfilled a sacred duty."[97] Very rarely, a "woman of genius" was absolved from

---

[92] *The American Frugal Housewife* (New York, 1838), p. 111.

[93] "Female Influence," in *The Ladies' Pearl and Literary Gleaner: A Collection of Tales, Sketches, Essays, Anecdotes, and Historical Incidents* (Lowell), I (1841), 10.

[94] Mrs. S. T. Martyn, "The Wife," *Ladies' Wreath*, II (1848–49), 171.

[95] *The Young Ladies' Oasis*, p. 26.

[96] "On Marriage," *Ladies' Repository*, I (1841), 133; "Old Maids," *Ladies' Literary Cabinet* (Newburyport), II (1822) (Microfilm), 141; "Matrimony," *Godey's*, II (Sept. 1831), 174; and "Married or Single," *Peterson's Magazine* (Philadelphia) IX (1859), 36, all express the belief that while marriage is desirable for a woman it is not essential. This attempt to reclaim the status of the unmarried woman is an example of the kind of mild crusade which the women's magazines sometimes carried on. Other examples were their strictures against an overly-genteel education and against the affectation and aggravation of ill health. In this sense the magazines were truly conservative, for they did not oppose all change but only that which did violence to some cherished tradition. The reforms they advocated would, if put into effect, make woman even more the perfect female, and enhance the ideal of True Womanhood.

[97] *Girlhood and Womanhood*, p. 100. Mrs. Graves tells the stories in the book in the person of an "Old Maid" and her conclusions are that "single life has its happiness too," for the single woman "can enjoy all the pleasures of maternity without its pains and trials" (p. 140). In an-

the necessity of marriage, being so extraordinary that she did not need the security or status of being a wife.[98] Most often, however, if girls proved "difficult," marriage and a family were regarded as a cure.[99] The "sedative quality" of a home could be counted on to subdue even the most restless spirits.

George Burnap saw marriage as "that sphere for which woman was originally intended, and to which she is so exactly fitted to adorn and bless, as the wife, the mistress of a home, the solace, the aid, and the counsellor of that ONE, for whose sake alone the world is of any consequence to her."[100] Samuel Miller preached a sermon on women:

> How interesting and important are the duties devolved on females as WIVES . . . the counsellor and friend of the husband; who makes it her daily study to lighten his cares, to soothe his sorrows, and to augment his joys; who, like a guardian angel, watches over his interests, warns him against dangers, comforts him under trials; and by her pious, assiduous, and attractive deportment, constantly endeavors to render him more virtuous, more useful, more honourable, and more happy.[101]

A woman's whole interest should be focused on her husband, paying him "those numberless attentions to which the French give the title of *petits soins* and which the woman who loves knows so well how to pay . . . she should consider nothing as trivial which could win a smile of approbation from him."[102]

Marriage was seen not only in terms of service but as an increase in authority for woman. Burnap concluded that marriage improves the female character "not only because it puts her under the best possible tuition, that of the affections, and affords scope to her active energies, but because it gives her higher aims, and a more dignified position."[103] *The Lady's Amaranth* saw it as a balance of power: "The man bears rule over his wife's person and conduct. She

---

other one of her books, *Woman in America* (New York, 1843), Mrs. Graves speaks out even more strongly in favor of "single blessedness" rather than "a loveless or unhappy marriage" (p. 130).

[98] A very unusual story is Lela Linwood, "A Chapter in the History of a Free Heart," *Ladies' Wreath*, III (1853), 349. The heroine, Grace Arland, is "sublime" and dwells "in perfect light while we others struggle yet with the shadows." She refuses marriage and her friends regret this but are told her heart "is rejoicing in its *freedom*." The story ends with the plaintive refrain:

> But is it not a happy thing,
> All fetterless and free,
> Like any wild bird, on the wing,
> To carol merrily?

But even in this tale the unusual, almost unearthly rarity of Grace's genius is stressed; she is not offered as an example to more mortal beings.

[99] Horace Greeley even went so far as to apply this remedy to the "dissatisfactions" of Margaret Fuller. In his autobiography, *Recollections of a Busy Life* (New York, 1868), he says that "noble and great as she was, a good husband and two or three bouncing babies would have emancipated her from a deal of cant and nonsense" (p. 178).

[100] *Sphere and Duties of Woman*, p. 64.

[101] *A Sermon: Preached March 13, 1808, for the Benefit of the Society Instituted in the City of New-York, For the Relief of Poor Widows with Small Children* (New York, 1808), pp. 13, 14.

[102] *Lady's Magazine and Museum: A Family Journal* (London) IV (Jan. 1831), 6. This magazine is included partly because its editorials proclaimed it "of interest to the English speaking lady at home and abroad" and partly because it shows that the preoccupation with True Womanhood was by no means confined to the United States.

[103] *Sphere and Duties of Woman*, p. 102.

bears rule over his inclinations: he governs by law; she by persuasion. . . .
The empire of the woman is an empire of softness . . . her commands are
caresses, her menaces are tears."[104]

Woman should marry, but not for money. She should choose only the high
road of true love and not truckle to the values of a materialistic society. A story
"Marrying for Money" (subtlety was not the strong point of the ladies' magazines) depicts Gertrude, the heroine, rueing the day she made her crass choice:
"It is a terrible thing to live without love. . . . A woman who dares marry for
aught but the purest affection, calls down the just judgments of heaven upon
her head."[105]

The corollary to marriage, with or without true love, was motherhood,
which added another dimension to her usefulness and her prestige. It also
anchored her even more firmly to the home. "My Friend," wrote Mrs. Sigourney, "If in becoming a mother, you have reached the climax of your happiness, you have also taken a higher place in the scale of being . . . you have
gained an increase of power."[106] The Rev. J. N. Danforth pleaded in *The Ladies'
Casket,* "Oh, mother, acquit thyself well in thy humble sphere, for thou mayest
affect the world."[107] A true woman naturally loved her children; to suggest
otherwise was monstrous.[108]

America depended upon her mothers to raise up a whole generation of
Christian statesmen who could say "all that I am I owe to my angel mother."[109]
The mothers must do the inculcating of virtue since the fathers, alas, were too
busy chasing the dollar. Or as *The Ladies' Companion* put it more effusively,
the father, "weary with the heat and burden of life's summer day, or trampling
with unwilling foot the decaying leaves of life's autumn, has forgotten the
sympathies of life's joyous springtime. . . . The acquisition of wealth, the advancement of his children in worldly honor—these are his self-imposed tasks."
It was his wife who formed "the infant mind as yet untainted by contact with
evil . . . like wax beneath the plastic hand of the mother."[110]

The Ladies' Wreath offered a fifty-dollar prize to the woman who submitted
the most convincing essay on "How May An American Woman Best Show
Her Patriotism." The winner was Miss Elizabeth Wetherell, who provided
herself with a husband in her answer. The wife in the essay of course asked
her husband's opinion. He tried a few jokes first—"Call her eldest son George

[104] "Matrimony," *Lady's Amaranth,* II (Dec. 1839), 271.
[105] Elizabeth Doten, "Marrying for Money," *The Lily of the Valley,* n. v. (1857), p. 112.
[106] *Letters to Mothers,* p. 9.
[107] "Maternal Relation," *Ladies' Casket* (New York, 1850?), p. 85. The importance of the
mother's role was emphasized abroad as well as in America. *Godey's* recommended the book by
the French author Aimeé-Martin on the education of mothers to "be read five times," in the
original if possible (XIII, Dec. 1842, 201). In this book the highest ideals of True Womanhood
are upheld. For example: "Jeunes filles, jeunes épouses, tendres mères, c'est dans votre âme bien
plus que dans les lois du législateur que reposent aujourd'hui l'avenir de l'Europe et les destinées
du genre humain," L. Aimeé-Martin, *De l'Education des Meres de famille ou De la civilisation du
genre humain par les femmes* (Bruxelles, 1857), II, 527.
[108] *Maternal Association of the Amity Baptist Church:* Annual Report (New York, 1847), p. 2:
"Suffer the little children to come unto me and forbid them not, is and must ever be a sacred
commandment to the Christian woman."
[109] For example, Daniel Webster, "The Influence of Woman," in *The Young Ladies' Reader*
(Philadelphia, 1851), p. 310.
[110] Mrs. Emma C. Embury, "Female Education," *Ladies' Companion,* VIII (Jan. 1838), 18.
Mrs. Embury stressed the fact that the American woman was not the "mere plaything of passion"
but was in strict training to be "the mother of statesmen."

Washington," "Don't speak French, speak American"—but then got down to telling her in sober prize-winning truth what women could do for their country. Voting was no asset, since that would result only in "a vast increase of confusion and expense without in the smallest degree affecting the result." Besides, continued this oracle, "looking down at their child," if "we were to go a step further and let the children vote, their first act would be to vote their mothers at home." There is no comment on this devastating male logic and he continues: "Most women would follow the lead of their fathers and husbands," and the few who would "fly off on a tangent from the circle of home influence would cancel each other out."

The wife responds dutifully: "I see all that. I never understood so well before." Encouraged by her quick womanly perception, the master of the house resolves the question—an American woman best shows her patriotism by staying at home, where she brings her influence to bear "upon the right side for the country's weal." That woman will instinctively choose the side of right he has no doubt. Besides her "natural refinement and closeness to God" she has the "blessed advantage of a quiet life" while man is exposed to conflict and evil. She stays home with "her Bible and a well-balanced mind" and raises her sons to be good Americans. The judges rejoiced in this conclusion and paid the prize money cheerfully, remarking "they deemed it cheap at the price."[111]

If any woman asked for greater scope for her gifts the magazines were sharply critical. Such women were tampering with society, undermining civilization. Mary Wollstonecraft, Frances Wright and Harriet Martineau were condemned in the strongest possible language—they were read out of the sex. "They are only semi-women, mental hermaphrodites." The Rev. Harrington knew the women of America could not possibly approve of such perversions and went to some wives and mothers to ask if they did want a "wider sphere of interest" as these nonwomen claimed. The answer was reassuring. " 'No!' they cried simultaneously, 'Let the men take care of politics, *we will take care of the children!* '" Again female discontent resulted only from a lack of understanding: women were not subservient, they were rather "chosen vessels." Looked at in this light the conclusion was inescapable: "Noble, sublime is the task of the American mother."[112]

"Women's Rights" meant one thing to reformers, but quite another to the True Woman. She knew her rights,

> The right to love whom others scorn,
> The right to comfort and to mourn,
> The right to shed new joy on earth,
> The right to feel the soul's high worth . . .
> Such women's rights, and God will bless
> And crown their champions with success.[113]

The American woman had her choice—she could define her rights in the way of the women's magazines and insure them by the practice of the

<hr>

[111] "How May An American Woman Best Show Her Patriotism?" *Ladies' Wreath*, III (1851), 313. Elizabeth Wetherell was the pen name of Susan Warner, author of *The Wide Wide World* and *Queechy*.

[112] Henry F. Harrington, "Female Education," *Ladies' Companion*, IX (1838), 293, and "Influence of Woman—Past and Present," *Ladies' Companion*, XIII (1840), 245.

[113] Mrs. E. Little, "What Are the Rights of Women?" *Ladies' Wreath*, II (1848–49), 133.

requisite virtues, or she could go outside the home, seeking other rewards than love. It was a decision on which, she was told, everything in her world depended. "Yours it is to determine," the Rev. Mr. Stearns solemnly warned from the pulpit, "whether the beautiful order of society . . . shall continue as it has been" or whether "society shall break up and become a chaos of disjointed and unsightly elements."[114] If she chose to listen to other voices than those of her proper mentors, sought other rooms than those of her home, she lost both her happiness and her power—"that almost magic power, which, in her proper sphere, she now wields over the destinies of the world."[115]

But even while the women's magazines and related literature encouraged this ideal of the perfect woman, forces were at work in the nineteenth century which impelled woman herself to change, to play a more creative role in society. The movements for social reform, westward migration, missionary activity, utopian communities, industrialism, the Civil War—all called forth responses from woman which differed from those she was trained to believe were hers by nature and divine decree. The very perfection of True Womanhood, moreover, carried within itself the seeds of its own destruction. For if woman was so very little less than the angels, she should surely take a more active part in running the world, especially since men were making such a hash of things.

Real women often felt they did not live up to the ideal of True Womanhood: some of them blamed themselves, some challenged the standard, some tried to keep the virtues and enlarge the scope of womanhood.[116] Somehow through this mixture of challenge and acceptance, of change and continuity, the True Woman evolved into the New Woman—a transformation as startling in its way as the abolition of slavery or the coming of the machine age. And yet the stereotype, the "mystique" if you will, of what woman was and ought to be persisted, bringing guilt and confusion in the midst of opportunity.[117]

The women's magazines and related literature had feared this very dislocation of values and blurring of roles. By careful manipulation and interpretation they sought to convince woman that she had the best of both worlds —power and virtue—and that a stable order of society depended upon her maintaining her traditional place in it. To that end she was identified with everything that was beautiful and holy.

"Who Can Find a Valiant Woman?" was asked frequently from the pulpit and the editorial pages. There was only one place to look for her—at home. Clearly and confidently these authorities proclaimed the True Woman of the nineteenth century to be the Valiant Woman of the Bible, in whom the heart of her husband rejoiced and whose price was above rubies.

---

[114] *Female Influence*, p. 18.   [115] *Ibid.*, p. 23.

[116] Even the women reformers were prone to use domestic images, i.e. "sweep Uncle Sam's kitchen clean," and "tidy up our country's house."

[117] The "Animus and Anima" of Jung amounts almost to a catalogue of the nineteenth-century masculine and female traits, and the female hysterics whom Freud saw had much of the same training as the nineteenth-century American woman. Betty Friedan, *The Feminine Mystique* (New York, 1963), challenges the whole concept of True Womanhood as it hampers the "fulfillment" of the twentieth-century woman.

Romantic Reform in America
1815–1865

John L. Thomas

INTRODUCTION

The following article deserves close reading for a number of reasons. It discusses the religious spirit that manifested itself in so many aspects of American reform in the nineteenth century, and it traces the complex ramifications of this basically conservative impulse in movements for far-reaching social reform. By focusing upon the romantic aspects of ante-bellum reform, Thomas provides a detailed analysis of such widespread nineteenth-century reformist assumptions and goals as perfectionism, immediatism, and anti-institutionalism as well as their strong belief in individualism. These forces are too frequently disregarded or ignored by the tendency to view Jacksonian democracy or the slavery controversy in exclusively political terms. Thomas briefly but perceptively explores the disruptive impact that the Civil War had upon these earlier reformist impulses and the role it had in shaping post-bellum reform. Finally, this essay establishes a historical framework within which the reform spirit so widespread among a growing segment of young Americans in the 1960's and early 1970's can be more readily understood.

Alice Felt Tyler, *Freedom's Ferment: Phases of American Social History to 1860** (1944), is a valuable overview of the reform ethos in the first half of the nineteenth century. John W. Ward, *Andrew Jackson: Symbol for an Age** (1955), is a superb attempt to recreate the ethos and analyze the ideology of Jacksonian America. Marvin Meyers, *The Jacksonian Persuasion: Politics and Belief** (1957), emphasizes the nostalgia of the period. Whitney R. Cross, *The Burned-Over District** (1950), is an important study of the genesis of reform movements in New York, with particular stress on the role of evangelical religion. Also important for the relationship of evangelicalism to reform in this period are Bernard Weisberger, *They Gathered at the River** (1958); William McLoughlin, *Modern Revivalism* (1959); C. C. Cole, Jr., *The Social Ideals of the Northern Evangelists, 1826–1860* (1954); and Timothy

L. Smith, *Revivalism and Social Reform in Mid-Nineteenth Century America* (1957).

Perry Miller's collection of transcendentalist writings, *The Transcendentalists** (1950), is a good introduction to their thought, as are two of the best literary histories of the period, F. O. Matthiessen, *American Renaissance* (1941), and Van Wyck Brooks, *The Flowering of New England, 1815–1865** (1936). Almost every aspect of the complex abolitionist movement is covered in the following studies: Dwight L. Dumond, *Antislavery** (1961); Gilbert H. Barnes, *The Anti-Slavery Impulse, 1833–1844** (1933); Aileen Kraditor, *Means and Ends in American Abolitionism* (1969); John L. Thomas, *The Liberator: William Lloyd Garrison* (1963); and Martin Duberman's collection of original essays, *The Antislavery Vanguard** (1965). Other reform movements of the period are covered in John A. Krout, *The Origins of Prohibition* (1925); Merle Curti, *The American Peace Crusade* (1929); Eleanor Flexner, *Century of Struggle** (1959); Paul Monroe, *The Founding of the American Public School System* (1940); and Blake McKelvey, *American Prisons* (1936). George M. Frederickson, *The Inner Civil War** (1965), is an illuminating discussion of the effects of the Civil War upon the reform impulse.

C ONFRONTED by the bewildering variety of projects for regenerating American society, Emerson concluded his survey of humanitarian reform in 1844 with the observation that "the Church, or religious party, is falling away from the Church nominal, and . . . appearing in temperance and nonresistance societies; in movements of abolitionists and of socialists . . . of seekers, of all the soul of the soldiery of dissent." Common to all these planners and prophets, he noted, was the conviction of an "infinite worthiness" in man and the belief that reform simply meant removing "impediments" to natural perfection.[1]

Emerson was defining, both as participant and observer, a romantic revolution which T. E. Hulme once described as "split religion."[2] A romantic faith in perfectibility, originally confined by religious institutions, overflows these barriers and spreads across the surface of society, seeping into politics and culture. Perfectibility—the essentially religious notion of the individual as a "reservoir" of possibilities—fosters a revolutionary assurance "that if you can so rearrange society by the destruction of oppressive order then these possibilities will have a chance and you will get Progress." Hulme had in mind the destructive forces of the French Revolution, but his phrase is also a particularly accurate description of the surge of social reform which swept across Emerson's America in the three decades before the Civil War. Out of a seemingly conservative religious revival there flowed a spate of perfectionist ideas for the improvement and rearrangement of American society. Rising rapidly in the years after 1830, the flood of social reform reached its crest at mid-century only to be checked by political crisis and the counterforces of the Civil War. Reform after the Civil War, though still concerned with individual perfectibility, proceeded from new and different assumptions as to the nature of individualism and its preservation in an urban industrial society. Romantic reform ended with the Civil War and an intellectual counterrevolution which discredited the concept of the irreducible self and eventually redirected reform energies.

Romantic reform in America traced its origins to a religious impulse which was both politically and socially conservative. With the consolidation of independence and the arrival of democratic politics the new nineteenth-century generation of American churchmen faced a seeming crisis. Egalitarianism and rising demands for church disestablishment suddenly appeared to threaten an inherited Christian order and along with it the preferred status of the clergy.

FROM John L. Thomas, "Romantic Reform in America, 1815–1865," *American Quarterly*, XVII (Winter 1965), 656–81. Copyright, 1965, Trustees of the University of Pennsylvania. Reprinted by permission.

[1] Ralph Waldo Emerson, "The New England Reformers," *Works* (Centenary ed.), III, 251; "Man the Reformer," *Works*, I, 248–49.

[2] T. E. Hulme, "Romanticism and Classicism," *Speculations: Essays on Humanism and the Philosophy of Art*, ed. Herbert Read (London, 1924), reprinted in *Critiques and Essays in Criticism, 1920–1948*, ed. Robert Wooster Stallman (New York, 1949), pp. 3–16.

Lyman Beecher spoke the fears of more than one of the clerical party when he warned that Americans were fast becoming "another people." When the attempted alliance between sound religion and correct politics failed to prevent disestablishment or improve waning Federalist fortunes at the polls, the evangelicals, assuming a defensive posture, organized voluntary benevolent associations to strengthen the Christian character of Americans and save the country from infidelity and ruin. Between 1815 and 1830 nearly a dozen moral reform societies were established to counter the threats to social equilibrium posed by irreligious democrats. Their intense religious concern could be read in the titles of the benevolent societies which the evangelicals founded: the American Bible Society, the American Sunday School Union, the American Home Missionary Society, the American Tract Society. By the time of the election of Andrew Jackson the benevolent associations formed a vast if loosely coordinated network of conservative reform enterprises staffed with clergy and wealthy laymen who served as self-appointed guardians of American morals.[3]

The clerical diagnosticians had little difficulty in identifying the symptoms of democratic disease. Infidelity flourished on the frontier and licentiousness bred openly in seaboard cities; intemperance sapped the strength of American workingmen and the saving word was denied their children. Soon atheism would destroy the vital organs of the republic unless drastic moral therapy prevented. The evangelicals' prescription followed logically from their diagnosis: large doses of morality injected into the body politics under the supervision of Christian stewards. No more Sunday mails or pleasure excursions, no more grog-shops or profane pleasures, no family without a Bible and no community without a minister of the gospel. Accepting for the moment their political liabilities, the moral reformers relied on the homeopathic strategy of fighting democratic excess with democratic remedies. The Tract Society set up three separate printing presses which cranked out hundreds of thousands of pamphlets for mass distribution. The Home Missionary Society subsidized seminarians in carrying religion into the backcountry. The Temperance Union staged popular conventions; the Peace Society sponsored public debates; the Bible Society hired hundreds of agents to spread its propaganda.

The initial thrust of religious reform, then, was moral rather than social, preventive rather than curative. Nominally rejecting politics and parties, the evangelicals looked to a general reformation of the American character achieved through a revival of piety and morals in the individual. By probing his conscience, by convincing him of his sinful ways and converting him to right conduct they hoped to engineer a Christian revolution which would leave the foundations of the social order undisturbed. The realization of their dream of a nonpolitical "Christian party" in America would ensure a one-party system open to moral talent and the natural superiority of Christian leadership. Until their work was completed, the evangelicals stood ready as servants of the Lord to manage their huge reformational apparatus in behalf of order and sobriety.

But the moral reformers inherited a theological revolution which in under-

---

[3] For discussions of evangelical reform see John R. Bodo, *The Protestant Clergy and Public Issues, 1812–1848* (Princeton, 1954), and Clifford S. Griffin, *Their Brothers' Keepers* (New Brunswick, N.J., 1960).

mining their conservative defenses completely reversed their expectations for a Christian America. The transformation of American theology in the first quarter of the nineteenth century released the very forces of romantic perfectionism that conservatives most feared. This religious revolution advanced along three major fronts: first, the concentrated anti-theocratic assault of Robert Owen and his secular utopian followers, attacks purportedly atheistic and environmentalist but in reality Christian in spirit and perfectionist in method; second, the revolt of liberal theology beginning with Unitarianism and culminating in transcendentalism; third, the containment operation of the "new divinity" in adapting orthodoxy to the criticism of liberal dissent. The central fact in the romantic reorientation of American theology was the rejection of determinism. Salvation, however variously defined, lay open to everyone. Sin was voluntary: men were not helpless and depraved by nature but free agents and potential powers for good. Sin could be reduced to the selfish preferences of individuals, and social evils, in turn, to collective sins which, once acknowledged, could be rooted out. Perfectionism spread rapidly across the whole spectrum of American Protestantism as different denominations and sects elaborated their own versions of salvation. If man was a truly free agent, then his improvement became a matter of immediate consequence. The progress of the country suddenly seemed to depend upon the regeneration of the individual and the contagion of example.

As it spread, perfectionism swept across denominational barriers and penetrated even secular thought. Perfection was presented as Christian striving for holiness in the "new heart" sermons of Charles Grandison Finney and as an immediately attainable goal in the come-outer prophecies of John Humphrey Noyes. It was described as an escape from outworn dogma by Robert Owen and as the final union of the soul with nature by Emerson. The important fact for most Americans in the first half of the nineteenth century was that it was readily available. A romantic religious faith had changed an Enlightenment doctrine of progress into a dynamic principle of reform.

For the Founding Fathers' belief in perfectibility had been wholly compatible with a pessimistic appraisal of the present state of mankind. Progress, in the view of John Adams or James Madison, resulted from the planned operation of mechanical checks within the framework of government which balanced conflicting selfish interests and neutralized private passions. Thus a properly constructed governmental machine might achieve by artifact what men, left to their own devices, could not—gradual improvement of social institutions and a measure of progress. Perfectionism, on the contrary, as an optative mood demanded total commitment and immediate action. A latent revolutionary force lay in its demand for immediate reform and its promise to release the new American from the restraints of institutions and precedent. In appealing to the liberated individual, perfectionism reinforced the Jacksonian attack on institutions, whether a "Monster Bank" or a secret Masonic order, entrenched monopolies or the Catholic Church. But in emphasizing the unfettered will as the proper vehicle for reform it provided a millenarian alternative to Jacksonian politics. Since social evils were simply individual acts of selfishness compounded, and since Americans could attempt the perfect society any time they were so inclined, it followed that the duty of the true reformer consisted in educating them and making them models of good behavior. As the sum of individual sins social wrong would disappear when enough people had been converted and rededicated to right conduct. Deep and lasting reform, therefore, meant an educational crusade based on the assumption that when a sufficient number of individual Americans had seen the light, they would automatically solve the country's social problems. Thus formulated, perfectionist reform offered a program of mass conversion achieved through educational rather than political means. In the opinion of the romantic reformers the regeneration of American society began, not in legislative enactments or political manipulation, but in a calculated appeal to the American urge for individual self-improvement.

Perfectionism radically altered the moral reform movement by shattering the benevolent societies themselves. Typical of these organizations was the American Peace Society founded in 1828 as a forum for clerical discussions of the gospel of peace. Its founders, hoping to turn American attention from the pursuit of wealth to the prevention of war, debated the question of defensive war, constructed hypothetical leagues of amity, and in a general way sought to direct American foreign policy into pacific channels. Perfectionism, however, soon split the Peace Society into warring factions as radical nonresistants, led by the Christian perfectionist Henry C. Wright, denounced all use of force and demanded the instant creation of an American society modeled on the precepts of Jesus. Not only war but all governmental coercion fell under the ban of the nonresistants who refused military service and political office along with the right to vote. After a series of skirmishes the nonresistants seceded in 1838 to form their own New England Non-Resistant Society; and by 1840 the institutional strength of the peace movement had been completely broken.

The same power of perfectionism disrupted the temperance movement. The founders of the temperance crusade had considered their reform an integral part of the program of moral stewardship and had directed their campaign against "ardent spirits" which could be banished "by a correct and efficient public sentiment." Until 1833 there was no general agreement on a pledge of total abstinence: some local societies required it, others did not. At the first national convention held in that year, however, the radical advocates of temperance, following their perfectionist proclivities, demanded a pledge of total abstinence and hurried on to denounce the liquor traffic as "morally wrong." Soon both the national society and local and state auxiliaries were split between moderates content to preach to the consumer and radicals bent on extending moral suasion to public pressure on the seller. After 1836 the national movement disintegrated into scattered local societies which attempted with no uniform program and no permanent success to establish a cold-water America.

By far the most profound change wrought by perfectionism was the sudden emergence of abolition. The American Colonization Society, founded in 1817 as another key agency in the moral reform complex, aimed at strengthening republican institutions by deporting an inferior and therefore undesirable Negro population. The cooperation of Southerners hoping to strengthen the institution of slavery gave Northern colonizationists pause, but they succeeded in repressing their doubts until a perfectionist ethic totally discredited their program. The abolitionist pioneers were former colonizationists who took sin and redemption seriously and insisted that slavery constituted a flat denial of perfectibility to both Negroes and whites. They found in immediate emancipation a perfectionist formula for casting off the guilt of slavery and bringing the Negro to Christian freedom. Destroying slavery, the abolitionists argued, depended first of all on recognizing it as sin: and to this recognition they bent their efforts. Their method was direct and intensely personal. Slaveholding they considered a deliberate flouting of the divine will for which there was no remedy but repentance. Since slavery was sustained by a system of interlocking personal sins, their task was to teach Americans to stop sinning. "We shall send forth agents to lift up the voice of remonstrance, of warning, of entreaty, and of rebuke," the Declaration of Sentiments of the American Anti-Slavery Society announced. Agents, tracts, petitions and conventions—all the techniques of the moral reformers—were brought to bear on the consciences of Americans to convince them of their sin.

From the beginning, then, the abolitionists mounted a moral crusade rather than an engine of limited reform. For seven years, from 1833 to 1840, their society functioned as a loosely coordinated enterprise—a national directory of antislavery opinion. Perfectionist individualism made effective organization difficult and often impossible. Antislavery delegates from state and local societies gathered at annual conventions to frame denunciatory resolutions, listen to endless rounds of speeches and go through the motions of electing officers. Nominal leadership but very little power was vested in a self-perpetuating executive committee. Until its disruption in 1840 the national society was riddled with controversy as moderates, disillusioned by the failure of moral suasion, gradually turned to politics, and ultras, equally disenchanted by public hostility, abandoned American institutions altogether. Faced with the resistance of Northern churches and state legislatures, the perfectionists, led by William Lloyd Garrison, deserted politics for the principle of secession. The come-outer abolitionists, who eventually took for their motto "No Union with Slaveholders," sought an alternative to politics in the command to cast off church and state for a holy fraternity which would convert the nation by the power of example. The American Anti-Slavery Society quickly succumbed to the strain of conflicting philosophies and warring personalities. In 1840 the Garrisonians seized control of the society and drove their moderate opponents out. Thereafter neither ultras nor moderates were able to maintain an effective national organization.

Thus romantic perfectionism altered the course of the reform enterprise by appealing directly to the individual conscience. Its power stemmed from a millennial expectation which proved too powerful a moral explosive for the reform agencies. In one way or another almost all of the benevolent societies felt the force of perfectionism. Moderates, attempting political solutions, scored temporary gains only to receive sharp setbacks. Local option laws passed one year were repealed the next. Despite repeated attempts the Sunday School Union failed to secure permanent adoption of its texts in the public schools. The Liberty Party succeeded only in electing a Democratic president in 1844. Generally, direct political action failed to furnish reformers with the moral leverage they believed necessary to perfect American society. The conviction spread accordingly that politicians and legislators, as Albert Brisbane put it, were engaged in "superficial controversies and quarrels, which lead to no practical results."[4] Political results, a growing number of social reformers were convinced, would be forthcoming only when the reformation of society at large had been accomplished through education and example.

---

[4] Arthur Brisbane, *Social Destiny of Man: or, Association and Reorganization of Industry* (Philadelphia, 1840), introduction, p. vi.

The immediate effects of perfectionism, therefore, were felt outside politics in humanitarian reforms. With its confidence in the liberated individual perfectionism tended to be anti-institutional and exclusivist; but at the same time it posited an ideal society in which this same individual could discover his power for good and exploit it. Such a society would tolerate neither poverty nor suffering; it would contain no condemned classes or deprived citizens, no criminals or forgotten men. Impressed with the necessity for saving these neglected elements of American society, the humanitarian reformers in the years after 1830 undertook a huge rescue operation.

Almost to a man the humanitarians came from moral reform backgrounds. Samuel Gridley Howe was a product of Old Colony religious zeal and a Baptist education at Brown; Thomas Gallaudet a graduate of Andover and an ordained minister; Dorothea Dix a daughter of an itinerant Methodist minister, school mistress and Sunday school teacher-turned-reformer; E. M. P. Wells, founder of the reform school, a pastor of a Congregational church in Boston. Louis Dwight, the prison reformer, had been trained for the ministry at Yale and began his reform career as a traveling agent for the American Tract Society. Robert Hartley, for thirty years the secretary of the New York Association for Improving the Condition of the Poor, started as a tract distributor and temperance lecturer. Charles Loring Brace served as a missionary on Blackwell's Island before founding the Children's Aid Society.

In each of these cases of conversion to humanitarian reform there was a dramatic disclosure of deprivation and suffering which did not tally with preconceived notions of perfectibility—Dorothea Dix's discovery of the conditions in the Charlestown reformatory, Robert Hartley's inspection of contaminated milk in New York slums, Samuel Gridley Howe's chance conversation with Dr. Fisher in Boston. Something very much like a conversion experience seems to have forged the decisions of the humanitarians to take up their causes, a kind of revelation which furnished them with a ready-made role outside politics and opened a new career with which they could become completely identified. With the sudden transference of a vague perfectionist faith in self-improvement to urgent social problems there emerged a new type of professional reformer whose whole life became identified with the reform process.

Such, for example, was the conversion of Dorothea Dix from a lonely and afflicted schoolteacher who composed meditational studies of the life of Jesus into "D. L. Dix," the militant advocate of the helpless and forgotten. In a very real sense Miss Dix's crusade for better treatment of the insane and the criminal was one long self-imposed subjection to suffering. Her reports, which recorded cases of unbelievable mistreatment, completed a kind of purgative rite in which she assumed the burden of innocent suffering and passed it on as guilt to the American people. The source of her extraordinary energy lay in just this repeated submission of herself to human misery until she felt qualified to speak out against it. Both an exhausting schedule and the almost daily renewal of scenes of suffering seemed to give her new energies for playing her romantic reform role in an effective and intensely personal way. Intense but not flexible: there was little room for exchange and growth in the mood of atonement with which she approached her work. Nor was her peculiarly personal identification with the victims of American indifference easily matched in reform circles. Where other reformers like the abolitionists often made abstract pleas for "bleeding humanity" and "suffering millions," hers was the real thing—a perfectionist fervor which strengthened her will at the cost of psychological isolation. Throughout her career she preferred to work alone, deploring the tendency to multiply reform agencies and ignoring those that existed either because she disagreed with their principles, as in the case of Louis Dwight's Boston Prison Discipline Society, or because she chose the more direct method of personal appeal. In all her work, even the unhappy and frustrating last years as superintendent of nurses in the Union Army, she saw herself as a solitary spokesman for the deprived and personal healer of the suffering.

Another reform role supplied by perfectionism was Bronson Alcott's educator-prophet, the "true reformer" who "studied man as he is from the hand of the Creator, and not as he is made by the errors of the world." Convinced that the self sprang from divine origins in nature, Alcott naturally concluded that children were more susceptible to good than people imagined and set out to develop a method for uncovering that goodness. With the power to shape personality the teacher, Alcott was sure, held the key to illimitable progress and the eventual regeneration of the world. The teacher might literally make society over by teaching men as children to discover their own divine natures. Thus true education for Alcott consisted of the process of self-discovery guided by the educator-prophet. He sharply criticized his contemporaries for their fatal mistake of imposing partial and therefore false standards on their charges. Shades of the prison house obscured the child's search for perfection, and character was lost forever. "Instead of following it in the path pointed out by its Maker, instead of learning by observation, and guiding it in that path, we unthinkingly attempt to shape its course to our particular wishes. . . ."[5]

To help children avoid the traps set by their elders Alcott based his whole system on the cultivation of self-awareness through self-examination. His pupils kept journals in which they scrutinized their behavior and analyzed their motives. Ethical problems were the subject of frequent and earnest debate at the Temple School as the children were urged to discover the hidden springs of perfectibility in themselves. No mechanical methods of rote learning could bring on the moment of revelation; each child was unique and would find himself in his own way. The real meaning of education as reform, Alcott realized, came with an increased social sense that resulted from individual self-discovery. As the creator of social personality Alcott's teacher was bound by no external rules of pedagogy: as the primary social reformer he had to cast off "the shackles of form, of mode, and ceremony" in order to play the required roles in the educational process.

Alcott's modernity lay principally in his concept of the interchangeability of roles—both teacher and pupils acquired self-knowledge in an exciting give-and-take. Thus defined, education became a way of life, a continuing process through which individuals learned to obey the laws of their own natures and in so doing to discover the laws of the good society. This identification of individual development with true social unity was crucial for Alcott, as for the other perfectionist communitarians, because it provided the bridge over which they passed from self to society. The keystone in Alcott's construction was supplied by the individual conscience which connected with the "common

---

[5] For a careful analysis of Alcott's educational theories see Dorothy McCuskey, *Bronson Alcott, Teacher* (New York, 1940), particularly pp. 25–40 from which these quotations are taken.

conscience" of mankind. This fundamental identity, he was convinced, could be demonstrated by the learning process itself which he defined as "sympathy and imitation, the moral action of the teacher upon the children, of the children upon him, and each other." He saw in the school, therefore, a model of the good community where self-discovery led to a social exchange culminating in the recognition of universal dependency and brotherhood. The ideal society —the society he hoped to create—was one in which individuals could be totally free to follow their own natures because such pursuit would inevitably end in social harmony. For Alcott the community was the product rather than the creator of the good life.

Fruitlands, Alcott's attempt to apply the lessons of the Temple School on a larger scale, was designed to prove that perfectionist educational reform affected the "economies of life." In this realization lay the real import of Alcott's reform ideas; for education, seen as a way of life, meant the communitarian experiment as an educative model. Pushed to its limits, the perfectionist assault on institutions logically ended in the attempt to make new and better societies as examples for Americans to follow. Communitarianism, as Alcott envisioned it, was the social extension of his perfectionist belief in education as an alternative to politics.

In the case of other humanitarian reformers like Samuel Gridley Howe perfectionism determined even more precisely both the role and intellectual content of their proposals. Howe's ideal of the good society seems to have derived from his experiences in Greece where, during his last year, he promoted a communitarian plan for resettling exiles on the Gulf of Corinth. With government support he established his colony, "Washingtonia," on two thousand acres of arable land, selected the colonists himself, bought cattle and tools, managed its business affairs, and supervised a Lancastrian school. By his own admission these were the happiest days of his life: "I laboured here day & night in season & out; & was governor, legislator, clerk, constable, & everything but a patriarch."[6] When the government withdrew its support and brigands overran the colony, Howe was forced to abandon the project and return home. Still, the idea of an entire community under the care of a "patriarch" shouldering its collective burden and absorbing all its dependents in a cooperative life continued to dominate the "Doctor's" reform thinking and to determine his methods.

The ethical imperatives in Howe's philosophy of reform remained constant. "Humanity demands that every creature in human shape should command our respect; we should recognise as a brother every being upon whom God has stamped the human impress." Progress he likened to the American road. Christian individualism required that each man walk separately and at his own pace, but "the rear should not be left too far behind . . . none should be allowed to perish in their helplessness . . . the strong should help the weak, so that the whole should advance as a band of brethren." It was the duty of society itself to care for its disabled or mentally deficient members rather than to shut them up in asylums which were "offsprings of a low order of feeling." "The more I reflect upon the subject the more I see objections in principle and practice to asylums," he once wrote to a fellow-reformer. "What right have we

[6] Letter from Howe to Horace Mann, 1857, quoted in Harold Schwartz, *Samuel Gridley Howe* (Cambridge, 1956), p. 37.

to pack off the poor, the old, the blind into asylums? They are of us, our brothers, our sisters—they belong in families. . . ."[7]

In Howe's ideal society, then, the handicapped, criminals and defectives would not be walled off but accepted as part of the community and perfected by constant contact with it. Two years of experimenting with education for the feeble-minded convinced him that even "idiots" could be redeemed from what he called spiritual death. "How far they can be elevated, and to what extent they may be educated, can only be shown by the experience of the future," he admitted in his report to the Massachusetts legislature but predicted confidently that "each succeeding year will show even more progress than any preceding one."[8] He always acted on his conviction that "we shall avail ourselves of special institutions less and the common schools more" and never stopped hoping that eventually all blind children after proper training might be returned to families and public schools for their real education. He also opposed the establishment of reformatories with the argument that they only collected the refractory and vicious and made them worse. Nature mingled the defective in common families, he insisted, and any departure from her standards stunted moral growth. He took as his model for reform the Belgian town of Geel where mentally ill patients were boarded at public expense with private families and allowed maximum freedom. As soon as the building funds were available he introduced the cottage system at Perkins, a plan he also wanted to apply to reformatories. No artificial and unnatural institution could replace the family which Howe considered the primary agency in the perfection of the individual.

Howe shared his bias against institutions and a preference for the family unit with other humanitarian reformers like Robert Hartley and Charles Loring Brace. Hartley's "friendly visitors" were dispatched to New York's poor with instructions to bring the gospel of self-help home to every member of the family. Agents of the AICP dispensed advice and improving literature along with the coal and groceries. Only gradually did the organization incorporate "incidental labors"—legislative programs for housing reform, health regulations and child labor—into its system of reform. Hartley's real hope for the new urban poor lay in their removal to the country where a bootstrap operation might lift them to sufficiency and selfhood. "Escape then from the city," he told them, "—for escape is your only recourse against the terrible ills of beggary; and the further you go, the better."[9] In Hartley's formula the perfectionist doctrine of the salvation of the individual combined with the conservative appeal of the safety-valve.

A pronounced hostility to cities also marked the program of Charles Loring Brace's Children's Aid Society, the central feature of which was the plan for relocating children of the "squalid poor" on upstate New York farms for "moral disinfection." The Society's placement service resettled thousands of slum children in the years before the Civil War in the belief that a proper family environment and a rural setting would release the naturally good

---

[7] Letter from Howe to William Chapin, 1857, quoted in Laura E. Richards, *Letters and Journals of Samuel Gridley Howe* (2 vols.; New York, 1909), II, 48.

[8] Second Report of the Commissioners on Idiocy to the Massachusetts Legislature (1849), quoted in Richards, *Howe,* II, 214.

[9] New York A.I.C.P., *The Mistake* (New York, 1850), p. 4, quoted in Robert H. Bremner, *From the Depths: the Discovery of Poverty in the United States* (New York, 1956), p. 38.

tendencies in young people so that under the supervision of independent and hard-working farmers they would save themselves.[10]

There was thus a high nostalgic content in the plans of humanitarians who emphasized pastoral virtues and the perfectionist values inherent in country living. Their celebration of the restorative powers of nature followed logically from their assumption that the perfected individual—the truly free American —could be created only by the reunification of mental and physical labor. The rural life, it was assumed, could revive and sustain the unified sensibility threatened by the city. A second assumption concerned the importance of the family as the primary unit in the reconstruction of society. As the great debate among social reformers proceeded it centered on the question of the limits to which the natural family could be extended. Could an entire society, as the more radical communitarians argued, be reorganized as one huge family? Or were there natural boundaries necessary for preserving order and morality? On the whole, the more conservative humanitarians agreed with Howe in re-jecting those communal plans which, like Fourier's, stemmed from too high an estimate of "the capacity of mankind for family affections."[11]

That intensive education held the key to illimitable progress, however, few humanitarian reformers denied. They were strengthened in their certainty by the absolutes inherited from moral reform. Thus Howe, for example, con-sidered his work a "new field" of "practical religion." The mental defective, he was convinced, was the product of sin—both the sin of the parents and the sin of society in allowing the offspring to languish in mental and moral dark-ness. Yet the social evils incident to sin were not inevitable; they were not "inherent in the very constitution of man" but the "chastisements sent by a loving Father to bring his children to obedience to his beneficent laws."[12] These laws—infinite perfectibility and social responsibility—reinforced each other in the truly progressive society. The present condition of the dependent classes in America was proof of "the immense space through which society has yet to advance before it even approaches the perfection of civilization which is attainable."[13] Education, both the thorough training of the deprived and the larger education of American society to its obligations, would meet the moral challenge.

The perfectionist uses of education as an alternative to political reform were most thoroughly explored by Horace Mann. Mann's initial investment in pub-lic school education was dictated by his fear that American democracy, lacking institutional checks and restraints, was fast degenerating into "the spectacle of gladiatorial contests" conducted at the expense of the people. Could laws save American society? Mann thought not.

With us, the very idea of legislation is reversed. Once, the law prescribed the actions and shaped the wills of the multitude; here the wills of the multitude prescribe and shape the law . . . now when the law is weak, the passions of the multitude have gathered irresistible strength, it is fallacious and insane to

[10] Brace's views are set forth in his *The Dangerous Classes of New York and Twenty Years Among Them* (New York, 1872). For a brief treatment of his relation to the moral reform move-ment see Bremner, *From the Depths*, chap. iii.

[11] Letter from Howe to Charles Sumner, Apr. 8, 1847, quoted in Richards, *Howe*, II, 255–56.

[12] First Report of the Commissioners on Idiocy (1848), quoted in Richards, *Howe*, II, 210–11.

[13] *Ibid.*, pp. 210–11.

look for security in the moral force of law. Government and law . . . will here be moulded into the similitude of the public mind. . . .[14]

In offering public school education as the only effective countervailing force in a democracy Mann seemingly was giving vent to a conservative dread of unregulated change in a society where, as he admitted, the momentum of hereditary opinion was spent. Where there was no "surgical code of laws" reason, conscience and benevolence would have to be provided by education. "The whole mass of mind must be instructed in regard to its comprehensive and enduring interests." In a republican government, however, compulsion was theoretically undesirable and practically unavailable. People could not be driven up a "dark avenue" even though it were the right one. Mann, like his evangelical predecessors, found his solution in an educational crusade.

> Let the intelligent visit the ignorant, day by day, as the oculist visits the blind mind, and detaches the scales from his eyes, until the living sense leaps to light. . . . Let the love of beautiful reason, the admonitions of conscience, the sense of religious responsibility, be plied, in mingled tenderness and earnestness, until the obdurate and dark mass of avarice and ignorance and prejudice shall be dissipated by their blended light and heat.[15]

Here in Mann's rhetorical recasting was what appeared to be the old evangelical prescription for tempering democratic excess. The chief problem admittedly was avoiding the "disturbing forces of party and sect and faction and clan." To make sure that education remained nonpartisan the common schools should teach on the *"exhibitory"* method, "by an actual exhibition of the principle we would inculcate."

Insofar as the exhibitory method operated to regulate or direct public opinion, it was conservative. But implicit in Mann's theory was a commitment to perfectionism which gradually altered his aims until in the twelfth and final report education emerges as a near-utopian device for making American politics simple, clean and, eventually, superfluous. In the Twelfth Report Mann noted that although a public school system might someday guarantee "sufficiency, comfort, competence" to every American, as yet "imperfect practice" had not matched "perfect theory." Then in an extended analysis of social trends which foreshadowed Henry George's classification he singled out "poverty" and "profusion" as the two most disturbing facts in American development. "With every generation, fortunes increase on the one hand, and some new privation is added to poverty on the other. We are verging toward those extremes of opulence and penury, each of which unhumanizes the mind."[16] A new feudalism threatened; and unless a drastic remedy was discovered, the "hideous evils" of unequal distribution of wealth would cause class war.

[14] Horace Mann, "The Necessity of Education in a Republican Government," *Lectures on Education* (Boston, 1845), pp. 152, 158.

[15] "An Historical View of Education; Showing Its Dignity and Its Degradation," *Lectures on Education*, pp. 260, 262.

[16] This quotation and the ones from Mann that follow are taken from the central section of the *Twelfth Report* entitled "Intellectual Education as a Means of Removing Poverty, and Securing Abundance," Mary Peabody Mann, *Life of Horace Mann* (4 vols.; Boston, 1891), IV, 245–68. See also the perceptive comments on Mann in Rush Welter, *Popular Education and Democratic Thought in America* (New York, 1962), pp. 97–102, from which I have drawn.

Mann's alternative to class conflict proved to be nothing less than universal education based on the exhibitory model of the common school. Diffusion of education, he pointed out, meant wiping out class lines and with them the possibility of conflict. As the great equalizer of condition it would supply the balance-wheel in the society of the future. Lest his readers confuse his suggestions with the fantasies of communitarians Mann hastened to point out that education would perfect society through the individual by creating new private resources. Given full play in a democracy, education gave each man the "independence and the means by which he can resist the selfishness of other men."

Once Mann had established education as an alternative to political action, it remained to uncover its utopian possibilities. By enlarging the "cultivated class" it would widen the area of social feelings—"if this education should be universal and complete, it would do more than all things else to obliterate factitious distinctions in society." Political reformers and revolutionaries based their schemes on the false assumption that the amount of wealth in America was fixed by fraud and force, and that the few were rich because the many were poor. By demanding a redistribution of wealth by legislative fiat they overlooked the power of education to obviate political action through the creation of new and immense sources of wealth.

Thus in Mann's theory as in the programs of the other humanitarians the perfection of the individual through education guaranteed illimitable progress. The constantly expanding powers of the free individual ensured the steady improvement of society until the educative process finally achieved a harmonious, self-regulating community. "And will not the community that gains its wealth in this way . . . be a model and a pattern for nations, a type of excellence to be admired and followed by the world?" The fate of free society, Mann concluded, depended upon the conversion of individuals from puppets and automatons to thinking men who were aware of the strength of the irreducible self and determined to foster it in others.

As romantic perfectionism spread across Jacksonian society it acquired an unofficial and only partly acceptable philosophy in the "systematic subjectivism" of transcendental theory.[17] Transcendentalism, as its official historian noted, claimed for all men what a more restrictive Christian perfectionism extended only to the redeemed. Seen in this light, self-culture—Emerson's "perfect unfolding of our individual nature"—appeared as a secular amplification of the doctrine of personal holiness. In the transcendentalist definition, true reform proceeded from the individual and worked outward through the family, the neighborhood and ultimately into the social and political life of the community. The transcendentalist, Frothingham noted in retrospect, "was less a reformer of human circumstances than a regenerator of the human spirit. . . . With movements that did not start from this primary assumption of individual dignity, and come back to that as their goal, he had nothing to do."[18] Emerson's followers, like the moral reformers and the humanitarians, looked to individuals rather than to institutions, to "high heroic example" rather than to political programs. The Brook-Farmer John Sullivan Dwight summed up

[17] The phrase is Santayana's in "The Genteel Tradition in American Philosophy." For an analysis of the anti-institutional aspects of transcendentalism and reform see Stanley Elkins, *Slavery* (Chicago, 1959), chap. iii.
[18] Octavius Brooks Frothingham, *Transcendentalism in New England* (Harper Torchbooks ed.: New York, 1959), p. 155.

their position when he protested that "men are anterior to systems. Great doctrines are not the origins, but the product of great lives."[19]

Accordingly the transcendentalists considered institutions—parties, churches, organizations—so many arbitrarily constructed barriers on the road to self-culture. They were lonely men, Emerson admitted, who repelled influences. "They are not good citizens; not good members of society. . . ."[20] A longing for solitude led them out of society, Emerson to the woods where he found no Jacksonian placards on the trees, Thoreau to his reclusive leadership of a majority of one. Accepting for the most part Emerson's dictum that one man was a counterpoise to a city, the transcendentalists turned inward to examine the divine self and find there the material with which to rebuild society. They wanted to avoid at all costs the mistake of their Jacksonian contemporaries who in order to be useful accommodated themselves to institutions without realizing the resultant loss of power and integrity.

The most immediate effect of perfectionism on the transcendentalists, as on the humanitarians, was the development of a set of concepts which, in stressing reform by example, opened up new roles for the alienated intellectual. In the first place, self-culture accounted for their ambivalence toward reform politics. It was not simply Emerson's reluctance to raise the siege on his hencoop that kept him apart, but a genuine confusion as to the proper role for the reformer. If government was simply a "job" and American society the senseless competition of the marketplace, how could the transcendentalist accept either as working premises? The transcendentalist difficulty in coming to terms with democratic politics could be read in Emerson's confused remark that of the two parties contending for the presidency in 1840 one had the better principles, the other the better men. Driven by their profound distaste for manipulation and chicanery, many of Emerson's followers took on the role of a prophet standing aloof from elections, campaigns and party caucuses and dispensing wisdom (often in oblique Emersonian terminology) out of the vast private resources of the self. In this sense transcendentalism, like Christian perfectionism, represented a distinct break with the prevailing Jacksonian views of democratic leadership and the politics of compromise and adjustment.

One of the more appealing versions of the transcendental role was the hero or genius to whom everything was permitted, as Emerson said, because "genius is the character of illimitable freedom." The heroes of the world, Margaret Fuller announced, were the true theocratic kings: "The hearts of men make music at their approach; the mind of the age is like the historian of their passing; and only men of destiny like themselves shall be permitted to write their eulogies, or fill their vacancies."[21] Margaret Fuller herself spent her transcendentalist years stalking the American hero, which she somehow confused with Emerson, before she joined the Roman Revolution in 1849 and discovered the authentic article in the mystic nationalist Mazzini.

Carlyle complained to Emerson of the "perilous altitudes" to which the transcendentalists' search for the hero led them. Despite his own penchant for hero-worship he came away from reading the *Dial* "with a kind of shudder." In their pursuit of the self-contained hero they seemed to separate themselves

---

[19] John Sullivan Dwight is quoted in Frothingham, *Transcendentalism*, p. 147.
[20] "The Transcendentalist," *Works*, I, 347–48.
[21] Such was her description of Lamennais and Beranger as quoted in Mason Wade, *Margaret Fuller* (New York, 1940), p. 195.

from "this same cotton-spinning, dollar-hunting, canting and shrieking, very wretched generation of ours."[22] The transcendentalists, however, were not trying to escape the Jacksonian world of fact, only to find a foothold for their perfectionist individualism in it. They sought a way of implementing their ideas of self-culture without corrupting them with the false values of materialism. They saw a day coming when parties and politicians would be obsolescent. By the 1850s Walt Whitman thought that day had already arrived and that America had outgrown parties.

> What right has any one political party, no matter which, to wield the American government? No right at all . . . and every American young man must have sense enough to comprehend this. I have said the old parties are defunct; but there remains of them empty flesh, putrid mouths, mumbling and speaking the tones of these conventions, the politicians standing back in shadow, telling lies, trying to delude and frighten the people. . . .[23]

Whitman's romantic alternative was a "love of comrades" cementing an American brotherhood and upholding a redeemer president.

A somewhat similar faith in the mystical fraternity informed Theodore Parker's plan for spiritual revolution. Like the other perfectionists, Parker began by reducing society to its basic components—individuals, the "monads" or "primitive atoms" of the social order—and judged it by its tendency to promote or inhibit individualism. "Destroy the individuality of those atoms, . . . all is gone. To mar the atoms is to mar the mass. To preserve itself, therefore, society is to preserve the individuality of the individual."[24] In Parker's theology perfectionist Christianity and transcendental method merged to form a loving brotherhood united by the capacity to apprehend primary truths directly. A shared sense of the divinity of individual man held society together; without it no true community was possible. Looking around him at antebellum America, Parker found only the wrong kind of individualism, the kind that said, "I am as good as you, so get out of my way." The right kind, the individualism whose motto was "You are as good as I, and let us help one another,"[25] was to be the work of Parker's spiritual revolution. He explained the method of revolution as one of *"intellectual, moral* and *religious* education —everywhere and for all men." Until universal education had done its work Parker had little hope for political stability in the United States. He called instead for a new "party" to be formed in society at large, a party built on the idea that "God still inspires men as much as ever; that he is immanent in spirit as in space." Such a party required no church, tradition or scripture. "It believes God is near the soul as matter to the sense. . . . It calls God father and mother, not king; Jesus, brother, not redeemer, heaven home, religion nature."[26]

---

[22] Quoted in Wade, *Margaret Fuller,* pp. 88–89.

[23] Walt Whitman, "The Eighteenth Presidency," an essay unpublished in Whitman's lifetime, in *Walt Whitman's Workshop,* ed. Clifton Joseph Furness (Cambridge, 1928), pp. 104–5.

[24] Quoted in Daniel Aaron, *Men of Good Hope* (Oxford paperback ed.: New York, 1961), p. 35.

[25] Theodore Parker, "The Political Destination of America and the Signs of the Times" (1848) excerpted in *The Transcendentalists,* ed. Perry Miller (Anchor ed.: Garden City, N.Y., 1957), p. 357.

[26] Quoted in R. W. B. Lewis, *The American Adam* (Chicago, 1955), p. 182.

Parker believed that this "philosophical party in politics," as he called it, was already at work in the 1850s on a code of universal laws from which to deduce specific legislation "so that each statute in the code shall represent a fact in the universe, a point of thought in God; so . . . that legislation shall be divine in the same sense that a true system of astronomy be divine." Parker's holy band represented the full fruition of the perfectionist idea of a "Christian party" in America, a party of no strict political or sectarian definition, but a true reform movement, apostolic in its beginnings but growing with the truths it preached until it encompassed all Americans in a huge brotherhood of divine average men. Party members, until time-serving Whigs and Democrats, followed ideas and intuitions rather than prejudice and precedent, and these ideas led them to question authority, oppose legal injustice and tear down rotten institutions. The philosophical party was not to be bound by accepted notions of political conduct or traditional attitudes toward law. When unjust laws interpose barriers to progress, reformers must demolish them.

So Parker himself reasoned when he organized the Vigilance Committee in Boston to defeat the Fugitive Slave Law. His reasoning epitomized perfectionist logic: every man may safely trust his conscience, properly informed, because it is the repository for divine truth. When men learn to trust their consciences and act on them, they naturally encourage others to do the same with the certainty that they will reach the same conclusions. Individual conscience thus creates a social conscience and a collective will to right action. Concerted right action means moral revolution. The fact that moral revolution, in its turn, might mean political revolt was a risk Parker and his perfectionist followers were willing to take.

Both transcendentalism and perfectionist moral reform, then, were marked by an individualist fervor that was disruptive of American institutions. Both made heavy moral demands on church and state; and when neither proved equal to the task of supporting their intensely personal demands the transcendentalists and the moral reformers became increasingly alienated. The perfectionist temperament bred a come-outer spirit. An insistence on individual moral accountability and direct appeal to the irreducible self, the faith in self-reliance and distrust of compromise, and a substitution of universal education for partial reform measures, all meant that normal political and institutional reform channels were closed to the perfectionists. Alternate routes to the millennium had to be found. One of these was discovered by a new leadership which made reform a branch of prophecy. Another was opened by the idea of a universal reawakening of the great god self. But there was a third possibility, also deeply involved with the educational process, an attempt to build the experimental community as a reform model. With an increasing number of reformers after 1840 perfectionist anti-institutionalism led to heavy investments in the communitarian movement.

The attraction that drew the perfectionists to communitarianism came from their conviction that the good society should be simple. Since American society was both complicated and corrupt, it was necessary to come out from it; but at the same [time] the challenge of the simple life had to be met. Once the true principles of social life had been discovered they had to be applied, some way found to harness individual perfectibility to a social engine. This urge to form the good community, as John Humphrey Noyes experienced it himself and perceived it in other reformers, provided the connection between perfectionism and communitarianism, or, as Noyes put it, between "Revivalism" and "Socialism." Perfectionist energies directed initially against institutions were diverted to the creation of small self-contained communities as educational models. In New England two come-outer abolitionists, Adin Ballou and George Benson, founded cooperative societies at Hopedale and Northampton, while a third Garrisonian lieutenant, John Collins, settled his followers on a farm in Skaneateles, New York. Brook Farm, Fruitlands and the North American Phalanx at Redbank acquired notoriety in their own day; but equally significant, both in terms of origins and personnel, were the experiments at Raritan Bay under the guidance of Marcus Spring, the Marlboro Association in Ohio, the Prairie Home Community of former Hicksite Quakers, and the Swedenborgian Brocton Community. In these and other experimental communities could be seen the various guises of perfectionism.

Communitarianism promised drastic social reform without violence. Artificiality and corruption could not be wiped out by partial improvements and piecemeal measures but demanded a total change which, as Robert Owen once explained, "could make an immediate, and almost instantaneous, revolution in the minds and manners of society in which it shall be introduced." Communitarians agreed in rejecting class struggle which set interest against interest instead of uniting them through association. "Whoever will examine the question of social ameliorations," Albert Brisbane argued in support of Fourier, "must be convinced that *the gradual perfecting of Civilization* is useless as a remedy for present social evils, and that the only effectual means of doing away with indigence, idleness and the dislike for labor is to do away with civilization itself, and organize Association . . . in its place."[27] Like the redemptive moment in conversion or the experience of self-discovery in transcendentalist thought, the communitarian ideal pointed to a sharp break with existing society and a commitment to root-and-branch reform. On the other hand, the community was seen as a controlled experiment in which profound but peaceful change might be effected without disturbing the larger social order. Massive change, according to communitarian theory, could also be gradual and harmonious if determined by the model.

Perfectionist religious and moral reform shaded into communitarianism, in the case of a number of social reformers, with the recognition that the conversion of the individual was a necessary preparation for and logically required communal experimentation. Such was John Humphrey Noyes' observation that in the years after 1815

> the line of socialistic excitement lies parallel with the line of religious Revivals. . . . The Revivalists had for their one great idea the regeneration of the soul. The great idea of the Socialists was the regeneration of society, which is the soul's environment. These ideas belong together and are the complements of each other.[28]

So it seemed to Noyes' colleagues in the communitarian movement. The course from extreme individualism to communitarianism can be traced in George

---

[27] Albert Brisbane, *Social Destiny of Man,* p. 286, quoted in Arthur Eugene Bestor, *Backwoods Utopias: The Sectarian and Owenite Phases of Communitarian Socialism in America: 1663–1829* (Philadelphia, 1950), p. 9.
[28] John Humphrey Noyes, *History of American Socialism* (Philadelphia, 1870), p. 26.

Ripley's decision to found Brook Farm. Trying to win Emerson to his new cause, he explained that his own personal tastes and habits would have led him away from plans and projects.

> I have a passion for being independent of the world, and of every man in it. This I could do easily on the estate which is now offered. . . . I should have a city of God, on a small scale of my own. . . . But I feel bound to sacrifice this private feeling, in the hope of the great social good.

That good Ripley had no difficulty in defining in perfectionist terms:

> . . . to insure a more natural union between intellectual and manual labor than now exists; to combine the thinker and the worker, as far as possible, in the same individual; to guarantee the highest mental freedom, by providing all with labor, adapted to their tastes and talents, and securing to them the fruits of their industry; to do away with the necessity of menial services, by opening the benefits of education and the profits of labor to all; and thus to prepare a society of liberal, intelligent, and cultivated persons, whose relations with each other would permit a more simple and wholesome life, than can be led amidst the pressure of our competitive institutions.[29]

However varied their actual experiences with social planning, all the communitarians echoed Ripley's call for translating perfectionism into concerted action and adapting the ethics of individualism to larger social units. Just as the moral reformers appealed to right conduct and conscience in individuals the communitarians sought to erect models of a collective conscience to educate Americans. Seen in this light, the communitarian faith in the model was simply an extension of the belief in individual perfectibility. Even the sense of urgency characterizing moral reform was carried over into the communities where a millennial expectation flourished. The time to launch their projects, the social planners believed, was the immediate present when habits and attitudes were still fluid, before entrenched institutions had hardened the American heart and closed the American mind. To wait for a full quota of useful members or adequate supply of funds might be to miss the single chance to make the country perfect. The whole future of America seemed to them to hinge on the fate of their enterprises.

Some of the projects were joint-stock corporations betraying a middle-class origin; others were strictly communistic. Some, like the Shaker communities, were pietistic and rigid; others, like Oneida and Hopedale, open and frankly experimental. Communitarians took a lively interest in each others' projects and often joined one or another of them for a season before moving on to try utopia on their own. The division between religious and secular attempts was by no means absolute: both types of communities advertised an essentially religious brand of perfectionism. Nor was economic organization always an accurate means of distinguishing the various experiments, most of which were subjected to periodic constitutional overhauling and frequent readjustment, now in the direction of social controls and now toward relaxation of those controls in favor of individual initiative.

---

[29] Letter from Ripley to Ralph Waldo Emerson, Nov. 9, 1840, in *Autobiography of Brook Farm*, ed. Henry W. Sams (Englewood Cliffs, N.J., 1958), pp. 5–8.

The most striking characteristic of the communitarian movement was not its apparent diversity but the fundamental similarity of educational purpose. The common denominator or "main idea" Noyes correctly identified as *"the enlargement of home—the extension of family union beyond the little man-and-wife circle to large corporations."*[30] Communities as different as Fruitlands and Hopedale, Brook Farm and Northampton, Owenite villages and Fourier phalansteries were all, in one way or another, attempting to expand and apply self-culture to groups. Thus the problem for radical communitarians was to solve the conflict between the family and society. In commenting on the failure of the Brook Farmers to achieve a real community, Charles Lane, Alcott's associate at Fruitlands, identified what he considered the basic social question of the day—"whether the existence of the marital family is compatible with that of the universal family, which the term 'Community' signifies."[31] A few of the communitarians, recognizing this conflict, attempted to solve it by changing or destroying the institution of marriage. For the most part, the perfectionist communitarians shied away from any such radical alteration of the family structure and instead sought a law of association by which the apparently antagonistic claims of private and universal love could be harmonized. Once this law was known and explained, they believed, then the perfect society was possible—a self-adjusting mechanism constructed in accordance with their recently discovered law of human nature.

Inevitably communitarianism developed a "science of society," either the elaborate social mathematics of Fourier or the constitutional mechanics of native American perfectionists. The appeal of the blueprint grew overwhelming: in one way or another almost all the communitarians succumbed to the myth of the mathematically precise arrangement, searching for the perfect number or the exact size, plotting the precise disposition of working forces and living space, and combining these estimates in a formula which would ensure perfect concord. The appeal of Fourierism stemmed from its promise to reconcile productive industry with "passional attractions." "Could this be done," John Sullivan Dwight announced, "the word 'necessity' would acquire an altogether new and pleasanter meaning; the outward necessity and the inward prompting for every human being would be one and identical, and his life a living harmony."[32] Association fostered true individuality which, in turn, guaranteed collective accord. In an intricate calculation involving ascending and descending wings and a central point of social balance where attractions equalled destinies the converts to Fourierism contrived a utopian alternative to politics. The phalanx represented a self-perpetuating system for neutralizing conflict and ensuring perfection. The power factor—politics—had been dropped out; attraction alone provided the stimulants necessary to production and progress. Here in the mathematical model was the culmination of the "peaceful revolution" which was to transform America.

The communitarian experiments in effect were anti-institutional institutions. In abandoning political and religious institutions the communitarians were

---

[30] Noyes, *American Socialisms*, p. 23.

[31] Charles Lane, "Brook Farm," *Dial*, IV (Jan. 1844), 351–57, reprinted in Sams, *Brook Farm*, pp. 87–92.

[32] John Sullivan Dwight, "Association in its Connection with Education," a lecture delivered before the New England Fourier Society, in Boston, Feb. 29, 1844. Excerpted in Sams, *Brook Farm*, pp. 104–5.

driven to create perfect societies of their own which conformed to their perfectionist definition of the free individual. Their communities veered erratically between the poles of anarchism and collectivism as they hunted feverishly for a way of eliminating friction without employing coercion, sure that once they had found it, they could apply it in a federation of model societies throughout the country. In a limited sense, perhaps, their plans constituted an escape from urban complexity and the loneliness of alienation. But beneath the nostalgia there lay a vital reform impulse and a driving determination to make American society over through the power of education.

The immediate causes of the collapse of the communities ranged from loss of funds and mismanagement to declining interest and disillusionment with imperfect human material. Behind these apparent reasons, however, stood the real cause in the person of the perfectionist self, Margaret Fuller's "mountainous me," that proved too powerful a disruptive force for even the anti-institutional institutions it had created. It was the perfectionist ego which allowed the communitarian reformers to be almost wholly nonselective in recruiting their membership and to put their trust in the operation of an atomistic general will. Constitution-making and paper bonds, as it turned out, were not enough to unite divine egoists in a satisfactory system for the free expression of the personality. Perfectionist individualism did not make the consociate family. The result by the 1850s was a profound disillusionment with the principle of association which, significantly, coincided with the political crisis over slavery. Adin Ballou, his experiment at Hopedale in shambles, summarized the perfectionist mood of despair when he added that "few people are near enough right in heart, head and habits to live in close social intimacy."[33] Another way would have to be found to carry divine principles into social arrangements, one that took proper account of the individual.

The collapse of the communitarian movement in the 1850s left a vacuum in social reform which was filled by the slavery crisis. At first their failure to consolidate alternative social and educational institutions threw the reformers back on their old perfectionist individualism for support. It was hardly fortuitous that Garrison, Mann, Thoreau, Howe, Parker, Channing, Ripley and Emerson himself responded to John Brown's raid with a defense of the liberated conscience. But slavery, as a denial of freedom and individual responsibility, had to be destroyed by institutional forces which could be made to sustain these values. The antislavery cause during the secession crisis and throughout the Civil War offered reformers an escape from alienation by providing a new identity with the very political institutions which they had so vigorously assailed.

The effects of the Civil War as an intellectual counterrevolution were felt both in a revival of institutions and a renewal of an organic theory of society. The war brought with it a widespread reaction against the seeming sentimentality and illusions of perfectionism. It saw the establishment of new organizations like the Sanitary and the Christian Commissions run on principles of efficiency and professionalism totally alien to perfectionist methods. Accompanying the wartime revival of institutions was a theological reorientation directed by Horace Bushnell and other conservative churchmen whose longstanding opposition to perfectionism seemed justified by the war. The extreme

[33] Letter from Ballou to Theodore Weld, Dec. 23, 1856, quoted in Benjamin P. Thomas, *Theodore Weld: Crusader for Freedom* (New Brunswick, N.J., 1950), p. 229.

individualism of the ante-bellum reformers was swallowed up in a Northern war effort that made private conscience less important than saving the Union. Some of the abolitionists actually substituted national unity for freedom for the slave as the primary war aim. Those reformers who contributed to the war effort through the Sanitary Commission or the Christian Commission found a new sense of order and efficiency indispensable. Older perfectionists, like Dorothea Dix, unable to adjust to new demands, found their usefulness drastically confined. Young Emersonians returned from combat convinced that professionalism, discipline and subordination, dubious virtues by perfectionist standards, were essential in a healthy society. A new emphasis on leadership and performance was replacing the benevolent amateurism of the perfectionists.

Popular education and ethical agitation continued to hold the post-war stage, but the setting for them had changed. The three principal theorists of social reform in post-war industrial America—Henry George, Henry Demarest Lloyd and Edward Bellamy—denounced class conflict, minimized the importance of purely political reform, and, like their perfectionist precursors, called for moral revolution. The moral revolution which they demanded, however, was not the work of individuals in whom social responsibility developed as a by-product of self-discovery but the ethical revival of an entire society made possible by the natural development of social forces. Their organic view of society required new theories of personality and new concepts of role-playing, definitions which appeared variously in George's law of integration, Lloyd's religion of love, and Bellamy's economy of happiness. And whereas Nemesis in the perfectionist imagination had assumed the shape of personal guilt and estrangement from a pre-established divine order, for the post-war reformers it took on the social dimensions of a terrifying relapse into barbarism. Finally, the attitudes of the reformers toward individualism itself began to change as Darwinism with the aid of a false analogy twisted the prewar doctrine of self-reliance into a weapon against reform. It was to protest against a Darwinian psychology of individual isolation that Lloyd wrote his final chapter of *Wealth Against Commonwealth,* declaring that the regeneration of the individual was only a half-truth and that "the reorganization of the society which he makes and which makes him is the other half."

> We can become individual only by submitting to be bound to others. We extend our freedom only by finding new laws to obey. . . . The isolated man is a mere rudiment of an individual. But he who has become citizen, neighbor, friend, brother, son, husband, father, fellow-member, in one is just so many times individualized.[34]

Lloyd's plea for a new individualism could also be read as an obituary for perfectionist romantic reform.

[34] Henry Demarest Lloyd, *Wealth Against Commonwealth* (Spectrum paperback ed.: Englewood Cliffs, N.J., 1963), pp. 174, 178.

Slave Songs and Slave Consciousness

An Exploration in Neglected Sources

Lawrence W. Levine

INTRODUCTION

Throughout American history, whites have viewed the Negro through the prism of their own expectations and desires; they have seen the Negro they wanted to see: the docile, infantile slave, the fawning, head-scratching, cackling "Uncle Tom," the disorganized, rhythmic, oversexed denizen of the Southern town and the urban ghetto. Whenever significant numbers of Negroes have visibly and unmistakably departed from these generalized behavior patterns, as in the years after both world wars, whites have exclaimed loudly and often fearfully about the rise of a "New Negro." Rarely, however, have they been motivated to reexamine the stereotype itself by looking more carefully and more sensitively at Negro life and culture.

During and after the period of slavery, black Americans built up an impressive body of folk materials—tales, sermons, jokes, religious and secular music—that constitutes an indispensable source of information for those interested in the history and psychology of Negroes in America. Scholars have thus far been remiss in using such materials. In the following article, Lawrence W. Levine examines the content and meaning of the slave spirituals and sees in them evidence of a viable cultural integrity that provided slaves with an outlet for many of their tensions and frustrations and allowed them to maintain important elements of their individual and communal dignity.

The questions Levine raises and the methods he utilizes are relevant not only for black history but for large areas of American history and culture in general. American historians have tended to ignore the history of those who were not represented by the abundant traditional sources—those who might most accurately be referred to as the "historically inarticulate," not because they were necessarily inarticulate in their own lifetimes but because they have been rendered so by the neglect of historians. To re-create their lives and their consciousness historians are going to have to learn to use materials they have thus far largely ignored and to deal with problems they have too easily abandoned to the folklorist, anthropologist, sociologist, psychologist, and demographer. The following article is a step in this direction.

Kenneth Stampp, *The Peculiar Institution** (1956), is the most comprehensive and perceptive history of slavery yet published. Recent attempts to deal with the cultural forms of slave resistance include: Bernard Wolfe, "Uncle Remus and the Malevolent Rabbit," *Commentary* (July 1949), 31–41; Vincent Harding, "Religion and Resistance Among Ante-Bellum Negroes, 1800–1860," in August Meier and Elliott Rudwick, eds., *The Making of Black America** (1969), Vol. 2, 179–97; George M. Frederickson and Christopher Lasch, "Resistance to Slavery," *Civil War History*, XIII (December 1967), 315–29; Eugene D. Genovese, "American Slaves and Their History," *New York Review of Books* (December 3, 1970), 34–43.

The earliest and still one of the most valuable collections of slave songs, William Francis Allen, Charles Pickard Ware, and Lucy McKim Garrison, *Slave Songs of the United States** (1867), has recently been made available in a paperback reprint. Two important collections of contemporary articles on the folklore and folk music of slaves and freedmen are Bruce Jackson, ed., *The Negro and His Folklore in Nineteenth-Century Periodicals* (1967), and Bernard Katz, ed., *The Social Implications of Early Negro Music in the United States** (1969). A useful introduction to the narratives written by ex-slaves in the nineteenth century is Charles Nichols, *Many Thousand Gone: The Ex-Slaves' Account of Their Bondage and Freedom** (1963). A number of these narratives have recently been reprinted in paperback editions. See, for instance, Gilbert Osofsky, ed., *Puttin' On Ole Massa** (1969); Arna Bontemps, ed., *Great Slave Narratives** (1969); and William Loren Katz, ed., *Five Slave Narratives** (1969). Also valuable are the narratives collected during the 1930's by the Federal Writers' Project in interviews with ex-slaves. Excerpts from these 2,000 narratives appear in B. A. Botkin, ed., *Lay My Burden Down: A Folk History of* Slavery* (1945), and Norman R. Yetman, ed., *Life Under the "Peculiar Institution"** (1970). Stanley Feldstein, *Once a Slave: The Slaves' View of Slavery* (1971), is based upon both kinds of narratives.

NEGROES in the United States, both during and after slavery, were anything but inarticulate. They sang songs, told stories, played verbal games, listened and responded to sermons, and expressed their aspirations, fears, and values through the same medium of an oral tradition that had characterized the West African cultures from which their ancestors had come. By largely ignoring this tradition, much of which has been preserved, historians have rendered an articulate people historically inarticulate, and have allowed the record of their consciousness to go unexplored.

Having worked my way carefully through thousands of Negro songs, folktales, jokes, and games, I am painfully aware of the problems inherent in the use of such materials. They are difficult, often impossible, to date with any precision. Their geographical distribution is usually unclear. They were collected belatedly, most frequently by men and women who had little understanding of the culture from which they sprang, and little scruple about altering or suppressing them. Such major collectors as John Lomax, Howard Odum, and Newman White all admitted openly that many of the songs they collected were "unprintable" by the moral standards which guided them and presumably their readers. But historians have overcome imperfect records before. They have learned how to deal with altered documents, with consciously or unconsciously biased firsthand accounts, with manuscript collections that were deposited in archives only after being filtered through the overprotective hands of fearful relatives, and with the comparative lack of contemporary sources and the need to use their materials retrospectively. The challenge presented by the materials of folk and popular culture is neither totally unique nor insurmountable.

In this essay I want to illustrate the possible use of materials of this kind by discussing the contribution that an understanding of Negro songs can make to the recent debate over slave personality. In the process I will discuss several aspects of the literature and problems related to the use of slave songs.

The subject of Negro music in slavery has produced a large and varied literature, little of which has been devoted to questions of meaning and function. The one major exception is Miles Mark Fisher's 1953 study, *Negro Slave Songs in the United States,* which attempts to get at the essence of slave life through an analysis of slave songs. Unfortunately, Fisher's rich insights are too often marred by his rather loose scholarly standards, and despite its continuing value his study is in many respects an example of how *not* to use Negro songs. Asserting, correctly, that the words of slave songs "show both accidental and intentional errors of transmission," Fisher changes the words almost at will to

FROM Lawrence W. Levine, "Slave Songs and Slave Consciousness," in Tamara K. Hareven, ed., *Anonymous Americans: Explorations in Nineteenth-Century Social History,* © 1971, 99–126. Reprinted by permission of Prentice-Hall, Inc., Englewood Cliffs, N.J. An earlier version of this essay was presented as a paper at the American Historical Association meetings on December 28, 1969. The author is indebted to the two commentators on that occasion, Professors J. Saunders Redding and Mike Thelwell, and to Nathan I. Huggins, Robert Middlekauff, and Kenneth M. Stampp for their penetrating criticisms and suggestions.

fit his own image of their pristine form. Arguing peruasively that "transplanted Negroes continued to promote their own culture by music," Fisher makes their songs part of an "African cult" which he simply wills into existence. Maintaining (again, I think, correctly), that "slave songs preserved in joyful strains, the adjustment which Negroes made to their living conditions within the United States," Fisher traces the major patterns of that adjustment by arbitrarily dating these songs, apparently unperturbed by the almost total lack of evidence pertaining to the origin and introduction of individual slave songs.[1]

Fisher aside, most other major studies of slave music have focused almost entirely upon musical structure and origin. This latter question especially has given rise to a long and heated debate.[2] The earliest collectors and students of slave music were impressed by how different that music was from anything familiar to them. Following a visit to the Sea Islands in 1862, Lucy McKim despaired of being able

> to express the entire character of these negro ballads by mere musical notes and signs. The odd turns made in the throat; and that curious rhythmic effect produced by single voices chiming in at different irregular intervals, seem almost as impossible to place on score, as the singing of birds, or the tones of an Aeolian Harp.[3]

Although some of these early collectors maintained, as did W. F. Allen in 1865, that much of the slave's music "might no doubt be traced to tunes which they have heard from the whites, and transformed to their own use, . . . their music . . . is rather European than African in its character,"[4] they more often stressed the distinctiveness of the Negro's music and attributed it to racial characteristics, African origins, and indigenous developments resulting from the slave's unique experience in the New World.

This tradition, which has had many influential twentieth-century adherents,[5] was increasingly challenged in the early decades of this century. Such scholars as Newman White, Guy Johnson, and George Pullen Jackson argued that the earlier school lacked a comparative grounding in Anglo-American folk song. Comparing Negro spirituals with Methodist and Baptist evangelical religious music of the late eighteenth and early nineteenth centuries, White, Johnson, and Jackson found similarities in words, subject matter, tunes, and musical structure.[6] Although they tended to exaggerate both qualitatively and quantitatively the degrees of similarity, their comparisons were often a persuasive and important corrective to the work of their predecessors. But their studies

---

[1] Miles Mark Fisher, *Negro Slave Songs in the United States* (New York, 1963, orig. pub. 1953), 14, 39, 132, and *passim*.

[2] The contours of this debate are judiciously outlined in D. K. Wilgus, *Anglo-American Folksong Scholarship Since 1898* (New Brunswick, 1959), App. One, "The Negro-White Spirituals."

[3] Lucy McKim, "Songs of the Port Royal Contrabands," *Dwight's Journal of Music*, XXII (November 8, 1862), 255.

[4] W. F. Allen, "The Negro Dialect," *The Nation*, I (December 14, 1865), 744–745.

[5] See, for instance, Henry Edward Krehbiel, *Afro-American Folksongs* (New York, 1963, orig. pub. 1914); James Wesley Work, *Folk Song of the American Negro* (Nashville, 1915); James Weldon Johnson, *The Book of American Negro Spirituals* (New York, 1925), and *The Second Book of Negro Spirituals* (New York, 1926); Lydia Parrish, *Slave Songs of the Georgia Sea Islands* (Hatboro, Penna., 1965, orig. pub. 1942); LeRoi Jones, *Blues People* (New York, 1963).

[6] Newman I. White, *American Negro Folk-Songs* (Hatboro, Penna., 1965, orig. pub. 1928); Guy B. Johnson, *Folk Culture on St. Helena Island, South Carolina* (Chapel Hill, 1930); George Pullen Jackson, *White and Negro Spirituals* (New York, 1943).

were inevitably weakened by their ethnocentric assumption that similarities alone settled the argument over origins. Never could they contemplate the possibility that the direction of cultural diffusion might have been from black to white as well as the other way. In fact, insofar as white evangelical music departed from traditional Protestant hymnology and embodied or approached the complex rhythmic structure, the percussive qualities, the polymeter, the syncopation, the emphasis on overlapping call and response patterns that characterized Negro music both in West Africa and the New World, the possibility that it was influenced by slaves who attended and joined in the singing at religious meetings is quite high.

These scholars tended to use the similarities between black and white religious music to deny the significance of slave songs in still another way. Newman White, for example, argued that since white evangelical hymns also used such expressions as "freedom," the "Promised Land," and the "Egyptian Bondage," "without thought of other than spiritual meaning," these images when they occurred in Negro spirituals could not have been symbolic "of the Negro's longing for physical freedom."[7] The familiar process by which different cultural groups can derive varied meanings from identical images is enough to cast doubt on the logic of White's argument.[8] In the case of white and black religious music, however, the problem may be much less complex, since it is quite possible that the similar images in the songs of both groups in fact served similar purposes. Many of those whites who flocked to the camp meetings of the Methodists and Baptists were themselves on the social and economic margins of their society, and had psychic and emotional needs which, qualitatively, may not have been vastly different from those of black slaves. Interestingly, George Pullen Jackson, in his attempt to prove the white origin of Negro spirituals, makes exactly this point:

> I may mention in closing the chief remaining argument of the die-hards for the Negro source of the Negro spirituals. . . . How could any, the argument runs, but a natively musical and sorely oppressed race create such beautiful things as "Swing Low," "Steal Away," and "Deep River"? . . . But were not the whites of the mountains and the hard-scrabble hill country also "musical and oppressed"? . . . Yes, these whites were musical, and oppressed too. If their condition was any more tolerable than that of the Negroes, one certainly does not get that impression from any of their songs of release and escape.[9]

If this is true, the presence of similar images in white music would merely heighten rather than detract from the significance of these images in Negro songs. Clearly, the function and meaning of white religious music during the late eighteenth and early nineteenth centuries demands far more attention than it has received. In the interim, we must be wary of allowing the mere fact of similarities to deter us from attempting to comprehend the cultural dynamics of slave music.

Contemporary scholars, tending to transcend the more simplistic lines of the

[7] White, *American Negro Folk-Songs*, 11–13.

[8] Professor John William Ward gives an excellent example of this process in his discussion of the different meanings which the newspapers of the United States, France, and India attributed to Charles Lindbergh's flight across the Atlantic in 1927. See "Lindbergh, Dos Passos, and History," in Ward, *Red, White, and Blue* (New York, 1969), 55.

[9] George Pullen Jackson, "The Genesis of the Negro Spiritual," *The American Mercury*, XXVI (June 1932), 248.

old debate, have focused upon the process of syncretism to explain the development of Negro music in the United States. The rich West African musical tradition common to almost all of the specific cultures from which Negro slaves came, the comparative cultural isolation in which large numbers of slaves lived, the tolerance and even encouragement which their white masters accorded to their musical activities, and the fact that, for all its differences, nothing in the European musical tradition with which they came into contact in America was totally alien to their own traditions—all these were conducive to a situation which allowed the slaves to retain a good deal of the integrity of their own musical heritage while fusing to it compatible elements of Anglo-American music. Slaves often took over entire white hymns and folk songs, as White and Jackson maintained, but altered them significantly in terms of words, musical structure, and especially performance before making them their own. The result was a hybrid with a strong African base.[10]

One of the more interesting aspects of this debate over origins is that no one engaged in it, not even advocates of the white derivation theory, denied that the slaves possesed their own distinctive music. Newman White took particular pains to point out again and again that the notion that Negro song is purely an imitation of the white man's music "is fully as unjust and inaccurate, in the final analysis, as the Negro's assumption that his folk-song is entirely original." He observed that in the slaves' separate religious meetings they were free to do as they would with the music they first learned from the whites, with the result that their spirituals became "the greatest single outlet for the expression of the Negro folk-mind."[11] Similarly, George Pullen Jackson, after admitting that he could find no white parallels for over two-thirds of the existing Negro spirituals, reasoned that these were produced by Negro singers in true folk fashion "by endless singing of heard tunes and by endless, inevitable and concomitant singing differentiation." Going even further, Jackson asserted that the lack of deep roots in Anglo-American culture left the black man "even freer than the white man to make songs over unconsciously as he sang . . . the free play has resulted in the very large number of songs which, though formed primarily in the white man's moulds, have lost all recognizable relationship to known individual white-sung melodic entities."[12] This debate over origins indicates clearly that a belief in the direct continuity of African musical traditions or in the process of syncretism is not a necessary prerequisite to the conclusion that the Negro slaves' music was their own, regardless of where they received the components out of which it was fashioned—a conclusion which is crucial to any attempt to utilize these songs as an aid in reconstructing the slaves' consciousness.

Equally important is the process by which slave songs were created and transmitted. When James McKim asked a freedman on the Sea Islands during the Civil War where the slaves got their songs, the answer was eloquently

---

[10] Richard Alan Waterman, "African Influence on the Music of the Americas," in Sol Tax (ed.), *Acculturation in the Americas: Proceedings and Selected Papers of the XXIXth International Congress of Americanists* (Chicago, 1952), 207–218; Wilgus, *Anglo-American Folksong Scholarship Since 1898*, 363–364; Melville H. Herskovits, "Patterns of Negro Music" (pamphlet, no publisher, no date); Gilbert Chase, *America's Music* (New York, 1966), Chap. 12; Alan P. Merriam, "African Music," in William R. Bascom and Melville J. Herskovits (eds.), *Continuity and Change in African Cultures* (Chicago, 1959), 76–80.

[11] "White, *American Negro Folk-Songs,* 29, 55.

[12] Jackson, *White and Negro Spirituals,* 266–267.

simple: "Dey make em, sah."[13] Precisely *how* they made them worried and fascinated Thomas Wentworth Higginson, who became familiar with slave music through the singing of the black Union soldiers in his Civil War regiment. Were their songs, he wondered, a "conscious and definite" product of "some leading mind," or did they grow "by gradual accretion, in an almost unconscious way"? A freedman rowing Higginson and some of his troops between the Sea Islands helped to resolve the problem when he described a spiritual which he had a hand in creating:

> Once we boys went for some rice and de nigger-driver he keep a-callin' on us; and I say, "O de ole nigger-driver!" Den anudder said, "Fust ting my mammy tole me was, notin' so bad as nigger-driver." Den I made a sing, just puttin' a word, and den anudder word.

He then began to sing his song:

> *O, de ole nigger-driver!*
> *O, gwine away!*
> *Fust ting my mammy tell me,*
> *O, gwine away!*
>
> *Tell me 'bout de nigger-driver,*
> *O, gwine away!*
> *Nigger-driver second devil,*
> *O, gwine away!*

Higginson's black soldiers, after a moment's hesitation, joined in the singing of a song they had never heard before as if they had long been familiar with it. "I saw," Higginson concluded, "how easily a new 'sing' took root among them."[14]

This spontaneity, this sense of almost instantaneous community which so impressed Higginson, constitutes a central element in every account of slave singing. The English musician Henry Russell, who lived in the United States in the 1830's, was forcibly struck by the ease with which a slave congregation in Vicksburg, Mississippi, took a "fine old psalm tune" and, by suddenly and spontaneously accelerating the tempo, transformed it "into a kind of negro melody."[15] "Us old heads," an ex-slave told Jeanette Robinson Murphy, "use ter make 'em up on de spurn of de moment. Notes is good enough for you people, but us likes a mixtery." Her account of the creation of a spiritual is typical and important:

> We'd all be at the "prayer house" de Lord's day, and de white preacher he'd splain de word and read whar Esekial done say—
>
> *Dry bones gwine ter lib ergin.*
>
> And, honey, de Lord would come a-shinin' thoo dem pages and revive dis ole nigger's heart, and I'd jump up dar and den and holler and shout and sing

[13] James Miller McKim, "Negro Songs," *Dwight's Journal of Music*, XXI (August 9, 1862), 149.
[14] Thomas Wentworth Higginson, *Army Life in a Black Regiment* (Beacon Press edition, Boston, 1962, orig. pub. 1869), 218–219.
[15] Henry Russell, *Cheer! Boys, Cheer!*, 84–85, quoted in Chase, *America's Music*, 235–236.

and pat, and dey would all cotch de words and I'd sing it to some ole shout song I'd heard 'em sing from Africa, and dey'd all take it up and keep at it, and keep a-addin' to it, and den it would be a spiritual.[16]

This "internal" account has been verified again and again by the descriptions of observers, many of whom were witnessing not slave services but religious meetings of rural southern Negroes long after emancipation. The essential continuity of the Negro folk process in the more isolated sections of the rural South through the early decades of the twentieth century makes these accounts relevant for the slave period as well. Natalie Curtis Burlin, whose collection of spirituals is musically the most accurate one we have, and who had a long and close acquaintance with Negro music, never lost her sense of awe at the process by which these songs were molded. On a hot July Sunday in rural Virginia, she sat in a Negro meeting house listening to the preacher deliver his prayer, interrupted now and then by an "O Lord!" or "Amen, Amen" from the congregation.

> Minutes passed, long minutes of strange intensity. The mutterings, the ejaculations, grew louder, more dramatic, till suddenly I felt the creative thrill dart through the people like an electric vibration, that same half-audible hum arose, —emotion was gathering atmospherically as clouds gather—and then, up from the depths of some "sinner's" remorse and imploring came a pitiful little plea, a real "moan," sobbed in musical cadence. From somewhere in that bowed gathering another voice improvised a response: the plea sounded again, louder this time and more impassioned; then other voices joined in the answer, shaping it into a musical phrase; and so, before our ears, as one might say, from this molten metal of music a new song was smithied out, composed then and there by no one in particular and by everyone in general.[17]

Clifton Furness has given us an even more graphic description. During a visit to an isolated South Carolina plantation in 1926, he attended a prayer meeting held in the old slave cabins. The preacher began his reading of the Scriptures slowly, then increased his tempo and emotional fervor, assuring his flock that "Gawd's lightnin' gwine strike! Gawd's thunder swaller de ert!"

> Gradually moaning became audible in the shadowy corners where the women sat. Some patted their bundled babies in time to the flow of the words, and began swaying backward and forward. Several men moved their feet alternately, in strange syncopation. A rhythm was born, almost without reference to the words that were being spoken by the preacher. It seemed to take shape almost visibly, and grow. I was gripped with the feeling of a mass-intelligence, a self-conscious entity, gradually informing the crowd and taking possession of every mind there, including my own.

In the midst of this increasing intensity, a black man sitting directly in front of Furness, his head bowed, his body swaying, his feet patting up and down,

[16] Jeanette Robinson Murphy, "The Survival of African Music in America," *Popular Science Monthly*, 55 (1899), 660–672, reprinted in Bruce Jackson (ed.), *The Negro and His Folklore in Nineteenth-Century Periodicals* (Austin, 1967), 328.
[17] Natalie Curtis Burlin, "Negro Music at Birth," *Musical Quarterly*, V (January 1919), 88. For Mrs. Burlin's excellent reproductions of Negro folk songs and spirituals, see her *Negro Folk-Songs* (New York, 1918–1919), Vol. I–IV.

suddenly cried out: "Git right—sodger! Git right—sodger! Git right—wit Gawd!"

> Instantly the crowd took it up, moulding a melody out of half-formed familiar phrases based upon a spiritual tune, hummed here and there among the crowd. A distinct melodic outline became more and more prominent, shaping itself around the central theme of the words, "Git right, sodger!"
>
> Scraps of other words and tunes were flung into the medley of sound by individual singers from time to time, but the general trend was carried on by a deep undercurrent, which appeared to be stronger than the mind of any individual present, for it bore the mass of improvised harmony and rhythms into the most effective climax of incremental repetition that I have ever heard. I felt as if some conscious plan or purpose were carrying us along, call it mob-mind, communal composition, or what you will.[18]

Shortly after the Civil War, Elizabeth Kilham witnessed a similar scene among the freedmen, and described it in terms almost identical to those used by observers many years later. "A fog seemed to fill the church," she wrote, ". . . an invisible power seemed to hold us in its iron grasp; . . . A few moments more, and I think we should have shrieked in unison with the crowd."[19]

These accounts and others like them make it clear that spirituals both during and after slavery were the product of an improvisational communal consciousness. They were not, as some observers thought, totally new creations, but were forged out of many preexisting bits of old songs mixed together with snatches of new tunes and lyrics and fit into a fairly traditional but never wholly static metrical pattern. They were, to answer Higginson's question, *simultaneously* the result of individual and mass creativity. They were products of that folk process which has been called "communal re-creation," through which older songs are constantly recreated into essentially new entities.[20] Anyone who has read through large numbers of Negro songs is familiar with this process. Identical or slightly varied stanzas appear in song after song; identical tunes are made to accommodate completely different sets of lyrics; the same song appears in different collections in widely varied forms. In 1845 a traveler observed that the only permanent elements in Negro song were the music and the chorus. "The blacks themselves leave out old stanzas, and introduce new ones at pleasure. Travelling through the South, you may, in passing from Virginia to Louisiana, hear the same tune a hundred times, but seldom the same words accompanying it."[21] Another observer noted in 1870 that during a single religious meeting the freedmen would often sing the words of one spiritual to several different tunes, and then take a tune that particularly pleased them and fit the words of several different songs to it.[22] Slave songs, then, were

[18] Clifton Joseph Furness, "Communal Music Among Arabians and Negroes," *Musical Quarterly*, XVI (January 1930), 49–51.

[19] Elizabeth Kilham, "Sketches in Color: IV," *Putnam's Monthly*, XV (March 1870), 304–311, reprinted in Jackson, *The Negro and His Folklore in Nineteenth-Century Periodicals*, 127–128.

[20] Bruno Nettl, *Folk and Traditional Music of the Western Continents* (Englewood Cliffs, 1965), 4–5; Chase, *America's Music*, 241–243.

[21] J. K., Jr., "Who Are Our National Poets?," *Knickerbocker Magazine*, 26 (October 1845), 336, quoted in Dena J. Epstein, "Slave Music in the United States Before 1860: A Survey of Sources (Part I)," *Music Library Association Notes*, XX (Spring 1963), 208.

[22] Elizabeth Kilham, "Sketches in Color: IV," *Putnam's Monthly*, XV (March 1870), 304–311, reprinted in Jackson, *The Negro and His Folklore in Nineteenth-Century Periodicals*, 129.

never static; at no time did Negroes create a "final" version of any spiritual. Always the community felt free to alter and recreate them.

The two facts that I have attempted to establish thus far—that slave music, regardless of its origins, was a distinctive cultural form, and that it was created or constantly recreated through a communal process—are essential if one is to justify the use of these songs as keys to slave consciousness. But these facts in themselves say a good deal about the nature and quality of slave life and personality. That black slaves could create and continually recreate songs marked by the poetic beauty, the emotional intensity, the rich imagery which characterized the spirituals—songs which even one of the most devout proponents of the white man's origins school admits are "the most impressive religious folk songs in our language"[23]—should be enough to make us seriously question recent theories which conceive of slavery as a closed system which destroyed the vitality of the Negro and left him a dependent child. For all of its horrors, slavery was never so complete a system of psychic assault that it prevented the slaves from carving out independent cultural forms. It never pervaded all of the interstices of their minds and their culture, and in those gaps they were able to create an independent art form and a distinctive voice. If North American slavery eroded the African's linguistic and institutional life, if it prevented him from preserving and developing his rich heritage of graphic and plastic art, it nevertheless allowed him to continue and to develop the patterns of verbal art which were so central to his past culture. Historians have not yet come to terms with what the continuance of the oral tradition meant to blacks in slavery.

In Africa, songs, tales, proverbs, and verbal games served the dual function of not only preserving communal values and solidarity, but also of providing occasions for the individual to transcend, at least symbolically, the inevitable restrictions of his environment and his society by permitting him to express deeply held feelings which he ordinarily was not allowed to verbalize. Among the Ashanti and the Dahomeans, for example, periods were set aside when the inhabitants were encouraged to gather together and, through the medium of song, dance, and tales, to openly express their feelings about each other. The psychological release this afforded seems to have been well understood. "You know that everyone has a *sunsum* (soul) that may get hurt or knocked about or become sick, and so make the body ill," an Ashanti high priest explained to the English anthropologist R. S. Rattray:

> Very often . . . ill health is caused by the evil and the hate that another has in his head against you. Again, you too may have hatred in your head against another, because of something that person has done to you, and that, too, causes your *sunsum* to fret and become sick. Our forebears knew this to be the case, and so they ordained a time, once every year, when every man and woman, free man and slave, should have freedom to speak out just what was in their head, to tell their neighbors just what they thought of them, and of their actions, and not only their neighbours, but also the king or chief. When a man has spoken freely thus, he will feel his *sunsum* cool and quieted, and the *sunsum* of the other person against whom he has now openly spoken will be quieted also.

[23] White, *American Negro Folk-Songs,* 57.

Utilization of verbal art for this purpose was widespread throughout Africa, and was not confined to those ceremonial occasions when one could directly state one's feelings. Through innuendo, metaphor, and circumlocution, Africans could utilize their songs as outlets for individual release without disturbing communal solidarity.[24]

There is abundant internal evidence that the verbal art of the slaves in the United States served many of these traditional functions. Just as the process by which the spirituals were created allowed for simultaneous individual and communal creativity, so their very structure provided simultaneous outlets for individual and communal expression. The overriding antiphonal structure of the spirituals—the call and response pattern which Negroes brought with them from Africa and which was reinforced by the relatively similar white practice of "lining out" hymns—placed the individual in continual dialogue with his community, allowing him at one and the same time to preserve his voice as a distinct entity and to blend it with those of his fellows. Here again slave music confronts us with evidence which indicates that however seriously the slave system may have diminished the strong sense of community that had bound Africans together, it never totally destroyed it or left the individual atomized and emotionally and psychically defenseless before his white masters. In fact, the form and structure of slave music presented the slave with a potential outlet for his individual feelings even while it continually drew him back into the communal presence and permitted him the comfort of basking in the warmth of the shared assumptions of those around him.

Those "shared assumptions" can be further examined by an analysis of the content of slave songs. Our preoccupation in recent years with the degree to which the slaves actually resembled the "Sambo" image held by their white masters has obscured the fact that the slaves developed images of their own which must be consulted and studied before any discussion of slave personality can be meaningful. The image of the trickster, who through cunning and unscrupulousness prevails over his more powerful antagonists, pervades slave tales. The trickster figure is rarely encountered in the slave's religious songs, though its presence is sometimes felt in the slave's many allusions to his narrow escapes from the Devil.

> *The Devil's mad and I'm glad,*
> *He lost the soul he thought he had.*[25]
>
> *Ole Satan toss a ball at me.*
> *O me no weary yet . . .*
>
> *Him tink de ball would hit my soul.*
> *O me no weary yet . . .*

[24] Alan P. Merriam, "Music and the Dance," in Robert Lystad (ed.), *The African World: A Survey of Social Research* (New York, 1965), 452–468; William Bascom, "Folklore and Literature," in *Ibid.*, 469–488; R. S. Rattray, *Ashanti* (Oxford, 1923), Chap. XV; Melville Herskovits, "Freudian Mechanisms in Primitive Negro Psychology," in E. E. Evans-Pritchard *et al.* (eds.), *Essays Presented to C. G. Seligman* (London, 1934), 75–84; Alan P. Merriam, "African Music," in Bascom and Herskovits, *Continuity and Change in African Cultures*, 49–86.

[25] William Francis Allen, Charles Pickard Ware, and Lucy McKim Garrison, compilers, *Slave Songs of the United States* (New York, 1867, Oak Publications ed., 1965), 164–165.

De ball for hell and I for heaven.
O me no weary yet . . .[26]

Ole Satan thought he had a mighty aim;
He missed my soul and caught my sins.
Cry Amen, cry Amen, cry Amen to God!

He took my sins upon his back;
Went muttering and grumbling down to hell.
Cry Amen, cry Amen, cry Amen to God![27]

The single most persistent image the slave songs contain, however, is that of
the chosen people. The vast majority of the spirituals identify the singers as
"de people dat is born of God," "We are the people of God," "we are de
people of de Lord," "I really do believe I'm a child of God," "I'm a child ob
God, wid my soul sot free," "I'm born of God, I know I am." Nor is there
ever any doubt that "To the promised land I'm bound to go," "I walk de
heavenly road," "Heav'n shall-a be my home," "I gwine to meet my Saviour,"
"I seek my Lord and I find Him," "I'll hear the trumpet sound/In that morning."[28]

The force of this image cannot be diminished by the observation that similar
images were present in the religious singing of white evangelical churches during the first half of the nineteenth century. White Americans could be expected to sing of triumph and salvation, given their long-standing heritage of
the idea of a chosen people which was reinforced in this era by the belief in
inevitable progress and manifest destiny, the spread-eagle oratory, the bom-
bastic folklore, and, paradoxically, the deep insecurities concomitant with the
tasks of taming a continent and developing an identity. But for this same
message to be expressed by Negro slaves who were told endlessly that they
were members of the lowliest of races *is* significant. It offers an insight into
the kinds of barriers the slaves had available to them against the internaliza-
tion of the stereotyped images their masters held and attempted consciously
and unconsciously to foist upon them.

The question of the chosen people image leads directly into the larger problem of what role religion played in the songs of the slave. Writing in 1862,
James McKim noted that the songs of the Sea Island freedmen "are all religious, barcaroles and all. I speak without exception. So far as I heard or was
told of their singing, it was all religious." Others who worked with recently
emancipated slaves recorded the same experience, and Colonel Higginson reported that he rarely heard his troops sing a profane or vulgar song. With a
few exceptions, "all had a religious motive."[29] In spite of this testimony, there
can be little doubt that the slaves sang nonreligious songs. In 1774, an English
visitor to the United States, after his first encounter with slave music, wrote in

[26] *Ibid.,* 43.
[27] Harriet Jacobs, *Incidents in the Life of a Slave Girl* (Boston, 1861), 109.
[28] Lines like these could be quoted endlessly. For the specific ones cited, see the songs in the
following collections: Higginson, *Army Life in a Black Regiment,* 206, 216–217; Allen *et al.,*
Slave Songs of the United States, 33–34, 44, 106–108, 131, 160–161; Thomas P. Fenner, compiler, *Religious Folk Songs of the Negro as Sung on the Plantations* (Hampton, Virginia, 1909,
orig. pub. 1874), 10–11, 48; J. B. T. Marsh, *The Story of the Jubilee Singers; With Their Songs*
(Boston, 1880), 136, 167, 178.
[29] McKim, "Negro Songs," 148; H. G. Spaulding, "Under the Palmetto." *Continental Monthly,*
IV (1863), 188–203, reprinted in Jackson, *The Negro and His Folklore in Nineteenth-Century
Periodicals,* 72; Allen, "The Negro Dialect," 744–745; Higginson, *Army Life in a Black Regiment,* 220–221.

his journal: "In their songs they generally relate the usage they have received from their Masters or Mistresses in a very satirical stile and manner."[30] Songs fitting this description can be found in the nineteenth-century narratives of fugitive slaves. Harriet Jacobs recorded that during the Christmas season the slaves would ridicule stingy whites by singing:

> *Poor Massa, so dey say;*
> *Down in de heel, so dey say;*
> *Got no money, so dey say;*
> *God A'mighty bress you, so dey say.*[31]

"Once in a while among a mass of nonsense and wild frolic," Frederick Douglass noted, "a sharp hit was given to the meanness of slaveholders."

> *We raise de wheat,*
> *Dey gib us de corn;*
> *We bake de bread,*
> *Dey gib us de crust;*
> *We sif de meal,*
> *Dey gib us de huss;*
> *We peal de meat,*
> *Dey gib us de skin;*
> *And dat's de way*
> *Dey take us in;*
> *We skim de pot,*
> *Dey gib us de liquor,*
> *And say dat's good enough for nigger.*[32]

Both of these songs are in the African tradition of utilizing song to bypass both internal and external censors and give vent to feelings which could be expressed in no other form. Nonreligious songs were not limited to the slave's relations with his masters, however, as these rowing songs, collected by contemporary white observers, indicate:

> *We are going down to Georgia, boys,*
>   *Aye, aye.*
> *To see the pretty girls, boys,*
>   *Yoe, yoe.*
> *We'll give 'em a pint of brandy, boys,*
>   *Aye, aye.*
> *And a hearty kiss, besides, boys,*
>   *Yoe, yoe.*[33]
>
> *Jenny shake her toe at me,*
> *Jenny gone away;*

[30] *Journal of Nicholas Cresswell, 1774–1777* (New York, 1934), 17–19, quoted in Epstein, *Music Library Association Notes*, XX (Spring 1963), 201.
[31] Jacobs, *Incidents in the Life of a Slave Girl*, 180.
[32] *Life and Times of Frederick Douglass* (rev. ed., 1892, Collier Books edition, 1962), 146–147.
[33] John Lambert, *Travels Through Canada and the United States of North America in the Years, 1806–1807 and 1808* (London, 1814), II, 253–254, quoted in Dena J. Epstein, "Slave Music in the United States Before 1860: A Survey of Sources (Part 2)," *Music Library Association Notes,* XX (Summer 1963), 377.

Jenny shake her toe at me,
Jenny gone away.
Hurrah! Miss Susy, oh!
Jenny gone away;
Hurrah! Miss Susy, oh!
Jenny gone away.[34]

The variety of nonreligious songs in the slave's repertory was wide. There were songs of in-group and out-group satire, songs of nostalgia, nonsense songs, songs of play and work and love. Nevertheless, our total stock of these songs is very small. It is possible to add to these by incorporating such post-bellum secular songs which have an authentic slavery ring to them as "De Blue-Tail Fly," with its ill-concealed satisfaction at the death of a master, or the ubiquitous

My ole Mistiss promise me,
W'en she died, she'd set me free,
She lived so long dat 'er head got bal',
An' she give out'n de notion a dyin' at all.[35]

The number can be further expanded by following Constance Rourke's suggestion that we attempt to disentangle elements of Negro origin from those of white creation in the "Ethiopian melodies" of the white minstrel shows, many of which were similar to the songs I have just quoted.[36] Either of these possibilities, however, forces the historian to work with sources far more potentially spurious than those with which he normally is comfortable.

Spirituals, on the other hand, for all the problems associated with their being filtered through white hands before they were published, and despite the many errors in transcription that inevitably occurred, constitute a much more satisfactory source. They were collected by the hundreds directly from slaves and freedmen during the Civil War and the decades immediately following, and although they came from widely different geographical areas they share a common structure and content, which seems to have been characteristic of Negro music wherever slavery existed in the United States. It is possible that we have a greater number of religious than nonreligious songs because slaves were more willing to sing these ostensibly innocent songs to white collectors

[34] Frances Anne Kemble, *Journal of a Residence on a Georgian Plantation in 1838–1839* (New York, 1863), 128.

[35] For versions of these songs, see Dorothy Scarborough, *On the Trail of Negro Folk-Songs* (Cambridge, 1925), 194, 201–203, 223–225, and Thomas W. Talley, *Negro Folk Rhymes* (New York 1922), 25–26. Talley claims that the majority of the songs in his large and valuable collection "were sung by Negro fathers and mothers in the dark days of American slavery to their children who listened with eyes as large as saucers and drank them down with mouths wide open," but offers no clue as to why he feels that songs collected for the most part in the twentieth century were slave songs.

[36] Constance Rourke, *The Roots of American Culture and Other Essays* (New York, 1942), 262–274. Newman White, on the contrary, has argued that although the earliest minstrel songs were Negro derived, they soon went their own way and that less than ten per cent of them were genuinely Negro. Nevertheless, these white songs "got back to the plantation, largely spurious as they were and were undoubtedly among those which the plantation-owners encouraged the Negroes to sing. They persist to-day in isolated stanzas and lines, among the songs handed down by plantation Negroes . . ." White, *American Negro Folk-Songs*, 7–10 and Appendix IV. There are probably valid elements in both theses. A similarly complex relationship between genuine Negro folk creations and their more commercialized, partly white-influenced imitations was to take place in the blues of the twentieth century.

who in turn were more anxious to record them, since they fit easily with their positive and negative images of the Negro. But I would argue that the vast preponderance of spirituals over any other sort of slave music, rather than being merely the result of accident or error, is instead an accurate reflection of slave culture during the ante-bellum period. Whatever songs the slaves may have sung before their wholesale conversion to Christianity in the late eighteenth and early nineteenth centuries, by the latter century spirituals were quantitatively and qualitatively their most significant musical creation. In this form of expression slaves found a medium which resembled in many important ways the world view they had brought with them from Africa, and afforded them the possibility of both adapting to and transcending their situation.

It is significant that the most common form of slave music we know of is sacred song. I use the term "sacred" not in its present usage as something antithetical to the secular world; neither the slaves nor their African forebears ever drew modernity's clear line between the sacred and the secular. The uses to which spirituals were put are an unmistakable indication of this. They were not sung solely or even primarily in churches or praise houses, but were used as rowing songs, field songs, work songs, and social songs. On the Sea Islands during the Civil War, Lucy McKim heard the spiritual "Poor Rosy" sung in a wide variety of contexts and tempos.

> On the water, the oars dip "Poor Rosy" to an even andante; a stout boy and girl at the hominy-mill will make the same "Poor Rosy" fly, to keep up with the whirling stone; and in the evening, after the day's work is done, "Heab'n shall-a be my home" [the final line of each stanza] peals up slowly and mournfully from the distant quarters.[37]

For the slaves, then, songs of God and the mythic heroes of their religion were not confined to any specific time or place, but were appropriate to almost every situation. It is in this sense that I use the concept sacred—not to signify a rejection of the present world but to describe the process of incorporating within this world all the elements of the divine. The religious historian Mircea Eliade, whose definition of sacred has shaped my own, has maintained that for men in traditional societies religion is a means of extending the world spatially upward so that communication with the other world becomes ritually possible, and extending it temporally backward so that the paradigmatic acts of the gods and mythical ancestors can be continually reenacted and indefinitely recoverable. By creating sacred time and space, man can perpetually live in the presence of his gods, can hold on to the certainty that within one's own lifetime "rebirth" is continually possible, and can impose order on the chaos of the universe. "Life," as Eliade puts it, "is lived on a twofold plane; it takes its course as human existence and, at the same time, shares in a trans-human life, that of the cosmos or the gods."[38]

This notion of sacredness gets at the essence of the spirituals, and through them at the essence of the slave's world view. Denied the possibility of achiev-

---

[37] McKim, "Songs of the Port Royal Contrabands," 255.

[38] Mircea Eliade, *The Sacred and the Profane* (New York, 1961), Chaps. 2, 4, and *passim*. For the similarity of Eliade's concept to the world view of West Africa, see W. E. Abraham, *The Mind of Africa* (London, 1962), Chap. 2, and R. S. Rattray, *Religion and Art in Ashanti* (Oxford, 1927).

ing an adjustment to the external world of the ante-bellum South which involved meaningful forms of personal integration, attainment of status, and feelings of individual worth that all human beings crave and need, the slaves created a new world by transcending the narrow confines of the one in which they were forced to live. They extended the boundaries of their restrictive universe backward until it fused with the world of the Old Testament, and upward until it became one with the world beyond. The spirituals are the record of a people who found the status, the harmony, the values, the order they needed to survive by internally creating an expanded universe, by literally willing themselves reborn. In this respect I agree with the anthropologist Paul Radin that

> The ante-bellum Negro was not converted to God. He converted God to himself. In the Christian God he found a fixed point and he needed a fixed point, for both within and outside of himself, he could see only vacillation and endless shifting. . . . There was no other safety for people faced on all sides by doubt and the threat of personal disintegration, by the thwarting of instincts and the annihilation of values.[39]

The confinement of much of the slave's new world to dreams and fantasies does not free us from the historical obligation of examining its contours, weighing its implications for the development of the slave's psychic and emotional structure, and eschewing the kind of facile reasoning that leads Professor Elkins to imply that, since the slaves had no alternatives open to them, their fantasy life was "limited to catfish and watermelons."[40] Their spirituals indicate clearly that there *were* alternatives open to them—alternatives which they themselves fashioned out of the fusion of their African heritage and their new religion—and that their fantasy life was so rich and so important to them that it demands understanding if we are even to begin to comprehend their inner world.

The God the slaves sang of was neither remote nor abstract, but as intimate, personal, and immediate as the gods of Africa had been. "O when I talk I talk wid God," "Mass Jesus is my bosom friend," "I'm goin' to walk with [talk with, live with, see] King Jesus by myself, by myself," were refrains that echoed through the spirituals.[41]

> *In de mornin' when I rise,*
> *Tell my Jesus huddy [howdy] oh,*
> *I wash my hands in de mornin' glory,*
> *Tell my Jesus huddy oh.*[42]

> *Gwine to argue wid de Father and chatter wid de son,*
> *The last trumpet shall sound, I'll be there.*

[39] Paul Radin, "Status, Phantasy, and the Christian Dogma," in Social Science Institute, Fisk University, *God Struck Me Dead: Religious Conversion Experiences and Autobiographies of Negro Ex-Slaves* (Nashville, 1945, unpublished typescript).
[40] Stanley M. Elkins, *Slavery* (Chicago, 1959), 136.
[41] Allen *et al.*, *Slave Songs of the United States*, 33–34, 105; William E. Barton, *Old Plantation Hymns: A Collection of Hitherto Unpublished Melodies of the Slave and the Freedmen* (Boston, 1899), 30.
[42] Allen *et al.*, *Slave Songs of the United States*, 47.

> *Gwine talk 'bout de bright world dey des' come from.*
> *The last trumpet shall sound, I'll be there.*[43]
>
> *Gwine to write to Massa Jesus,*
> *To send some Valiant soldier*
> *To turn back Pharaoh's army, Hallelu!*[44]

The heroes of the Scriptures—"Sister Mary," "Brudder Jonah," "Brudder Moses," "Brudder Daniel"—were greeted with similar intimacy and immediacy. In the world of the spirituals, it was not the masters and mistresses but God and Jesus and the entire pantheon of Old Testament figures who set the standards, established the precedents, and defined the values; who, in short, constituted the "significant others." The world described by the slave songs was a black world in which no reference was ever made to any white contemporaries. The slave's positive reference group was composed entirely of his own peers: his mother, father, sister, brother, uncles, aunts, preacher, fellow "sinners" and "mourners" of whom he sang endlessly, to whom he sent messages via the dying, and with whom he was reunited joyfully in the next world.

The same sense of sacred time and space which shaped the slave's portraits of his gods and heroes also made his visions of the past and future immediate and compelling. Descriptions of the Crucifixion communicate a sense of the actual presence of the singers: "Dey pierced Him in the side . . . Dey nail Him to de cross . . . Dey rivet His feet . . . Dey hanged him high . . . Dey stretch Him wide. . . ."

> *Oh sometimes it causes me to tremble,—tremble,—tremble,*
> *Were you there when they crucified my Lord?*[45]

The Slave's "shout"—that counterclockwise, shuffling dance which frequently occurred after the religious service and lasted long into the night—often became a medium through which the ecstatic dancers were transformed into actual participants in historic actions: Joshua's army marching around the walls of Jericho, the children of Israel following Moses out of Egypt.[46]

The thin line between time dimensions is nowhere better illustrated than in the slave's visions of the future, which were, of course, a direct negation of his present. Among the most striking spirituals are those which pile detail upon detail in describing the Day of Judgment: "You'll see de world on fire . . . see de element a meltin', . . . see the stars a fallin' . . . see the moon a bleedin' . . . see the forked lightning, . . . Hear the rumblin' thunder . . . see the righteous marching, . . . see my Jesus coming . . . ," and the world to come where "Dere's no sun to burn you . . . no hard trials . . . no whips a crackin' . . . no stormy weather . . . no tribulation . . . no evil-doers . . . All is glad-

---

[43] Barton, *Old Plantation Hymns*, 19.

[44] Marsh, *The Story of the Jubilee Singers*, 132.

[45] Fenner, *Religious Folk Songs of the Negro*, 162; E. A. McIlhenny, *Befo' De War Spirituals: Words and Melodies* (Boston, 1933), 39.

[46] Barton, *Old Plantation Hymns*, 15; Howard W. Odum and Guy B. Johnson, *The Negro and His Songs* (Hatboro, Penn., 1964, orig. pub. 1925), 33–34; for a vivid description of the "shout" see *The Nation*, May 30, 1867, 432–433; see also Parrish, *Slave Songs of the Georgia Sea Islands*, Chap. III.

ness in de Kingdom."[47] This vividness was matched by the slave's certainty that he would partake of the triumph of judgment and the joys of the new world:

> *Dere's room enough, room enough, room enough in de heaven, my Lord*
> *Room enough, room enough, I can't stay behind.*[48]

Continually, the slaves sang of reaching out beyond the world that confined them, of seeing Jesus "in de wilderness," of praying "in de lonesome valley," of breathing in the freedom of the mountain peaks:

> *Did yo' ever*
> *Stan' on mountun,*
> *Wash yo' han's*
> *In a cloud?*[49]

Continually, they held out the possibility of imminent rebirth; "I look at de worl' an de worl' look new, . . . I look at my hands an' they look so too . . . I looked at my feet, my feet was too."[50]

These possibilities, these certainties were not surprising. The religious revivals which swept large numbers of slaves into the Christian fold in the late eighteenth and early nineteenth centuries were based upon a *practical* (not necessarily theological) Armianism: God would save all who believed in Him; Salvation was there for all to take hold of if they would. The effects of this message upon the slaves who were exposed to and converted by it have been passed over too easily by historians. Those effects are illustrated graphically in the spirituals which were the products of these revivals and which continued to spread the evangelical word long after the revivals had passed into history.

The religious music of the slaves is almost devoid of feelings of depravity or unworthiness, but is rather, as I have tried to show, pervaded by a sense of change, transcendence, ultimate justice, and personal worth. The spirituals have been referred to as "sorrow songs," and in some respects they were. The slaves sang of "rollin' thro' an unfriendly world," of being "a-trouble in de mind," of living in a world which was a "howling wilderness," "a hell to me," of feeling like a "motherless child," "a po' little orphan chile in de worl'," a "home-e-less child," of fearing that "Trouble will bury me down."[51]

But these feelings were rarely pervasive or permanent; almost always they were overshadowed by a triumphant note of affirmation. Even so despairing a wail as "Nobody Knows the Trouble I've Had" could suddenly have its mood transformed by lines like: "One morning I was a-walking down, . . .

---

[47] For examples of songs of this nature, see Fenner, *Religious Folk Songs of the Negro*, 8, 63–65; Marsh, *The Story of the Jubilee Singers*, 240–241; Higginson, *Army Life in a Black Regiment*, 205; Allen *et al., Slave Songs of the United States*, 91, 100; Burlin, *Negro Folk-Songs*, I, 37–42.

[48] Allen *et al., Slave Songs of the United States*, 32–33.

[49] *Ibid.*, 30–31; Burlin, *Negro Folk-Songs*, II, 8–9; Fenner, *Religious Folk Songs of the Negro*, 12.

[50] Allen *et al., Slave Songs of the United States*, 128–129; Fenner, *Religious Folk Songs of the Negro*, 127; Barton, *Old Plantation Hymns*, 26.

[51] Allen *et al., Slave Songs of the United States*, 70, 102–103, 147; Barton, *Old Plantation Hymns*, 9, 17–18, 24; Marsh, *The Story of the Jubilee Singers*, 133, 167; Odum and Johnson, *The Negro and His Songs*, 35.

Saw some berries a-hanging down, . . . I pick de berry and I suck de juice, . . . Just as sweet as de honey in de comb."[52] Similarly, amid the deep sorrow of "Sometimes I feel like a Motherless chile," sudden release could come with the lines: "Sometimes I feel like/ A eagle in de air. . . . Spread my wings an'/ Fly, fly, fly."[53] Slaves spent little time singing of the horrors of hell or damnation. Their songs of the Devil, quoted earlier, pictured a harsh but almost semicomic figure (often, one suspects, a surrogate for the white man), over whom they triumphed with reassuring regularity. For all their inevitable sadness, slave songs were characterized more by a feeling of confidence than of despair. There was confidence that contemporary power relationships were not immutable: "Did not old Pharaoh get lost, get lost, get lost, . . . get lost in the Red Sea?"; confidence in the possibilities of instantaneous change: "Jesus make de dumb to speak. . . . Jesus make de cripple walk. . . . Jesus give de blind his sight. . . . Jesus do most anything"; confidence in the rewards of persistence: "Keep a' inching along like a poor inch-worm,/ Jesus will come by'nd bye"; confidence that nothing could stand in the way of the justice they would receive: "You kin hender me here, but you can't do it dah," "O no man, no man, no man can hinder me"; confidence in the prospects of the future: "We'll walk de golden streets/ Of de New Jerusalem." Religion, the slaves sang, "is good for anything, . . . Religion make you happy, . . . Religion gib me patience . . . O member, get Religion . . . Religion is so sweet."[54]

The slaves often pursued the "sweetness" of their religion in the face of many obstacles. Becky Ilsey, who was 16 when she was emancipated, recalled many years later:

> 'Fo' de war when we'd have a meetin' at night, wuz mos' always 'way in de woods or de bushes some whar so de white folks couldn't hear, an' when dey'd sing a spiritual an' de spirit 'gin to shout some de elders would go 'mongst de folks an' put dey han' over dey mouf an' some times put a clof in dey mouf an' say: "Spirit don talk so loud or de patterol break us up." You know dey had white patterols what went 'roun' at night to see de niggers didn't cut up no devilment, an' den de meetin' would break up an' some would go to one house an' some to er nudder an' dey would groan er w'ile, den go home.[55]

Elizabeth Ross Hite testified that although she and her fellow slaves on a Louisiana plantation were Catholics, "lots didn't like that 'ligion."

> We used to hide behind some bricks and hold church ourselves. You see, the Catholic preachers from France wouldn't let us shout, and the Lawd done said you gotta shout if you want to be saved. That's in the Bible.
> Sometimes we held church all night long, 'til way in the mornin'. We burned some grease in a can for the preacher to see the Bible by. . . .
> See, our master didn't like us to have much 'ligion, said it made us lag in our work. He jest wanted us to be Catholicses on Sundays and go to mass and not study 'bout nothin' like that on week days. He didn't want us shoutin' and

---

[52] Allen *et al., Slave Songs of the United States,* 102–103.
[53] Mary Allen Grissom, compiler, *The Negro Sings a New Heaven* (Chapel Hill, 1930), 73.
[54] Marsh, *The Story of the Jubilee Singers,* 179, 186; Allen *et al., Slave Songs of the United States,* 40–41, 44, 146; Barton, *Old Plantation Hymns,* 30.
[55] McIlhenny, *Befo' De War Spirituals,* 31.

moanin' all day'-long, but you gotta shout and you gotta moan if you wants to be saved.[56]

The slaves clearly craved the affirmation and promise of their religion. It would be a mistake, however, to see this urge as exclusively otherworldly. When Thomas Wentworth Higginson observed that the spirituals exhibited "nothing but patience for this life,—nothing but triumph in the next," he, and later observers who elaborated upon this judgment, were indulging in hyperbole. Although Jesus was ubiquitous in the spirituals, it was not invariably the Jesus of the New Testament of whom the slaves sang, but frequently a Jesus transformed into an Old Testament warrior: "Mass' Jesus" who engaged in personal combat with the Devil; "King Jesus" seated on a milk-white horse with sword and shield in hand. "Ride on, King Jesus," "Ride on, conquering King," "The God I serve is a man of war," the slaves sang.[57] This transformation of Jesus is symptomatic of the slaves' selectivity in choosing those parts of the Bible which were to serve as the basis of their religious consciousness. Howard Thurman, a Negro minister who as a boy had the duty of reading the Bible to his grandmother, was perplexed by her refusal to allow him to read from the Epistles of Paul.

> When at length I asked the reason, she told me that during the days of slavery, the minister (white) on the plantation was always preaching from the Pauline letters—"Slaves, be obedient to your masters," etc. "I vowed to myself," she said, "that if freedom ever came and I learned to read, I would never read that part of the Bible!"[58]

Nor, apparently, did this part of the Scriptures ever constitute a vital element in slave songs or sermons. The emphasis of the spirituals, as Higginson himself noted, was upon the Old Testament and the exploits of the Hebrew children.[59] It is important that Daniel and David and Joshua and Jonah and Moses and Noah, all of whom fill the lines of the spirituals, were delivered in *this* world and delivered in ways which struck the imagination of the slaves. Over and over their songs dwelt upon the spectacle of the Red Sea opening to allow the Hebrew slaves past before inundating the mighty armies of the Pharaoh. They lingered delightedly upon the image of little David humbling the great Goliath with a stone—a pretechnological victory which post-bellum Negroes were to expand upon in their songs of John Henry. They retold in endless variation the stories of the blind and humbled Samson bringing down

[56] *Gumbo Ya-Ya: A Collection of Louisiana Folk Tales,* compiled by Lyle Saxon, Edward Dreyer, and Robert Tallant from materials gathered by workers of the WPA, Louisiana Writer's Project (Boston, 1945), 242.

[57] For examples, see Allen *et al., Slave Songs of the United States,* 40–41, 82, 97, 106–108; Marsh, *The Story of the Jubilee Singers,* 168, 203; Burlin, *Negro Folk-Songs,* II, 8–9; Howard Thurman, *Deep River* (New York, 1945), 19–21.

[58] Thurman, *Deep River,* 16–17.

[59] Higginson, *Army Life in a Black Regiment,* 202–205. Many of those northerners who came to the South to "uplift" the freedmen were deeply disturbed at the Old Testament emphasis of their religion. H. G. Spaulding complained that the ex-slaves needed to be introduced to "the light and warmth of the Gospel," and reported that a Union army officer told him: "Those people had enough of the Old Testament thrown at their heads under slavery. Now give them the glorious utterances and practical teachings of the Great Master." Spaulding, "Under the Palmetto," reprinted in Jackson, *The Negro and His Folklore in Nineteenth-Century Periodicals,* 66.

the mansions of his conquerors; of the ridiculed Noah patiently building the ark which would deliver him from the doom of a mocking world; of the timid Jonah attaining freedom from his confinement through faith. The similarity of these tales to the situation of the slave was too clear for him not to see it; too clear for us to believe that the songs had no worldly content for the black man in bondage. "O my Lord delivered Daniel," the slaves observed, and responded logically: "O why not deliver me, too?"

> He delivered Daniel from de lion's den,
> Jonah from de belly ob de whale,
> And de Hebrew children from de fiery furnace,
> And why not every man?[60]

These lines state as clearly as anything can the manner in which the sacred world of the slaves was able to fuse the precedents of the past, the conditions of the present, and the promise of the future into one connected reality. In this respect there was always a latent and symbolic element of protest in the slave's religious songs which frequently became overt and explicit. Frederick Douglass asserted that for him and many of his fellow slaves the song, "O Canaan, sweet Canaan,/I am bound for the land of Canaan," symbolized "something more than a hope of reaching heaven. We meant to reach the *North,* and the North was our Canaan," and he wrote that the lines of another spiritual, "Run to Jesus, shun the danger,/I don't expect to stay much longer here," had a double meaning which first suggested to him the thought of escaping from slavery.[61] Similarly, when the black troops in Higginson's regiment sang:

> We'll soon be free, [three times]
> When de Lord will call us home.

a young drummer boy explained to him, "Dey think *de Lord* mean for say *de Yankees.*"[62] Nor is there any reason to doubt that slaves could have used their songs as a means of secret communication. An ex-slave told Lydia Parrish that when he and his fellow slaves "suspicioned" that one of their number was telling tales to the driver, they would sing lines like the following while working in the field:

> O Judyas he wuz a 'ceitful man
> He went an' betray a mos' innocen' man.
> Fo' thirty pieces a silver dal it wuz done
> He went in de woods an' e' self he hung.[63]

And it is possible, as many writers have argued, that such spirituals as the commonly heard "Steal away, steal away, steal away to Jesus!" were used as explicit calls to secret meetings.

[60] Allen *et al., Slave Songs of the United States,* 148; Fenner, *Religious Folk Songs of the Negro,* 21; Marsh, *The Story of the Jubilee Singers,* 134–135; McIlhenny, *Befo' De War Spirituals,* 248–249.
[61] *Life and Times of Frederick Douglass,* 159–160; Marsh, *The Story of the Jubilee Singers,* 188.
[62] Higginson, *Army Life in a Black Regiment,* 217.
[63] Parrish, *Slave Songs of the Georgia Sea Islands,* 247.

But it is not necessary to invest the spirituals with a secular function only at the price of divesting them of their religious content, as Miles Mark Fisher has done.[64] While we may make such clear-cut distinctions, I have tried to show that the slaves did not. For them religion never constituted a simple escape from this world, because their conception of the world was more expansive than modern man's. Nowhere is this better illustrated than during the Civil War itself. While the war gave rise to such new spirituals as "Before I'd be a slave/I'd be buried in my grave,/And go home to my Lord and be saved!" or the popular "Many thousand Go," with its jubilant rejection of all the facets of slave life—"No more peck o' corn for me, . . . No more driver's lash for me, . . . No more pint o' salt for me, . . . No more hundred lash for me, . . . No more mistress' call for me"[65]—the important thing was not that large numbers of slaves now could create new songs which openly expressed their views of slavery; that was to be expected. More significant was the ease with which their old songs fit their new situation. With so much of their inspiration drawn from the events of the Old Testament and the Book of Revelation, the slaves had long sung of wars, of battles, of the Army of the Lord, of Soldiers of the Cross, of trumpets summoning the faithful, of vanquishing the hosts of evil. These songs especially were, as Higginson put it, "available for camp purposes with very little strain upon their symbolism." "We'll cross de mighty river," his troops sang while marching or rowing,

> We'll cross de danger water, . . .
> O Pharaoh's army drowned!
> My army cross over.

"O blow your trumpet, Gabriel," they sang,

> Blow your trumpet louder;
> And I want dat trumpet to blow me home
> To my new Jerusalem.

But they also found their less overtly militant songs quite as appropriate to warfare. Their most popular and effective marching song was:

> Jesus call you, Go in de wilderness,
> Go in de wilderness, go in de wilderness,
> Jesus call you. Go in de wilderness
> To wait upon de Lord.[66]

Black Union soldiers found it no more incongruous to accompany their fight for freedom with the sacred songs of their bondage than they had found it inappropriate as slaves to sing their spirituals while picking cotton or shucking corn. Their religious songs, like their religion itself, was of this world as well as the next.

Slave songs by themselves, of course, do not present us with a definitive key to the life and mind of the slave. They have to be seen within the context of

---

[64] "Actually, not one spiritual in its primary form reflected interest in anything other than a full life here and now." Fisher, *Negro Slave Songs in the United States*, 137.

[65] Barton, *Old Plantation Hymns*, 25; Allen *et al.*, *Slave Songs of the United States*, 94; McKim, "Negro Songs," 149.

[66] Higginson, *Army Life in a Black Regiment*, 201–202, 211–12.

the slave's situation and examined alongside such other cultural materials as folk tales. But slave songs do indicate the need to rethink a number of assumptions that have shaped recent interpretations of slavery, such as the assumption that because slavery eroded the linguistic and institutional side of African life it wiped out almost all the more fundamental aspects of African culture. Culture, certainly, is more than merely the sum total of institutions and language. It is also expressed by something less tangible, which the anthropologist Robert Redfield has called "style of life." Peoples as different as the Lapp and the Bedouin, Redfield has argued, with diverse languages, religions, customs and institutions, may still share an emphasis on certain virtues and ideals, certain manners of independence and hospitality, general ways of looking upon the world, which give them a similar life style.[67] This argument applies to the West African cultures from which the slaves came. Though they varied widely in language, institutions, gods, and familial patterns, they shared a fundamental outlook toward the past, present, and future and common means of cultural expression which could well have constituted the basis of a sense of community and identity capable of surviving the impact of slavery.

Slave songs present us with abundant evidence that in the structure of their music and dance, in the uses to which music was put, in the survival of the oral tradition, in the retention of such practices as spirit possession which often accompanied the creation of spirituals, and in the ways in which the slaves expressed their new religion, important elements of their shared African heritage remained alive not just as quaint cultural vestiges but as vitally creative elements of slave culture. This could never have happened if slavery was, as Professor Elkins maintains, a system which so completely closed in around the slave, so totally penetrated his personality structure as to infantalize him and reduce him to a kind of *tabula rasa* upon which the white man could write what he chose.[68]

Slave songs provide us with the beginnings of a very different kind of hypothesis: that the preliterate, premodern Africans, with their sacred world view, were so imperfectly acculturated into the secular American society into which they were thrust, were so completely denied access to the ideology and dreams which formed the core of the consciousness of other Americans, that they were forced to fall back upon the only cultural frames of reference that made any sense to them and gave them any feeling of security. I use the word "forced" advisedly. Even if the slaves had had the opportunity to enter fully into the life of the larger society, they might still have chosen to retain and perpetuate certain elements of their African heritage. But the point is that they really had no choice. True acculturation was denied to most slaves. The alternatives were either to remain in a state of cultural limbo, divested of the old cultural patterns but not allowed to adopt those of their new homeland—which in the long run is no alternative at all—or to cling to as many as possible of the old ways of thinking and acting. The slaves' oral tradition, their music, and their religious outlook served this latter function and constituted a cultural refuge at least potentially capable of protecting their personalities from some of the worst ravages of the slave system.

The argument of Professors Tannenbaum and Elkins that the Protestant churches in the United States did not act as a buffer between the slave and his

[67] Robert Redfield, *The Primitive World and Its Transformations* (Ithaca, 1953), 51–53.
[68] Elkins, *Slavery,* Chap. III.

master is persuasive enough, but it betrays a modern preoccupation with purely institutional arrangements.[69] Religion is more than an institution, and because Protestant churches failed to protect the slave's inner being from the incursions of the slave system, it does not follow that the spiritual message of Protestantism failed as well. Slave songs are a testament to the ways in which Christianity provided slaves with the precedents, heroes, and future promise that allowed them to transcend the purely temporal bonds of the Peculiar Institution.

Historians have frequently failed to perceive the full importance of this because they have not taken the slave's religiosity seriously enough. A people cannot create a music as forceful and striking as slave music out of a mere uninternalized anodyne. Those who have argued that Negroes did not oppose slavery in any meaningful way are writing from a modern, political context. What they really mean is that the slaves found no *political* means to oppose slavery. But slaves, to borrow Professor Hobsbawm's term, were prepolitical beings in a prepolitical situation.[70] Within their frame of reference there were other—and from the point of view of personality development, not necessarily less effective—means of escape and opposition. If mid-twentieth-century historians have difficulty perceiving the sacred universe created by slaves as a serious alternative to the societal system created by southern slaveholders, the problem may be the historians' and not the slaves'.

Above all, the study of slave songs forces the historian to move out of his own culture, in which music plays a peripheral role, and offers him the opportunity to understand the ways in which black slaves were able to perpetuate much of the centrality and functional importance that music had for their African ancestors. In the concluding lines of his perceptive study of primitive song, C. M. Bowra has written:

> Primitive song is indispensable to those who practice it. . . . they cannot do without song, which both formulates and answers their nagging questions, enables them to pursue action with zest and confidence, brings them into touch with gods and spirits, and makes them feel less strange in the natural world. . . . it gives to them a solid centre in what otherwise would be almost chaos, and a continuity in their being, which would too easily dissolve before the calls of the implacable present . . . through its words men, who might otherwise give in to the malice of circumstances, find their old powers revived or new powers stirring in them, and through these life itself is sustained and renewed and fulfilled.[71]

This, I think, sums up concisely the function of song for the slave. Without a general understanding of that function, without a specific understanding of the content and meaning of slave song, there can be no full comprehension of the effects of slavery upon the slave or the meaning of the society from which slaves emerged at emancipation.

[69] *Ibid.*, Chap. II; Frank Tannenbaum, *Slave and Citizen* (New York, 1946).
[70] E. J. Hobsbawm, *Primitive Rebels* (New York, 1959), Chap. I.
[71] C. M. Bowra, *Primitive Song* (London, 1962), 285–286.

The Southern Road to Appomattox

Kenneth M. Stampp

INTRODUCTION

In 1960, a collection of essays appeared which summed up almost one hundred years of controversy over the defeat of the Southern Confederacy. That collection, *Why the North Won the Civil War,* edited by David Donald, rehearsed explanations long since familiar that concentrate upon Southern economic weakness and Northern strength, especially in manpower and industry, and upon Southern political failure and Northern political aptitude. Historians emphasizing political failure have pointed to inept and uninspired leadership of the Confederacy, a people so devoted to democratic rights as to be paralyzed by the need for wartime discipline and further crippled by the doctrine of state rights. Kenneth M. Stampp dismisses none of these possible explanations, but rather argues that they all gain coherence when they are placed in the proper psychological context. Physical and industrial weakness along with problems of leadership and state and individual rights might all have been overcome, he suggests, had not "many seemingly loyal Confederates lacked a deep commitment to the southern cause" and had not others "unconsciously even desired to lose the war." How Stampp works out this intriguing argument is a fascinating exercise involving both intuition and evidence. The reader of this essay should also think about its suggestive comments about the character of ante-bellum Southern society.

The Donald collection cited above provides an excellent discussion of several of the problems Stampp takes up. In addition, see Clement Eaton, *A History of the Southern Confederacy** (1954); C. P. Roland, *The Confederacy** (1960); R. W. Patrick, *Jefferson Davis and His Cabinet* (1944); F. L. Owsley, *King Cotton Diplomacy** (1931). There are many military histories; among the best are D. S. Freeman's great *R. E. Lee, A Biography* (4 vols., 1934–35); and a series of books by Bruce Catton, *Mr. Lincoln's Army** (1951), *Glory Road** (1952), and *A Stillness at Appomattox** (1954).

Nοτ long ago one of America's best political commentators made an observation about the problem of causation in history that every responsible historian would surely endorse:

> I hold a kind of Tolstoyan view of history and believe that it is hardly ever possible to determine the real truth about how we got from here to there. Since I find it extremely difficult to uncover my own motives, I hesitate to deal with those of other people, and I positively despair at the thought of ever being really sure about what has moved whole nations and whole generations of mankind. No explanation of the causes and origins of any war—of any large happening in history—can ever be for me much more than a plausible one, a reasonable hypothesis.[1]

This is a position to which I fully subscribe, and I believe that it is as valid for explanations of why a war was won or lost as for explanations of why a war began.

With this cautionary statement in mind, I am going to suggest one of the conditions, among several, that may help to explain why the South lost the Civil War. I think there is reason to believe that many Southerners—how many I cannot say, but enough to affect the outcome of the war—who outwardly appeared to support the Confederate cause had inward doubts about its validity, and that, in all probability, some unconsciously even hoped for its defeat. Like all historical explanations, my hypothesis is not subject to definitive proof; but I think it can be established as circumstantially plausible, because it is a reasonable explanation for a certain amount of empirical evidence.

All interpretations of the defeat of the Confederacy fall into two broad categories: those that stress the South's physical handicaps, and those that stress human failings. Explanations in the first category emphasize the overwhelming preponderance of northern manpower and economic resources. To some historians it is enough to note that the North had four times as many men of military age as the South, ten times as productive an industrial plant, three times as many miles of railroads in operation, and far greater supplies of raw materials. Moreover, the North had a large merchant marine and sufficient naval power to establish an effective blockade of southern ports, whereas the South had virtually no merchant marine and no navy at all. "The prime cause [of Confederate defeat] must have been economic," argues Richard N. Current. "Given the vast superiority of the North in men and materials, in instruments of production, in communication facilities, in business organization and skill—and assuming for the sake of the argument no more than rough equality in statecraft and generaliship—the final outcome seems all but inevitable."[2]

And yet, as Professor Current observes, "the victory is not always to the

FROM Kenneth M. Stampp, "The Southern Road to Appomattox," *Cotton Memorial Papers*, No. 4 (February 1969), 3–22. © 1969 by Texas Western Press. Reprinted by permission.

[1] Richard H. Rovere in *The New Yorker*, October 28, 1967, p. 87.
[2] David Donald, ed., *Why the North Won the Civil War* (Baton Rouge, 1960), p. 19.

rich," for history provides some striking examples of wealthy nations losing to economically poorer adversaries. "In terms of economic logic," David M. Potter writes, "it can perhaps be demonstrated that the Confederacy, hopelessly overmatched by almost every measure of strength, was doomed to defeat. But history not only shows that in war the lighter antagonist sometimes defeats the heavier, it also shows that what seems logically certain often fails to happen." Professor Potter believes that for at least the first two years of the war the outcome was in doubt; therefore the analysis of Confederate defeat must "go beyond the *a priori* arguments of economic determinism," for "other countervailing factors" might possibly have offset northern economic superiority.[3] He thus introduces the second category of explanations for Confederate defeat: those that compare and evaluate the behavior of Northerners and Southerners under the stresses of war.[4]

The behavioral factor that Potter has in mind is political leadership. He suggests that superior Confederate leadership might have counterbalanced the North's economic power, but he finds instead another area of decisive Confederate weakness. Potter emphasizes Abraham Lincoln's brilliant record as a war leader and compares it to the dismal record of Jefferson Davis—a discrepancy "as real and as significant as the inequality in mileage between Union and Confederate railroad systems." Indeed, Potter believes that Lincoln contributed so much to the ultimate Union victory that "if the Union and the Confederacy had exchanged presidents with one another, the Confederacy might have won its independence." Moreover, because the South failed to develop a two-party system, no constructive leadership emerged from the opposition to Davis in Congress or in the state governments. Instead, the "petulant, short-sighted, narrow-gauge, negativistic, vindictive quality of the criticism of Davis made him seem, with all his shortcomings, a better man than most of those who assailed him."[5]

Professor Potter argues the political failure of the Confederacy so convincingly that, for the purposes of my own argument, I need make only one additional point: It is odd that the South, with its long tradition of leadership in political affairs, should have thus given the appearance of political bankruptcy during the four years of the Civil War. Among the politicians who created the Confederate States of America were men of superior talent, and many of them had considerable legislative and administrative experience. One wonders what happened to them. A study of the political history of the Confederacy leaves one with the impression that the South was afflicted with what Roy F. Nichols has described as "an undefined and stultifying force of some sort which inhibited effective statesmanship."[6] Political failure does help to

---

[3] Donald, ed., *Why the North Won the Civil War*, pp. 19–20, 92–93.

[4] Physical factors, such as manpower, railroads, and resources, can be argued more easily with empirical evidence than behavioral factors; but it does not follow that the former are therefore more readily proved as historical causes than the latter. In neither case does the evidence establish a cause-effect relationship outside the historian's mind, in both cases it is easy for the historian to fall into the logical fallacy of *post hoc, ergo propter hoc. Both* physical and behavioral explanations can only be reasonable hypotheses, and it is as valid to explore one as the other.

[5] Donald, ed., *Why the North Won the Civil War*, pp. 91–114. Eric McKitrick has developed more fully Potter's thesis that the Confederacy suffered from the lack of a two-party system. William N. Chambers and Walter D. Burnham, eds., *The American Party Systems: Stages of Political Development* (New York, 1967), pp. 117–51.

[6] Roy F. Nichols, unpublished paper delivered at the annual meeting of the American Historical Association, December, 1960.

explain Confederate defeat, but it also raises some questions that need to be answered.

The theme of political failure has several variations. According to one of them, the widespread assertion of the constitutional doctrine of state rights during the war crisis made southern defeat certain. Frank L. Owsley maintains that "if the political system of the South had not broken down under the weight of an impracticable doctrine put into practice in the midst of a revolution, the South might have established its independence." He suggests that on the gravestone of the Confederacy should be carved these words: "Died of State Rights." Owsley provides ample illustrations of the extremes to which some Confederate politicians went in defense of the sovereignty of the states.[7]

Unquestionably the state-rights doctrinaires helped to paralyze the hands of the Confederate government and thus grievously injured their own cause. But this explanation of Confederate defeat also raises questions, because before the war most southern politicians had not been consistent state-rights doctrinaires. Instead, like Northerners, they had shown a good deal of flexibility in their constitutional theories, and they had been willing to tolerate a relatively vigorous federal government as long as it heeded southern needs. They had not objected to a federally subsidized transcontinental railroad—along a southern route; they had not objected to federal appropriations for internal improvements—if the appropriations were for the improvement of transportation along southern rivers; and they showed no fear of creeping federal tyranny when they demanded effective federal action to recover fugitive slaves or to protect slavery in the territories. Indeed, some southern politicians seemed to show less constitutional flexibility in dealing with a government of their own creation than they had in dealing with the federal government before 1861.

David Donald offers another variation on the theme of Confederate political failure. He argues that the basic weakness of the Confederacy was that "the Southern people insisted upon retaining their democratic liberties in wartime. If they were fighting for freedom, they asked, why should they start abridging it? As soldiers, as critics of the government, and as voters they stuck to their democratic, individualistic rights." In the North civil rights were more severely compromised, the soldier was better disciplined, and regimentation was more readily accepted. Therefore, Professor Donald concludes, "we should write on the tombstone of the Confederacy: 'Died of Democracy.'"[8]

Before the Civil War, needless to say, the South had not been notably more democratic than the North; and at some points Donald seems to equate democracy with poor organization, political ineptitude, and chaos. But there is truth in his generalization, which raises still another question: Why was it that Northerners, who were every bit as democratic and almost as individualistic as Southerners, by and large were willing to tolerate more regimentation for the sake of their cause than Southerners appeared ready to tolerate for the sake of theirs? The question, of course, is one of degree, for many Northerners also resisted war measures such as conscription and encroachments on civil liberties.

Bell I. Wiley adds a final touch to the behavioral approach to Confederate defeat. "Perhaps the most costly of the Confederacy's shortcomings," he suggests,

[7] Frank L. Owsley, *State Rights in the Confederacy* (Chicago, 1925).
[8] Donald, ed., *Why the North Won the Civil War*, pp. 77–90.

was the disharmony among its people. A cursory glance at the Confederacy reveals numerous instances of bitter strife. . . . Behind the battle of bullets waged with the invaders was an enormous war of words and emotions among Confederates themselves which began before secession and which eventually became so intense that it sapped the South's vitality and hastened Northern victory.

In a recent study of Confederate politics, Eric L. McKitrick was also struck by the bickering "that seeped in from everywhere to soften the very will of the Confederacy."[9]

Collectively, all these behavioral problems—the failure of political leadership, the absurd lengths to which state rights was carried, the reluctance of Southerners to accept the discipline that war demanded, and the internal conflicts among the southern people—point to a Confederate weakness that matched in importance its physical handicaps. This was a weakness of morale. Assuming rough equality in military training and similar military traditions, a country with inferior resources and manpower can hope to defeat a more powerful adversary only if it enjoys decidedly superior morale in its civilian population. High morale is the product of passionate dedication to a cause, which creates a willingness to subordinate personal interests to its success. This is what has sometimes enabled small states to resist successfully the aggression of stronger neighbors, and nationalist movements to succeed against colonial powers. In such cases the fires of patriotism, fed by a genuine national identity, burned fiercely, and the longing for political freedom produced a spirit of self-sacrifice. When the partisans of a cause have no doubts about its validity, when they view the consequences of defeat as unbearable, morale is likely to be extremely high.

Such was not the case in the Confederacy, as numerous historians have observed. "The collapse of the Confederacy," Charles H. Wesley concludes, "was due in part to a lack of resources, but more directly to the absence of a wholehearted and sustained resistance, . . . without which no revolution has been successful."[10] E. Merton Coulter, though admitting physical handicaps, insists that "the Confederacy never fully utilized the human and material resources it had," because it "never succeeded in developing an *esprit de corps,* either in its civil or military organization." The reason for this, according to Coulter, was that the Confederacy "was not blessed with a 'one for all and all for one' patriotism with which future generations of sentimental romancers were to endow it." Coulter concludes succinctly: "The forces leading to defeat were many but they may be summed up in this one fact: The people did not will hard enough and long enough to win."[11]

The problem of morale to which I am referring here should not be confused with another persistent but separate Confederate problem: that of disloyalty among southern Unionists. Nor should it be confused with the defeatism and demoralization that grew out of military reverses, shortages of civilian supplies, and financial collapse during the closing stages of the war. In the Confederacy weak morale was not simply the ultimate consequence of war

[9] Bell I. Wiley, *The Road to Appomattox* (Memphis, 1956), p. 78; Chambers and Burnham, eds., *The American Party Systems,* p. 142.

[10] Charles H. Wesley, *The Collapse of the Confederacy* (Washington, D.C., 1937).

[11] E. Merton Coulter, *The Confederate States of America, 1861–1865* (Baton Rouge, 1950), pp. 374, 566.

weariness, for the problem was there at its birth. It was the product of uncertainty about the South's identity, of the peculiar circumstances that led to secession and the attempt at independence, and of widespread doubts and apprehensions about the validity of the Confederate cause. The problem was obscured for a time by the semi-hysteria that swept the Deep South in the months after Lincoln's election, and to some extent by early military successes. But it was always there and soon began to make itself felt, for the South was ill-equipped for a long war not only physically but spiritually and ideologically as well.

That southern morale was not high enough and dedication to the cause fierce enough to offset the Confederacy's physical handicaps has sometimes been attributed to the failure of its leaders to perform their duties as propagandists and morale builders. Charles W. Ramsdell holds the politicians responsible for failing to build an efficient propaganda organization or to portray some compelling issue for which the southern people would have made great sacrifices.[12] Similarly, Bell I. Wiley blames both Jefferson Davis and the Confederate Congress for not realizing "the necessity of winning the hearts and minds of the people."[13] To David M. Potter the prime responsibility for the failure to dramatize the southern cause belonged to President Davis. One of his major shortcomings was his inability to "communicate with the people of the Confederacy. He seemed to think in abstractions and to speak in platitudes."[14]

If Davis had a penchant for abstract and platitudinous discourse, most other Confederate politicians and publicists, when upholding the Confederate cause, seemed to suffer from the same defect. Yet the South had more than its share of able speakers and editors, who exploited as best they could the available issues: the menace of a ruthless northern invader, the need to defend the constitutional principles of the Founding Fathers, and the threat to southern civilization posed by northern abolitionists and their doctrine of racial equality. Significantly, however, only occasionally did they identify the Confederacy with slavery. "Our new Government," Vice President Alexander H. Stephens once boldly proclaimed,

> is founded upon . . . the great truth that the negro is not equal to the white man; that slavery, subordination to the superior race, is his natural and moral condition. This, our new Government, is the first, in the history of the world, based upon this great physical, philosophical and moral truth.

In his message to Congress, April 29, 1861, President Davis declared that "the labor of African slaves was and is indispensable" to the South's economic development. "With interests of such overwhelming magnitude imperiled, the people of the Southern States were driven by the conduct of the North to the adoption of some course of action to avert the danger with which they were openly menaced." This rhetoric was hardly inspiring, but, more important, neither was the cause it supported. Confederate propagandists apparently found

[12] See J. Cutler Andrew, "The Confederate Press and Public Morale," *Journal of Southern History*, XXXII (1966), pp. 445–46, for a summary of Ramsdell's unpublished paper read before the annual meeting of the American Historical Association, December, 1924. See also James W. Silver, "Propaganda in the Confederacy," *ibid.*, XI (1945), pp. 487–503.

[13] Wiley, *The Road to Appomattox*, p. 106.

[14] Donald, ed., *Why the North Won the Civil War*, p. 104.

the defense of slavery a poor tool with which to build southern morale, and they usually laid stress on other issues.

This reluctance of southern propagandists candidly to identify the Confederacy with slavery helps to explain their sterile rhetoric and their dismal failure; for, in my opinion, slavery was the key factor that gave the ante-bellum South its distinct identity, and the supposed northern threat to slavery was the basic cause of secession. To understand why southern propagandists failed, one must, in addition to evaluating their skill and techniques, compare the issues at their disposal with those at the disposal of their antagonists. Northern propagandists exploited all the historic traditions associated with the federal Union; reaffirmed America's mission and manifest destiny; proclaimed that democracy and self-government were on trial; above all, identified their cause with the principles of the Declaration of Independence. These were the themes that Lincoln developed in the letters, speeches, and state papers which we remember a century later. It is of the utmost significance that no southern leader, even if he had had Lincoln's skill with words, could have claimed for the Confederacy a set of war aims that fired the nineteenth-century imagination as did those described in the Gettysburg Address. One wonders what Lincoln could have done with the issues available to him in the South, what even Jefferson Davis might have done with those that every northern politician had available to him.

When southern propagandists found it expedient, for reasons of domestic policy as well as foreign, to soft-pedal the very *cause* of the war, the Confederacy was at a considerable disadvantage as far as its moral position was concerned. This may help to explain why the Confederate Congress contained no group as fiercely dedicated to the southern cause as the Radical Republicans were to the northern cause. It illuminates Roy F. Nichols' impression that southern leaders were "beset by psychological handicaps."[15] In short, it locates one of the fundamental reasons for the weakness of southern morale. It was due not only to the failure of those who tried to uphold the cause, important as that may have been; but, viewed as an appeal to the minds and emotions of nineteenth-century Americans, it was also due to the inherent frailty of the cause itself.

At this point, keeping the southern morale problem in mind, I would like to introduce my hypothesis that many seemingly loyal Confederates lacked a deep commitment to the southern cause and that some unconsciously even desired to lose the war. In the study of human behavior we frequently encounter cases of persons involved in conflicts which outwardly they seem to be striving to win, when, for reasons of which they are hardly conscious, they are in fact inviting defeat. I believe that there is considerable circumstantial evidence indicating that an indeterminate but significant number of Southerners were behaving in this manner, and I would like to suggest two reasons why unconsciously they might have welcomed defeat, or at least declined to give that "last full measure" which might have avoided it.

The first reason is related to the circumstances of southern secession. Fundamentally this movement was not the product of genuine southern nationalism; indeed, except for the institution of slavery, the South had little to give it a clear national identity. It had no natural frontiers; its white population came

---

[15] Nichols, unpublished paper.

from the same stocks as the northern population; its political traditions and religious beliefs were not significantly different from those of the North; and the notion of a distinct southern culture was largely a figment of the imaginations of proslavery propagandists. Few of the conditions that underlay nineteenth- and twentieth-century nationalist movements in other parts of the world were present in the ante-bellum South. As Charles G. Sellers, Jr., has observed: "No picture of the Old South as a section confident and united in its dedication to a neo-feudal social order, and no explanation of the Civil War as a conflict between 'two civilizations' can encompass the complexity and pathos of the ante-bellum reality." Southerners, notwithstanding the paradox of slavery, shared the ideals of other Americans. From the Revolution on, for Northerners and Southerners alike,

> liberty was the end for which the Union existed, while the Union was the instrument by which liberty was to be extended to all mankind. Thus the Fourth of July . . . became the occasion for renewing the liberal idealism and the patriotic nationalism which united Americans of all sections at the highest levels of political conviction.[16]

Even after a generation of intense sectional conflict over slavery, the South was still bound to the Union by a heritage of national ideals and traditions. Nothing was more common in southern political rhetoric than boasts of the South's manifold contributions to the building of the nation and of the national heroes it had produced. Southerners knew that the American dream was to have its fulfillment not in a regional confederacy but in the federal Union. Few could resist the appeal of American nationalism; few found a viable substitute in that most flimsy and ephemeral of dreams: southern nationalism.

This is not to say that the people of the Deep South were dragged out of the Union against their will. In all probability secession had the approval of the overwhelming majority, but most of them were driven to secession not by some mystical southern nationalism but by fear and anger, feeling that secession was not so much a positive good as a painful last resort. At his inauguration as provisional President, Jefferson Davis spoke of the "sincerity" with which Southerners had "labored to preserve the government of our fathers" and explained that they had turned finally to secession as "a necessity not a choice." A New Orleans editor believed that many left the Union "with feelings akin to those they would experience at witnessing some crushing national calamity." Nearly all the public celebrations in the seceded states during the dismal winter of 1860–1861 had about them a quality of forced gaiety, and much of the flamboyant oratory had a slightly hollow sound. Whatever was to be gained from independence, Southerners knew that some priceless things would inevitably be lost. They could hate the Yankees, but that was not quite the same as hating the Union.

They hated the Yankees for questioning their fidelity to American traditions and for denying them a share of the American dream; and they held the Yankees responsible for driving them out of the Union. As they departed, Southerners announced their determination to cherish more faithfully than Northerners the sacred heritage of the Founding Fathers. In the Confederate

[16] Charles G. Sellers, Jr., ed., *The Southerner as American* (Chapel Hill, 1960), pp. 40–41.

Constitution, said Alexander H. Stephens, "all the essentials of the old Constitution, which have endeared it to the hearts of the American people, have been preserved and perpetuated." By 1861 Southerners could no longer escape this heritage, and rather than seeking to escape it they claimed it as their own. But in doing so they confessed rather pathetically the speciousness of southern nationalism.

This being the case, it may well be that for many Southerners secession was not in fact the ultimate goal. Roy F. Nichols suggests that even among the active secessionsts "it may be doubted if all had the same final objective —namely, an independent republic, a confederacy of slave states." Nichols believes that some southern politicians were looking for a device that would enable them to negotiate for a better and stronger position in the old Union and that they thought of secession in these terms. "The real motive and object of many . . . was the creation of the Confederacy as a bargaining agency more effective than a minority group negotiating within the Union. As Thomas R. R. Cobb expressed it, better terms could be secured out of the Union than in it." John Bell of Tennessee described the secession movement as a stratagem to alarm the North, force it to "make such concessions as would be satisfactory and therefore the seceding states would return to the fold of the Union."[17] In fact, an argument repeatedly used by some secessionists was that an independent Confederacy would be the first step toward a reconstructed Union on southern terms. On December 5, 1860, the New Orleans *Bee* reported:

> Moderate men . . . are now forced painfully, reluctantly, with sorrow and anguish, to the conclusion that it is wholly impossible for the South tamely to tolerate the present, or indulge the slightest hope of an improvement in the future. They now see clearly that there are but two alternatives before the South, . . . either a final separation from the section which has oppressed and aggrieved her, or a new compact under which her rights will be amply secured. The one may take place, and still eventually prepare for the other.

Southerners who went out of the Union in anguish hoping for negotiations and peaceful reunion were bitterly disappointed by events. The Union did not negotiate with the Confederacy, and two months after its birth the Confederacy was involved in a war for which it was poorly equipped both physically and morally. Those who had expected reunion through negotiation found themselves trapped in a war they had not anticipated, fighting for an independence they had never sought; and, in spite of their indignation at northern "aggression," they may well have turned now unconsciously to reunion through defeat. The game had to be played out, the war had to be fought—and the men who served in the Confederate armies displayed their share of gallantry—but a contestant suffering from a lack of national identity and a serious morale problem, as well as from inferior resources, was involved in a lost cause from the start. Defeat restored to the South its traditions, its long-held aspirations, and, as part of the federal Union, the only national identity it ever had. It is instructive to contrast the myth of a special southern national identity with the reality of, say, Polish nationalism, which survived more than a century of

[17] Roy F. Nichols, *Blueprint for Leviathan: American Style* (New York, 1963), pp. 143–47, 160–63, 239–41.

occupation, partition, and repression. After Appomattox the myth of southern nationalism died remarkably soon.[18]

Defeat gave Southerners another reward: a way to rid themselves of the moral burden of slavery. This is the second reason why I think that some of them, once they found themselves locked in combat with the North, unconsciously wanted to lose. To suggest as I do that slavery gave the South such identity as it had, caused secession and war, and at the same time gave some Southerners a reason for wanting to lose the war will, I admit, take some explaining.

Let me begin with what I believe to be a fact, namely, that a large number of white Southerners, however much they tried, could not persuade themselves that slavery was a positive good, defensible on Christian and ethical principles. In spite of their defense of slavery and denial of its abuses, many of them, as their unpublished records eloquently testify, knew that their critics were essentially right. In saying this, I do not think I am judging nineteenth-century men by twentieth-century standards, for among the romanticists of the nineteenth century there was no greater moral good than individual liberty. Hence, the dimensions of the South's moral problem cannot be appreciated unless one understands that slavery was, by the South's own values, an abomination. The problem would not have been nearly as serious for Southerners if abolitionist criticism, strident and abrasive though it often was, had not been a mere echo of their own consciences.

No analysis of the Old South, writes Professor Sellers, "that misses the inner turmoil of the ante-bellum Southerner can do justice to the central tragedy of the southern experience. . . . Southerners were at least subconsciously aware of the 'detestable paradox' of 'our every-day sentiments of liberty' while holding beings in slavery." Their general misgivings about slavery "burrowed beneath the surface of the southern mind, where they kept gnawing away the shaky foundations on which Southerners sought to rebuild their morale and self-confidence as a slave-holding people."[19] Wilbur J. Cash insists that the Old South

> in its secret heart always carried a powerful and uneasy sense of the essential rightness of the nineteenth century's position on slavery. . . . This Old South, in short, was a society beset by the specters of defeat, of shame, of guilt—a society driven by the need to bolster its morale, to nerve its arm against waxing odds, to justify itself in its own eyes and in those of the world.[20]

To be sure, a basic purpose of the proslavery argument, with its historical, biblical, philosophical, and scientific defenses, was to soothe the troubled consciences of slaveholders. This is evident in the frequency with which they recited the argument to themselves and to each other in their diaries and letters. But it did not seem to be enough. No people secure in their conviction that slavery was indeed a positive good and unaware of any contradictions between theory and practice would have quarreled with the outside world so

---

[18] The myth of ante-bellum southern nationalism should not be confused with the twentieth-century concept of regionalism. That the South has distinct regional characteristics is undeniable, but these characteristics never have given the South anything remotely resembling a national identity.

[19] Sellers, ed., *The Southerner as American*, pp. 40, 44, 47.

[20] W. J. Cash, *The Mind of the South* (New York, 1941), pp. 60–61.

aggressively and reassured themselves so often as the slaveholders did. "The problem for the South," William R. Taylor believes,

> was not that it lived by an entirely different set of values and civic ideals but rather that it was forced either to live with the values of the nation at large or—as a desperate solution—to invent others, others which had even less relevance to the Southern situation. . . . More and more it became difficult for Southerners to live in peace with themselves: to accept the aspirations and the ideals of the nation and, at the same time, accept the claims and rationalizations produced by the South's special pleaders. Almost invariably they found themselves confronted with contradictions of the most troubling and disquieting kind.[21]

I do not mean to suggest that every slaveholder was guilt-ridden because of slavery. The private papers of many of them give no sign of such a moral crisis—only a nagging fear of slave insurrections and bitter resentment at outside meddling in the South's affairs. Countless slaveholders looked upon Negroes as subhuman, or at least so far inferior to whites as to be suited only for bondage, and some showed little sensitivity about the ugly aspects of slavery. On the other hand, many slaveholders, perhaps most, were more or less tormented by the dilemma they were in. They could not, of their own volition, give up the advantages of slavery—a profitable labor system in which they had a $2 billion capital investment. They dreaded the adjustments they would have to make if they were to live in the same region with four million free Negroes, for their racial attitudes were much like those of most other white Americans, North and South. Yet they knew that slavery betrayed the American tradition of individual liberty and natural rights and that the attack on it was in the main valid.

In their extremity sensitive Southerners joined their less sensitive neighbors in angry attacks on their tormentors, until, finally, driven by their inner tensions, they were ready to seek an escape from their problems by breaking up the Union, or at least by threatening to do so. Professor Sellers argues persuasively that this moral crisis eventually converted Southerners into an "aggressive slavocracy." "The almost pathological violence of their reaction to northern criticism indicated that their misgivings about their moral position on slavery had become literally intolerable under the mounting abolitionist attack." Slavery was doomed, Sellers concludes, but Southerners were so caught in its contradictions "that they could neither deal with it rationally nor longer endure the tensions and anxieties it generated. Under these circumstances the Civil War or something very like it was unavoidable."[22]

Indeed, I believe that under these circumstances not only the Civil War but the outcome as we know it was unavoidable. Southerners, many of whom were unsure of their goals and tormented by guilt about slavery, having founded a nation on nothing more substantial than anger and fear, were in no position to overcome the North's physical advantages. Moreover, at least some of them must have been troubled, at some conscious or unconscious level, by the question of what precisely was to be gained from winning the war—whether more in fact might be gained from losing it. For it soon became evident that, in

---

[21] William R. Taylor, *Cavalier and Yankee* (New York, 1961), pp. 17–18.
[22] Sellers, ed., *The Southerner as American,* pp. 67–71.

addition to restoring the South to the Union, defeat would be the doom of slavery. Thus President Lincoln and the Union Congress would do for the slaveholders what even the more sensitive among them seemed unable to do for themselves—resolve once and for all the conflict between their deeply held values and their peculiar and archaic institution.

What circumstantial evidence is there to suggest that Southerners lost the Civil War in part because a significant number of them unconsciously felt that they had less to gain by winning than by losing? There is, first of all, the poor performance of some of the South's talented and experienced political leaders; the uninspiring record of the Confederate Congress; the aggressive assertion of state rights even though it was a sure road to defeat; and the internal bickering and lack of individual commitment that would have made possible the discipline essential to victory. The history of the Confederacy is not that of a people with a sense of deep commitment to their cause—a feeling that without victory there is no future—for too many of them declined to make the all-out effort that victory would have required.

Equally significant was the behavior of Confederate civilians in areas occupied by Union military forces. One must be cautious in the use of historical analogies, but it is worth recalling the problems that plagued the German Nazis in the countries they occupied during the second World War. Everywhere they met resistance from an organized underground that supplied information to Germany's enemies, committed acts of sabotage, and made life precarious for collaborators and German military personnel. At the same time, bands of partisans gathered in remote places to continue the war against the Nazis. The French had a similar experience in Algeria after the second World War. The Algerian nationalists struggled with fanatical devotion to their cause; every village was a center of resistance, and no Frenchman was safe away from the protection of the French army. The country simply could not be pacified, and France, in spite of its great physical superiority, had to withdraw.

In the Confederate South, apart from border-state bushwhacking, there was only one example of underground resistance even remotely comparable to that demonstrated in Nazi-occupied Europe or French-occupied Algeria. This example was provided not by southern nationalists but by East Tennessee Unionists against the Confederacy itself. The counties of East Tennessee had been strongly opposed to secession, and so great was the disaffection that by the fall of 1861 some 11,000 Confederate infantry, cavalry, and artillery occupied them. In response some two thousand Union partisans fled to Kentucky to begin training as an army of liberation, while others drilled in mountain fastnesses in preparation for the arrival of federal forces. Still other East Tennesseans organized an underground and engaged in such activities as cutting telegraph wires and burning bridges. The most strenuous Confederate efforts at pacification failed to suppress these dedicated Unionists, and East Tennessee remained a cancer in the vitals of the Confederacy.[23]

Nowhere in the South was there impressive resistance to the federal occupation, even making allowance for the fact that most able-bodied men of military age were serving in the Confederate armies. In 1862 Middle Tennessee, West Tennessee, part of northern Mississippi, and New Orleans fell under federal

[23] E. Merton Coulter, *William G. Brownlow* (Chapel Hill, 1937), pp. 154–77.

military occupation, but no significant underground developed. In 1864, General Sherman marched through Georgia and maintained long lines of communication without the semblance of a partisan resistance to trouble him. In commenting on this remarkable phenomenon, Governor Zebulon Vance of North Carolina wrote:

> With a base line of communication of 500 miles in Sherman's rear, through our own country, not a bridge has been burnt, a car thrown from its track, nor a man shot by our people whose country has been desolated! They seem everywhere to submit. . . . It shows what I have always believed, that the great *popular heart* is not now and never has been in this war!

The absence of civilian resistance was quite as remarkable when, early in 1865, Sherman's army turned northward from Savannah into South Carolina. In the spring, when the Confederate armies surrendered, there were no partisans to take refuge in the mountains for a last desperate defense of southern nationalism. The Confederate States of America expired quietly, and throughout the South most people were reconciled to its death with relative ease. We hear much of unreconstructed southern rebels, but the number of them was not very large; the great majority of Southerners made haste to swear allegiance to the Union.

Finally, and to me most significant of all, was the readiness, if not always good grace, with which most Southerners accepted the abolition of slavery—a readiness that I do not think is explained entirely by the circumstances of defeat. Probably historians have given too much emphasis to the cases of recalcitrance on this matter in the months after Appomattox, when, actually, slavery collapsed with remarkably little resistance. Just a few years earlier it had been impossible publicly to oppose slavery in all but the border slave states, and southern politicians and publicists had aggressively asserted that slavery was a positive good; yet soon after the Confederate surrender no Southerner except an occasional eccentric would publicly affirm the validity of the proslavery argument. Indeed, I believe that even in the spring of 1866, if Southerners had been permitted to vote for or against the reestablishment of slavery, not one southern state would have mustered a favorable majority. Only two weeks after Appomattox, when a group of South Carolina aristocrats looked to the years ahead, though one of them could see only "poverty, no future, no hope," another found solace in the fact that at least there would be "no slaves, thank God!" In July another South Carolinian said more crudely: "It's a great relief to get rid of the horrid negroes."

Very soon, as a matter of fact, white Southerners were publicly expressing their satisfaction that the institution had been abolished and asserting that the whites, though perhaps not the blacks, were better off without it. Many were ready now to give voice to the private doubts they had felt before the war. They denied that slavery had anything to do with the Confederate cause, thus decontaminating it and turning it into something they could cherish. After Appomattox Jefferson Davis claimed that slavery "was in no wise the cause of the conflict," and Alexander H. Stephens argued that the war "was not a contest between the advocates or opponents of that Peculiar Institution." The speed with which white Southerners dissociated themselves from the cause of slavery is an indication of how great a burden it had been to them before Appomattox.

The acceptance of emancipation, of course, did not commit Southerners to a policy of racial equality. Rather, they assumed that the free Negroes would be an inferior caste, exposed to legal discrimination, denied political rights, and subjected to social segregation. They had every reason to assume this, because these, by and large, were the politices of most of the northern states toward their free Negro populations, and because the racial attitudes of the great majority of Northerners were not much different from their own. White Southerners were understandably shocked, therefore, when Radical Republicans, during the Reconstruction years, tried to impose a different relationship between the races in the South—to give Negroes legal equality, political rights, and, here and there, even social equality. Now for the first time white Southerners organized a powerful partisan movement and resisted more fiercely than they ever had during the war. The difference, I think, was that in rejecting Radical race policy they felt surer of their moral position, for they were convinced that Northerners were perpetrating an outrage that Northerners themselves would not have endured. Thus the morale problem was now on the other side; and the North, in spite of its great physical power, lacked the will to prevail. Unlike slavery, racial discrimination did not disturb many nineteenth-century white Americans, North or South. Accordingly, in a relatively short time, chiefly because of the unrelenting opposition of white Southerners, Radical Reconstruction collapsed.

The outcome of Reconstruction is significant: it shows what a people can do against overwhelming odds when their morale is high, when they believe in their cause, and when they are convinced that defeat means catastrophe. The fatal weakness of the Confederacy was that not enough of its people really thought that defeat would be a catastrophe; and, moreover, I believe that many of them unconsciously felt that the fruits of defeat would be less bitter than those of success.

A Democratic Society Emerges from Total War

Eric McKitrick

INTRODUCTION

The importance of the following essay by Eric McKitrick lies in both the nature of the questions he raises and the methods he utilizes to answer them. Rather than accept the inevitability of the situation that prevailed between the North and the South during Reconstruction, he examines the immediate postwar scene and explores the expectations and psychic needs of the Northerners after the war. What, he asks, were the "symbolic requirements" of victory, and to what extent were they met or frustrated? His technique is to analyze the problem in part through historical analogy —by examining the relations between the United States, Germany, and Japan after the Second World War. Improperly used, of course, this kind of strategy can lead to gross distortion, for no two situations are ever exactly parallel. But when utilized with the care and intelligence that McKitrick exhibits, this methodology holds great promise, since it provides historians with a comparative frame of reference that can do much to illuminate the phenomena they are examining.

One intriguing question that McKitrick does not explicitly raise or attempt to answer, because it is peripheral to his major interests in this study, is *why* the South seemed so incapable of accepting defeat. Borrowing McKitrick's own technique, one might well attempt to explore this problem by putting it beside a parallel case, say Germany's failure to fully accept its defeat in the First World War, or by comparing France's ability to accept defeat in Indo-China in the early 1950's with the apparent inability of the United States to do so in the 1960's and early 1970's. This is not to say that the Confederate South was Imperial Germany nor that the contemporary United States is the Third French Republic. The differences between these societies might well prove to be so great as to make any comparisons misleading. On the other hand, a minute examination of the actions of these societies in similar circumstances could reveal certain common or at least similar needs, expectations, and responses that would enable the history of one society to illuminate that of the other.

For McKitrick's views on the entire postwar period, see his *Andrew Johnson and Reconstruction* (1960). Kenneth M. Stampp, *The Era of Reconstruction** (1965), is the best one-volume synthesis of the period. Other important recent accounts include: LaWanda and John H. Cox, *Politics, Principle, and Prejudice, 1865–1866* (1963); W. R. Brock, *An American Crisis: Congress and Reconstruction, 1865–1867** (1963); David Donald, *The Politics of Reconstruction* (1965); and James M. McPherson, *The Struggle for Equality: Abolitionists and the Negro in the Civil War and Reconstruction** (1964). Kenneth M. Stampp and Leon F. Litwack, eds., *Reconstruction: An Anthology of Revisionist Writings** (1969), is an excellent introduction to recent historiography.

For studies focusing on the Negro in Reconstruction, see W. E. B. DuBois, *Black Reconstruction** (1935); Vernon L. Wharton, *The Negro in Mississippi, 1865–1890** (1947); Joel R. Williamson, *After Slavery: The Negro in South Carolina During Reconstruction, 1861–1877* (1965); Willie Lee Rose, *Rehearsal for Reconstruction: The Port Royal Experiment* (1964); George R. Bentley, *A History of the Freedmen's Bureau,* 2nd ed. (1970); Leon F. Litwack, "Free at Last," in Tamara K. Hareven, ed., *Anonymous Americans: Explorations in Nineteenth-Century Social History** (1971); and Alrutheus A. Taylor's three studies, *The Negro in South Carolina During the Reconstruction* (1924), *The Negro in the Reconstruction of Virginia* (1926), and *The Negro in Tennessee, 1865–1880* (1941).

B y the end of the summer and fall of 1865 an uneasy conviction had spread throughout most of the North that somehow the South had never really surrendered after all. This was hardly a "rational" persuasion in the ordinary sense: the evidence was overwhelming that the Southerners had had their fill of fighting. There was no way in which the military security of the North was in the least threatened; the Southern armies had fully dispersed; no legitimate forum for the expression of Southern sentiment, not one of the agencies of government, state or local, showed the least inclination to rebel further against the authority of the United States. And yet Northern feeling, well before the meeting of Congress could give it any clear leadership, had already become noticeably poisoned with fear and suspicion.

Of course, there were many men in the North of violent radical proclivities who would have been quite willing that sectional bitterness be prolonged until such time as thoroughgoing changes might be effected in Southern society. But it would be difficult, this early, to locate any such group of men sufficiently well organized, and exerting enough general influence and authority throughout the North at large, to have manufactured such asperities themselves. Indeed, these feelings were neither focused nor organized; they were pervasive, they seemed to ooze from everywhere, and they invaded the repose of weary men who would have given much to be rid of them. Charles Sumner, to be sure, wrote letters to his friends all summer long, tirelessly sounding the alarm. But Charles Sumner was hardly the tribune of the Northern people and never had been; if the Northern people had a tribune at this time, it was still Andrew Johnson. Probably this phenomenon of feeling did not have much direct connection with the work of individual Northern or Southern leaders. It may actually have had more to do with the meaning of victory itself, and with the peripheral meanings that hover about the notion of surrender.

Centuries ago, men gave much thought and effort to the problem of bringing a kind of *de jure* sanctity to the *de facto* brutality of conquest in war. They were oppressed by the realization that, right or no right, it was in the nature of war that the conqueror was somehow not to be thwarted from having his will in the end. Many of the things written by the commentators upon the ancient laws of war were therefore based on the implicit question of why, in fact, this had to be. Though the victor ought to use prudence in his exactions and temper his demands with mercy, the arbitrary inequity of "might makes right" flowed from the very nature of conquest. The victor in any war emerges from his conquest preoccupied with a whole set of requirements, and in his hour of triumph he is in the supreme position to insist upon their fulfilment. Both victor and vanquished desire peace and a return to peaceful occupations.

FROM Eric McKitrick, "A Democratic Society Emerges from Total War," *Andrew Johnson and Reconstruction,* Chicago: University of Chicago Press, 1960, 21–41. Reprinted by permission. The footnotes have been renumbered.

But the conqueror's conception of peace is of a far more sweeping character than that of the conquered: the latter expects nothing, the former expects all. He requires a kind of total security; his idea of "peace" is a function of his sense of security.

These barbaric thoughts of a former age are implicit, for example, in the writings of Grotius, who assures the conqueror that he "is entitled to impose ANY terms upon the conquered, who is now placed, by the external laws of war, in a situation to be deprived of every thing, even personal liberty or life, much more then, of all his property, either of a public or private kind." But now that the conqueror knows his rights to be absolute, he should in practice observe limits:

> . . . *as far as security allows,* it is always laudable to incline to moderation and clemency. Sometimes even circumstances may require such a line of conduct and the best conclusion of any war is that, which reconciles all contending claims by a fair adjustment, and a general amnesty. The moderation and clemency to which the vanquished appeal, are by no means in abolition but only a mitigation of the conqueror's absolute right.[1]

Such principles have their shortcoming as international jurisprudence.[2] But although they have little to tell us about the right and the good, there has been many a garbled insight into men's psychic needs hidden away in the old categories of political economy, philosophy, and law. Here we seem to have a glimpse of certain "spiritual" requirements with which men have perennially emerged from battle, and of the appropriate behavior which may follow upon their satisfaction. Let the conqueror feel that his victory and dominion—and therefore his security—are absolute, so that the granting of clemency, if it suits his pleasure, may itself be absolute.

This "security" concept has a significance that goes beyond the gross fact of physical conquest and disarming of the enemy. There are deeper requirements: the victor needs to be assured that his triumph has been invested with the fullest spiritual and ceremonial meaning. He must know that his expenditures have gone for something, that his objectives have been accomplished, and that the righteousness of his principles has been given its vindication. The assurances must be accorded him in terms that go well beyond the physical and objective; he must have ritual proofs. The conquered enemy must be prepared to give symbolic satisfactions as well as physical surrender; he must—in some

---

[1] Hugo Grotius, "On Good Faith between Enemies," in *The Rights of War and Peace*, trans. A. C. Campbell (London: M. W. Dunne, 1901), p. 399; italics added. Grotius' original treatise was published in 1625. Most of the classical treatises on international law (including the rights of conquest), beginning with the fourteenth-century *De bello, de repraesalis et de duello* of Giovanni da Legnano, have been handsomely republished both in photographic reproductions of the originals and in translation, under the auspices of the Carnegie Endowment for International Peace. The series title is "Classics of International Law," ed. James Brown Scott (Oxford: Clarendon Press, 1911–).

[2] They were attacked and discredited by Locke and, following him, by the writers of the Enlightenment. Rousseau quotes the Marquis d'Argenson in support of his own attack on Grotius: "Learned researches upon public right are often only the history of ancient abuses; and it is lost labor to take the trouble to study them too much." See Jean Jacques Rousseau, *The Social Contract*, trans. Rose M. Harrington (New York: G. P. Putnam's Sons, 1893), p. 5. The value of such writings as those of Hobbes and Grotius certainly does not lie in their adequacy as law and right but rather in their refracted descriptions of men's actual behavior in situations where different sets of values (such as clemency and security) appear at loggerheads.

way appropriate to his customs and his culture—"act out" his defeat.[3] This properly done, with satisfying gestures, the conditions are created wherein peace and clemency, if they are to obtain at all, will have their most auspicious setting. The foolish doubts which may still congest the victor's mind regarding the completeness of his victory—and which may cloud his impulses toward mercy, if he has any—could thereby be swept away at the very outset.

War being what it always has been—a species of ritual slaughter—there is much reason to think that the ceremonial requirements of earlier days still find some echo in those of more modern and enlightened warfare. Our war with Japan, judging from the results, affords considerable proof of the point.[4] What is one to think, then, coming upon an instance in which the passions, hatreds, and suspicions of war have not been swept away at all but seem to have been unduly and abnormally prolonged? It may be that in such a case the victor has had his "security"—in this enlarged, symbolic sense—withheld from him. His principles may never have been vindicated at all; he may have wrested the enemy's arms from him, but nothing more: perhaps no rituals of submission were performed to satisfy his deeper needs. Something of this sort seems to have been involved between North and South in 1865. In this case, the psychic fulfilments needed for a proper transition from war to peace were experienced by no martial sovereign but by an entire people. It is here that the quality of total commitment in a modern, democratic war becomes of particular importance.

The Civil War could in a way be called the most democratic of all our wars —conceivably the most democratic war of all time. The *levée en masse* was not the feature which made it so; many another culture has had that. The war was democratic in a kind of total, political sense: it was carried on within an intensely democratic political culture, and its democratic and its political features are impossible to separate. Unlike our foreign wars, this one had to be prosecuted and promoted—"campaigned for," as it were—almost as an expanded political platform. Consequently the sense of a "cause" (vital to any war) was not to be imposed by remote authority. The cause had to be something whose effectiveness, from both without and within the individual citizen, depended to a remarkable degree on its being voluntarily assumed. The moral coercions flowed not from the fiat of the state but from consensus in the community. Such coercions, of course, are the hardest of all to resist, for no one can really personify their source: they emanate, in the ultimate sense, from "the people."[5]

[3] It was thus, for instance, that the victory processions of ancient times would include the enemy chieftains, followed by files of captives loaded with chains, who would at the appropriate moment throw themselves upon the clemency of the conquering sovereign.

[4] See below, pp. 234–36.

[5] We may imagine a counter-instance in the loyal Austrian peasant of 1914 being conscripted into the imperial army. "The powers above," he might have said, "tell me that I must go and do my duty; therefore, of course, I must." This is in the tradition of authority, acceptance, and obedience. The same tradition can also be one of revolution and mutiny: there is something removed from the community scene, yet something focused and personified in the heads of the state, that can specifically be resisted. Indeed, there have been thousands of cases, among our own European immigrant forebears, where such resistance to military authority has been a matter of great pride. And yet in our own military tradition, such as it is, there are no such themes, either of implicit acquiescence to authority or of revolt. The conviction that our military enterprises are just and righteous does not flow automatically from on high. At the same time, one does not point with pride to an ancestor who evaded duty in any of our wars. Where, then, are the coercions? They emanate, in a special sense, from ourselves. Nobody, for instance, wants very

The principles that justify such a war must thus strike very deep. They must be strong enough and safe enough to be carried about in the individual's own conscience throughout all vicissitudes, and they must constantly be refreshed, renewed, and re-created by a process essentially political in nature.

The consequences of this democratic quality in our Civil War can be illustrated in a number of ways. There was a very intimate relationship, for instance, between battles and elections. Throughout the war, the political prospects of almost anyone running for major state and federal offices depended upon the military situation. It was more imperative than ever in wartime that the government remain sensitive to public feeling; both state and federal administrations had to carry the population with them in order to prevent being hamstrung, in their conduct of the war, by the elections. Military campaigns had to be "ratified," in effect, at the polls. Conversely, the administration party's success, or lack of it, was one fairly dependable criterion for judging how things were going in the field.[6]

Another feature of the war was that of full and constant communication. There were few aspects of the war's military progress—the location of troops, their disposition, the attributes of their commanders, and so on—which were not most of the time a matter of general knowledge. An extraordinary amount of information was carried simply by men going back and forth on furlough, and since units were made up geographically rather than at random, news of the regiment would be cherished at home by the entire community. Above all, there were the newspapers. One has only to follow for a week or two the reports, the dispatches, and the maps in the wartime files of any leading daily to be convinced that this was the best-reported war in history.[7] Hand in hand with this pitch of awareness and sensitivity to every development in the military situation, so fully diffused among the entire population, went the widest

---

much to be drafted for military service, but the sanctions are hard to "mutiny" against; they come not so much from the President as from "a local board composed of your neighbors." The principle of "conformity," for all its odium, is a democratic concept (the odium is itself symptomatic of the individualistic as well as the mass themes of democracy); "conformity" does not, in any case, mean the same thing as "obedience to authority." It means conformity to standards that one has one's own part in maintaining, if only negatively, and that would collapse if substantial numbers of one's friends and neighbors refused to support them.

[6] This connection between battlefield success and success at the polls may be tested by noting that the two lowest points of the war for the North coincided with ebb tides in the fortunes of the Union party. In 1862, after the abortive Peninsular campaign and Second Bull Run, the Democrats won extensive victories which included the governorships of New York and New Jersey. They made similar inroads in the legislatures and congressional delegations of Ohio, Pennsylvania, Illinois, and Wisconsin. Republican Governor Oliver Morton was faced with an antiwar majority in the Indiana legislature, against which his heroic efforts to maintain his state's troops in the field have become part of the wartime legend. See William B. Hesseltine, *Lincoln and the War Governors* (New York: Alfred A. Knopf, 1948), pp. 265–71; also Kenneth Stampp, *Indiana Politics during the Civil War* (Indianapolis: Indiana Historical Commission, 1949), pp. 179–85, and William Dudley Foulke, *Life of Oliver P. Morton* (Indianapolis: Bowen-Merrill, 1899), I, 203 ff. The second low point for the Union party came in the summer of 1864 with the desperate and apparently fruitless bloodletting of Grant's army in Virginia. Seldom had Lincoln's political future looked so dark. His subsequent success at the polls, and in effect the administration's mandate to continue the war, were directly related, as everyone knows, to Sherman's capture of Atlanta and the victories of Sheridan and Farragut. The people did, of course, have a clear alternative: they could have voted for the "peace plank" of the Democratic party.

[7] For much interesting material on the fiercely competitive efforts of the New York dailies to outdo each other both in the completeness of their war coverage and in the speed with which they got their stories before their readers, see Bernard A. Weisberger, *Reporters for the Union* (Boston: Little, Brown, 1953); and Louis M. Starr, *Bohemian Brigade* (New York: Alfred A. Knopf, 1954).

latitude for criticism of the war effort.[8] Principles, objectives, and dedication to the cause would have been put to the sternest of tests amid so minute a process of communication. The commitments, to survive such a process and retain their vitality and meaning, would have had to reach great depths in the popular soul.

Even the procurement of troops depended, in a way that would never again be so direct, upon the maintenance of these principles and commitments as justification for re-enlistment. The nucleus of the Union army in 1864 was composed of veterans who had enlisted in 1861 and whose three-year terms were then running out. Only persuasion could keep them in; they could not be conscripted. Yet nearly three-fourths of them did re-enlist; to the end, only about 6 per cent of the Union troops would be brought in by the draft. The 1864 re-enlistment of three-year volunteers was thus in effect a ratification, by the army itself, of the war and its principles.[9]

The most important point of all, in considering the democratic, shared quality of this war and its effect on the sense of dedication necessary to prosecute it, is the aspect of sacrifice. There is no very precise way to measure dedication, but there is a rough way of indicating its ultimate test. The people had to be convinced, and to convince themselves, that the cause for which their sons were fighting was worth sacrifices that would go well beyond the experience of any other generation of Americans, before or since. The Union casualty rate was between six and seven times heavier than the comparable percentage of American losses in the Second World War.[10] It is well and just that war should be pronounced the most depraved and useless of all modes of human enterprise. But there are special times when such a judgment is better withheld than uttered. Not much is gained in telling a people that the ordeal from which they have just emerged is without moral meaning; nor does one ever say these things to a Gold Star mother. Once the sacrifice is made, the principles themselves, despite the corrosions and disillusionments of time, become in some way consecrated. They become, like the young man in death, incorruptible.

[8] "Despite great provocation there was no Espionage Act and no Sedition Act during the Lincoln administration. During a time when disloyalty was widespread and defiant, the anti-Lincoln and anti-Union organs were, as a rule, left undisturbed; and the continuous stream of abuse which the opposition papers emitted was in itself a standing evidence of the fact that liberty of the press, even to the point of license, did exist." James G. Randall, *Constitutional Problems under Lincoln* (New York: D. Appleton, 1926), p. 508.

[9] "Union armies in the Civil War did not sign up for the duration. They enlisted by regiments, and the top term was three years. This meant—since the hard core of the United States Army was made up of volunteers who had enlisted in 1861—that as the climactic year of 1864 began, the army was on the verge of falling apart. Of 956 volunteer infantry regiments, as 1863 drew to a close, 455 were about to go out of existence because their time would very soon be up. Of 158 volunteer batteries 81 would presently cease to exist.

"There was no way on earth by which these veterans could be made to remain in the army if they chose not to stay. If they took their discharges and went home—as they were legally and morally entitled to do—the war effort would simply collapse." Bruce Catton, *This Hallowed Ground* (New York: Doubleday, 1956), p. 317. "Astoundingly, 136,000 three year veterans re-enlisted. They were the men who had seen the worst of it—men who had eaten bad food, slept in the mud and the rain, made killing marches, and stood up to Rebel fire in battles like Antietam and Stone's River, Chickamauga and Gettysburg—and they had long since lost the fine flush of innocent enthusiasm that had brought them into the army in the first place." *Ibid.,* p. 318.

[10] In round figures, Union casualties have been estimated at 360,000 deaths from all causes, out of a population of about 20 million. American losses in World War II came to 384,000 deaths from all causes, from a population of 135 million. This is a comparison of 1.8 per cent to 0.28 per cent. A casualty rate in World War II comparable to that of the Civil War would have required nearly 2.5 million deaths.

The meaning of victory, then, would be to declare all the ideals successful. The nation had told itself that, with victory, the war principles would be vindicated, and now, with the collapse of the rebellion, they were presumably vindicated and secured beyond all question. The logic of military events, at least, would appear to have made them so. As for just what these principles were, it was not that easy to say. The fundamental thing about them was not their precision, for they had none; it was rather their pervasiveness and depth. Lincoln, as poet, had given them their fittest expression at Gettysburg. The basic symbol was that of the Union, whose sub-theme was freedom. The poet himself had become a sacrifice, and it was now required of the beaten enemy that he pay some form of homage to the symbol. The thing could not be fully consummated with the surrender of the Confederate army. It was somehow necessary that the South go a little farther in acting out its defeat, though no one had much of a notion as to just when the curtain should be allowed to fall. But among the millions of witnesses there would have to be at least a consensus of sorts that the effort had been made—and that reunion had been accepted with appropriate and satisfying ritual gestures. Peace on the battle-field must be followed by a willingness to bring peace to the Northern mind.

There were no precedents at all for the case of two American communities facing each other in the attitudes of victory and defeat. In the North, men talked of "guarantees," knowing that they did not quite mean guarantees for their homes and firesides. They longed for "reassurances," but knowing the courage of the men who had fought them, they hardly expected abject and groveling servility. On "reconstruction," some form of which was universally anticipated, there were many variations of opinion and much muddled reasoning in matters of both procedure and principle. But they did want something in the way of satisfaction; they wanted a security that was more than military. In the things they said, it is possible to make out at least some pattern of consistency.

For one thing, the fire-eating "secesh" style in Southern manners would have to be repudiated and discredited. There must be some transcendent assurance, willingly given by all of society, not only that the South was "loyal" in the passive sense, but also that the act of secession was somehow wrong. No blood sacrifice was asked. Nothing really overwhelming was demanded—but the notion of "repentance" kept recurring like a leitmotif.[11] Meanwhile those who had been active secessionists should be "firmly ostracised for the time being,"[12] and "excluded from all participation in political affairs,"[13] so that they might have leisure to reflect upon their errors.

> We hold that repentance, a repentance not to be repented of, should go before absolution and perfect pardon. We believe in the conversion of sinners, but we

[11] "Let them take their own time in coming in to supper. We can stand it as long as they can; and besides, we can rely upon the repentance of men who have been cured of their folly upon empty stomachs and cool reflection." New York *Herald*, May 3, 1865.
[12] Washington *Evening Star*, June 12, 1865.
[13] *Illinois State Journal*, May 29, 1865. "But there are, and long will be, bad men in every Southern State, who are filled with the most rancorous hate of the government, and whose whole study hereafter will be how to do it injury. All such men can be shut out of Congress by the very stringent oath of allegiance which is now required before allowing a seat in either body. But they should also be precluded so far as possible, from all eligibility to State offices, and from the elective franchise. A State ruled by such men would become a nest for hatching new treason." New York *Times*, May 5, 1865.

are slow to believe in instantaneous conversions. Let fruits meet for repentance be first brought forth, and then let the repentant prodigals be restored to the rights of sonship and brotherhood and not before.[14]

Directly related to this need for some visible and articulate rejection of secessionism was the requirement that Southern Unionists be given some kind of security for having been Unionists. Not only must they receive protection, but upon them should fall the responsibility of forming the postwar governments.

The reorganization of the several Southern States' governments must necessarily be exclusively entrusted to men who have played no active parts in the rebellion, who besides being against it originally, have at no time and in no manner given it the countenance of their willing support.[15]

The Unionist position must now in some way be redefined as "right." No doubt practical considerations would render an utter revolution in leadership impossible; perhaps it would sooner or later be realized that there were not so many Southern Unionists as one had initially thought and that the South's best men had been rebels. But at least the new values of postwar Southern society should to some extent be imparted by the men who had been loyal and Unionist throughout; society should accord them some kind of meaningful honor.

In the third place, it was of great symbolic importance that the masses of Southern Negroes, especially the ex-soldiers,[16] be conceded full protection in their newly conferred freedom. Slavery and its appurtenances should be fully repudiated. The new society must be based on a system of free labor which would include the ex-slave's freedom to work where he pleased, physical security in his comings and goings, and fair treatment in all matters pertaining to legal rights. The period of victory's immediate aftermath coincided with the period of least pessimism in Northern minds over this entire question. This was the time when the North's sense of responsibility for the freedmen was at its maximum, and the question had a moral clarity then that was later to disintegrate when the issue of Negro suffrage became a political football in partisan battles.

This sense of responsibility flowed from two sources, both full of coercion for the Northern conscience. Emancipation had become one of the war principles and was now an accomplished fact whose rightness had been sanctioned by victory. The Negro population, moreover, represented a strong salient of loyalty to the Union. "It is the duty of the government," asserted the *Illinois State Journal* of Springfield, "not only to protect its friends among the white population of the South, but to maintain the rights of the freedmen also, who have been solemnly clothed with the privileges of citizenship."[17] But although

14 *Nation*, I (Oct. 19, 1865), 485.

15 Washington *Evening Star*, June 12, 1865.

16 "From first to last there were 178,975 Negroes in the United States Volunteer army, and of this number 36,847 were killed, wounded, and missing. They participated in four hundred and forty-nine battles, and served in nearly every military department of the United States Army. Besides this large military force there were at least one hundred and fifty thousand Negro laborers in the Quartermaster and Engineering departments." George W. Williams, *A History of the Negro Troops* (New York: Harper & Bros., 1888), p. 324.

17 May 29, 1865. This thought (the Negro as a responsibility, implied in both emancipation

the prime responsibility for this protection and security should lie with the federal government, it must somehow be morally certified by the South itself. It was not simply that the Southern constituent assemblies were being asked to ratify the new emancipation amendment. The North was really concerned with how the thing would be done. Northerners wanted to see it acted out, and to judge its style.[18]

Finally, there were expectations, vague but palpable, regarding the reception of Northerners in Southern communities. Such expectations could not be announced in any manifestoes, but they were there. "A reunion of hands and hearts" was a note sounded surprisingly often in the immediate post-victory period. This did not necessarily represent a simple willingness to forgive and forget. It is rather that one may, reading a little between the lines, think of such a sentiment as yet another function of victory. The Northern conquest should be, among other things, a conquest of hands and hearts. "There must be a change of heart": the victor was coming, and he would have to be welcomed. The North had besieged the South with arms and she had submitted; the South, now in her defenseless, "feminine" entity, had no further right to repel the North, should the North now assume the role, as it were, of suitor. The South would henceforth be disarmed in all ways: not only was she to receive armies of occupation, of whose authority there was to be no question, but a new era of hospitality to Northern immigrants, Northern enterprise, and Northern ideas was about to be inaugurated.[19]

Before considering how these requirements were responded to, let us experiment briefly with a kind of analogy. In many ways, the German and Japanese occupations in 1945 may constitute a bad parallel for the post-surrender situation that followed the Civil War. But in at least one limited respect the parallel, such as it is, can be enlightening. It seems to show that there is such a thing as "symbolic" needs and that their fulfilment does make a great difference in the quality of feeling that will characterize the postwar behavior of former enemies toward each other. The analogy can show nothing specific about which ceremonial affirmations of defeat may be peculiarly proper but simply that the need for them exists. These requirements were fulfilled so automatically and so completely after World War II that they never consti-

---

and the Negro's own loyalty) was elaborately discussed in a New York *Times* editorial of May 5, 1865, entitled "The Points To Be Secured before Reconstruction." "Some security," the *Times* insisted, "must be provided for the freedmen of the South. They have been unswervingly loyal to the government from the beginning of the rebellion, and that alone is enough to entitle them to its special protection. However, the government, for its own purposes, made them what they are, and it therefore is bound to take care that emancipation shall be a blessing to them, and not a curse. The fulfillment of these duties is really the hardest difficulty, the very gordian knot of reconstruction."

18 "They [the delegates to the Southern state conventions] will signify unconditional submission to the Union—they will surrender slavery, by ratifying the constitutional amendment providing for its abolition, and last, but not least they will adopt such measures toward the freedmen —their recent slaves—as will guarantee them full protection in their persons and the enjoyment, prospectively, if not at once, of all their political rights. If, on the other hand, the Southern people are not yet prepared to accept the position of faithful citizens under a Government, which is not only founded upon common ideas of National sovereignty and unity, but under which all men shall be, in the spirit of the Declaration, free and equal, that fact will doubtless be manifested, not only in a failure to do the things above specified, but in the display of a hostile temper which will betray the treason lurking in their souls." *Bureau County* (Ill.) *Republican*, Oct. 5, 1865.

19 As the *Nation* put it, "They must deal better with . . . the stranger that may be within their gates, than they have ever yet done. . . ." I (Oct. 19, 1865), 485.

tuted a problem for us; this in itself may be a good reason for making a point of it, and for suggesting that the point is applicable to more than one war.

Societies with a long tradition of accommodating themselves to power will have acquired, in the course of things, a deep knowledge of power in all its forms and meanings. They will know, for example, how to recognize superior power and how to appreciate and respond to it when they meet it. They will have little need of instruction on the requirements of a conqueror, and even less need of being told that he has them. Such societies, schooled in the ways of power, will know by instinct the cleanest ways of liquidating defeat; they will recognize, as a matter of self-interest, that when the requirements are met, the willingness (whatever its limits) of the conqueror to be merciful, to grant clemency, forgiveness, and oblivion, is at its maximum. So there is a sense in which the ancient law of conquest, to the extent that it makes the matter explicit, need not be thought of as entirely inhumane. It is here that our experience of victory in World War II seems particularly illuminating.

Those who participated in the last stages of the offensive against Germany in 1945, and subsequently in the occupation, will remember their surprise at the total collapse of all forms of resistance, civilian as well as military. The lack of sullenness on the part of the population was most remarkable; respect and deference, bordering on the obsequious, to the occupying power was everywhere in evidence. Before long there was even a willingness by the Germans themselves to try, and to convict, their own "war criminals." In the light of their supposedly arrogant ways, the people at large showed an amazing spirit of accommodation to the presence of our army; and the friendliness of the women was especially notable.[20]

And yet all this pales before the tableau that was acted out, in virtually pure form, by the Japanese. The chronology of the first year's occupation of Japan, taken in sequence through the pages of one of the news magazines, will evoke renewed amazement at the week-by-week story of how all the horror and loathing of the Japanese, and all the wartime hatreds, simply melted away. Before the first landings, early in September, 1945, the Americans were filled with misgivings. Perhaps we as a nation had been tricked in our decision to retain the Emperor. We were outnumbered, as General MacArthur later put it, "a thousand to one." There seemed no reason why the Japanese, with an undefeated army of several million—many of whom would shortly be unemployed brigands—could not carry on underground activity indefinitely. The troops were given dire warnings against the women: ". . . they have been taught to hate you. . . . The Geisha girl . . . may entice you only to poison you."[21]

---

[20] Here is one point (among several) at which it is important not to let the analogy get out of hand. It is true that the overpowering and occupying of one country by another has both figuratively and literally all sorts of "sexual" overtones. But on the more literal level, the community morals of nineteenth-century America, even under conditions of fullest hospitality, would not have allowed anything like the freedom that existed between American soldiers and the women of post–World War II Germany. And yet that need not banish the parallel altogether. Allowing for the differences in mores, one can still ask what happened, in the South of 1865, to the *ad hoc* society that seems to spring up on the spot, in all times and places, whenever there are young people. The fact was that in 1865 not even the normal and accepted gradings in relationship between men and women were sanctioned by Southern society vis-à-vis the Northern occupying force—and here it was the women themselves who made the law.

[21] *Time,* Aug. 27, 1945, pp. 27–29.

Meanwhile, the peacemaking government decreed the banishment of autocracy and the inauguration of democracy, all of which was legalized by the Diet, while the *Nippon Times* pronounced the death of the old order and called for all haste in the work of building the new. Coming ashore was "like a veteran's dream of victory" for the tautly apprehensive Americans. Advance detachments were smothered with attentions which included turtle soup, roast beef, cold beer, and beds with clean linen sheets. A sign on a factory roof read, "Three cheers for the U.S. Navy and Army." The arrival of the conqueror was as extravagantly heralded in the newspapers as had been the early victories of the imperial forces. Three weeks later in the United States it was being reported, with bated optimism, that "the big news from Japan was what had not happened." Not a single demonstration of enmity had occurred; on the contrary, the people were giving every evidence of sincere accommodation and submission.[22]

Almost immediately, the Japanese repudiated their militarist leadership, and even before the official war criminal lists were prepared, the Japanese themselves were suggesting names for them. They reacted with unfeigned symptoms of guilt to the stories of atrocities to American prisoners, published in their own newspapers, and asked to set up their own courts for the punishment of those responsible.[23]

In October, General MacArthur "decreed revolution," which involved the most sweeping changes in Japanese life: full civil liberties, free speech and free thought, release of political prisoners, abolishment of all totalitarian powers, the inauguration of democratic government, the organization of labor, and the dissolution of the zaibatsu, or great family business combines. "Japanese officialdom bowed low, smiled, and consented," and a new cabinet was formed by Baron Shidehara, one of the few surviving prewar liberal leaders. New parties sprang into existence, and the general election which was held in the spring brought 27 million voters to the polls. With Olympian understatement, the Supreme Commander pronounced it "satisfactory."[24]

The Japanese eagerness to please was manifested in a hundred ways. The Tokyo theater featured such plays as Drinkwater's *Abraham Lincoln* and Lillian Hellman's anti-Fascist *Watch on the Rhine*. With the decrees of female equality came an influx of women into politics; there was a flood of new business for the divorce courts; and the Emperor himself asked for an American woman tutor for the crown prince. The first contingent of Navy wives was welcomed at the pier by a delegation of Japanese women announcing their desire to learn American ways. The popular songs became heavily American in style; the efforts at Americanization extended even to the underworld.[25] On the anniversary of Hiroshima's destruction a tremendous "Peace and Re-

---

[22] *Ibid.*, Sept. 3, 1945, p. 28; Sept. 10, 1945, pp. 28–29; Sept. 24, 1945, p. 21.

[23] *Ibid.*, Sept. 10, 1945, p. 29; Sept. 17, 1945, p. 27; Sept. 24, 1945, p. 22; Nov. 19, 1945, p. 31.

[24] *Ibid.*, Oct. 1, 1945, p. 28; Oct. 15, 1945, p. 29; Apr. 22, 1946, p. 32.

[25] *Ibid.*, Feb. 25, 1946, p. 50; July 1, 1946, p. 50; Apr. 1, 1946, p. 32; May 6, 1946, p. 35; Sept. 9, 1946, pp. 59–60; July 1, 1946, p. 25; Apr. 29, 1946, p. 48; June 24, 1946, p. 35. Giichi Matsuda, boss of the Matsuzakaya gang, tried to get his followers to wear Western-style sack suits and pursue more democratic and progressive business methods. When an outraged henchman assassinated Matsuda, the latter's widow was elected as the first woman gang chief ever known in Japan.

construction Festival" was joyously staged by the city's boosters.[26] And finally, nothing was half so well suited to softening the asperities of war as the way in which the girls of Japan welcomed their American suitors. It was necessary at one point for General Eichelberger, in the interests of propriety and good military order, to issue a directive against "public displays of affection."[27]

After one year, the progress report on occupation could sum up a great success, from anyone's viewpoint. The Japanese had magnificently acted out all that was required of them;[28] the symbolic satisfactions of occupation had changed everything between the two peoples. With our Oriental enemies of over a generation, there now existed something closer to a "union of hands and hearts" than any American, in the bitter days of Bataan, Corregidor, and Guadalcanal, could very well have imagined.[29]

To expect from the conquered South any such behavior as that just described would have been grotesque. It would have been not only impossible but probably undesirable; it might conceivably have undermined a more permanent objective, that of remaking two peoples into one. Indeed, neither side had more than the dimmest idea of what was proper under the circumstances: Americans had never been conquered before, had never really known authority, had had no real experience or appreciation of power, in either the active or the passive sense, and no instinct was sharp enough to warn of the behavior appropriate to any given instance of it. Such things lay outside the realm of anyone's experience. So the South could not in the truest sense submit, not really knowing how, and that was the way things had to be. But there would

[26] *Ibid.*, Aug. 19, 1946, p. 36. A child whose mother and sister had been killed by the bomb said to a *Time* correspondent: "American soldier good. American number one." *Ibid.*, July 15, 1946, p. 38.

[27] *Ibid.*, Apr. 1, 1946, p. 25. A few months later, however, the military authorities were issuing phrase books with hints on "sweet talk." *Ibid.*, July 15, 1946, p. 38.

[28] "Last September MacArthur came to a Japan whose people were imprisoned in feudalism and superstitution, whose cities were ashen ruins, whose militarist traditions had no place for such concepts as defeat and war guilt. The Supreme Commander's first job was to destroy what was left of Japan's war potential. But he said: 'I am not concerned with how to keep Japan down but how to get her on her feet again.'

". . . By last week the U.S. imprint was strong on Japan. Japanese girls strolled hand in hand with G.I.s beside the imperial moat. Children played with toy models of American 'jeepu'; women copied U.S. fashion. In Tokyo a special school taught U.S. slang, and cinema fans queued up to see Hollywood movies (biggest hit: *Tall in the Saddle*, a Western). In geisha houses, the girls gaily crooned *You Are My Sunshine.*

"The Japs, long used to following the leader, followed American democracy in much the same spirit as they accepted U.S. jazz. When MacArthur ordered them to hold an election, 27 million of them trooped to the polls. They organized Western-style political parties and prepared to accept a Western-style constitution. When they were ordered to cease worshiping their Emperor as a god, they willingly obliged." *Ibid.*, Sept. 2, 1946, p. 27.

[29] It is being argued that the experience of victory, together with the appropriate tokens of acquiescence, constitutes the most effective—and indeed the indispensable—ritual catharsis for the liquidation of prior hatreds. A final example of its profundity, before leaving the point, might come out of a few comparisons between American attitudes toward wartime "friends" and toward defeated enemies. In 1898, after the close of hostilities in Cuba, our hearts went out to the gallant Spaniards, whose submission was perfect, while we quickly perceived what an unsavory lot our friends, the suffering Cuban rebels, had been. On this point see Walter Millis, *The Martial Spirit* (New York: Literary Guild, 1931), pp. 363–64. (The same thing, of course, happened in the Philippines.) In Europe, our unsteady friendship for the French and Russians in World War II paled beside the real warmth which developed in our feelings for the prostrated Germans. And in Asia our relationship with our wartime friends, the Chinese, has become odious in every way conceivable.

still have to be a price: the North still realized—dimly, perhaps, but somehow —that something was missing.

As the North waited, first in expectancy and then in deepening mortification, it began to dawn on the people that they were being somehow cheated of all the truly meaningful satisfactions of their victory. The South "accepted the situation," but this, as Northerners came to realize, was an idiomatic phrase brought into being especially for the purpose; it covered, with a special nicety, military defeat and no more.[30] As the reports came in, it began to appear that the deeper gratifications, even in their mildest form, could never be accorded by the erstwhile enemy.

Representative James Garfield of Ohio, by the fall and early winter of 1865, was one of the numerous public men receiving letters from the Southern states, with details of the political activities going on there, and it was made clear to him that in none of these states could the late enemy help glorying in his secessionism. "The 'secesh' ticket in this county was elected throughout," wrote Joseph R. Putnam from Huntsville, Alabama.[31] L. A. Sheldon, a conservative Northern businessman, wrote from New Orleans that "politically the state is in the hands of the men who voted her out of the Union."[32] "In a word," declared James Atkins, writing from Atlanta,

> the control of everything down here is in the hands of the thoroughly disloyal. At a distance I felt a great sympathy for the people here: now that I am here and know how the pulse of the people beat, I have lost a great portion of my sympathy. The people have suffered terribly and are in a pitiable condition for

[30] This point was explained by E. O. Dunning to the Joint Committee on Reconstruction. *Report of the Joint Committee on Reconstruction,* 39 Cong., 1 sess., Part II, "Virginia, North Carolina, South Carolina," p. 48.

Of all the groups in society, however, that element closest to the full ritual requirements of war appears perennially to be the military. The ceremonial of surrender made its deepest impression on those who actually participated in it—namely the armies—and those Southerners most convinced of defeat, and of the need for performing the gestures appropriate to it, were the Confederate soldiers. This should be taken mainly, of course, as a matter of degree, since no one class in a democratic society can be expected to remain aloof very long from the moral coercions of the rest of society. But the attitude was still noticeable enough, in the first six months or so following the war, that any number of otherwise critical Northern observers made a point of commenting on it, simply to emphasize the recalcitrance of Southern society at large. "Indeed," wrote Whitelaw Reid, "nothing was more touching, in all that I saw in Savannah, than the almost painful effort of the rebels from Generals down to privates, to conduct themselves so as to evince respect for our soldiers. . . ." *After the War: A Southern Tour* (London: Sampson Low, Son, & Marston, 1866), p. 156. Sidney Andrews wrote, "I found it almost everywhere true in Georgia and the Carolinas that the best citizens of to-day are the Confederate soldiers of yesterday." "Three Months among the Reconstructionists," *Atlantic Monthly,* XVII (Feb., 1866), 242. Conversely, the Union armies constituted the most conservative class in all Northern society, so far as further exactions on the South were concerned. This is not fully explained simply by saying that the soldiers had had their fill of war and its horrors and now wanted to end it once and for all. The point is rather that the armies had participated in a very profound and compelling experience which was denied the respective civilian populations—the experience of surrender. The ceremony had, of course, opposite meanings for the opposing participants, but for a moment it brought them spiritually very close together. It prepared the Southern soldier for submission, the Northern soldier for magnanimity. But then, the meaning of such an occasion has to be tremendously enlarged and extended for the civilian who could not be there, or for the man whose son was sacrificed in order that it might take place. That is why, for full satisfaction, the gestures of surrender could not end with Appomattox.

[31] Joseph R. Putnam to James Garfield, Nov. 10, 1865, Garfield MSS, Library of Congress. Putnam was a Union soldier whose regiment, stationed at Huntsville, was about to be mustered out.

[32] L. A. Sheldon to Garfield, Nov. 21, 1865, Garfield MSS.

the most part. Nevertheless all their sympathy is with those who distinguished themselves in behalf of the Confederacy. Men are advocated for such virtues openly. . . .[33]

Conversely, Southern Unionists found, even after the South's defeat, that their Unionism not only conferred no moral status whatever in their home communities but actually made their very existence intolerable there. The first test occurred in Virginia, where a large number of local elections, held late in May and early in June, brought solid rebel victories. "There is no security here for such men as me," flatly declared J. E. Brush of Norfolk,[34] and James H. Clements assured Charles Sumner that "if the Rebels continue to have the same privileges as now appears to be the policy to give them in this State, God help the Union men."[35] "The real Union men of this state," lamented G. W. Welker of North Carolina, "are but few and are so situated that they must look abroad for aid. . . . We entreet Congress never to place us again under the power of the men who betrayed us, plundered us & oppressed us."[36] It was observed by Sidney Andrews that "In Barnwell and Anderson districts, South Carolina, official records show the murder of over a dozen Union men in the months of August and September. . . ."[37] And Gillet Watson wrote imploringly to Thaddeus Stevens from Richmond: "We represent the loyal people of this section, many of whom have fought and bled, and lost their all in defence of the stars and stripes. Are these men to be turned over to an excited and infuriated mob, by the U.S. Representatives?"[38]

[33] James Atkins to Garfield, Dec. 7, 1865, Garfield MSS. Atkins was a federal officeholder in the Department of Internal Revenue.

[34] J. E. Brush to Sumner, June 9, 1865, Sumner MSS, Harvard College Library. "The undersigned is a Native of this Town, but left immediately after hostilities commenced destined for the City of Memphis with high hopes of being able to reach the Federal lines, but failed, was in Memphis 26 months, was there when the city was captured, absent from my family that length of time, 9 months of which did not hear from them. . . . Was born and reared here, but have bitter enemies because of the decided stand which I took and the liberal opinions which I now entertain. Many things I could tell you about [conditions] here provided I could get a hearing from you or some other influential man in the Congress of the U. States."

[35] James H. Clements to Sumner, June 11, 1865, Sumner MSS. Clements, who called himself "simply a Mechanic," had left Portsmouth, Virginia, at the outbreak of the war in order to join the Union Forces. "I hope sir," he said to Sumner, "you will excuse the freedom I take in addressing you, but sir the interest I feel in my future welfare and that of my family justifies me in calling on the rulers of my country."

[36] G. W. Welker to Thaddeus Stevens, Dec. 2, 1865, Stevens MSS, Library of Congress. Another North Carolina Unionist, who signed himself only "Union," summarized for Stevens the result of the recent congressional election in his district:

" 'I cannot take the oath, if I would' & (defiantly) 'I would not, if I could.' Stubbs.

" 'I cannot take the oath.' Speed.

" 'I can honestly and truthfully take the oath, having never done any thing inconsistent with it except *involuntarily* under military or mobocratic coercion.' Bond.

"The result was—Stubbs 2783, Speed 2013, Bond 450!!! Speed and Stubbs won simply on the hope, that the oath would be repealed. Let Congress do that, & the seats from the South will be occupied by the 'Secesh,' the Unionist in the South forever proscribed by them & the Group in constant danger from their plots & intrigues." "Union" to Stevens, Nov. 27, 1865, Stevens MSS.

[37] Andrews, "Three Months among the Reconstructionists," p. 238. "I spent the months of September, October, and November, 1865," Andrews wrote, "in the States of North Carolina, South Carolina, and Georgia. I travelled over more than half the stages and railway routes therein, visited a considerable number of towns and cities in each State, attended the so-called reconstruction conventions at Raleigh, Columbia, and Milledgeville, and had much conversation with many individuals of nearly all classes."

[38] Gillet Watson to Stevens, Dec. 5, 1865, Stevens MSS. Watson was chairman of the Union League of Virginia. "Sir," wrote a Louisiana correspondent of Nathaniel P. Banks, "the present Legislature boast on the streets that they intend to *ostracise* all so called loyal men to the United

Meanwhile, whatever illusions the North may have cherished regarding the future of the Southern Negro began to dissolve. The ideals of emancipation and free labor, as well as the hope of an incorruptible Unionist bulwark (which required at least some form of citizenship), faded before the reports. Even the most sanguine Northerner became heavy-hearted at what he read and heard. "As for your niggers," said a Virginia ex-colonel to Whitelaw Reid,

> you've got 'em on your hands. They won't work, unless you force them to it, and they'll steal rather than starve. You even talk about giving them suffrage! There are no words to express the infamy of such a proposition. This is a white man's government, and must be kept so till the end of time.[39]

"Three-fourths of the people," wrote Sidney Andrews,

> assume that the negro will not labor, except on compulsion; and the whole struggle between the whites on the one hand and the blacks on the other hand is a struggle for and against compulsion. The negro insists . . . that he shall be free to come and go as he pleases; the white insists that he shall come and go only at the pleasure of his employer. . . . I did not anywhere find a man who could see that laws should be applicable to all persons alike; and hence even the best men held that each State must have a negro code.[40]

Such a movement, indeed, was well under way by December. The hitherto circumspect *Nation,* confronted with the codes of South Carolina, Alabama, and Missisippi, was appalled at these "disgraceful statutes." "Such are some of the open manifestations of the mood of 'our Southern brethren' in circumstances when they would have been tempted to make a show at least of complete acquiescence in the will of their magnanimous conqueror."[41]

Finally, in receiving her triumphant conqueror, the South was unable to tender even the civilly measured hospitality that accompanies a forced submission.[42] Northerners with plans for emigration were chilled to discover that their arrivals were openly discouraged[43] and that there were no guarantees,

---

States Government by giving them no private or public employment, & thus force them to leave the State for more agreeable quarters." J. P. Henderson to Banks, Nov. 26, 1865, Banks MSS, Essex Institute.

[39] *After the War*, p. 318.

[40] "Three Months among the Reconstructionists," p. 243.

[41] *Nation*, I (Dec. 28, 1865), 806.

[42] Sidney Andrews, who did more listening than talking and therefore got into less trouble than many Northern travelers, reported that he had had much less to complain of than most of his fellow Yankees. Yet there were numerous snubs and humiliations at hotels and boarding houses; "at one house in South Carolina," he noted, "when I sought accommodations for two or three days at a boarding-house, I was asked by the woman in charge, 'Are you a Yankee or a Southerner?' and when I answered, 'Oh, a Yankee, of course,' she responded, 'No Yankee stops in this house!' and turned her back upon me and walked off. In another town in the same State I learned that I was the first Yankee who had been allowed to stop at the hotel since the close of the war." "Three Months among the Reconstructionists," p. 237. This was easily the most commonly shared experience of Northern travelers. It even extended to the military. General Grant's aide, Cyrus Comstock, at New Orleans with the General's party, laconically wrote in his diary for February 5, 1866: "Saw Gen. Baird. Says feeling in Nov. & Oct. was very bad, that officers were insulted at St. Charles, that officers wives at St. Charles table were not waited on and that on remonstrances being made were told they were not desired there as it might affect the custom of the house." Diary of Cyrus B. Comstock, Feb. 5, 1866, Library of Congress.

[43] "At the time I am writing, the owners of property in Richmond are holding it at such high rates as to repel Northern purchasers. Letters from that city say, the residents have determined to

except for the presence of federal troops, that they were even safe in their persons.[44] But what really must have struck the Northerner to the heart, in all the flush and pride of his victory, was the implacability of the Southern women. The women, far from performing for their people any of the gentler rites of peace, were the bitterest of all. "A day or two ago," wrote Carl Schurz from Savannah,

> a Union officer, yielding to an impulse of politeness, handed a dish of pickles to a Southern lady at the dinner-table of a hotel in this city. A look of unspeakable scorn and indignation met him. "So you think," said the lady, "a Southern woman will take a dish of pickles from a hand that is dripping with the blood of her countrymen?"[45]

The Northern and Southern hands were not to join, even over the sour formality of a dish of pickles.

In no case were specific violations of the Confederate surrender involved in any of these stories. It was the protocol of defeat for an entire people that had been violated, a protocol whose spirit and overtones could hardly be specified in any articles of surrender. Under the circumstances, there may have been

---

sell no property to Northern men, when they can possibly avoid it." Thomas W. Knox, *Camp-Fire and Cotton Field: Southern Adventure in Time of War* (New York: Blelock, 1865), p. 497. "One of our firm, Jos. Glenn," wrote Richard Smith (of the Cincinnati *Gazette*) to James Garfield, "has been travelling in Miss. and Louisiana for some time and bought a cotton plantation, which he now regrets. He says that if the troops are withdrawn Northern men could neither live nor travel there. . . ." Smith to Garfield, Jan. 14, 1866, Garfield MSS.

[44] John Murray Forbes declared that "if you withdraw the army, and give back the local government to the Governors and Mayors and Magistrates and Constables who have been fighting us, any northern man who wishes to emigrate south must either cut out his tongue and his conscience, or provide himself with an India rubber neck and a ball proof jacket!" Forbes to N. M. Beckwith, Aug. 6, 1865, Carl Schurz MSS, Library of Congress. "It follows, of course," wrote Sidney Andrews in milder vein, "that safety of person is not assured. Very likely one might travel through every county of either State without harm; but any Union man must expect to hear insulting words; and any Northern man is sure to find his principles despised, his people contemned, and himself subjected to much disagreeable contumely; while any man holding and openly advocating even moderately radical sentiments on the negro question, stands an excellent chance, in many counties of Georgia and South Carolina, of being found dead some morning,—shot from behind, as is the custom of the country. Of course the war has not taught its full lesson till even Mr. Wendell Phillips can go into Georgia and proclaim 'The South Victorious.'" *The South since the War, As Shown by Fourteen Weeks of Travel and Observation in Georgia and the Carolinas* (Boston: Ticknor & Fields, 1866), p. 385.

[45] Carl Schurz, "Letters from the South, No. 4" July 31, 1865, Schurz MSS. "As we rode through the city," wrote Grant's aide at Charleston, "I saw several who called themselves ladies make faces at the Yankee officers with us. It is useless to say they are only women—they express openly what their husbands & brothers feel but do not show." Diary of Cyrus B. Comstock, Dec. 1, 1865. Even President Johnson's emissary, Benjamin Truman—whose report was specifically designed to present Southern conditions sympathetically—corroborated other witnesses on this point. "There is a prevalent disposition not to associate too freely with northern men," Truman wrote, "or to receive them into the circles of society; but it is far from insurmountable. Over Southern society, as over every other, woman reigns supreme, and they are more embittered against those whom they deem the authors of all their calamities than are their brothers, sons and husbands." *Senate Executive Documents*, 39 Cong., 1 sess., No. 43, "Report of Benjamin Truman," p. 6. Here Truman was assuming that with the melting of that insignificant barrier, all would be changed. He little appreciated the formidability of the women: they did *not* melt. Joseph LeConte of Columbia, South Carolina, writing of the later reconstruction period, said that the men of Columbia were very cordial to the officers stationed there, "but the ladies were inexorable." "I became quite friendly with some of the officers," he wrote, "but I could never induce my wife to invite one of the gentlemen to the house for a social meal." *Autobiography of Joseph LeConte*, ed. William D. Armes (New York: D. Appleton, 1903), pp. 236–37.

very little help for it: there were no cues in the national experience to follow in setting matters to rights once they had gone awry. But whatever the cause, there were poisons in the Northern bosom by December, 1865, that had not been there in May. In one sense they had been carried over from a long, costly, and bitter war. But something had now been added, a new malaise, created not so much by war as by peace. It had been a most irregular peace, very uncertainly managed, a peace whose quality was quite different from anything that had been expected. Many were saying, by early 1866, that the wartime principles were now tarnished, the fruits of victory soured, and the sacrifices rendered meaningless; there seemed little left to show for the overwhelming moral commitment which the war had once represented. The moral victory which the North imagined itself to have won had come to nothing.

Although the above themes may tell us something important about the new turn in sectional feeling that occurred in the latter half of 1865, they still make up only a part of the story. The Southerners in the beginning could hardly have been so blind to their own deepest interests; nor could Northerners have been quite so muddled about what they required of the South. Still other things were involved during that summer of 1865, among them the fact that the most important channels of communication between the North and the South were not really open. The United States government, whose most authoritative agency at this time was the Republican party, was not in full functioning for the settlement of Southern problems, nor would it be until the end of the year. No one, meanwhile, could be expected to know how much difference this made; nor was it clear to what extent President Johnson considered himself the spokesman of that agency. Each of the interested parties had quite different notions on this point. Indeed, the entire period—the summer and fall of 1865—might be seen from a later viewpoint as a season of self-delusion on nearly all sides. So if Southerners misconceived the accuracy with which the Northern will was being communicated to them, there remains the question of how much of this was properly their responsibility. Other explanations must be sought, more perspectives established, further trial balances struck.

A 2
B 3
C 4
D 5
E 6
F 7
G 8
H 9
I 0
J 1

well you don't know
where you'll meet her
Out door or together